THE NUCLEAR ORACLES

THE NUCLEAR ORACLES

A political history of the General Advisory Committee of the Atomic Energy Commission, 1947–1977

RICHARD T. SYLVES

WITH AN INTRODUCTION BY ANTHONY A. TOMEI

IOWA STATE UNIVERSITY PRESS  AMES

Dedicated to the memory of

ORLO DAVID SYLVES (1895–1960)

A devoted father, husband, grandfather, and public servant who mastered areas of science and engineering through his singular drive and thirst for knowledge

Richard T. Sylves is an Associate Professor of Political Science at the University of Delaware.

© 1987 Iowa State University Press, Ames, Iowa   50010
All rights reserved

Composed by Iowa State University Press
Printed in the United States of America

First edition, 1987

Library of Congress Cataloging-in-Publication Data

Sylves, Richard Terry.
    The nuclear oracles.

    Bibliography: p.
    Includes index.
    1. U.S. Atomic Energy Commission. General Advisory Committee — History.   2. Nuclear energy — United States — History.   3. Nuclear engineering — United States — History.   I. Title.
QC773.3.U5S95   1987   353.0087'22   87-2845
ISBN 0-8138-0062-5

CONTENTS

PREFACE

THE GENERAL ADVISORY COMMITTEE (GAC) of the Atomic Energy Commission (AEC), which operated from 1947 to 1977, was composed of the nation's foremost scientists and engineers. Working under conditions of official secrecy, the GAC critically analyzed, and produced recommendations in, every area of AEC responsibility. The decision to approve or reject hydrogen bomb development, advice on the decade-long problem of radioactive fallout from above-ground nuclear tests, evaluation of the progress of the Nuclear Plowshare program, priority setting in developing major particle accelerators, and oversight of the AEC's huge network of contract research laboratories were all taken up by the GAC.

This study takes the reader inside GAC meetings, escorted by Anthony A. Tomei, who was GAC secretary for twenty-eight years. To what degree did GAC advice involve critical political issues? On what basis did GAC members render their advice—as representatives of academic, corporate, and government laboratory interests or as advocates of their individual disciplinary fields? What do scientists and engineers say and do when they hold the highest security clearance, have access to the most sensitive defense and national security documents, and can be assured that their confidential advice will not be publicly divulged for decades?

The recently declassified unpublished records of numerous GAC meetings provided the primary source basis of this study. First is presented a biographical analysis of each of the fifty-five people who served on the nine-member Committee from 1947 to 1977. This is followed by a careful and balanced review of the major topical problems addressed by the GAC.

Chapter 1 reviews the general character of government science advising—the dynamics and types of federal advisory committees and how the GAC operated within this system. In Chapter 2 are discussed the origin, purpose, and procedures of the GAC, the formal information about the mechanics of the Committee's operation.

Chapters 3 and 4 address GAC membership issues. Career histories and knowledge specializations of each GAC member are presented in Chapter 3, as well as the chief reasons for each member's selection to the body. In addition, the disciplinary composition of the GAC membership over time is analyzed. Understanding the conflict and accommodation between the basic and the applied sciences is essential in understanding how the Committee conducted its advice activities through the years. Chapter 3 describes GAC members as individuals with special types of knowledge qualifications. Chapter 4 discusses GAC members as groups of people who had established relationships with one another through university education, work in the wartime Manhattan Project, work for the early AEC, and service on related federal advisory committees such as the President's Science Advisory Committee. Chapter 4 describes the elite nature of the GAC membership and suggests how patterns of interaction may have influenced the nomination of appointees to fill vacancies on the Committee.

Chapters 5 through 9 address the work of the GAC. The Committee's role in oversight of the great atomic energy laboratories is the heart of Chapter 5, including a special case example of the GAC role in the Aircraft Nuclear Propulsion project, one in which the Oak Ridge National Laboratory had a major stake. Chapter 6 takes up the Committee's most controversial and sensational issue, the question of whether to recommend a program of accelerated development of the superbomb, a code word for the thermonuclear or hydrogen bomb. Special attention is given to J. Robert Oppenheimer's moral and ethical concerns, which were shared by many of his colleagues on the GAC. Appended to this analysis is a follow-up of GAC actions after President Truman approved a crash program of H-bomb development. The Committee's transactions with Edward Teller over the matter of a second weapons lab documents the creation of the Lawrence Livermore National Laboratory.

Chapter 7 presents GAC recommendations in the matter of thermonuclear weapon testing, particularly the problem of radioactive fallout. A major dilemma involved how to continue above-ground testing to maintain an advantage over the Soviet Union and at the same time avert a potential ecological catastrophe caused by the increased fallout from this testing. The Committee tried to help the AEC find suitable alternatives to above-ground detonations while at the same time it sought to allay public fears about the possible carcinogenic effects of radioactive fallout over the continent. Radioactive fallout was a topic regularly on the GAC agenda from 1953 until 1963, when the Partial Test Ban Treaty took effect.

Chapter 8 examines the checkered history of Project Plowshare, the peaceful use of nuclear explosives, which was a regular agenda item from 1956 until 1973. The GAC played a promotional and regulatory role in this civilian-oriented enterprise. Chapter 9 investigates a long-standing bread-and-butter interest of the GAC's physicists: the siting, construction, operation, maintenance, expansion, and user-dedication of various types of high-energy particle accelerators. This affords a be-hind-the-scenes look at how scientific advisers behave in discussions of subjects crucial to their personal research and to the advance of their knowledge disciplines.

Chapter 10 presents a general analysis of the GAC's life cycle. The rise and decline of various knowledge specializations represented on the GAC is of particular importance in understanding how the GAC offered advice. This chapter summarizes some of the general findings of the work and examines the effects of the AEC's dissolution on the Committee. Relatively recent rules governing the operation of federal advisory bodies, such as the Federal Advisory Committee Act of 1972, profoundly affected the composition and operation of the GAC of the Energy Research and Development Agency.

By considering the history of GAC operation it may be possible to better anticipate, and to gauge the impact of, scientific and technical advice in current government domestic and defense programs. The history of the AEC GAC, which was quite possibly the most important scientific advisory body ever impaneled by the U.S. government, also reveals much about the influence and motives of scientific and technical advisers.

INTRODUCTION

ANTHONY A. TOMEI
Former Secretary of the AEC General Advisory Committee

ESSENTIAL TO OUR UNDERSTANDING of the immediate post–World War II period is knowledge of the people who successfully steered the United States through what President Harry S. Truman called "the years of trial and hope." Among those people were the members of the General Advisory Committee (GAC) of the Atomic Energy Commission (AEC), an extraordinary group of accomplished individuals who possessed the knowledge and foresight required to advise the AEC through that period.

Although numerous books have been written about atomic energy, this one can be regarded as unique by virtue of its special contents, that is, a carefully documented account of GAC scientific activities together with a detailed analysis of political issues raised in Committee deliberations. The work draws from declassified primary source documents that few have yet examined, as well as the expertise and experience of those who were closely involved with the AEC. The investigation also uses biographical information about each person who served on the GAC in order to demonstrate how and why certain individuals were appointed to the Committee. This study will help provide an understanding of how we have progressed to the present. Atomic energy applications, all intended to improve human welfare, include electrical power, weapons, propulsion, and medical and industrial uses; a political history of advice and recommendations on selected nuclear technologies is both necessary and warranted.

The author's account of the GAC's operation can easily be considered to be generally fair and complete insofar as is possible in any single book on this complex and far-ranging topic. The twenty-eight years of the AEC involved countless important programs and projects, which would require many volumes to record in every detail. The author has selected a sample of topics that afford the reader a good perspective of the entire field. I have enjoyed working with such a capable, dedicated, and enthusiastic professional. I consider this manuscript to be among the best in this field.

The GAC was truly a noteworthy organization in that it was appointed by the president without Senate approval to advise an essential federal commission on scientific and technical matters relating to materials, production, and research and development. It also made the recommendations for the AEC Fermi and Lawrence awards as authorized by law. It elected its own chairman annually and was required by statute to meet at least four times every calendar year. The Committee was composed of nine members appointed to six-year terms. The mix of disciplines of the overlapping membership depended on the need thereof as determined by the AEC and, in turn, the president, with occasional advice furnished by the GAC upon request.

The caliber of the GAC membership remained consistently high throughout the period. Its investigations of AEC problem areas were thorough, and its advice acceptable to the AEC in great measure. The GAC had no responsibilities for deciding issues or for supervision and operated accordingly, leaving such responsibilities to the AEC. In its early days the GAC was relied upon most heavily for advice by the largely inexperienced Commission. Later, with AEC commissioner and staff experiences on the increase, the Commission operated more independently. My experiences of many years indicate that the relationship between the GAC and the Commission was harmonious and differences were minimal.

Together with the AEC, the GAC wrestled with numerous major ongoing issues. Some examples were foreign distribution of radioisotopes, prospects for civilian nuclear power, AEC personnel policy, the outlook on raw materials production, materials flow, the composition and functions of laboratories, the weapons/submarine/aircraft programs, peaceful uses of atomic energy, radioactive fallout, and high-level nuclear waste disposal.

On June 13, 1949, a GAC statement was released that stated, "The improvement which has been achieved during the Commission's administration appears to us to offer clear proof of competence and devotion to duty by the Commission." This view was extant during the remaining years.

Following six years of operation, the GAC released to the public via the AEC a statement of its modus operandi throughout its history, to June 1952. The statement concluded,

> We do not wish to suggest that the procedures we have adopted are the only ones or the best ones, either for the past or for the

future. In fact, we make this report partly with the thought that if our past way of work is understood, it may be helpful in determining how to proceed in the future.

The statement also listed agenda topics, some of which are related below:

> . . . the organization of the Commission's development work in reactors, the organization of the Commission's research and development efforts in the field of raw materials, the need for weapons tests, the relation between the problem of custody of atomic weapons and the combat readiness of such weapons, the creation of an informed general understanding of the prospects of civil power, the objectives of the thermonuclear program, the need for an accessible atomic proving ground, and the technical benefits to be derived from collaboration with our wartime partners, the United Kingdom and Canada.

The method of operation outlined in the statement was followed in the AEC GAC years, to 1974.

The GAC often met with other committees, such as the AEC–Department of Defense Military Liaison Committee, the Committee on Exploration and Mining, the Industrial Advisory Group, the Joint Congressional Committee on Atomic Energy, the Security Survey Panel, and the Advisory Committee on Biology and Medicine. It was customary for the GAC to hold half of its meetings of the full Committee at AEC field installations, frequently alternating between these meetings and those in Washington. Moreover, it was common practice for the GAC to socialize with local personnel one evening per meeting. The GAC itself and individual members also hosted parties, as well as formal dinners, at personal expense.

The country is fortunate to have had the benefit of the knowledge and wisdom of those who served on the GAC. All were outstanding in their fields, and they gave unstintingly of their time. I am pleased to have had the opportunity to work with, and be responsible to, the AEC GAC for all but the first few months of its existence. Whenever asked how it felt to work with a particularly famous GAC person, I readily recall the response of Mrs. Rose Kennedy to a similar question. When asked in the early 1960s how it felt to be with her famous son, she said, "Which one?"

ACKNOWLEDGMENTS

A POLITICAL SCIENTIST WHO ATTEMPTS TO WRITE a political history of a federal advisory committee composed of some of the nation's foremost physical scientists and engineers has to have help. I would like to express my thanks and appreciation to two individuals who provided unflagging support.

Dr. Thomas B. Priest, Chairman of the Sociology Department at Johnson C. Smith University in Charlotte, gave me the initial encouragement needed to embark on this investigation. Dr. Priest read and critiqued early draft work and provided important assistance in field research and data collection. His insight and collegial interest helped to shape the entire manuscript. He has collaborated with me in a number of research endeavors regarding government advisory committees, and I can think of no better friend and colleague.

Anthony A. Tomei's assistance was constant, rigorous, and editorially invaluable. Mr. Tomei worked for the AEC from 1947 to 1975, devoting most of his career to working for and with the GAC. He served as administrative assistant and for a period as secretary. It was Tomei's job to record and keep the minutes of the GAC, which comprise much of the original primary source material of this study. Tomei attended nearly all the AEC GAC meetings conducted between 1947 and 1975. In the preparation of this study, he furnished advice about how to obtain special categories of declassified GAC records from the U.S. Department of Energy Archives and helped authenticate names, dates, biographical data, and official records.

Tomei painstakingly reviewed every component of the original and revised draft manuscripts. We essentially agree in matters of interpretation. However, opinions, analyses, and conclusions offered in this study are those of the author, not necessarily those of Tomei. The author owes a very great debt to him for volunteering his knowledge and experience in matters regarding the GAC. The minutes and record keeping of GAC meetings and sessions reflect his exacting transcriptive skills and superb writing ability. His 1956 in-house AEC study, "An Account of the Administrative and Organizational Practices and Procedures of the General Advisory Committee," was very useful in preparation of this study. Mr. Tomei's enthusiasm and encouragement buoyed the author on more than one occasion. The best features of this study should be considered Mr. Tomei's legacy to the GAC and the AEC, to which he dedicated himself. Any critical references in this study to the GAC or its members and deficiencies in the study itself should be attributed exclusively to the author.

John H. Manley, the GAC's first secretary, volunteered an exacting critique of the Project Super chapter, as did Carson Mark and former Los Alamos director Norris E. Bradbury. I am also grateful to Francoise Ulam, wife of the late Stanislaw M. Ulam.

There were many polite and cooperative public servants of the U.S. Department of Energy (DOE) to whom I owe considerable thanks. I want to make special note of the assistance provided by Roger M. Anders, archivist of the DOE History Division, who unselfishly devoted his time and effort in my field research at the Germantown, Maryland, DOE offices where virtually all the AEC GAC records are stored. I am also grateful to Dr. Jack M. Holl, acting historian of the DOE. Both Anders and Holl provided congenial assistance and pleasant research conditions despite their many other work obligations and despite the need to conform with security restrictions. I would also like to thank William Woodard, who followed Mr. Tomei in working with the GAC. Mr. Woodard furnished valuable information about the GAC of the Energy Research and Development Administration (ERDA), 1975–1977. He permitted me to inspect and duplicate the public meeting records of the ERDA GAC, and his suggestions made possible significant improvements in the scientific awards portion of the book. I would also like to express my appreciation for the assistance provided by Dr. Lawrence K. Akers of the Laboratory Management Branch of the DOE. Dr. Akers has followed the progress of this research endeavor from the outset. He ably critiqued early draft work regarding the national energy laboratories, and he identified appropriate contact people within the DOE who could answer the author's questions. Dr. Akers has been both a helpful professional and a devoted friend.

Other government employees assisted the author. Herbert Kinney, who works in the office of the director at Brookhaven National Laboratory (BNL), read and critiqued the full manuscript, provided the author with several original documents, and spent a full day with the author discussing the GAC at his BNL offices. Mr. Kinney was a longtime AEC employee with considerable Capitol Hill experience. He worked for the GAC Research Subcommittee in the 1960s and lent his expertise to the "particle accelerator debates" section of the study. I would also like to note the assistance provided by Jerome Saltzman of the Nuclear Regulatory Commission.

In acknowledging the help furnished by university scholars in the fields addressed by this book, I want to emphasize the tremendous intellectual debt I owe to the previously published scholarship of Don K. Price, W. Henry Lambright, Harold Orlans, Irvin C. Bupp, Herbert York, and most particularly, Richard G. Hewlett and his coauthors Oscar E. Anderson and Francis Duncan. Works very useful in the preparation of this study include those by Hans A. Bethe, Joan Lisa Bromberg, Harvey Brooks, David Brown, Thomas E. Cronin and Norman C. Thomas, Steven Del Sesto, Robert Devine, David Dickson, Daniel Ford, Robert Gilpin and Christopher Wright, William T. Golden, Peter Goodchild, Harold P. Green and Alan Rosenthal, Daniel S. Greenberg, Sanford D. Greenberg, Steven Hilgartner (et al.), George F. Kennan, James R. Killian, George B. Kistiakowsky, David E. Lilienthal, Grant McConnell, Dorothy Nelkin, Martin L. Perl, Joseph A. Pika, Joel Primack and Frank von Hippel, Randall Ripley and Grace A. Franklin, Elizabeth S. Rolph, Jonathan Schell, Dean Schooler, Jr., Glenn T. Seaborg, Albert H. Teich, Edward Teller, Thaddeus J. Trenn, David Truman, Robert C. Williams and Philip L. Cantelon, Jerome B. Weisner, Thomas R. Wolanin, and Sir Solly (Lord) Zuckerman.

Many people who read the manuscript material and offered valuable advice deserve special mention, among them Robert A. Rothman, Norman C. Thomas, Richard G. Hewlett, Henry Steck, Carl Grafton, Conrad Trumbore, Lloyd Musolf, George Basalla, and William W. Boyer, Jr. My friend and mentor, Barry S. Rundquist, has been a source of support and encouragement. I am also grateful for the thorough advice offered by two anonymous readers of this work.

I would also like to acknowledge the help furnished to me by the University of Delaware. Resources have been generously made available by Department of Political Science Chairs James K. Oliver and Marian L. Palley. The university approved a General Faculty Research Grant that subsidized the cost of work time and field research undertaken in 1984, and for this I would like to thank Provost L. Leon Campbell and Research Coordinator Robert D. Varrin. Arts and Science Dean Helen Gouldner approved a typing grant that paid for the excellent first draft typing services of Jo Arena. Anne E. Webster volunteered extensive computing service consulting aid during preparation of the draft manuscript. Bill Silag and Marilyn Keller of Iowa State University Press ably assisted the author through several stages of editing and production.

I also thank students of my graduate and undergraduate classes who have listened to presentations of my chapter work, read portions of that work, and volunteered sound advice and comment. I express gratitude to my parents, Robert and Joanne. My wife, Claire, and my sons, Nathan and Eric, have been understanding and patient in tolerating my long and frequent absences from home life, sometimes shouldering too much of the burden of this enterprise.

THE NUCLEAR ORACLES

1 Government science advice and the GAC

SCIENTISTS HAVE LONG VOLUNTEERED ADVICE to their government. Modern science advice to government may well have begun in 1695, when England's Regency Council decided to consult a number of leading intellectuals about a monetary crisis. Among those consulted were Sir Isaac Newton and John Locke. Newton not only rendered expert advice but went on to serve the English Mint and later won election to a seat in the House of Commons.[1] Since World War II scientific advice to the U.S. government has evolved into a "scientific advisory system." Scientists and engineers who wish to serve the country in the technical decision making process have joined the advisory system and by so doing have become "insiders."[2]

Why are scientists needed as advisers? It has been argued: "If we have a reliable method for discovering the truth, namely, science, should we not use it to solve all of our most important problems? If we propose to do so, should not those who make our most important decisions be selected for their understanding of the most relevant science?"[3] The U.S. government has responded affirmatively and has drawn on the skills and talents of those who worked for universities or private firms. Those scientific experts most in demand for their advisory services and consultations are likely to be drawn from a scientific establishment composed of "heads of professional societies, heads of university or industrial laboratories, and chairmen of university science departments."[4]

The semipublic world of the scientific adviser blends science and politics. The scientific advisory system "provides a facade of prestige which tends to legitimize technical decisions made by the President" or by administrative officials.[5] Correspondingly service on major federal advisory committees is a source of status for those who serve, and when those recruited to serve have major stature, the agency sponsoring the

3

advisory committee may enjoy added respect and influence.

The world of the science adviser is an elite and exclusive one. There is little doubt that the politics of science has been generally conducted by a remarkably small number of people.[6] Only prominent scientists have been invited to join science advisory committees, and most owe their fame to research accomplishments, rather than to administrative, business, or teaching success.

Science advisers to government have not always been described in flattering terms. It has been said that in the years after World War II, leading scientists "turned into celebrities by the news media, were looked upon as high priests of a state religion that promised social progress by means of made-to-order technological advances."[7] The first chairman of the Atomic Energy Commission (AEC), David E. Lilienthal, claimed that the atomic establishment "had the added thrust of official mystery and complexity of atomic energy. They were the experts; they knew it all; it was over the head of the public, and public critics were held in disdain."[8]

Why did the federal government grow to depend on scientists and the advice they could offer? The scientific revolution refashioned the basic sciences and demonstrated the ability to produce new technology. In turn, the government came to depend on the technical innovations that science made possible; this was particularly so for the military. In fact, "When politicians became persuaded that basic research held the key to our future security and material welfare, the basic relation of government to private institutions changed."[9] The public and private sectors moved closer together. National policy today assumes that a great deal of our new enterprise is likely to flow from technological developments financed by the government and directed in response to government policy.[10] A prime example of the government's ability to stimulate technological advancement was the Apollo project of the National Aeronautics and Space Administration.[11]

In producing technological progress, science posed a challenge to accepted routines of political decision making. Science brought so much complexity into public policy that public issues could no longer be determined by the "parliamentary competition of opposing doctrines."[12] Scientific phenomena were not translatable subjects of partisan political debate. If science, particularly atomic science, was incomprehensible to members of Congress, it was equally mystifying to many of the federal government's senior administrative officials. As more and more public problems had to be left not to administrative discretion but to scientific discovery, the judgment of scientists and their professional colleagues became essential. In making judgments, scientists were "likely to be influenced by the opinion of their fellow scientists," and a chief opinion source was, and continues to be, the "many advisory networks which . . . link public and private interests."[13]

Some advisory groups have achieved strong influence over, or even control of, public policy in certain domains. The line between offering advice and making policy has become indistinct for many advisory committee members.[14] This is particularly the case in science advice. For many public administrators and elected officials, science has become something very close to an establishment, "a set of institutions supported by tax funds, but largely on faith, and without direct responsibility to political control."[15] This establishment tends to guide the direction that research takes and designates research subjects as fashionable or unfashionable. Members of the establishment often serve as models, as well, for young scientists and engineers interested in research.

Dynamics of federal advisory committees

What purposes are served by federal advisory committees? For one thing, they facilitate acceptance of agency actions by groups represented on the committee.[16] In a sense, an advisory committee is an arena for testing agency policy "trial balloons." The advisory committee may save the agency considerable embarrassment by deflating flawed or inappropriate proposals. Agency decisions endorsed by an advisory committee (or committees) may be accorded greater procedural legitimacy.[17] Advisory committee members sometimes prove to be welcome allies in debates that concern agency proposals in legislative or executive political arenas.

Advisory committees can be valuable in the public relations work of government organizations. In 1959, for example, the AEC encouraged the General Advisory Committee (GAC) to issue a report to help assuage public fears about the danger of radioactive fallout from atmospheric testing of nuclear weapons. The GAC accommodated the Commission and released a statement declaring that most media reports about dangers from exposure to nuclear bomb fallout were both exaggerated and unsubstantiated.[18] This was a valuable service to AEC officials who, at the time, were being bombarded by public inquiries and fears about the danger of exposure to radioactivity.

For federal administrators, an advisory committee is a source of expert advice and information rendered by accomplished individuals who work outside of government. This consultative advice is usually secured at very low cost to the host agency. As volunteers, many advisory committee members serve with little or no pay, perhaps receiving only reimbursement for the expenses incurred in traveling to and from meetings and for food and lodging costs.

Despite nominal compensation for their time and effort, advisory committee members do realize indirect gains from their service. Advisory committee service furnishes access to federal political and administrative officials, which creates unique opportunities to discover the immediate concerns of these officials. Also, the agenda of business submitted by the department to the advisory committee may convey information that is professionally, commercially, or academically useful to committee members. Furthermore, service on an advisory committee may be expected to carry some weight in the adviser's business transactions or in the efforts to secure research grant funding. Advisory committee service can also help elevate the status of those invited to serve.[19] In some cases, advisory committees are delegated considerable authority and responsibility in monitoring administrative actions. Usually, the broader an advisory committee's charge happens to be, the greater the possibility that the committee will act independently in its oversight of agency work. The degree of influence an advisory committee possesses in its relations with its host agency is associated with the degree of expertise represented by committee members individually and as a whole and is strongest when the agency lacks the in-house expertise that advisory committee members possess.

The personal status that enhances an advisory committee member's influence on agency officials and committee colleagues comes in a variety of ways. If an individual has achieved a powerful executive or managerial position, his or her status may be largely a function of the post occupied. For example, Robert E. Wilson, an AEC GAC member from 1956 to 1960, was an esteemed chemical engineer who had also been chairman of the board of Standard Oil of Indiana. During his GAC term he assumed the board chairmanship of the American Oil Co. It is clear that the institutional position he occupied at the time of his service helped enhance his recommendations.

Similarly, an individual's distinguished record of scientific or technical achievement may confer status of a scholarly nature. Advisory committee members with such status may be influential because of expertise unmatched by other committee members or by other agency personnel. For example, Enrico Fermi's unprecedented academic credentials, his scientific accomplishments that culminated in the winning of a Nobel Prize in 1938, and his ongoing achievements in the research of high-energy physics beyond 1938 must have given Fermi immense influence on the GAC and with the Commission itself. Given the almost academic nature of many GAC meetings, scholastic status was often more important than institutional status. Influence in the deliberations of any federal advisory committee is likely to be related to one or both forms of status.

Another dynamic of federal advisory committees involves the issue of representation. By identifying the backgrounds of those who served on a federal advisory committee, it is possible to determine which interests, institutions, and academic disciplines have advised federal officials. Changes in the membership of an advisory committee over time should reveal which interests, institutions, or academic disciplines have gained or lost representation.

An interest group or corporation with one or more employees serving on a prestigious federal advisory committee has a variety of opportunities. At the very least, the organization or interest has potential access to inside administrative information, and advisory committee members may even become advocates or proponents of committee-reviewed proposals that are advantageous to their organizations or interests. Loss of representation on a federal advisory committee results in diminished access to federal officials for a corporation, university, research lab, or special interest organization.

Types of federal advisory committees

A general advisory committee is only one of a number of types of federal advisory committees. These committees can be classified by the level of government they serve, by their task or function, and by the length of time of their existence.

Within the executive branch of the federal government are two categories of advisory committees, presidential and departmental. Authors of studies that examine the function and operation of presidential advisory committees generally conclude that these committees are more vulnerable to politicization than are departmental advisory committees.[20] Each time a new president takes office, for example, executive office advisory committees are subject to virtually complete membership turnover. In addition, although presidential advisory committees may be assigned a variety of advisory tasks, they are likely to be influential only to the extent that they are used, and listened to, by the president and the White House staff.

The second category, departmental advisory committees, are impaneled to advise specific departments or agencies of the federal bureaucracy. Some of these committees have their origin in specific statutes that mandate their operation and continuation by law; others are created by the federal agencies they serve. A study describing the elaborate array of committees and councils established to advise administrators of the Department of Health, Education, and Welfare (HEW) national education offices indicated that many of these bodies were temporary and malleable, and individuals recruited to serve on them were often hand-picked by HEW administrators themselves.[21]

Not all department advisory committees have members chosen directly by host agency officials. In many instances agency officials must have appointments cleared by the White House, and sometimes the president makes direct appointments to a departmental advisory committee. In the case of the AEC GAC, the president relied on a list of nominees proposed by the AEC chairman to make new GAC appointments or reappoint GAC members whose terms expired, and he rarely deviated from choosing nominees endorsed by the Commission.

The GAC of the AEC, and later the Energy Research and Development Administration (ERDA), was a departmental advisory committee created by law, although its members were appointed by the president. Because it had its origin in law, the AEC and ERDA could not simply terminate or disband the committee. This statutory foundation enabled the GAC to operate almost independently, which sometimes resulted in controversy. Moreover, GAC members did not slavishly follow the agenda prepared by its host agency; the Committee occasionally embarked on independent reviews of certain AEC or ERDA operations. Because the GAC was a departmental rather than a presidential committee, it was subject to less political interference than the President's Science Advisory Committee (PSAC), which may be one reason why the GAC outlasted the PSAC.

A second classification of advisory committees is by task or function. There are six general types of federal advisory committees distinguishable by task or function: (1) committees of a general advisory nature, (2) scientific and technical advisory committees, (3) special clientele (usually industry) advisory committees, (4) special task (or action) advisory committees, (5) research committees (usually called commissions), and (6) public conferences.[22]

In brief, general advisory committees are usually appointed by an executive or by a legislature. They advise the agency on all matters that concern the agency's missions. Committees of this type have seven to fifteen members, are expected to meet at least once a year, and "are likely to be formed when programs are controversial, costly, complex, and unfamiliar."[23] Presumably, members of such committees are not only fully knowledgeable in the agency's major fields of activity but may also have political influence that can be brokered on behalf of the agency.

Scientific and technical advisory committees, as expected, are composed of individuals with professional, scientific, or technical qualifications. Through this type of professional entity a public organization or agency may acquire talent or expertise that it is unable to obtain in other ways. In addition, this type of committee is an impartial and capable group that can judge major project proposals for the agency.

Certain special advisory committees represent a specific clientele or constituency group of the host agency. "Unlike members of the general committee, who are expected to serve a public as apart from a private or an industry interest, the point of view of the members of the industry committee is primarily a selfish one."[24] Many industrial advisory committees originated in World War II, when it was essential that the government gain the active support of industries with facilities critical to the war effort.[25] Many have alleged that special clientele advisory committees "enlist the support of the regulated in the process of regulation."[26]

Special task force advisory committees handle discrete operational assignments for their host agencies, particularly when an agency is precluded from doing the work "in-house." These bodies often hold hearings, conduct inquiries, and perform quasi-judicial functions. Many of these committees are subject to automatic termination when the task they are assigned is definitely completed or if their assignment is time-bound and a deadline has passed. Sometimes specific task force groups are used by the agency to judge and rank grant proposals prepared by individuals or organizations outside of government. The objectivity and disinterestedness of task force members is often an asset for public agency officials who either are prohibited from judging outside proposals or are unwilling to do so.[27]

Research or study committees do fact-finding work and are commonly employed at the presidential level. Usually impaneled as commissions, these councils deal with important political and societal problems. Commissions in recent history, for example, have investigated political assassinations, urban riots, racial problems, national security, and government reorganization. Research committees have from five to as many as twenty or more members, including both private citizens and government officials. These bodies may build the groundwork for a new administration approach or program or serve to refute criticism of the president made by those who believe that the president has failed to respond to a major problem. The final report issued by a research committee or commission may have considerable influence on public policy as well as be of great scholarly value.

Another type of advisory body is the public conference, which may be convened at the presidential level to deal with a subject of urgent concern. Usually the topic addressed is not as controversial or as sensitive as those assigned to a commission; education, conservation, mental retardation, and national economic issues have been conference subjects in recent history. Conferences, which can involve a few hundred to several thousand people, are often conducted with no well-developed system for formulating recommendations or governing participation. They afford the possibility of meaningful dialogue between citizens and government officials and are useful in presidential problem identification.[28] Conferences can permit administration critics to express their views and to vent their frustration and provide these critics with the hope that their recommendations may finally get consideration.

The third factor used in classifying advisory committees concerns time. Some advisory committees have been chartered as "permanent" statutory bodies not subject to dismissal or termination by their host institutions. The GAC and the Advisory Committee on Reactor Safeguards both originated with the AEC and operated as permanent, legally constituted committees.[29] Only a federal law, or a change in federal law, can terminate such permanent bodies. On the other hand, many advisory committees are impaneled as temporary entities by the president or by other federal officials who have that authority. Either definite or indefinite time limits can be fixed on the committee's length of operation. Sometimes ad hoc, task-oriented working groups operate with preset termination dates.

The Federal Advisory Committee Act of 1972 subjects nearly all federal advisory committees to automatic termination dates and mandates termination after two years for the bulk of federal advisory committees. However, this act does not prohibit the routine reauthorization of these committees at the time of this biennial review. The GAC was judged by the Justice Department to be exempt from this biennial termination process.

When analyzing the GAC according to these three categories, it is important to recognize that the GAC was a departmental, not a presidential, advisory body, although its members were appointed or reappointed by the president and appointments were not subject to Senate confirmation. The GAC operated as a permanent advisory body explicitly created by the Atomic Energy Act of 1946, the same law that created the Joint Committee on Atomic Energy of the U.S. Congress. The GAC closely conformed to the "general advisory" type of committee, as its title denotes. However, the GAC also possessed some of the characteristics of a scientific-technical and a special clientele committee.

The role of scientific federal advisory committees in public policy-making has often been discounted or ignored. Because of the stature of the members, its important advisory responsibilities, and its many years of operation, this type of committee is particularly noteworthy.

The AEC General Advisory Committee

The General Advisory Committee of the U.S. Atomic Energy Commission had an extraordinary organizational longevity and exceptional advisory powers. Created by statute with the AEC in 1946, the Committee continued in operation for thirty years. It survived the dissolution of the AEC in 1974 and, with a reconstituted membership, went on to advise Energy Research and Development Administration officials. The GAC was terminated in the statutory reorganization that absorbed the ERDA staff into the U.S. Department of Energy (DOE) in 1977. The final group of GAC members were invited to join the ad hoc Solar Working Group in the new DOE.

Over its thirty-year history the GAC played a central role in the development and use of atomic energy in a variety of ways. The Committee fulfilled an important advisory role for the AEC through its oversight of projects and programs undertaken by the great AEC laboratories. In addition, it not only advised the AEC on matters pertaining to research and development of fission and thermonuclear atomic weapons but offered advisories on how those weapons could be tested and used. Morcover, it was instrumental in charting the future of high-energy physics through its review of the basic research budgets and projects of the AEC, through its recommendations regarding the creation, location, and maintenance of particle accelerator facilities, and through its AEC laboratory recruitment efforts and personnel training.

The GAC held 130 meetings from 1947 through 1974, and another 12 meetings to advise ERDA from 1975 to late 1977 (see Appendix A). Required by law to meet at least four times a year, in some years the GAC met five, six, or seven times. Each meeting covered two or three days, usually lasting the entire workday. The frequency and regularity of this thirty-year meeting schedule produced a huge volume of minutes, letter reports, subcommittee reports, memoranda, and other records, all stored at the U.S. Department of Energy Archives, Germantown, Maryland. Although a substantial portion of these records and documents remains classified by the U.S. government, an increasing amount of GAC material has been declassified.

In order to produce a balanced assessment of the work of the GAC, documentary material, published information gathered from books, periodical literature, other government documents and AEC records, and interviews were used. This study answers two cardinal questions: (1) Who served on the GAC and when? and (2) What AEC matters were Committee members asked to advise on and what recommendations did they make?

Embodied in the first question are several collateral questions. How were people recruited to serve on the GAC? What qualifications did they possess to justify appointment to such a prestigious body? For whom were they working during their terms of Committee service? From what disciplines and knowledge fields did members come? On what other advisory committees were members serving during their GAC terms? What determined turnover of Committee membership? How did the composition of the membership change over the years? What factors account for changes in the composition of the membership?

A total of fifty-five individuals served at various times on this nine-member body between January 1947 and September 1977, including six Nobel laureates, many corporation presidents, several university presidents, and in the later years a number of government research laboratory officials. The Committee was composed of some of the nation's most outstanding and renowned scientists and engineers. Many members were distinguished and respected physicists, chemists, chemical and electrical engineers, and mathematicians.

The distribution of academic disciplines represented on the panel over time suggests the general kinds of issues that the Committee was entrusted to address and the kind of advice the body was likely to offer. The membership history of the GAC also reveals the university, corporate, and government interests that were represented on the GAC, and when. Changes in the distribution of interest group representation over time illustrates to a degree how the Committee, appointed by the president, was perceived and used by the AEC and later by other federal administrative officials.

The second main question has two parts, On what subjects was the GAC asked to give advice? and What were the subsequent Committee recommendations? Three general issue domains serve as the topical focus of the study: (1) private versus public sector research and development, (2) military and national security issues, and (3) university versus AEC contract laboratory research. By investigating each domain individually, it is possible to better identify what the GAC did, as well as to analyze the participation in GAC meetings by individual members and the role of each member's interests and knowledge fields in meeting transactions. These transactions are analyzed through accounts of GAC meetings about selected AEC programs, including the superbomb controversy, the Project Gabriel radioactive fallout studies, Project Plowshare's peaceful use of nuclear explosives experiments, and high-energy particle accelerator physics.

Issues dealt with by the GAC

At the heart of the GAC's advisory responsibility was the constant supervision and oversight of the laboratory empire of the AEC, and later, the ERDA. Evidence gathered from records of over 142 GAC meetings consistently demonstrates that Committee members assiduously protected, promoted, exhorted, and sometimes reprimanded those responsible for scientific research and development conducted at the major federally funded AEC contract laboratories. Major contract laboratories such as Los Alamos, Brookhaven, Oak Ridge, Lawrence-Livermore, Lawrence-Berkeley, and Argonne were considered a national resource of scientific and technical talent and consequently play a central role in this study.

Private versus public sector research and development

The GAC had to determine which research and development activities should be performed by government contract laboratories and which should be undertaken by private corporations or universities outside of the government's official environment. While this was ostensibly a scientific or technical question, debate on this decision was often heatedly political and ideological. For example, the Committee had to arbitrate disputes and conflicts between the major research universities and the national laboratories.[30] Some of the most tension-ridden GAC meetings involved conflicts over whether a scientific or engineering research project should be assigned to a university-based research facility or to a government contractor–operated research laboratory. When officials employed by national laboratories were appointed to the Committee in the early 1960s, university influence began to diminish in these disputes and university GAC representation began a long decline.

Military and national security issues

Atomic energy's military and national security applications were ever present. The GAC shouldered major advice responsibilities in matters of national defense. Operating under the umbrella of official government secrecy, the Committee addressed issues of nuclear weapons research, development, and testing. Committee members were not asked to advise on matters of actual nuclear weapons deployment by the military, but they often volunteered their advice on this matter and therefore had to have an intimate knowledge of fission and thermonuclear weapons in terms of both production and capability. Members assumed an advisory role in defense nuclear power as well, as the AEC and the Defense Department explored a variety of ways to utilize atomic energy in the propulsion of submarines, surface ships, aircraft, and other military conveyances.

The GAC's scientific and technical discussions involving matters of national security resulted in the imposition of official secrecy restrictions, and the members wrestled with the problem of advising in conditions of official secrecy. Regularly cautioned that divulging too much information might jeopardize national security, GAC members responded that any overclassification of nuclear information would pose serious problems in the pursuit of new scientific knowledge. It could discourage and deter talented scientists from entering those fields because their achievements would not be publicly recognized or attributed, and it would inhibit the free flow of scientific information internationally. Furthermore, pursuing secret research on university campuses was seen to pose a serious challenge to traditional academic freedom.

The GAC's most controversial recommendations were those involving national defense, particularly with regard to H-bomb development and the later testing of thermonuclear bombs. Before the United States and the Soviet Union had successfully negotiated the 1963 Partial Test Ban Treaty, each country had pursued years of above-ground testing of fission and thermonuclear weapons. The huge amount of radioactive material discharged to the upper atmosphere posed a serious threat as radioactive nuclides descended back to earth. The GAC regularly investigated the dangers of radioactive fallout. The AEC relied on the members' expertise to quell public fears and to challenge public criticisms about these dangers. (The Committee's public pronouncements about atomic fallout, however, were not always consistent with what the Committee discussed under conditions of formal secrecy.)

The GAC doggedly attempted to find peaceful uses for nuclear technologies rooted in military application. For many years the Committee tried to foster Project Plowshare, an enterprise geared to finding peaceful uses for thermonuclear explosives.

University versus AEC contract laboratory research

A third issue domain arose from the question as to whether certain basic research projects should be assigned to universities or instead to AEC contract laboratories. Several national laboratories are managed under contract by large universities or by a consortium of universities, and this added another level of complexity. As basic scientific research demanded increasingly expensive equipment and facilities, often much beyond the financial means of universities or university groups, the GAC frequently recommended incorporation of basic research projects within AEC contract laboratories. This was particularly evident in the committee's deliberations on siting and construction of particle accelerators, or "atom smashers" as the popular press refers to them. These decisions from 1947 through 1977, which developed the pattern of U.S. support for basic scientific research, continue to have significant implications for the U.S. scientific community.

2 GAC origin, purpose, members, and procedures

GAC origin and purpose

The Atomic Energy Commission, the congressional Joint Committee on Atomic Energy, and the AEC General Advisory Committee were given legislative birth in the Atomic Energy Act of 1946, sometimes referred to as the McMahon Act. The charter of the GAC, which appeared in the 1946 law, is reproduced below from the amended Atomic Energy Act of 1954:

> There shall be a General Advisory Committee to advise the Commission on scientific and technical matters relating to materials, production, and research and development, to be composed of nine members, who shall be appointed from civilian life by the President. Each member shall hold office for a term of six years, except that (a) any member appointed to fill a vacancy occurring prior to the expiration of the term for which his predecessor was appointed, shall be appointed for the remainder of such term; and (b) the terms of office of the members first taking office after August 1, 1946, shall expire, as designated by the President at the time of appointment, three at the end of two years, three at the end of four years, and three at the end of six years, after August 1, 1946. The Committee shall designate one of its own members as Chairman. The Committee shall meet at least four times in every calendar year. The members of the Committee shall receive a per diem compensation for each day spent in meetings or conferences, and all members shall receive their necessary traveling or other expenses while engaged in the work of the Committee.[1]

The GAC's central purpose was contained in the phrase "on scientific and technical matters relating to materials, production, and research and development." The charter's rather bland and obscure mission statement does little to suggest the range and degree of GAC advisory responsibility. For many years the GAC served as the Atomic Energy Commission's chief repository of scientific and technical advice.[2] In the early years of AEC operation, when the agency had a small and inexperienced staff, the GAC functioned as "science directorate," although without formal line authority.

The Atomic Energy Act of 1954 repeated the wording of the original 1946 GAC charter but added this sentence: "The [Atomic Energy] Commission may also, upon recommendation of the General Advisory Committee, and with the approval of the President, grant an award for any especially meritorious contribution to the development, use or control of Atomic Energy."[3] This section was eventually used to found the Fermi Award (named in honor of Enrico Fermi, its first recipient), a scientific prize highly coveted by the science community and the most prestigious science prize awarded by the United States government. In the late 1950s, the GAC assumed similar responsibility in selecting the winners of the Lawrence Award, named for the late Ernest O. Lawrence, a highly esteemed physicist and creator-director of the University of California's Radiation Laboratory. While Fermi had been an original member of the GAC, Lawrence never served on the committee, although he occasionally met with the GAC in its early years. He made many contributions to the atomic sciences, developed one of the earliest cyclotrons, and served as teacher and mentor to many scientists who eventually were appointed to the GAC. Many eminent scientists were attracted to GAC service, in part, by the prospect of receiving nominations and choosing winners for these awards. (A subsequent section examines the Committee's work in conferring both awards.)

The General Advisory Committee was composed of nine "top" scientists and engineers who were to offer advice on all matters of research and applications of atomic energy.[4] GAC members were officially appointed by the president, but the Committee reported not to the president but rather to the Commission. The commissioners, in cooperation with sitting GAC members, suggested people to fill open positions on the Committee.[5] In the first ten to twelve years of the Committee's operation, sitting GAC members apparently had considerable say in who was chosen to fill vacant Committee seats. In later periods, the AEC chairman made an independent selection, merely having his choice confirmed by the president. Usually the president drew from a list of nominees prepared by the GAC, which had been passed on by the Commission chairman. The president was, of course, free to make an independent choice ignoring AEC- or GAC- endorsed candidates. There is some evidence that Presidents Johnson and Ford made independent choices.

One of the Commission's first acts was to consider appointments to the GAC. Robert F. Bacher, among the original five Commissioners and the AEC's first scientist commissioner, interpreted the GAC's mission statement to mean that it should be composed of physicists, chemists, metallurgists, and engineers.[6] Most commissioners of the 1940s and 1950s had had little scientific or technical training in matters of atomic energy and relied heavily on the advice and assistance of GAC scientists and engineers. The GAC provided "the AEC with scientific and technical guidance and advice, which allowed the Commission increased flexibility and greater opportunity to concentrate on basic policy matters."[7] Some have maintained that the GAC "largely determined AEC policy during the Commission's first few years."[8] Because the GAC commanded some of the best scientific and technical talent available in the nation, "certainly the (Atomic Energy) Commission [relied] heavily on the committee, at least until the Commissioners learned their jobs" and until the AEC general manager had assembled and trained his staff.[9]

When the AEC staff expanded in numbers of personnel and matured in technical expertise, the Commission's dependence on GAC advice and direction should have declined; it is difficult, however, to prove an inverse relationship between the GAC's degree of influence on the commissioners and the growth of AEC staff and technical expertise. For a number of reasons, GAC advisory powers may not have been eroded by improvements in the technical competence of the AEC staff. From the outset, the AEC employed extensive networks of advisers and advisory committees and enjoyed and benefited professionally from such contacts.[10] The AEC staff grew to depend on ongoing scientific and technical advice, such as from the Advisory Committee on Reactor Safeguards.

Moreover, the GAC did much more than simply dispense technical advice. In conjunction with other AEC advisory committees, the Committee counteracted the ill effects of secrecy and isolation common in the AEC operating environment. In many respects, the GAC and related advisory boards made for "safer if not speedier administration."[11] Despite criticisms that such heavy use of advisers was a way for timid AEC bureaucrats to avoid taking responsibility, the commissioners and management of the AEC found the benefits of committee advice far greater than the political costs. The Commission had much to gain in continuing to call on the advice and guidance of the GAC, even after the AEC staff had developed scientific and technical expertise.

Another factor to consider in gauging the degree of GAC influence throughout its existence is that of the appointment of sitting GAC members, or former members, to seats on the Commission itself (see Table 4.3). Three GAC members were appointed almost directly to the Commission after having served on the GAC: Willard F. Libby, John von Neumann, and Robert E. Wilson. Eleven years after leaving the GAC, Glenn T. Seaborg was appointed chairman of the AEC, a position he occupied for more than eleven years. There was movement in the other direction as well; Libby, T. Keith Glennan, John H. Williams, and Gerald F. Tape served as commissioners and were later appointed to the GAC.

This suggests a close association between Commission and GAC members. When Seaborg was appointed chairman of the AEC, Committee talent and expertise was in fact in command of the AEC. The transfer of GAC members to seats on the Commission diminished the need to regularly petition the Committee for help, and when former AEC commissioners were in service on the GAC, the Commission could continue to use the expertise and experience of these individuals by approaching the Committee for guidance.

The GAC did more than simply serve the internal interests of the AEC. The Committee, a highly independent and statutorily permanent federal advisory board, used this independence to reach out to other agencies within the executive branch. Often, top government officials were asked to participate in GAC meetings. There were times when the Joint Chiefs of the Armed Services participated in GAC meetings, as did members of the AEC Military Liaison Committee. Minutes of Meeting 17 of the GAC, held over a three-day period in October 1949, disclose that U.S. State Department counselor George F. Kennan was an invited participant. Among the matters discussed at this meeting was the role of atomic energy in the future of American foreign policy, particularly the impact of the anticipated "superbomb," or hydrogen bomb, on international affairs and U.S. foreign policy.[12]

There is evidence that the GAC met with President Harry S. Truman.[13] The Committee conferred with members of Congress, as well. The Joint Committee on Atomic Energy (JCAE), a powerful and long-standing committee of the Congress, regularly consulted GAC members.[14] Composed of nine representatives and nine senators, the JCAE exercised strong oversight power in its relationship with the AEC.[15] Yet, much like the early group of Atomic Energy commissioners, members of the JCAE lacked the expertise to assess highly scientific and technical issues.[16]

Many of the early GAC meetings were conducted in the presence of the assembled Atomic Energy commissioners. Throughout the thirty-year history of the body most, if not all five, commissioners were commonly in attendance at meetings held at Washington headquarters, and at least one commissioner usually attended the other meetings. When the GAC advised the Energy Research and Development Administration from 1975 into 1977, ERDA's chief administrator occasionally attended the GAC meetings. The participation of top AEC and ERDA officials in these meetings gave the Committee a privileged position as an advisory body.

The GAC's advice to the Commission was wide-ranging and often administrative and political as well as scientific and technical. For example, Meeting 2 of the GAC dealt with three central topics that presaged the GAC's main areas of advisory responsibility for many years: weapons, reactors, and the availability of isotopes for research.[17] The availability of isotopes topic falls under the GAC charter's reference to "materials, production, and research and development." "Materials" refers in a general sense to the radioactive substances or transuranic elements needed to pursue physical and chemical atomic research and necessary in the fabrication of atomic weapons.

Implicit in the responsibility to review weapon, reactor, and isotope issues was the need to examine the progress of research conducted by the major AEC laboratories. At its first meeting, GAC members agreed that the Commission should prepare and submit a report to the Committee on the status of research and development and materials and production before the Committee could "properly advise" the Commission.[18] Under this arrangement, the GAC could offer technical advice and guidance that afforded the Commission more flexibility and a chance to concentrate on basic policy matters it was better suited to address.[19] It has been observed that science may help refine our value judgments and may even determine the nature of goals themselves.[20] The science advice rendered by the GAC served this purpose for the AEC.

In planning how the GAC would operate, during the first GAC meeting, the commissioners and GAC members generally agreed "that it would not be feasible for the Committee to act as a technical consulting group to the Commission, but that the GAC might properly advise the Commission on major policy and program determinations."[21] In other words, the Committee would offer technical advice but would not shoulder the responsibilities of a scientific consultant engaged in the day-to-day management of AEC programs. The GAC would consider AEC staff reports and would be given AEC staff briefings at each meeting. Usually, the reports and briefings involved AEC project work conducted at the national laboratories or by other AEC-funded parties. For many years the AEC furnished the GAC with special monthly reports on the progress of activities, and also supplied the GAC with copies of the special semiannual and annual reports prepared for the JCAE. These classified reports were routed to those GAC members who had AEC-approved security storage facilities at their own offices.

The AEC inherited from the Manhattan Project of World War II an empire of laboratories and manufacturing facilities worth over $2.2 billion in public investment. This complex network, which employed about 40,000 people in 1947, was almost devoid of coherent central management.[22] As procedures evolved, AEC's contract laboratories furnished the Commission with reports on the status of their research and development projects that were almost routinely circulated to the GAC. Based on this and other information, the GAC used its collective scientific insight and technical expertise in drafting proposals and recommendations for the Commission. A regular system of correspondence emerged; the GAC chairman directed a letter report of each GAC meeting to the AEC chairman. This report was prepared almost immediately after each meeting and often was sent forward with appended documents. Frequently the report, as well as other GAC documents, requested a response at or before the GAC's next meeting. The responses produced by the AEC or its staff often became agenda items at the next GAC meeting. Consequently, while the AEC or its staff regularly approached the GAC with issues in an unprompted way, GAC correspondence often compelled the AEC or its staff to make some kind of response. In an unofficial way, this interaction helped make the AEC and its staff somewhat accountable to the GAC.

A vast range of issues was addressed by the GAC, either independently or at the request of the AEC. It was not uncommon for the Committee to discuss a topic as trivial as reimbursement policy for AEC-funded scientists traveling abroad and then move on to a review of global radioactive fallout deposition patterns resulting from thermonuclear bomb tests that the body had approved.

The GAC considered agendas of items prepared by the AEC; some agenda items, however, were products of independent GAC investigative action. In fact, the GAC may have acted with all the authority of a grand jury, able to look into any part of the AEC's scientific and technical work.[23] The GAC did not limit itself to technical problems but "freely volunteered advice on broad issues of national and international civilian nuclear policy."[24]

The GAC was not afraid to criticize the Commission or its scientific and technical projects. Sometimes Committee members expressed disappointment or dismay with AEC action or inaction. Lee A. DuBridge, one of the first GAC appointees, declared during one GAC meeting in 1947, "There is no technical reason for the absence of atomic energy" as a source of public power. DuBridge insisted that his assertion was widely held and that one conclusion that could be drawn from this "apparently slow progress is a failure of the Commission to be effective in this field."[25]

Appointments to the GAC

An important question is how people were appointed to the GAC. The GAC was composed of nine members appointed from civilian life by the president (Table 2.1). The first nine appointees had staggered

Table 2.1. GAC appointments, 1946-1977, including presidential reappointments and total length of service

Appointee	Date of Appointment	Date of Departure and Reason[a]	Length of Service
	Truman Appointees		
Oppenheimer, J. Robert	Dec. 12, 1946	Aug. 1, 1952 TE	5 yr, 7 mo
Conant, James B.	Dec. 12, 1946	Aug. 1, 1952 TE	5 yr, 7 mo
DuBridge, Lee A.	Dec. 12, 1946	Aug. 1, 1952 TE	5 yr, 7 mo
Fermi, Enrico	Dec. 12, 1946	Aug. 1, 1950 TE	3 yr, 7 mo
Rabi, Isidor I.	Dec. 12, 1946	Aug. 1, 1948 TE	1 yr, 7 mo
	July 31, 1948	Aug. 1, 1954 TE	6 yr
	Oct. 1, 1954[b]	Aug. 1, 1956 TE	1 yr, 10 mo
Rowe, Hartley	Dec. 12, 1946	Aug. 1, 1950 TE	3 yr, 7 mo
Seaborg, Glenn T.	Dec. 12, 1946	Aug. 1, 1950 TE	3 yr, 7 mo
Smith, Cyril S.	Dec. 12, 1946	Aug. 1, 1948 TE	1 yr, 7 mo
	July 31, 1948[b]	Jan. 25, 1952 RES	3 yr, 5 mo
Worthington, Hood	Dec. 12, 1946	Aug. 1, 1948 TE	1 yr, 7 mo
Buckley, Oliver E.	July 31, 1948	Aug. 1, 1954 TE	6 yr
Libby, Willard F.	Aug. 7, 1950	Sept. 30, 1954 RES	4 yr, 1 mo
	May 26, 1960[c]	Aug. 1, 1962 TE	2 yr, 2 mo
Murphree, Eger V.	Aug. 7, 1950	Aug. 1, 1956 TE	5 yr, 11 mo
	Apr. 4, 1957[c]	Aug. 1, 1958 TE	1 yr, 3 mo
	Oct. 27, 1958[c]	Oct. 29, 1962 D	4 yr
Whitman, Walter G.	Aug. 7, 1950	Aug. 1, 1956 TE	5 yr, 11 mo
von Neumann, John	Feb. 27, 1952	Aug. 1, 1954 TE	2 yr, 5 mo
Fisk, James B.	Sept. 22, 1952	Aug. 1, 1958 TE	5 yr, 10 mo
Warner, John C.	Sept. 22, 1952	Aug. 1, 1958 TE	5 yr, 10 mo
	Oct. 27, 1958[c]	Aug. 1, 1964 TE	5 yr, 9 mo
Wigner, Eugene P.	Sept. 22, 1952	Jan. 24, 1957 RES	4 yr, 4 mo
	Dec. 3, 1959[c]	Aug. 1, 1962 TE	2 yr, 7 mo
	Sept. 20, 1962[d]	May 1, 1964 RES	1 yr, 7 mo

Sources: U.S. Energy Research and Development Administration, "Memorandum: G.A.C. Members, Chairmen, and Technical Assistants," from Anthony A. Tomei to General Advisory Committee files, February 18, 1975.

[a]Reason symbols: TE = term expired, RES = resigned, D = deceased, and CTE = committee terminated (effective Sept. 30, 1977).

[b]Reappointed by Truman.

[c]Reappointed by Eisenhower.

[d]Reappointed by Kennedy.

Table 2.1. *(Continued)*

Appointee	Date of Appointment	Date of Departure and Reason[a]	Length of Service
Eisenhower Appointees			
Beams, Jesse W.	Oct. 23, 1954	Aug. 1, 1960 TE	5 yr, 9 mo
Johnson, Warren C.	Oct. 23, 1954	Aug. 1, 1960 TE	5 yr, 9 mo
McMillan, Edwin M.	Oct. 23, 1954	Oct. 7, 1958 RES	3 yr, 11 mo
Glennan, T. Keith	Oct. 26, 1956	Sept. 25, 1958 RES	1 yr, 11 mo
Teller, Edward	Oct. 26, 1956	Aug. 13, 1958 RES	1 yr, 9 mo
Wilson, Robert E.	Oct. 26, 1956	Mar. 22, 1960 RES	3 yr, 4 mo
Pitzer, Kenneth S.	Oct. 27, 1958	Aug. 1, 1964 TE	5 yr, 9 mo
	July 27, 1964[e]	July 31, 1965 RES	1 yr
McRae, James W.	Oct. 29, 1958	Feb. 2, 1960 D	1 yr, 3 mo
Benedict, Manson	Oct. 29, 1958	Aug. 1, 1962 TE	3 yr, 9 mo
	Sept. 20, 1962[d]	Aug. 1, 1968 TE	5 yr, 10 mo
Abelson, Philip H.	June 27, 1960	Nov. 15, 1963 RES	3 yr, 4 mo
Ramsey, Norman F., Jr.	Nov. 17, 1960	Aug. 1, 1966 TE	5 yr, 8 mo
	Sept. 1, 1966[e]	Aug. 1, 1972 TE	5 yr, 11 mo
Williams, John H.	Nov. 17, 1960	Apr. 17, 1966 D	5 yr, 5 mo
Kennedy Appointees			
Hafstad, Lawrence R.	Sept. 20, 1962	Aug. 1, 1968 TE	5 yr, 10 mo
Webster, William	Mar. 13, 1963	Aug. 1, 1964 TE	1 yr, 4 mo
	July 27, 1964[e]	Aug. 1, 1970 TE	6 yr
	June 30, 1970[f]	May 17, 1972 D	1 yr, 10 mo
Johnson Appointees			
Froman, Darol	Apr. 6, 1964	Aug. 1, 1966 TE	2 yr, 3 mo
Bugher, John C.	May 1, 1964	Aug. 1, 1968 TE	4 yr, 3 mo
	Aug. 16, 1968[e]	Sept. 19, 1970 D	2 yr, 1 mo
Lawroski, Stephen	July 27, 1964	Aug. 1, 1970 TE	6 yr
Vesper, Howard G.	Oct. 19, 1965	Aug. 1, 1970 TE	4 yr, 9 mo
	June 30, 1970[f]	Feb. 28, 1975 RES	4 yr, 7 mo
Goldwasser, Edwin L.	Sept. 1, 1966	Aug. 1, 1972 TE	5 yr, 11 mo
Hall, Jane H.	Sept. 1, 1966	Aug. 1, 1972 TE	5 yr, 11 mo
Friedman, Herbert	Aug. 16, 1968	Aug. 1, 1974 TE	5 yr, 11 mo
Squires, Lombard	Aug. 16, 1968	Aug. 1, 1974 TE	5 yr, 11 mo
Nixon Appointees			
Eliassen, Rolf	June 30, 1970	Feb. 28, 1975 RES	4 yr, 7 mo
Sterner, James H.	May 26, 1971	Aug. 1, 1974 TE	3 yr, 2 mo
Hayward, Evans V.	Oct. 6, 1972	Feb. 28, 1975 RES	2 yr, 5 mo
Heffner, Hubert	Oct. 6, 1972	Feb. 28, 1975 RES	2 yr, 5 mo
May, Michael M.	Oct. 6, 1972	Feb. 28, 1975 RES	2 yr, 5 mo
	Sept. 24, 1975[g]	Sept. 30, 1977 CTE	2 yr
Zinn, Walter H.	Oct. 6, 1972	Feb. 28, 1975 RES	2 yr, 5 mo
Ford Appointees			
Hansen, Arthur G.	Sept. 24, 1975	Aug. 1, 1976 TE	11 mo
Morse, Richard S.	Sept. 24, 1975	Aug. 1, 1976 TE	11 mo
Ward, Martin J.	Sept. 24, 1975	Aug. 1, 1976 TE	10 mo
	Jan. 19, 1977[g]	Sept. 30, 1977 CTE	1 yr, 2 mo
Gould, William R.	Sept. 24, 1975	Sept. 30, 1977 CTE	2 yr
Hitch, Charles J.	Sept. 24, 1975	Sept. 30, 1977 CTE	2 yr
Linden, Henry R.	Sept. 24, 1975	Sept. 30, 1977 CTE	2 yr
Patrick, Ruth	Sept. 24, 1975	Sept. 30, 1977 CTE	2 yr
Tape, Gerald F.	Sept. 24, 1975	Sept. 30, 1977 CTE	2 yr
Connor, James E.	Jan. 19, 1977	Sept. 30, 1977 CTE	9 mo
Zarb, Frank G.	Jan. 19, 1977	Sept. 30, 1977 CTE	9 mo

[e]Reappointed by Johnson.
[f]Reappointed by Nixon.
[g]Reappointed by Ford.

terms; J. Robert Oppenheimer, James B. Conant, and DuBridge had six-year terms; Fermi, Hartley Rowe, and Seaborg four-year terms, and Isidor I. Rabi, Cyril S. Smith, and Hood Worthington two-year terms.[26] The staggered terms were intended to provide a regular, incremental turnover in membership. Ideally, one-third of the GAC membership would be either replaced or subject to reappointment action every two years.

After 1946, when vacancies on the Committee were created by the expiration of terms, each new appointment was for six years. If a member resigned before his or her term expired, or if a member passed away, the president appointed a replacement to serve out the duration of an unexpired term. Appointment of replacements accounts for the significant number of the abbreviated terms of service listed in Table 2.1.

It was also permissible to reappoint members of the GAC whose terms had expired, either for another full term or for an abbreviated term as a replacement for someone leaving before a term's expiration. Ten GAC members appointed by one president were reappointed by other presidents. Rabi, Libby, Eger V. Murphree, and John C. Warner, originally appointed by President Truman, were later reappointed by President Dwight D. Eisenhower. First appointed by Truman, Eugene P. Wigner was reappointed first by Eisenhower and later by President John F. Kennedy. Kenneth S. Pitzer and Norman F. Ramsey, Jr., both Eisenhower appointees, were later reappointed by President Lyndon B. Johnson. Manson Benedict was appointed by Eisenhower and later by Kennedy. William Webster was first chosen by Kennedy and then was reappointed by Johnson and once more by President Richard M. Nixon. Howard G. Vesper began as a Johnson choice and was given another term by Nixon. As the AEC was about to be abolished and its personnel and facilities transferred to either the new Nuclear Regulatory Commission or the emerging ERDA, Michael M. May, a Nixon appointee, was reappointed by President Gerald R. Ford to serve on the reconstituted GAC that was to advise the ERDA.

Reappointment enabled Murphree, Warner, and Ramsey to serve nearly twelve continuous years on the GAC. Libby and Wigner, both Nobel laureates, resigned during their original terms and were reappointed to the GAC several years later. Twenty-one GAC members served at least one term of six years, and seven of these people served on the committee more than six years. The AEC GAC had a total of forty-five members, who served a total of 241.5 years from December 1946 until February 1975, an average 5.3 years of service. The ERDA GAC functioned for only two years; there were ten new appointees plus May. The average length of service for the final ERDA GAC cohort was only slightly longer than eighteen months. The two groups, a total of fifty-five members, gave 258.8 years service from 1946 into 1977, with an average length of service of 4.7 years.

The average length of AEC GAC service of those appointed between 1946 and 1960 and those appointed between 1961 and 1975 were similar. The first twenty-two GAC appointees had an average length of service of 5.47 years. The last twenty-two appointees (excluding May) had almost precisely the same average length of Committee service, 5.49 years. From 1946 through 1960, there were twenty-nine GAC appointments, with a 5.57-year average period of service. For those fifteen AEC GAC appointees (excluding May) who began their terms after 1960, the average period of service was 5.3 years, again showing similar lengths of service.

Presidential appointments

The original appointing president of each GAC member and, if members were reappointed to the committee, the name of the president who made the reappointment are listed in Table 2.1. In Table 2.2 are cumulated the appointment and reappointment actions of each president who served during the period of the Committee's existence.

President Truman made the first nine appointments to the GAC. He went on to reappoint Rabi and Smith, who were appointed originally to only two-year terms. He was able to make eight more original appointments. So from December 1946 until September 1952 Truman made seventeen appointments and two reappointment actions, more original appointments and total appointment actions than any of the five succeeding presidents.

President Eisenhower made the second largest number of original

Table 2.2. **Number of presidential appointments and reappointments to the GAC, 1947–1977**

President	Original Appointments	Reappointments	Total Appointment Actions
Truman (1946–1952)	17	2	19
Eisenhower (1953–1960)	12	6	18
Kennedy (1961–1963)	2	2	4
Johnson (1964–1968)	8	4	12
Nixon (1969–1974)	6	2	8
Ford (1975–1977)ª	10	2	12
	55	18	73

ªPresident Ford made two appointments and one reappointment to the GAC on January 19, 1977, immediately prior to leaving office. President Carter, anticipating the termination of the GAC, made no appointment or reappointment decisions in the Committee's final nine months of operation in 1977.

appointments and the largest number of reappointments during the years he was in office. A two-term president, Eisenhower was the longest-serving president during the GAC's thirty-year history. Clearly, Truman and Eisenhower could profoundly influence the membership composition of the Committee. Presidents Kennedy, Johnson, and Nixon had somewhat fewer opportunities to make wholesale changes in membership. Nevertheless, they left their mark on the Committee through the affiliations and disciplines of the appointees they did select.

President Ford, in making appointments to the ERDA GAC, effected a nearly complete change in GAC membership. As the AEC underwent a reorganization into the Nuclear Regulatory Commission and the ERDA, the AEC GAC members tendered "courtesy" resignations en masse when the new ERDA administrator, Robert C. Seamans, Jr., indicated that this was necessary in order to permit him and President Ford an opportunity to impanel a new GAC membership better suited to serve the missions of the ERDA. As a result Ford made eight new appointments simultaneously and invited AEC GAC member May to join the ERDA GAC. Ford's dramatic reshaping of the membership composition of the GAC allowed heretofore unrepresented disciplines to gain GAC seats.

Factors influencing GAC turnover

Members left GAC service for many reasons. Five members died during their terms of service. Sixteen more tendered their resignations prior to fulfillment of their terms. A few stepped down as they entered their retirement years. Some left to join the AEC or other advisory committees; for example, Edward Teller departed GAC service less than two years into his term in order to serve on the President's Science Advisory Committee (PSAC). Some left because they had assumed new positions that they believed would pose possible "conflict of interest" problems if they continued to serve on the Committee. In addition, as stated earlier, all GAC members tendered resignations when the AEC was abolished in early 1975. In August 1974 three GAC terms had expired, and none of these vacancies had been filled by early 1975; thus the "courtesy" resignation group consisted of six sitting members.

Of a total seventy-three terms of GAC service, in forty-three cases members served until their terms expired. So nearly 60 percent of the open terms were served to completion. (This calculation omits the nine terms that expired prematurely with the termination of the GAC itself on September 30, 1977.) The chief reasons for turnover in GAC membership were expiration of term, resignation, death, and agency reorganization.

GAC procedures

Meeting frequency and location

The GAC was required by law to meet at least four times every calendar year. In the epoch of the AEC, the Committee held 130 meetings. This covered the period between 1947 and 1974 (see Appendix A). In addition one special unnumbered meeting of the body was convened in Chicago in December 1947. When the GAC was carried over to the ERDA, an additional twelve meetings were held. When the Committee was officially terminated on September 30, 1977, its members joined an ad hoc Solar Working Group. The body was created to permit former GAC members to complete a solar energy project assigned by the ERDA. The date of GAC termination coincided with the last day of ERDA operation prior to its absorption into the new Department of Energy (DOE). By April 1, 1978, the group, having submitted its completed report, was officially disbanded by the DOE.

The GAC held four to five meetings a year, with a thirty-year average of about 4.5 meetings per year. In 1947, the Committee held an extraordinary eight meetings. The years 1949, 1959, and 1961 were years of very high meeting frequency. In 1949, the Committee was regularly consulted to help fashion the organization of the AEC and its scientific projects. Meetings in 1959 were necessary to address the problems posed by major increases in above-ground atomic testing by the United States and the Soviet Union. Problems of atomic testing were at the center of 1961 meetings as well, as the United States and the Soviet Union entered into negotiations to ban or restrict nuclear testing. Off-schedule GAC meetings were hastily called for other reasons, some of which remain officially classified.

Most GAC meetings covered a three-day period, with one of the three days including a Saturday or Sunday. This minimized disruption of the private work schedules of members and facilitated travel arrangements. Meetings were divided into morning and afternoon sessions; many records reflect a subdivision of meetings into numbered sessions. Over the course of a three-day meeting period, there may have been as many as six or more sessions.

Ninety-two of the AEC GAC meetings were conducted in the AEC Washington, D.C.–area offices. Some were held at AEC H Street offices downtown; after 1960 some were held at the AEC Germantown, Maryland, offices twenty miles from the downtown facility. The majority of ERDA GAC meetings were held at the Washington-area offices.

From 1949 to 1951 and in 1954 and 1956, the GAC held one meeting a year outside Washington, D.C. Beginning in 1957, it was customary for the Committee to hold two quarterly meetings each year at various major AEC contract laboratories. This made it possible for GAC members to stay better informed and more up-to-date about the progress of laboratory activities and in particular to allow interaction of Committee members with AEC laboratory directors, officials, and scientists. A visit by the GAC was an opportunity for a laboratory to show off new equipment and facilities. Almost invariably, a GAC meeting agenda at a lab site included tours and special briefings that enabled laboratory people to prove their expertise while pressing for additional AEC funding or support. Correspondingly, when the GAC conducted a meeting at a laboratory, it was in effect doing a field investigation for the AEC. Sometimes a GAC lab-based meeting revealed managerial difficulties, scientific errors, poor use of scarce resources, or just an irresolute application of scientific manpower. Lab directors had a chance to air their complaints freely about AEC practices in an environment away from AEC headquarters and under conditions of confidentiality.

GAC meetings held at sites away from AEC headquarters were almost always conducted at major AEC national laboratories. From 1947 to 1975, the panel met eight times in Los Alamos, New Mexico; frequently, these sessions were split between the Los Alamos Scientific Laboratory and the nearby Sandia National Laboratory. The Argonne National Laboratory, in a Chicago suburb, was the site of six GAC meetings. Another seven were convened in the San Francisco Bay area, where sessions often were divided between University of California's campus-based Berkeley Radiation Laboratory and its Livermore National Laboratory (after the death of Ernest O. Lawrence, these labs were renamed respectively the Lawrence Berkeley Radiation Laboratory and the Lawrence Livermore National Laboratory). The Oak Ridge National Laboratory in Tennessee hosted five GAC meetings, and the Brookhaven National Laboratory on Long Island in New York three meetings. Commission labs near Hanford, Washington, and the Savannah River lab outside of Aiken, South Carolina, were occasionally sites of GAC meetings in later years. The Committee's most unusual meeting locations were Mayaguez, Puerto Rico, in February 1966 and Scottsdale, Arizona, in February 1972. At Mayaguez the Committee included an inspection of the Puerto Rico Nuclear Centre directed by Dr. John C. Bugher, who was at the time a GAC member. At Scottsdale, the group held discussions in an environment away from the laboratories.

Committee staff aides and travel policy

The GAC was furnished a two- to seven-member staff of AEC employees and (later) ERDA employees.[27] This secretariat performed administrative duties and compiled records of each GAC meeting. All meetings were recorded; after each meeting, transcriptions were made of the tapes for the sole use of the Committee secretary, and then both transcriptions and tapes were destroyed.[28]

The GAC selected its own secretary, and the AEC or ERDA assigned an administrative liaison officer to attend each meeting. John H. Manley, a Los Alamos physicist, served as secretary from 1947 until early 1951. He was succeeded by Richard W. Dodson, a Brookhaven chemist, who served from 1951 to 1955. Jane H. Hall, another Los Alamos physicist and future GAC member, served as secretary until May 1959; in October 1959 Robert A. Charpie, an Oak Ridge physicist, replaced Hall. In 1963 Anthony A. Tomei, who had long served as the GAC administrative liaison, became the committee's full-time secretary until the dissolution of the AEC. When the GAC moved under the ERDA umbrella, Fisher Howe became the GAC secretary and William L. Woodard continued to serve as assistant secretary; these men coordinated the work of the committee up to and through its 1977 termination. When Tomei became secretary, Duane C. Sewell and Melvin A. Harrison of the Lawrence Livermore Laboratory served together as Committee technical officers.

The GAC secretary and the AEC liaison officer painstakingly recorded Committee deliberations and prepared transcriptions. They compiled documents needed for each meeting, made arrangements in fashioning each meeting's agenda, and helped the GAC's recommendations penetrate the AEC bureaucracy. In addition, they did the mundane work of handling the Committee's financial affairs and ensuring that invited witnesses appeared at meetings.

Those who served on the GAC received a per diem compensation for time devoted to meetings of the GAC or its subcommittees. Members were reimbursed for travel expenses incurred in attending meetings or in subcommittee-related field research. Financial compensation for serving on the Committee was less than what members earned at their home offices or laboratories, so GAC service was clearly not a source of direct financial enrichment.

Meeting confidentiality and secrecy restrictions

The AEC GAC played a key role in both the military and civilian realms of atomic energy. The Committee may best be remembered by the general public as one of the few internal governmental bodies to oppose development of the hydrogen bomb in 1949. In deliberating on these and other highly sensitive matters, each GAC member had to be issued an appropriate security clearance including authorization to read classified documents. Obviously, individuals who posed security risks, as determined by FBI background checks, could not be serious contenders for membership. Consequently, it can be assumed that all fifty-five people who served on the GAC were previously issued a security clearance, which they maintained for the duration of their service or longer.

The Committee itself held closed meetings for many years of its operation. On some rare occasions, portions of the meetings were opened to outside uncleared individuals and to the media. Open GAC meetings became more commonplace after enactment of the Federal Advisory Committee Act (FACA) of 1972 and the Freedom of Information Act of 1974. The FACA in particular compelled the GAC and other federal advisory committees to keep written records that could be made public. Secrecy or confidentiality of meetings was permitted only under specific circumstances, when the discussion involved secrets involving national defense or foreign policy, corporate or financial trade confidential information, certain facts that could not be revealed by law, law enforcement or federal investigatory files, or internal personnel rules or any other possible invasion of personal privacy.

GAC materials, records, minutes, and letters have in many instances been kept classified in the interests of national security. According to longtime GAC secretary and AEC administrative liaison officer Tomei, detailed minutes were written for every GAC meeting. Woodard, former assistant secretary of the ERDA GAC, confirmed that copious minutes and records were kept in the 1975–1977 period, as well. In a public statement issued in 1960, AEC Chairman Seaborg declared that he "had no reservations about making reports of the General Advisory Committee available to Congress."[29] Nevertheless, a congressional committee study in 1977 reported that ERDA GAC meetings from 1976 on were conducted without adequate transcripts or detailed minutes. The staff study castigated the Committee for failure to afford the public access to meetings and for poor compliance with provisions of the Freedom of Information Act.[30] In this regard, the GAC was not much different from other science advisory bodies. Advice given to a government official by such bodies "is almost always received under the condition that it be kept confidential by the official or by the agency."[31]

In planning an April 1976 ERDA GAC meeting at the Oak Ridge National Laboratory, the GAC secretary wrote,

> Because of the Federal Advisory Committee Act (FACA), it is necessary for us to declare which sessions are to be **CLOSED** to the public. All sessions must be **OPEN** unless exemption is authorized by the Freedom of Information Act . . . and **OPEN** sessions must be held at locations which are reasonably accessible to the public.

According to the FACA, tours are not "meetings," and therefore, need not be open to the public. "GAC Agenda" sessions are always **CLOSED**. (In the past, we have arbitrarily called the **CLOSED** sessions "discussions" and those in **OPEN** sessions we refer to as "briefings.")[32]

The GAC had great difficulty operating in an open, nonconfidential setting. Before enactment of the FACA and Federal Freedom of Information statutes, the GAC simply functioned as a closed elite body that opened its meetings only when the Committee itself decided it was necessary or desirable. Members were regularly warned or admonished to keep classified information from public disclosure. At its second meeting, AEC Chairman David E. Lilienthal alleged that someone on the Committee had been indiscreet with secret information and forcefully reminded members that "discussion of superbombs by those presumed to have access to classified information is still classified by the AEC."[33]

In 1947 GAC Chairman Oppenheimer was asked by the AEC to review and prepare an appropriate security policy.[34] This is ironic given the later challenge of Oppenheimer's loyalty in the AEC inquiries of 1953–1954 when AEC General Manager Kenneth D. Nichols informed Oppenheimer in a letter dated December 23, 1953, that his security clearance would not be renewed. Oppenheimer requested a hearing on the matter, and a three-member inquiry group headed by Gordon Gray undertook a lengthy and controversial investigation of Oppenheimer's loyalty, patriotism, and personal integrity, focusing on the period of his wartime service.[35] Ultimately the board of inquiry ruled against Oppenheimer in a split vote, and he was denied the security clearance he had held since the years of his work with the Manhattan Project. The Oppenheimer case must have had a chilling effect on GAC members, particularly those who had worked closely with him.

Matters of security and classification preoccupied Committee work on many occasions. Nevertheless, the insularity provided the Committee by closed meetings and classified meeting records permitted members to speak freely, confident that their remarks would not go beyond the Committee and a narrow set of agency officials restrained by the same restrictions they themselves were.

GAC subcommittees

Even though it was only a nine-member body, the GAC generated a limited number of subcommittees. At Meeting 2, members agreed that a subcommittee system was a good way to gather detailed knowledge about a variety of problems the Committee was to face. Three subcommittees were organized at this time, one on matters of research, another on atomic reactor matters, and a third on weapons matters.[36]

At this early point, DuBridge chaired the Research Subcommittee, which had as members Rabi, Conant, and Seaborg. Smith, a renowned metallurgist, chaired the Reactors Subcommittee, which also had as members Fermi and Du Pont Company's Worthington. Conant chaired the Weapons Subcommittee, which was also composed of Rowe, Rabi, and Fermi. GAC Committee Chairman Oppenheimer served as an ex officio member of each subcommittee.[37] While the membership of these three subcommittees changed over time, the subcommittees themselves were maintained for almost the whole of the AEC GAC's existence.

The GAC created a variety of other subcommittees over its organizational life span, usually of short duration. Most were project oriented or were joint panels fused with other committees. Subcommittees markedly increased the advisory capabilities of the full Committee. Between full GAC meeting periods, subcommittee members often conducted investigative field trips to AEC laboratory or research facilities. Subcommittee members often prepared elaborate reports later presented to the full Committee and to the Commission. The subcommittee mechanism was a logical division of labor in helping the full Committee shoulder its heavy responsibilities. It would be a mistake to conclude from the meeting frequency information in Appendix A that the GAC functioned only nine to twelve days each year. Subcommittee work by GAC members, with the assistance of the AEC staff, consumed substantial additional time, work, and travel. Subcommittees amplified the breadth of GAC responsibilities and influence and simultaneously produced an objective data base outside official AEC channels, much like an independent evaluator.

GAC chairmen

The GAC charter stated that the Committee designate one of its own members as chairman. Not all GAC chairmen were men; for a brief period a woman, Evans V. Hayward, chaired the Committee. The names and periods of service for each GAC chairman are listed in Table 2.3. Rowe, although not listed, presided as temporary GAC chairman at the first panel meeting until Oppenheimer arrived and learned he had been officially elected chairman.[38]

It is difficult to discern how much impact each GAC chairman had on the Committee during his or her tenure. Based on the comments of GAC insiders, however, Oppenheimer and Rabi seemed to have exerted substantial personal influence in GAC proceedings when they served as chairmen. The position of chairman was not inconsequential or merely ceremonial. Besides directing the course of meetings, the chairman had

Table 2.3.   GAC chairmen, 1947–1977

Chairman	From	To	Length of Service
J. Robert Oppenheimer	Jan. 1947 (Meeting 1)	June 1952 (Meeting 31)	5 yr, 7 mo (31 meetings)
I. I. Rabi	Oct. 1952 (Meeting 32)	July 1956 (Meeting 50)	4 yr (19 meetings)
Warren C. Johnson	Oct. 1956 (Meeting 51)	July 1960 (Meeting 70)	4 yr (20 meetings)
Kenneth S. Pitzer	Oct. 1960 (Meeting 71)	Jan. 1962 (Meeting 78)	1 yr, 6 mo (8 meetings)
Manson Benedict	March 1962 (Meeting 79)	Jan. 1964 (Meeting 87)	2 yr (9 meetings)
Lawrence R. Hafstad	April 1964 (Meeting 88)	July 1968 (Meeting 105)	4 yr, 6 mo (18 meetings)
Norman F. Ramsey, Jr. (temporary chairman)	Oct. 1968 (Meeting 106)	Feb. 1969 (Meeting 107)	7 mo (2 meetings)
Howard G. Vesper	April 1969 (meeting 108)	Feb. 1973 (Meeting 123)	4 yr (16 meetings)
Lombard Squires	May 1973 (Meeting 124)	July 1974 (Meeting 129)	1 yr, 5 mo (6 meetings)
Evans V. Hayward (acting chairman)	Nov. 1974 (Meeting 130)	Same	7 mo (1 meeting)
Charles Hitch	Oct. 1975 (ERDA GAC Meeting 1)	Sept. 1977 (ERDA GAC Meeting 12)	2 yr (12 meetings)

Source: For first ten chairmen, U.S. ERDA Memorandum to the General Advisory Committee files from Anthony A. Tomei, Secretary, February 18, 1975, p. 6.

considerable say as to what would go on the GAC meeting agenda and selected meeting sites, often determining which laboratory would have the honor of hosting a GAC meeting. The chairman also assigned members to specific subcommittees and determined who would be invited to attend closed GAC meetings and when public access to a meeting was permissible. It was customary for the GAC chairman to write a letter to the AEC chairman summarizing the proceedings of each completed GAC meeting. Often copies of this correspondence were routed to appropriate AEC staff officials and sometimes to individuals outside the AEC, as determined by the Commission.

The first five chairmen were affiliated with, or under the employ of, either a nonprofit research institute or a university (see Table 3.1). Oppenheimer worked for the Institute for Advanced Study at Princeton, New Jersey, where he was both director and professor of physics. While independent of Princeton University, the institute retains strong academic ties to the university. Rabi, a Nobel laureate in physics, key Manhattan Project scientist, and longstanding professor of physics at Columbia University, also was fundamentally an academician. Warren C. Johnson devoted wartime service between 1943 and 1946 to directing the Clinton (Oak Ridge) Laboratory's chemical division; with the exception of this time, Johnson spent nearly forty years as a professor of chemistry at the University of Chicago. Pitzer followed Johnson to the chairmanship; as a professor of chemistry and president of Rice University, he too should be considered an academician. Pitzer had directed AEC's Division of Research from 1949 to 1951. Benedict, the fifth GAC chairman, held a variety of university, corporate, and research institute posts. As a chemical and nuclear engineer, he had worked for the Kellex Corporation 1942–1946 and Hydrocarbon Research in 1946–1951, for the AEC's analytical staff in 1951–1952, and for the National Research Corporation in 1951–1957. However, from 1958 to 1971 and during his term as GAC chairman, Benedict was a professor who chaired the Massachusetts Institute of Technology Nuclear Engineering Department.[39] Benedict's chairmanship signified a shift in GAC attention away from basic research and toward more applied research.

The preponderance of university-affiliated people appointed to chair the GAC ended in 1964. The next three chairmen were associated with major private corporations. In 1964 Lawrence R. Hafstad, a physicist by training and vice president of General Motors Corporation research laboratories, became chairman. Hafstad had done distinguished work in the development of the naval nuclear reactor and was named the first director of the AEC Reactor Development Division, a position he occupied from 1949 to 1955. Howard G. Vesper assumed the chairmanship while he was vice president of Standard Oil of California. A graduate of California Institute of Technology, his career mainly was within the corporate world. Vesper was succeeded by Lombard Squires, a chemical engineer who had worked his way up to a key position as manager of Du Pont's Atomic Energy Division.

A few meetings in the period between 1964 and 1975 were chaired by people outside the corporate world. Ramsey, a Harvard professor of physics, chaired two GAC meetings overlapping 1968 and 1969. Evans V. Hayward, one of three women appointed to the GAC and an outstanding physicist employed by the National Bureau of Standards, chaired the final AEC GAC meeting in November 1974.

When the Committee resurfaced to advise ERDA, Charles J. Hitch, president of Resources for the Future in Washington, D.C., was selected to serve a one-year term as chairman.[40] He later agreed to serve a second year, which became the last year of GAC operation. Hitch worked for the Rand Corporation from 1948 to 1961 and then was selected to serve as assistant secretary of defense under Robert S. McNamara. Hitch later assumed an economics professorship at the University of California at Berkeley and was chosen president of that university in 1968.

The GAC and scientific awards

Some eight years after its creation, the GAC assumed responsibility for recommending nominees for scientific prizes. The Enrico Fermi Award and the Ernest O. Lawrence Award were authorized by the revised Atomic Energy Act of 1954, section 157b3, which stated in part, "The Commission may also, upon recommendation of the General Advisory Committee, and with the approval of the President, grant an award for any especially meritorious contribution to the development, use, or control of atomic energy.[41] Congress, particularly members of the JCAE, followed the progress of these awards and often commented on the monetary stipend each award carried with it.[42]

While scientific awards appear to be only of symbolic value, such symbols are nonetheless important. According to sociologist Amitai Etzioni, in a study of modern organizations,

> Pure symbols are those whose use does not constitute a physical threat or a claim on material rewards. These include normative symbols, those of prestige and esteem; and social symbols, those of love and acceptance. When physical contact is used to symbolize love, or material objects to symbolize prestige, such contacts or objects are viewed as symbols because their effect on the recipient is similar to that of "pure" symbols. The use of symbols for control purposes is referred to as normative, normative-social, or social power. Normative power is exercised by those in higher ranks to control the lower ranks directly as when an officer gives a pep talk to his men. Normative-social power is used indirectly, as when the higher in rank appeals to the peer group of a subordinate to control him. Social power is the power which peers exercise over one another.[43]

Scientific prizes represent normative symbols through which the professional scientific research community confers prestige and esteem. While the prize itself may not directly affect the behavior of the recipient, it certainly influences others in the research community. Science prizes are instruments of normative power in the sense that higher-ranking or eminent scientists send a signal to lower-ranking, as yet unestablished, aspiring scientists by the selection of award recipients. Moreover, conferrals of awards, as well as social gatherings, ceremonies, and speeches geared to motivating fellow professionals, are expressive activities, which "affect interpersonal relations within the organization and the establishment of and adherence to norms by organizational participants."[44]

The awarding of scientific prizes through the GAC was a means by which the scientists and engineers, working closely with the AEC, were able to acknowledge outstanding achievement, enhancing the status and prestige of the recipients. In many cases, the award was an expression of gratitude for outstanding scientific service to the U.S. government as well as to a field or discipline of science. Given the normative nature of scientific research organizations, the awarding of scientific prizes is indeed a significant activity.

The Enrico Fermi Award

In November 1954, as Enrico Fermi's health continued to worsen, the GAC met to consider appropriate wording of a citation that the group wanted the AEC to award to the renowned physicist. During this meeting, Commissioner Libby read three drafts of how the citation might be worded:

> For his contributions to basic neutron physics, particularly those which led to the achievement of controlled nuclear chain reaction.

> For his pioneering researches in nuclear physics, particularly those relating to neutrons, and for his brilliant leadership of the work that led to achievement of the first sustained nuclear reaction.

> For his pioneer researches in basic neutron physics, and for his especially meritorious contribution to the achievement of the first sustained nuclear chain reaction.[45]

Acting on the recommendation of the GAC, AEC Chairman Lewis L. Strauss wrote to President Eisenhower proposing the award to Fermi. Strauss indicated that the "Commission wants to grant $25,000 to Dr. Enrico Fermi in recognition of his contributions to basic neutron physics and particularly to the controlled nuclear chain reaction."[46]

Enrico Fermi died November 28, 1954, only a few days after he was told that the president had approved conferral of the award. To commemorate Fermi's achievements, the AEC instituted the Fermi Award, to be bestowed, with the approval of the president, each year a nominee is selected.[47] It recognizes "exceptional and altogether outstanding scientific and technical achievement in the development, use, or control of atomic energy (broadly interpreted) in scientific management or in engineering."[48] The Fermi Award is international, open to scientists and engineers of all nations. The procedures stipulate, "The Award is given only to one of international reputation whose career has been marked by continued outstanding achievement in the field, rather than a single prominent contribution."[49]

The Fermi Award originally consisted of a citation signed by the president and the AEC chairman, a gold medal, and a $50,000 monetary prize. The amount of the cash award periodically triggered controversy.

In early 1964, Commissioner Tape proposed reducing the cash award to a maximum of $25,000 per recipient, so two awards could be made in a single year if appropriate.[50] Tape's request was consistent with the wishes of GAC members at that time. In meetings with the JCAE in 1964, the criteria for awarding the Fermi Award were discussed. AEC Chairman Seaborg commented: "The Commission has discussed the provisions under which the Fermi Award is given and has concluded it will recommend a smaller amount this next year for the Fermi Award and also has concluded it would broaden the base for the award so that more scientists and especially engineers would be eligible for the award."[51]

As a consequence of this decision, the cash prize was set at $25,000 per recipient. Double awards were conferred in 1971, 1978, and 1980, and the $50,000 was divided among three corecipients in 1966. Twenty-seven scientists won the award (Table 2.4). Hyman G. Rickover (1964) and Benedict (1972) were the first and second engineers to win the Fermi, and Oppenheimer and Norris E. Bradbury, as well as Rickover, were lauded for their achievements in scientific administration.

Table 2.4. Recipients of the Enrico Fermi Award, 1954–1983

Winners	Year	Period of GAC Service[a]
Enrico Fermi	1954	Jan. 1947 to Aug. 1950
John von Neumann	1956	Feb. 1952 to Aug. 1954
Ernest O. Lawrence	1957	n.a.
Eugene P. Wigner	1958	Sept. 1952 to Jan. 1957, Dec. 1959 to May 1964
Glenn T. Seaborg	1959	Jan. 1947 to Aug. 1950
Hans A. Bethe	1961	n.a.
Edward Teller	1962	Oct. 1956 to Aug. 1958
J. Robert Oppenheimer	1963	Jan. 1947 to Aug. 1952
Hyman G. Rickover	1964	n.a.
Otto Hahn	1966	n.a.
Lise Meitner	1966	n.a.
Fritz Strassmann	1966	n.a.
John A. Wheeler	1968	n.a.
Walter H. Zinn	1969	Oct. 1972 to Feb. 1975
Norris E. Bradbury	1970	n.a.
Shields Warren	1971	n.a.
Stafford L. Warren	1972	n.a.
Manson Benedict	1972	Oct. 1958 to Aug. 1968
William L. Russell	1976	n.a.
Wolfgang K. H. Panofsky	1978	n.a.
Harold M. Agnew	1978	n.a.
Rudolf E. Peierls	1980	n.a.
Alvin M. Weinberg	1980	n.a.
W. Bennett Lewis	1981	n.a.
Seth Neddermeyer	1982	n.a.
Herbert Anderson	1982	n.a.
Alexander Hollaender	1983	n.a.
John H. Lawrence	1983	n.a.

Source: Letter announcement of Alvin W. Trivelpiece, Director, Office of Energy Research, U.S. Department of Energy, March 1, 1984.
[a]n.a. = not applicable, indicating no appointment to the GAC.

Nomination of candidates for the award is invited by public announcement. In addition, letters are directed to members of the National Academy of Sciences, officers of scientific and technical societies, research institutions, and other individuals "of special knowledge and competence, including heads of foreign government agencies with scientific missions."[52] Those who put forward nominees must supply a full letter of justification and, if possible, a bibliography. Unselected nominees have their names recorded on a list that maintains their eligibility for two additional years; if unchosen after three consecutive years of consideration, the nominee's name is removed from the list, but nominees can be renominated. The award can only go to living nominees.

Screening and selection processes for the Fermi Award rely on the assistance of "consultants drawn from the appropriate scientific fields." Deliberations are conducted in closed session where nominees are ranked according to merit, and no nominee for the award may sit on a screening panel. From 1956 to 1975, the members of the GAC screened the nominations and selected the recommendees. The ERDA GAC performed in the same fashion when conferring the award in 1976 and 1977. After 1977, this duty was assumed by the DOE Energy Research Advisory Board.

Before 1974, the GAC recommended and selected the Fermi Award winners subject to AEC and presidential concurrence. From 1974 on the AEC, and later ERDA, needed only to consult with the GAC before choosing award winners. There is no available evidence to show whether GAC-approved nominees and nominee rankings were disregarded by AEC, ERDA, or presidential officials, but it is highly unlikely that the Fermi went to anyone who was not the highest-ranked GAC-approved nominee.

Some AEC and ERDA officials familiar with the history of the GAC suggest that one reason scientists and engineers wanted to serve on the Committee was because members selected the Fermi and Lawrence awards winners.[53] Being part of the screening and selection process for the awards was viewed as an honor.[54]

Seven GAC members have won individual and unshared Fermi Awards. The first recipient after Fermi, von Neumann, won with special recognition of his contributions to game theory and to computer programming. Two years later, in 1958, Wigner was cited for his contributions to nuclear physics theory and nuclear reactor development. In 1959, Seaborg, then chancellor of the University of California at Berkeley, won for identifying plutonium, eight additional transuranium elements, and well over 100 isotopes. In 1962 Edward Teller won the award for his many contributions to nuclear physics and engineering, most particularly his work in development of the first thermonuclear bomb. Benedict won in 1972 for his outstanding achievements in isotope separation and in nuclear chemical technology.

Oppenheimer won the Fermi in 1963, as an acknowledgment of his many contributions to theoretical physics as well as his direction of the Los Alamos Scientific Laboratory, culminating in the creation of the first atomic bomb. President Kennedy had approved Oppenheimer's award in 1963 but was assassinated before the date of bestowal. President Johnson conferred the award on schedule. To many, Oppenheimer's Fermi Award symbolized an exoneration from the accusations made against him in the 1950s.

Walter H. Zinn, who won in 1969, was the only GAC member to win the Fermi Award before initial appointment to the Committee. Zinn had worked closely with Fermi at the University of Chicago in building and operating the first atomic pile and made innumerable contributions to the development of nuclear reactor technology and to nuclear physics in general. Zinn, like Bradbury, Alvin Weinberg, Oppenheimer, Lawrence, and other Fermi winners, had extensive experience as director of a major AEC research laboratory.

The Fermi Award not only confirmed the winners' success in having reached the pinnacle of their disciplines, but it was also, in the case of American winners, a testament to service to the U.S. government. Participation on major presidential or departmental advisory committees was considered by screening committees reviewing award nominees. By acknowledging and rewarding both scientific achievement and governmental service, GAC members and federal authorities hoped the award would exert enough normative power on the scientific and engineering professions to denote outstanding scientific achievement put forward in the national and international interest. While not as prestigious as the Nobel Prize, the Fermi Award has become one of the most highly coveted U.S. science prizes and is held in very high regard by the world scientific and engineering community.

The Ernest O. Lawrence Memorial Award

Dr. Ernest O. Lawrence was for many years director of the University of California's Berkeley Radiation Laboratory. At age thirty-eight, Lawrence won a Nobel Prize for his invention of the cyclotron and its applications in discovery of new elements and isotopes. Professor Lawrence attracted and educated many of the nation's finest physicists and chemists. When Lawrence died in August 1958, AEC Chairman John A. McCone petitioned President Eisenhower to establish an award in memory of this luminary of the scientific world.

The Ernest O. Lawrence Memorial Award, like the Fermi Award, is for "especially meritorious contributions to the development, use, or control of atomic energy (broadly interpreted)." However, the Lawrence Award has distinctive features. The award includes candidates not only from the physical sciences and engineering but also from the life science fields, particularly medicine, and from materials sciences, reactor technology, and national security areas.[55] The reference to national security opened up the possibility that scientists or engineers engaged in classified areas of research, such as nuclear weapons development, could be nominees for the award (as they are for the Fermi Award).

The Lawrence Award also stipulated the age and nationality of the nominee. Eligible candidates had to be "U.S. citizens less than 45 years old." Owing to concern about possible accusations of age discrimination raised in the mid-1970s, the strict age limit is no longer a requirement. Instead the qualifications state that nominations of scientists are sought "who are early in their careers and show exceptional promise of future development." Nominations are judged primarily on "the basis of scientific and technical competence and achievement, with secondary weight given to managerial ability or innovative talents."[56]

No more than five Lawrence Awards can be conferred in a single year. The award has been bestowed on five different scientists each year since the first award ceremony in 1960. Today as many as six Lawrence Awards can be made each year. The original award consisted of a citation, a gold medal, and a $5,000 cash prize for each recipient. Today the award stipend is $10,000 per recipient. Like the Fermi Award, the AEC's authority to confer the Lawrence Award resides in the Atomic Energy Act of 1954.

The establishment of the Lawrence Award emerged from negotiations between AEC Chairman John A. McCone, his fellow commissioners, and the GAC. McCone proposed the Lawrence Award in a letter to President Eisenhower dated August 28, 1958. The letter, however, did not set out criteria for conferring the award. In his response to McCone, the president cited the proposed award "as a means of helping carry forward [Lawrence's] work through inspiring others to dedicate their lives and talents to scientific effort."[57]

At about this time, members of the AEC staff began to advocate creation of an atomic energy award acknowledging "outstanding achievements in engineering, building, designing, etc." Harold D. Anamosa, acting secretary to the AEC, drafted a memorandum calling for creation of an award in honor of Gordon E. Dean, AEC chairman from 1950 to 1953. Anamosa pointed out that the Fermi Award, which could be granted for engineering development, project direction and program administration, and the Distinguished Service and Special Service awards, which were restricted to AEC employees, showed that "the slant of the past awards has been toward outstanding achievements in basic, fundamental scientific research." He argued: "Not covered, however, are outstanding achievements in the work that translates basic scientific theory into actual engineering realities — whether it be program direction, project direction, program administration, or architect engineering. It would be appropriate to expand the AEC's awards program to reflect the unique contribution of those responsible for such achievements."[58] Anamosa expected the Dean Award to carry the same monetary stipend and prestige as the Fermi Award. Since the Commission had received presidential approval to establish the Lawrence Award but had not yet specified criteria for choosing the recipients, the Commission and the AEC general manager decided that rather than propose creation of another award they would use some of the criteria proposed for the Dean Award in the Lawrence Award.

The Commission consulted with the GAC and through negotiation established the Lawrence Award criteria and by November 1959 had approved all elements of the award. It was to be conferred, on recommendation of the GAC and with the approval of the president, for "recent especially meritorious contributions to the development, use, or control of atomic energy in areas of all the sciences related to atomic energy, including medicine and engineering." It was to go to young men or young women who were not more than 45 years of age. No more than five recipients could be named each year, each recipient to receive a monetary prize of not less than $5,000. The GAC recommended, and the AEC approved, the provision that award recipients be U.S. citizens.

In GAC deliberations on the Lawrence Award proposal, "the view was expressed that the areas of competence of award recipients should at least be co-extensive with the range of expertise represented by GAC members." Over the history of the award, the GAC "as a matter of practice" has ensured that award recipients "in any given year have each represented different fields of scientific endeavor."[59] The GAC thus played a central role in designing the Lawrence Award in much the same way it had helped to craft the Fermi Award.

Screening and selection procedures used in conferring the Lawrence Award mirror the Fermi Award procedures.[60] There is a public solicitation of nominees, and the names of unselected nominees in any single year are carried forward on a list for three consecutive years. Only living nominees are eligible. Those submitting nominations that include classified material are asked to submit an unclassified summary of the documents they enclose.

From 1960 through 1977, about ninety people have received the Lawrence Award. Only two recipients in that era, Ramsey and May, ever served as GAC members, and they won the awards before they were appointed to the Committee. Both received their awards at approximately age forty-four, and both had done important work at major AEC laboratories.

Ramsey received his Lawrence Award in 1960 and later that year began a nearly twelve-year period of service on the GAC. He had an impressive record of achievement at the wartime Los Alamos lab. He later pursued research at Brookhaven while on the physics faculty of Columbia and then Harvard universities. Ramsey had high-level Washington contacts, which gave him the opportunity to serve on the international science panel of the PSAC in 1960. Before that, he had worked two years as science adviser in the North Atlantic Treaty Organization. In 1966 he became a chaired professor at Harvard. Ramsey is also credited with major contributions to the design of high-energy particle accelerators. In the early 1960s he chaired a joint panel of the GAC and the President's Science Advisory Committee (PSAC) that advised the president on the future of high-energy-physics research and the need for larger and newer types of particle accelerators.

May established his career at the Lawrence Berkeley radiation lab in the 1950s and 1960s and has been considered both a superior physicist and a politically sophisticated executive. In the 1960s he moved to the Lawrence Livermore lab where he emerged as a major executive and administrator. After 1974, May served as an advisor to the secretary of defense for the Strategic Arms Limitation Treaty talks and as a member of the U.S. delegation.

Both Ramsey and May have been integrally involved in defense-related work throughout the course of their careers, which suggests that the Lawrence Award criteria offers special provisions enabling scientists working in classified fields to compete. Approximately half the Lawrence Awards conferred under GAC consultation went to scientists who were connected with major AEC laboratories, showing that scientists and engineers working at these labs have been well equipped to promote strong nominations. The Lawrence Award has been a means of rewarding scientific and engineering as well as life science achievements. The award has also helped confer professional legitimacy on, and acclaim for, superior research conducted under the umbrella of official secrecy. In a sense this award is official acknowledgment by the professional research community that defense-related scientific achievement should be publicly rewarded.

Both the Fermi and Lawrence awards permitted the GAC's scientific and engineering elite to dispense status rewards to members of the scientific community. Winners were held up as role models in the research community. The ceremony surrounding conferment of the Fermi Award involves a visit to the White House where recipients, their families, GAC members, AEC officials, and other invited guests listen to the president read the official award citation. This is followed by the presentation of the citation, medal, and check. These proceedings accord award winners, the AEC, and the GAC public recognition and prestige, as the media coverage of the event is usually extensive. In helping to create and assign these awards, GAC members exercised normative power in their relationships with the national scientific and engineering research community.

The GAC owed its origin to the same law that created the Atomic Energy Commission itself. The law made explicit the method of Committee appointment but left deliberately vague the precise areas the Committee could address. This generality and imprecision gave the Committee wide latitude both to serve the AEC and to critically investigate its operations. The three major paths of GAC inquiry and recommendations involved research of necessary scientific materials (often involving provision for the production of transuranic elements), studies of reactor design and development projects, and review of weapons-related research, fabrication, and testing activities. This division of labor was reflected in the subcommittee structure. The GAC chairman possessed considerable authority in directing the work of the Committee and in promoting its findings and recommendations to the AEC.

The many preeminent scientists and engineers recruited to serve on the GAC ensured that the Committee's advice would carry great weight with the Commission and with the AEC staff. Moreover, the Committee reached out indirectly to consult and advise the president, the Congress (most particularly the JCAE), and the Department of Defense. Much GAC work entailed review of the progress of AEC national laboratory and contract laboratory research projects.

The Committee held four meetings or more each year for thirty years. The majority of these three-day meetings were held at AEC Washington headquarters offices, but many others were conducted at various

AEC national laboratories, furnishing the membership with site-visit opportunities. The Committee was provided with a capable staff that maintained careful records and organized Committee work. The GAC reviewed candidates and nominated individuals for the prestigious Fermi Award and for the highly coveted Lawrence Award.

Perhaps most significant in all considerations of Committee mechanics is the fact that this advisory body functioned for more than twenty-five years under conditions of strict secrecy. Members enjoyed high security clearance, and records remained sequestered from public scrutiny for decades after they were initially compiled, which made the GAC a unique scientific privy council. The oracular advice rendered by the panel was channeled to an even more highly placed body of executive officials.

3 Knowledge specializations and career histories of GAC members

The role of academic disciplines

What constitutes knowledge for scientists is what their discipline defines as knowledge. In turn, the methods and procedures of science as embodied in their disciplinary training determine the path and progress of research. Throughout the long history of the GAC one force remained constant, the motivational power of each member's academic discipline and training. The scientists and engineers invited to serve on the GAC represented the state of their art before Committee members and before others in attendance at the meetings.

This is logically what one would expect science advisers to do: "If we have a reliable method for discovering truth, namely, science, should we not use it to solve all of our important problems? If we propose to do so, should not those who make our important decisions be selected for their understanding of the most relevant science?"[1] GAC members were more committed to the interests of their disciplines, in fact, than they were to the interests of their employers. It was customary for members to use their scientific or engineering expertise to present views, interpretations, and arguments before the Committee. For example, GAC-prepared advisories pertaining to the AEC high-energy physics program gave the physicists on the Committee a chance to influence the future of their discipline by making key recommendations about how the AEC should administer its high-energy physics program.

Scientific advisers act as representatives of science in general.[2] They also, however, promote specific scientific or engineering disciplines and knowledge specializations. They are members "of the establishment" who represent "their professions, institutions, and organizations before the federal government in requesting funds for research and education."[3]

45

For many scientists, disciplinary training has been a decisive force in defining their profession (although there have been many cases in which scientists have crossed disciplines or moved on to new disciplines in the course of their professional lives). The behavior of scientists and engineers in GAC sessions can in many ways be understood as an advocacy and defense of their disciplines. (See Table 3.1 for a list of the GAC members and their disciplines.)

It seems clear that discipline, or knowledge specialization, was a variable given great weight in the appointment or reappointment of GAC members. The disciplines represented on the Committee over time serve as a general indication of the nature of the advice sought by the AEC and later by the ERDA. Changes in the nature or distribution of discipline representation signify a change in the kind of advice the Committee was expected to offer. Any analysis of discipline representation must address four general questions:

1. What was the disciplinary composition of the GAC membership and how did it change, if at all, over time?
2. Did some scientific or engineering disciplines enjoy multimember representation while other disciplines had only single-member representation?
3. How did the representation of basic science disciplines compare with that of applied science disciplines?
4. To what degree were disciplines outside the physical sciences and engineering represented?

As stated above, the demand for disciplinary advice was largely a function of what the AEC needed at any single time, and this was not only internally determined. When the president and Congress became willing and anxious to promote certain areas of research, it was necessary to consult members knowledgeable in those areas to best devise how to give assistance and direction.

Soon after World War II, the AEC began to organize its research and development programs. The success of the Manhattan Project helped to build confidence among public officials that increasing public funding for pure science and basic research was a wise course of action: "Basic research is influenced to the extent that the scientific disciplines that are given priority by technoscience agencies are those relevant to development goals."[4] Presumably, how the AEC went about recruiting the members of the GAC was directly related to the kind of help they sought in organizing the agency's basic research program. Given the demands imposed on the AEC in 1947, it is not surprising that Commissioner Robert F. Bacher interpreted the GAC charter to mean that the Committee should have a strong representation of physicists, chemists, and engineers.[5]

Conversely, once outside scientific and technical advisers are given an opportunity to help shape the programs of a technoscientific agency like the AEC, they also can shape agency developmental goals and advance the disciplines (usually their own) needed to realize those goals. For example, advising the government to pursue chemical engineering studies of light-water fission reactor technologies can serve a dual purpose. The agency directing the federally subsidized research and development effort (1) uses the product of the research to help in the development of safer, more reliable, and more efficient reactor technology and (2) funnels money and resources to researchers who use their findings to extend the boundaries of knowledge in, say, chemical engineering. As a result, chemical engineers working in universities or in private corporations are drawn to the government research program by the lure of funding, the prestige accorded to those who make breakthroughs, the opportunity to train and educate others in their discipline, underwritten by public funding support, and the personal satisfaction realized in making a contribution to their discipline.

Disciplinary representation on the GAC

Various science and engineering disciplines were represented on the GAC through appointment of those trained in those disciplines (Table 3.2). It is difficult to pigeonhole each GAC member because many straddled disciplines or fields in their research. Eugene P. Wigner, for example, was not only a brilliant mathematical physicist but a superb engineer as well. Isidor I. Rabi achieved success in a variety of fields and eventually was appointed Columbia University's first University Professor. This title signified that Rabi was established in a variety of disciplines and was therefore independent of any single academic disciplinary department.

Some GAC members pioneered the creation of new interdisciplinary or subdisciplinary fields quite different from the discipline of their original postgraduate training. Philip H. Abelson, like several of his GAC colleagues, moved adroitly from one field or discipline to another. Another factor complicating the disciplinary classification of GAC members was the fact that the training for a physics or chemistry doc-

Table 3.1. GAC members in the order of appointment

Appointee	Dates of Service	Affiliation at Time of GAC Service	Discipline
J. Robert Oppenheimer	Jan. 1947–Aug. 1952	Institute for Advanced Study, Princeton, N.J.	Physics
James B. Conant	Jan. 1947–Aug. 1952	Harvard University	Chemistry
Lee A. DuBridge	Jan. 1947–Aug. 1952	California Institute of Technology	Physics
Enrico Fermi	Jan. 1947–Aug. 1950	University of Chicago	Physics
Isidor I. Rabi	Jan. 1947–Aug. 1948	Columbia University	Physics
	July 1948–Aug. 1954		
	Oct. 1954–Aug. 1956		
Hartley Rowe	Jan. 1947–Aug. 1950	United Fruit Co.	Electrical engineering
Glenn T. Seaborg	Jan. 1947–Aug. 1950	University of California at Berkeley	Chemistry
Cyril S. Smith	Jan. 1947–Aug. 1948	University of Chicago	Physical metallurgy
	July 1948–Jan. 1952		
Hood Worthington	Jan. 1947–Aug. 1948	E. I. du Pont de Nemours & Co.	Chemical engineering
Oliver E. Buckley	July 1948–Aug. 1954	Bell Telephone Laboratories	Electrical engineering
Willard F. Libby	Aug. 1950–Sept. 1954	University of Chicago	Chemistry
	May 1960–Aug. 1962		
Eger V. Murphree	Aug. 1950–Aug. 1956	Standard Oil Development Co. (Esso-Exxon)	Chemistry
	Apr. 1957–Aug. 1958		
	Oct. 1958–Oct. 1962		
Walter G. Whitman	Aug. 1950–Aug. 1956	Massachusetts Institute of Technology	Chemical engineering
John von Neumann	Feb. 1952–Aug. 1954	Institute for Advanced Study, Princeton, N.J.	Mathematics
James B. Fisk	Sept. 1952–Aug. 1958	Bell Telephone Laboratories	Physics
John C. Warner	Sept. 1952–Aug. 1958	Carnegie Institute of Technology	Chemistry
	Oct. 1958–Aug. 1964		
Eugene P. Wigner	Sept. 1952–Jan. 1957	Princeton University	Mathematical physics, engineering
	Dec. 1959–Aug. 1962		
	Sept. 1962–May 1964		
Jesse W. Beams	Oct. 1954–Aug. 1960	University of Virginia	Physics
Warren C. Johnson	Oct. 1954–Aug. 1960	University of Chicago	Chemistry
Edwin M. McMillan	Oct. 1954–Oct. 1958	University of California at Berkeley	Physics
T. Keith Glennan	Oct. 1956–Sept. 1958	Case Institute of Technology	Electrical engineering
Edward Teller	Oct. 1956–Aug. 1958	University of California at Berkeley	Physics
Robert E. Wilson	Oct. 1956–Mar. 1960	Standard Oil of Indiana	Chemical engineering
Kenneth S. Pitzer	Oct. 1958–Aug. 1964	University of California at Berkeley	Physical chemistry
	July 1964–July 1965		
Manson Benedict	Oct. 1958–Aug. 1962	Massachusetts Institute of Technology	Chemical engineering
	Sept. 1962–Aug. 1968		

Table 3.1. (continued)

Appointee	Dates of Service	Affiliation at Time of GAC Service	Discipline
James W. McRae	Oct. 1958–Feb. 1960	American Telephone and Telegraph Co.	Electrical engineering
Philip H. Abelson	June 1960–Nov. 1963	Carnegie Institution of Washington	Physical chemistry
Norman F. Ramsey, Jr.	Nov. 1960–Aug. 1966	Harvard University	Physics
	Sept. 1966–Aug. 1972		
John H. Williams	Nov. 1960–Apr. 1966	University of Minnesota	Physics
Lawrence R. Hafstad	Sept. 1962–Aug. 1968	General Motors Corp.	Physics
William Webster	Mar. 1963–Aug. 1964	New England Electric System	Marine engineering
	July 1964–Aug. 1970		
	June 1970–May 1972		
Darol K. Froman	Apr. 1964–Aug. 1966	Los Alamos Scientific Laboratory	Physics
John C. Bugher	May 1964–Aug. 1968	Puerto Rico Nuclear Center	Pathology, biology
	Aug. 1968–Sept. 1970		
Stephen Lawroski	July 1964–Aug. 1970	Argonne National Laboratory	Chemical engineering
Howard G. Vesper	Oct. 1965–Aug. 1970	Standard Oil of California	Chemical engineering
	June 1970–Feb. 1975		
Edwin L. Goldwasser	Sept. 1966–Aug. 1972	University of Illinois, Urbana-Champaign	Physics
Jane H. Hall	Sept. 1966–Aug. 1972	Los Alamos Scientific Laboratory	Physics
Herbert Friedman	Aug. 1968–Aug. 1974	Naval Research Laboratory	Physics
Lombard Squires	Aug. 1968–Aug. 1974	E. I. du Pont de Nemours & Co.	Chemical engineering
Rolf Eliassen	June 1970–Feb. 1975	Stanford University, Metcalf Eddy Co.	Civil engineering
James H. Sterner	May 1971–Aug. 1974	University of Texas	Medicine
Evans V. Hayward	Oct. 1972–Feb. 1975	National Bureau of Standards, Linac Laboratory	Physics
Hubert Heffner	Oct. 1972–Feb. 1975	Stanford University	Electrical engineering
Michael M. May	Oct. 1972–Feb. 1975	Lawrence Livermore Laboratory	Physics
Walter H. Zinn	Oct. 1972–Feb. 1975	Combustion Engineering Co. (retired)	Physics
Arthur G. Hansen	Sept. 1975–Aug. 1976	Purdue University	Mechanical engineering
Richard S. Morse	Sept. 1975–Aug. 1976	Massachusetts Institute of Technology	Physics
Martin J. Ward	Sept. 1975–Aug. 1976	United Association of Plumbers and Pipefitters	Construction
	Jan. 1977–Sept. 1977		
William R. Gould	Sept. 1975–Sept. 1977	Southern California Edison Co.	Mechanical engineering
Charles J. Hitch	Sept. 1975–Sept. 1977	Resources for the Future	Economics
Henry R. Linden	Sept. 1975–Sept. 1977	Institute of Gas Technology	Chemical engineering
Ruth Patrick	Sept. 1975–Sept. 1977	Academy of Natural Sciences, University of Pennsylvania	Botany, limnology
Gerald F. Tape	Sept. 1975–Sept. 1977	Associated Universities, Inc.	Physics
James E. Connor	Jan. 1977–Sept. 1977	First Boston Corp.	Political science
Frank G. Zarb	Jan. 1977–Sept. 1977	Shearson Hayden Stone	Business

Table 3.2. Cumulation of GAC member discipline representation

Discipline[a]	% of GAC Members	Discipline Grouping (% of total)
Basic sciences		
Physics	20	
Mathematical physics	1	
Chemistry	6	
Physical chemistry	2	
Mathematics	1	
	30	(54.5)
Applied sciences		
Chemical engineering	8	
Electrical engineering	5	
Mechanical engineering[b]	3	
Civil (sanitary) engineering	1	
Physical metallurgy	1	
	18	(32.7)
Life and social sciences		
Biology, medicine	2	
Botany, limnology	1	
Economics	1	
Political science	1	
Business administration	1	
Construction trades	1	
	7	(12.8)

    [a]Determined by the subject area in which the highest academic degree was earned or by the major teaching or occupational field, as listed in *American Men and Women of Science* or other biographical directories.
    [b]Includes marine engineering.

torate from 1910 to 1930 was quite different from such training thereafter; GAC members who had earned their doctorates in the early part of this century may have moved well beyond their original disciplinary training because the discipline itself had dramatically changed. Over the course of their careers, some GAC members helped to reshape or extend their original scientific and engineering disciplines.

The basic sciences

The basic sciences were well represented on the Committee in its formative years. From the first group of appointments until 1963, basic science representation ranged from six to eight members each year. From 1965 until the Committee's termination in 1977, however, the only basic science represented was physics. After 1964 approximately four GAC seats seem to have been reserved for physicists, another four for engineering disciplines, and a single seat for a representative of the life sciences. The ERDA GAC reserved about three of its seats for basic science interests. The basic and applied sciences appear to have been in almost perfect numerical balance on the GAC from 1965 to 1977.

Physics rose into public prominence after World War II. Before the war, physicists interacted through societies that were intimate clubs of theoretical academicians. After the war, these societies "began to find that their members had moved into positions of managerial importance in a great academic-industrial complex, and were deeply involved in the affairs of government."[6]

The basic or pure sciences are at the center of a scientific estate, according to political scientist Don K. Price, and physics is one of the cardinal basic sciences. It is argued that members of the scientific estate seek truth for its own sake, freedom and self-government for their endeavors, and funding for the advancement of basic scientific research. The scientific estate is distinct from the professional estate, the administrative estate, and the political estate. When the scientific estate became paramount, basic science became a type of establishment "supported by tax funds, largely on faith, and without direct responsibility to political control."[7]

Estate theory addresses a spectrum of the politics of science that moves far beyond the realm of science advisory committees. However, advisory bodies, particularly science advisory bodies, act as a link between public and private interests when "more and more things have to be left not to administrative discretion, but to scientific discovery, or to the judgment of scientists and their professional colleagues."[8] The scientists interact with engineers and administrative officers. Scientists produce new knowledge which, for the engineer, defines what is becoming possible. They "also define what new knowledge is for administrative officers. Then, in an exchange relationship between engineers and administrative officials exclusively, engineers identify what is feasible and administrators indicate what they would like the engineers to produce."[9]

The early GAC membership (1947–1963) had six to eight basic scientists in any single year. In no other period were the basic sciences so heavily represented on the Committee. In this respect, the early GAC was dominated by the scientific estate.

If the scientific estate characterization is appropriate for the early GAC, what reasons can be given for the decline in the number of basic science representatives on the Committee in later years? One explanation is that the applied sciences, epitomized by the engineering disciplines, gained an increasing number of Committee seats in the 1960s as nuclear reactor technology matured from a theoretical and design stage to a development and application stage. The AEC became more solicitous of the advice offered by the engineers of the professional estate. One postulate holds that physicists and other basic science specialists lost interest in nuclear power when it moved out of the realm of theory and into one of application and construction; many academic theorists preferred to leave government advisory and research service to return to their universities and laboratories. In the 1950s, basic researchers were drawn to nuclear power, and to other dimensions of atomic energy, as the AEC promoted a variety of theoretical research projects and nuclear power experiments. Once the Commission decided that light-water fission reactor technology was the preferred approach to nuclear power, application studies of this technology replaced much of the general basic research that had been supported previously.[10]

Much of the 1950s and early 1960s involved competition for AEC research funding for building reactor prototypes. At this time each laboratory seemed to have a favorite concept, "and the object of the game was to persuade the AEC that theirs offered the best chance of economical nuclear power."[11] The GAC furnished these laboratory officials with a platform from which they could try to "persuade" AEC commissioners and staff. Others agree that basic scientists withdrew in significant numbers from advising the AEC once a specific reactor technology was assigned priority by the Commission: "Nobel prizes are not given to people who do plumbing, even if it is for the reactor's cooling system. . . . Scientists of the highest calibre automatically dismissed most of the tasks needed for reactor development as hack work that was not for them."[12] The question is whether these assertions hold true for GAC disciplinary representation over time.

There was clearly a wholesale departure of basic science disciplines in the early 1960s, with the exception of physics (Tables 3.3 and 3.4). By 1965, mathematical physicists, physical chemists, chemists, and mathematicians were no longer represented on the Committee. Applied science disciplines, however, were represented on the Committee for the whole of its thirty-year history. The applied science disciplines were strongest in the period 1965 to 1972; in each of those years, applied scientists held four GAC seats. Chemical engineers have long and strong GAC representation. In the period 1963 to 1972, mechanical and civil engineering disciplines, which had not been represented in the past, finally secured a place on the GAC. This partially affirms the argument that the late 1960s and early 1970s was a period in which applied scientists gained ascendance in the work of the AEC. However, the representation of physics as a discipline was as strong in the final fifteen years of GAC operation as it was in the first fifteen years.

Table 3.3.   Representation of discipline groups on the GAC, 1947–1977

Year[a]	Basic Sciences	Applied Sciences	Life and Social Sciences	Year-End Totals
1947	6	3	0	9
1948	6	3		9
1949	6	3		9
1950	6	3		9
1951	6	3		9
1952	7	2		9
1953	7	2		9
1954	7	1		8[b]
1955	7	2		9
1956	7	2		9
1957	7	2		9
1958	6	3		9
1959	6	3		9
1960	8	1		9
1961	8	1		9
1962	7	1		8[b]
1963	6	2		8[b]
1964	5	3	1	9
1965	4	4	1	9
1966	4	4	1	9
1967	4	4	1	9
1968	4	4	1	9
1969	4	4	1	9
1970	4	4	0	8[b]
1971	4	4	1	9
1972	3	4	1	8[b]
1973	3	4	1	8[b]
1974	3	3	0	6[c]
1975	3	3	3	9
1976	2	2	3	7[d]
1977[e]	2	2	5	9

[a]Figures for each year denote year-end totals, not within-year variations.

[b]The year ended with one unfilled seat.

[c]Three vacant seats appear for 1974 because this began a period of en masse resignations by GAC members as the AEC underwent a bifurcation into the Nuclear Regulatory Commission and the Energy Research and Development Administration.

[d]The year ended with two unfilled seats.

[e]Up to the GAC termination date, September 30, 1977.

GAC physicists

The GAC had a heavy and sustained representation of those trained in physics. Of the GAC's total fifty-five-person membership over thirty years, twenty members had earned doctoral degrees in physics (Table 3.2). This constitutes 36 percent of the Committee's life membership. If representation of those trained in physics is considered on an annual basis, the dominance of the discipline of physics is again obvious. In only two years (1958 and 1959) was the end-of-year disciplinary representation of physicists down to a single member. There were thirteen years in which four physicists served simultaneously on the nine-member

Table 3.4. Representation of all knowledge disciplines of GAC members, 1947-1977

Year[a]	Basic Sciences					Applied Sciences						Life and Social Sciences				
	Phys	Math phys	Chem	Phys chem	Math	Chem eng	Elec eng	Mech eng	Civil eng	Phys metal	Biol med	Bot limn	Econ	Pol sci	Bus adm	Bldg
1947	4		2			1				1						
1948	4		2				2			—						
1949	4		2				2			—						
1950	3		3				—			—						
1951	3		3			—	—									
1952	2	1	3		1	—	—									
1953	2	1	3		1	—	—									
1954	3	1	3			—										
1955	3	1	3			—										
1956	4	1	2			—										
1957	4	1	3			—	—									
1958	1	—	3	1		2										
1959	1	—	3	1		2	—									
1960	2	—	3	2		1										
1961	2	—	3	2		—										
1962	3	—	1	2		—										
1963	3	1	1	1		—		1								
1964	4					2		—			—					
1965	4					3		—			—					
1966	4					3		—			—					
1967	4					3		1			—					
1968	4					3		—			—					
1969	4					3			1		—					
1970	4					2	1	—	—		—					
1971	4					2		—	—		—					
1972	3					2	1		1		—					
1973	3					2	—		1		—					
1974	3					—		2								
1975	3					1		—				—	1			—
1976	2					—		1				—	—		1	—
1977	2					—		1				—	—			—

Note: Phys = physics, Math phys = mathematical physics, Chem = chemistry, Phys chem = physical chemistry, Math = mathematics, Chem eng = chemical engineering, Elec eng = electrical engineering, Mech eng = mechanical engineering, Civil eng = civil engineering, Phys metal = physical metallurgy, Biol med = biology-medicine, Bot limn = botany-limnology, Econ = economics, Pol sci = political science, Bus adm = business administration, Bldg = building trades.

[a]Refers to year-end totals, not within-year variations. For the precise year and months of GAC service by discipline, see Table 3.1.

The Los Alamos Scientific Laboratory, established during World War II to create the first atomic bombs.

Gen. Leslie R. Groves presenting Enrico Fermi with the Medal of Merit for his wartime service to the United States, March 20, 1946. (Courtesy of Argonne National Laboratory)

The Mike shot, a 10.4-megaton surface detonation at Eniwetok Atoll October 31, 1952 (GCT). This was the first thermonuclear bomb explosion. (Courtesy Los Alamos National Laboratory)

A GAC delegation arriving at the Santa Fe, N.M., airport April 3, 1947, to begin a visit at the Los Alamos Scientific Laboratory. *Left to right:* James B. Conant, J. Robert Oppenheimer, Brig. Gen. James E. McCormack, Hartley Rowe, John H. Manley, Isidor I. Rabi, and Roger S. Warner. (Courtesy Los Alamos National Laboratory)

GAC Meeting 41, held at the Sandia and Los Alamos laboratories in New Mexico July 12–15, 1954. *Seated, left to right:* Willard F. Libby, Isidor I. Rabi (chairman), and Oliver E. Buckley. *Standing, left to right:* John C. Warner, Eger V. Murphree, James B. Fisk, John von Neumann, and Walter G. Whitman. Absent was Eugene P. Wigner. (Courtesy U.S. Department of Energy, History Division)

Fireball of the Cherokee air drop shot, a thermonuclear explosion over Bikini Atoll May 21, 1956 (GCT), photographed from an aircraft at 12,000 feet altitude approximately 50 miles northwest of the target. (Courtesy U.S. Air Force)

AEC commissioners and GAC members at the Germantown, Md., offices of the AEC in early 1959. *Seated, left to right:* Alvin R. Luedecke (AEC general manager) and AEC Commissioners John S. Graham, Willard F. Libby, John A. McCone (AEC chairman), Harold S. Vance, John F. Floberg, and Paul F. Foster (AEC deputy manager). *Standing, left to right:* John C. Warner, Eger V. Murphree, Robert E. Wilson, Warren C. Johnson (GAC chairman), Kenneth S. Pitzer, James W. McRae, Jesse W. Beams, Eugene P. Wigner, and Manson Benedict. (Courtesy U.S. Department of Energy, History Division)

GAC Meeting 62, held at Savannah River, S.C., March 9–11, 1959. *Seated, left to right:* Anthony A. Tomei (GAC administrative officer), Edwin M. McMillan, Warren C. Johnson (GAC chairman), Jane H. Hall (GAC secretary), and Eger V. Murphree. *Standing, left to right:* Jesse W. Beams, Manson Benedict, Kenneth S. Pitzer, Robert E. Wilson, James W. McRae, and Eugene P. Wigner (consultant). Absent was John C. Warner. (Courtesy U.S. Department of Energy, History Division)

AEC Chairman John A. McCone reading the inscription on the 1959 Fermi Award won by Glenn T. Seaborg (*left*). The ceremony took place at AEC headquarters in December 1959. (Courtesy U.S. Department of Energy, History Division)

White House ceremony for 1961 Fermi Award recipient
Hans A. Bethe. *Left to right:* GAC member Manson
Benedict, AEC Chairman Glenn T. Seaborg, Dr. Bethe,
President John F. Kennedy, and Mrs. Hans A. Bethe.
(Courtesy U.S. Department of Energy, History Division,
official White House photograph)

The Sedan
crater, formed at
the Nevada test
site July 6, 1962,
as part of the
AEC Plowshare
Program. The
crater is 1280
feet in diameter
and 320 feet
deep. The lip
ranges from 20
to 105 feet high.
(Courtesy
Livermore
Radiation
Laboratory)

GAC Meeting 78, held in Washington, D.C., January 29–31, 1962. *Left to right:*
Kenneth S. Pitzer (GAC chairman), Robert A. Charpie (GAC secretary),
Norman F. Ramsey, Jr., John H. Williams, Eugene P. Wigner, Philip H. Abelson,
Willard F. Libby, Manson Benedict, Eger V. Murphree, John C. Warner (*leaning
forward*), and Anthony A. Tomei (GAC administrative officer). (Courtesy U.S.
Department of Energy, History Division)

Fermi Award ceremony at the White House for recipient Edward Teller, December 1962. *Left to right:* AEC Chairman Glenn T. Seaborg, Teller, and President John F. Kennedy. (Courtesy U.S. Department of Energy, History Division, official White House photograph)

GAC Meeting 83, held at the Sandia and Los Alamos scientific laboratories in New Mexico March 18–20, 1963. *Front left, left to right:* Robert E. Wilson (AEC commissioner), Anthony A. Tomei, and Eugene P. Wigner. *Seated at back table, left to right:* Lawrence R. Hafstad, Jane H. Hall, Kenneth S. Pitzer, Manson Benedict (GAC chairman), and John H. Williams. *Front right, left to right:* Philip H. Abelson (*leaning forward*), John C. Warner, and R. E. Schreiber (of the Los Alamos laboratory). Sitting in the back are members of the Los Alamos staff. Absent were William Webster and Norman F. Ramsey, Jr. (Courtesy U.S. Department of Energy, History Division)

White House ceremony for 1963 Fermi Award recipient
J. Robert Oppenheimer. *Left to right:* AEC Chairman
Glenn T. Seaborg, President Lyndon B. Johnson,
unidentified woman, Dr. Oppenheimer, Peter
Oppenheimer, Katherine Oppenheimer, Lady Bird
Johnson, AEC Commissioner Robert E. Wilson,
unidentified woman, AEC Commissioner James T. Ramey,
and Mrs. Glenn T. Seaborg. (Courtesy U.S. Department of
Energy, History Division)

Recipients of 1965 Lawrence Awards, with AEC Chairman Glenn T. Seaborg. *Left to right:* John Lawrence, Arthur C. Upton, George A. Cowan, Theodore B. Taylor, Floyd L. Culler, Milton C. Edlund, and Chairman Seaborg. (Courtesy U.S. Department of Energy, History Division)

GAC Meeting 106, held in Washington, D.C., October 14, 1968. *Seated, left to right:* Jane H. Hall, Norman F. Ramsey, Jr. (temporary GAC chairman), and Herbert Friedman. *Standing, left to right:* Anthony A. Tomei (GAC administrative officer), Stephen Lawroski, Howard G. Vesper, William Webster, Edwin L. Goldwasser, Lombard Squires, and Melvin A. Harrison (scientific officer). Absent was John C. Bugher. (Courtesy U.S. Department of Energy, History Division)

Aerial view of the Stanford Linear Accelerator Center, looking west from the beam switchyard (*foreground*). The two-mile-long 29-Bev linear accelerator on the Stanford University campus was dedicated September 9, 1967. (Courtesy Stanford University)

Committee. From 1947 to 1977, physicists held an annual average of three seats, or a third, of the membership, and two-thirds of all basic science members were physicists. In fact, the Committee was never without at least one physicist. This cannot be said for any other discipline.

One possible explanation for the extended representation of physicists on the Committee involves both demand for advice and disciplinary self-interest. Clearly the basic science advice offered by GAC physicists from 1947 to the mid-1960s was extremely valuable to the AEC. As the need for applied science advice displaced the need for basic science advice in the 1960s and beyond, physicists retained their favored GAC status because of their experience and knowledge in working with the major AEC contract laboratories. Moreover, because many of these laboratories required sustained AEC funding to continue scientific research projects, including money to build, operate, and maintain particle accelerators, laboratory-linked physicists found GAC service immensely important in shaping the future of their labs and the future of high-energy physics as a field.

Many of the physicists who served on the GAC were virtually legends in their own time. Three had won Nobel Prizes for their achievements, and many were renowned for managerial accomplishments as well. The physicists appointed to the GAC after 1964 were more closely associated with major AEC contract labs than those appointed earlier. Moreover, post-1964 physicist appointees seemed more closely linked to laboratory administration than to basic research.

J. ROBERT OPPENHEIMER (December 1946–August 1952). J. Robert Oppenheimer, the first GAC chairman, was respected for his direction of the Los Alamos Scientific Laboratory from 1943 to 1945. Placed in charge of work on the atomic bomb in 1942, he helped select the site for the laboratory, assisted in supervising construction of the facility, and managed to assemble a group of about 4500 scientists representing a wide range of fields to work at the lab. Trained as a physicist, Oppenheimer was sufficiently eclectic so that he could manage and supervise the work of this group of specialists. He planned the research program at Los Alamos and elected to have the lab pursue several competing designs in the process of assembling the bomb. Not long after conducting the first and successful test of an atomic weapon, in July 1945, he resigned his lab directorship.

Oppenheimer earned an A.B. in chemistry from Harvard University in 1925. He did graduate work under Lord Rutherford at Cambridge University and later under Max Born at the University of Gottingen, where he earned a doctorate in physics in 1927. Returning to the United States in 1929, he held concurrent appointments at the University of California at Berkeley and the California Institute of Technology, rising to the rank of professor of physics. After World War II he was appointed director of the Institute for Advanced Study in Princeton, New Jersey, and in this capacity worked as senior professor of physics. He advised and consulted with numerous agencies of the federal government and assumed great influence in the realm of atomic energy through his chairmanship of the GAC.

Oppenheimer made many original contributions to theoretical physics. He helped advance knowledge of cosmic rays, fundamental particles, and relativity. Included among his accomplishments in physics is his work in the development of a triggering mechanism for the atomic bomb.

LEE A. DUBRIDGE (December 1946–August 1952). Lee A. DuBridge earned a Ph.D. in physics from the University of Wisconsin in 1926. He held several academic appointments before joining the physical science division of the National Research Council (1936–1942). From 1940 to 1945 he directed the radiation laboratory at the Massachusetts Institute of Technology (MIT), where he helped to perfect radar technology. After the war DuBridge became the president of the California Institute of Technology (1946–1969) and continued to write and consult with government and private industry in a wide number of areas. His service on the GAC coincided with Oppenheimer's. He is noted for his work in biophysics, nuclear disintegration, direct current amplification, photoelectric and thermionic emission, the theory of photoelectric effect, and the energy distribution of photoelectrons.

ENRICO FERMI (December 1946–August 1950). Enrico Fermi earned his Ph.D. in physics at the University of Pisa in 1922. Like Oppenheimer, he studied under Max Born at Gottingen. At age twenty-five he won a position as professor of physics at the University of Rome where he worked until 1938. Fermi was a frequent visiting scholar to American universities in the prewar years. In 1939 he moved to the United States and became an American citizen in 1944. He worked at Columbia University and then the University of Chicago and did key design work on the atom bomb while at the Los Alamos Scientific Laboratory. After the war he returned to the University of Chicago where he continued to pursue research at the Institute for Nuclear Studies until he died in 1954.

Fermi's success in producing artificial radioactivity and in analyzing the decay products won him the 1938 Nobel Prize in physics. In 1926

Fermi and P. A. M. Dirac separately and independently derived the statistical mechanics of all indistinguishable particles (e.g., photons, electrons, and neutrons). In 1933 Fermi solved the beta-decay problem. He discovered a number of new radioactive elements and proved that nuclear reactions could be brought about by slow neutrons. His investigations of neutron bombardment led him to design and construct the first nuclear reactor. The lattice of graphite and uranium built in a squash court under the stands of an unused University of Chicago stadium and operated by Fermi and his colleagues achieved the first controlled nuclear chain reaction.

ISIDOR I. RABI (December 1946–August 1956). After earning a bachelor of chemistry at Cornell University in 1919, Isidor I. Rabi studied physics at Columbia University, obtaining a Ph.D. in 1927. He studied in Hamburg at Otto Stern's laboratory in 1927 and 1928 on a postdoctoral fellowship. In 1930 he joined the faculty at Columbia University, rose to full professor (1937), Higgins Professor (1951–1964), and University Professor (1964–1967). Before World War II he developed a new method for perfecting the measurement of atomic moments. Methods developed by Rabi have been applied to the atomic clock, nuclear magnetic resonance, and the maser and laser. For his work in identifying the anomalous magnetic moment of the electron, the quadrupole moment of the deuteron, and the Lamb shift associated with the polarizability of the vacuum, Rabi was awarded the Nobel Prize for physics in 1944.

From 1940 to 1945 Rabi focused his research on the development of microwave radar as associate director of the Radiation Laboratory in Cambridge, Mass. He periodically worked at Los Alamos between 1943 and 1945. In the postwar years Rabi helped to form the Brookhaven National Laboratory and its parent organization, Associated Universities, Inc. His expertise in high-energy physics and his work as a U.S. delegate to UNESCO helped establish the movement that culminated in CERN, the great international accelerator laboratory in Geneva. Rabi also did consulting work for numerous public and private organizations.

JAMES B. FISK (September 1952–August 1958). James B. Fisk received his undergraduate and graduate education at MIT, where he earned a Ph.D. in theoretical physics in 1935. He went on to become a teaching fellow in physics at MIT (1934–1936), a member of Harvard University's Society of Fellows (1936–1938), and an associate professor of physics at the University of North Carolina (1938–1939). From 1939 to 1945 Fisk worked as an electronics research engineer at Bell Telephone Laboratories and from 1945 to 1947 was assistant director of physical research there. He briefly returned to university life when he became McKay Professor of applied physics at Harvard from 1947 to 1949. In this period he became the first director of the AEC division of research (1947–1948). He returned to Bell Laboratories in 1949, becoming assistant research director, director of research in physical science (1952–1954), vice president of research (1954–1955), executive vice president (1955–1958), and finally president from 1959 to 1973. He became chairman of the board from 1973 to 1974 and then retired. Fisk was chairman of the GAC the last four years of his six-year membership.

Fisk was an outstanding aeronautical engineer who regularly furnished advice to the air force nuclear-powered-airplane program (see Chapter 5). He also supervised development of the microwave magnetron for use in high-frequency radar. He and William Shockley devised one of the first complete mathematical computations for operation of an atomic pile. Fisk also performed research on the internal conversion of gamma rays and on scattering problems in particle physics. His engineering ability set him apart from many other physicists of the GAC; he was clearly an applied physicist capable of exploiting a superb understanding of theoretical physics.

JESSE W. BEAMS (October 1954–August 1960). Jesse W. Beams earned a master's degree from the University of Wisconsin in 1922 and a doctorate in physics from the University of Virginia in 1925. He returned to the University of Virginia in 1928 and two years later was promoted to professor of physics. He served as department chair of physics from 1948 to 1963 and was the Francis H. Smith Professor of Physics.

During World War II Beams was a principal investigator with the Office of Scientific Research and Development (OSRD) where he did work on isotope separation, weapons, and ramjet engines. After the war he became a member of the board of directors of the Oak Ridge Institute of Nuclear Studies. His early research involved investigation of the initial stages of the electrical breakdown of gases and the initiation of the electric spark in air. He developed devices that made it possible to photograph light emitted in the initial stages of the electric spark in gases at various pressures and in a high vacuum. Shortly before the war, Beams, working with a team of scientists, developed a new type of high-energy particle accelerator that accelerated ions. He and E. G. Pickels developed a vacuum-type ultracentrifuge for purifying and characterizing substances used in biology, medicine, and chemistry. Beams and his colleagues accomplished the first separation of isotopes by centrifuging in 1935 and soon after successfully separated uranium isotopes in this manner. He was able to determine the molecular weights of a large number of substances, including proteins and viruses, through his magnetically suspended vacuum-type ultracentrifuge. Beams made contributions to the study of tensile strength of metals, low-temperature physics, and magnetic balances, and he helped perfect Kerr cells, ramjets, and cavity oscillators. During his six years of GAC service he played a very active role in high-energy physics advice and in review of particle accelerator proposals.

EDWIN M. MCMILLAN (October 1954–October 1958). Edwin M. McMillan studied physics at the California Institute of Technology, earning the B.S. in 1928 and the M.S. in 1929. He took his Ph.D. at Princeton in 1932 and spent two years as a National Research Fellow at the University of California at Berkeley as part of the staff of Ernest O. Lawrence's Radiation Laboratory. He became a member of the UC-Berkeley physics faculty in 1935. In World War II he contributed to development of radar at the MIT Radiation Laboratory (1940–1941), sonar at the Radio and Sound Laboratory of the U.S. Navy (1941–1942), and nuclear weapons at the Los Alamos Scientific Laboratory (1942–1945). After the war he returned to the Berkeley Radiation Laboratory where he became associate director in 1954 and director in 1958–1973.

Working with Philip H. Abelson, McMillan discovered element 93, neptunium, in the summer of 1940. The line of investigation set out by the pair was used by Glenn T. Seaborg and his colleagues when they discovered plutonium in early 1941. He shared the 1951 Nobel Prize with Seaborg. McMillan also developed a method for overcoming limitations on the energies that could be attained by the cyclotrons of the 1930s. In 1945, McMillan and Russian physicist V. I. Veksler separately proposed the theory of phase stability, which became the basis of the high-energy accelerators of the postwar period. McMillan coined the name "synchrotron" for accelerators based on the principle. The theory of phase stability is at the heart of the operation of proton accelerators at Berkeley, Brookhaven, and CERN. McMillan's theory and design work made possible numerous scientific advances in particle physics; synchrotron experimentation has led to discovery of antimatter, many new subatomic particles, and a host of knowledge about the ultimate structure of matter.

EDWARD TELLER (October 1956–August 1958). Edward Teller received his Ph.D. at the University of Leipzig in 1930 and was a researcher at the University of Gottingen from 1931 to 1933. He came to the United States in 1935 to become a professor of physics at George Washington University. In 1941 he assumed U.S. citizenship and became a staff member of the Manhattan Engineer District. He worked first at Columbia University (1941–1942), then at the University of Chicago (1942–1943), and finally at the Los Alamos Scientific Laboratory (1943–1946).

After World War II, Teller returned to the University of Chicago as a professor of physics. He continued his research there and then returned to Los Alamos in 1949. From 1949 to 1951 he served as assistant director of the Los Alamos lab. Dissatisfied with what he believed was the slow pace of research on thermonuclear weapons at Los Alamos, Teller returned to the University of Chicago and with Lawrence and Herbert York, succeeded in establishing a new AEC laboratory, the Livermore Radiation Laboratory, at Livermore, California. From 1953 to 1960 he was a professor of physics at the University of California at Berkeley where he worked mainly at the Livermore lab; in 1954 he became associate director of the Berkeley Radiation Laboratory. After resigning from the GAC he became director of the Livermore lab, occupying this post until 1960. He worked as a Berkeley professor at large from 1960 to 1975, which enabled him to work at Berkeley, Livermore, and the University of California at Davis at various times. By 1975 Teller had become an emeritus professor of physics at Berkeley and senior research fellow at the Hoover Institute on War, Peace, and Revolution at Stanford University. Teller has served on the U.S. Air Force Science Advisory Board and the President's Foreign Intelligence Advisory Board and in the early 1970s was a consultant to the Commission on Critical Choices of Americans. Teller continues to advise the president on matters of science and technology and was one of those who proposed the so-called "star wars" nuclear defense to President Ronald W. Reagan. Some elements of President Reagan's Strategic Defense Initiative were products of Teller's advice.

Teller's scientific accomplishments are prodigious. His early research in the 1930s involved quantum mechanics and physical chemistry. His work on the hydrogen molecular ion was considered a major advance in the development of the theory of molecular orbitals. This research successfully explained the phenomenon of the chemical bond. He collaborated with others in identifying the "BET" equation, which expressed the relation, at constant temperature, between the volume of gas adsorbed on a surface and the pressure of the gas above the adsorbent. He also explored molecular vibration, sound distribution, and the duration of the magnetic cooling process.

In the late 1930s Teller moved into the study of nuclear physics. He and George Gamow set out new selection rules for the beta-decay process, and they explained certain observed transitions that had been "forbidden" under earlier selection rules. His paper on the scattering of neutrons by ortho- and parahydrogen suggested experiments to test the spin dependence of the neutron-proton force, which eventually yielded information on the spin of the neutron and the range of nuclear forces.

In the 1940s Teller, Fermi, and others advanced the theoretical possibility of obtaining controlled fusion power through the confinement of hot plasma in a strong magnetic field. The AEC supported research of controlled nuclear fusion (called Project Sherwood), and Teller has been an active participant in this line of research. During his wartime service at Los Alamos, he made computations that were used in predicting how the atomic bomb would function. Most significantly, Teller was one of the first to study thermonuclear reactions. In the years 1946 to 1951, working with a group of scientists, he and Stanislaw M. Ulam developed the principle that led to the successful construction of the first hydrogen bomb. In the years following the explosion of the first thermonuclear bomb, he strongly advocated use of thermonuclear explosives for peaceful purposes and was one of the chief architects of Project Plowshare (see Chapter 8).

NORMAN F. RAMSEY, JR. (November 1960–August 1972). Norman F. Ramsey, Jr., earned his A.B. (1935), M.A. (1939), and Ph.D. (1940) from Columbia University and a B.A. (1937) and M.A. (1940) from Cambridge University in England. He joined Harvard University as a professor of physics from 1942 to 1966. From 1940 to 1942 he was a research associate at the MIT Radiation Laboratory where he headed groups that developed the first three-centimeter-wavelength magnetrons and the first radar systems at that wavelength. As a consultant to the secretary of war, Ramsey advised the air force on radar use. From 1943 to 1945 he was a group leader and associate division chief at the Los Alamos Scientific Laboratory. As chief scientist for the technical group detached to Tinian Island, he helped reassemble and load onto the B-29s the atomic bombs to be dropped on Hiroshima and Nagasaki.

After the war Ramsey helped to establish the Brookhaven National Laboratory. He served as the laboratory's first Physics Department chairman from 1946 to 1947, returned to Harvard University as an associate professor of physics in 1947, and became a full professor in 1950. From 1949 to 1956 Ramsey was a member of the U.S. Air Force Science Advisory Board and a member of the Defense Science Board from 1954 to 1958. He then became the science advisor to the North Atlantic Treaty Organization for two years. In 1963 he was chosen to chair a high-energy physics advisory panel composed of President's Science Advisory Committee (PSAC) members and GAC members, which came to be called the Ramsey panel (see Chapter 9). Among its recommendations was a call to build a new high-energy particle accelerator facility, which became known as the Enrico Fermi National Accelerator Laboratory.

Ramsey's scientific work concerned the properties of molecules, atoms, nuclei, and elementary particles. His Ph.D. thesis, written under Rabi, made the first accurate measurements of the rotational magnetic moments of molecules, demonstrating for the first time how magnetic moments depended on the weight of the nuclei. His work with Rabi identified the existence of a tensor force between the neutron and the proton. He researched the forces between elementary particles by measurements on the scattering of neutrons and protons from hydrogen, helium, and other nuclei. In research undertaken after the war, Ramsey studied the properties of molecules and nuclei by the molecular-beam resonance method he invented. He chaired the scientific committee for the 6-MeV (million electron volt) Cambridge electron accelerator during its period of construction in the late 1950s. Ramsey developed the theory of magnetic shielding of nuclei in molecules, investigated the thermodynamics and statistical mechanics of systems at negative absolute temperatures, and helped to rephrase the second law of thermodynamics to account for his findings in these experiments. He measured the magnetic moment of the neutron to high accuracy and helped to develop the atomic hydrogen maser, which made possible the measurement of hyperfine frequencies of hydrogen, deuterium, and tritium.

JOHN H. WILLIAMS (November 1960–April 1966). John H. Williams was born in Quebec, Canada, and became a U.S. citizen in 1928. He earned a B.A. (1928) from the University of British Columbia and an M.A. (1930) and Ph.D. (1931) in physics from the University of California at Berkeley. He built his academic career at the University of Minnesota, rising through the ranks from instructor (1933–1934) to assistant professor (1934–1937), associate professor (1937–1942), and full professor (1946–1966).

During World War II Williams worked as an official investigator for the OSRD (1942–1943) and then as group leader of the physics division at the Los Alamos Scientific Laboratory (1943–1946). After the war he returned to the University of Minnesota. From 1958 to 1959 he directed the AEC division of research and served as an AEC commissioner from 1959 to 1960. He retained his academic appointment and concurrently served as a vice president of the University of Minnesota.

Williams conducted research on the natural line width of x-rays and spectroscopy. He investigated light nuclei reactions and the scattering of light nuclei, and his design work advanced proton linear accelerator technology. He was associated with the Midwest Universities Research Association, or MURA (see Chapter 9).

LAWRENCE R. HAFSTAD (September 1962–August 1968). Lawrence R. Hafstad graduated from the University of Minnesota in 1926 with a B.S. in electrical engineering, continued graduate work there, and received his Ph.D. in physics from the Johns Hopkins University in 1933. In 1928 he began a fourteen-year period of research work with the Carnegie Institution in Washington, D.C. In 1942 he joined the Applied Physics Laboratory of Johns Hopkins and from 1945 to 1947 assumed directorship of that lab.

During World War II he served with the OSRD, working on ordnance projects such as the proximity fuze, ramjet engines, missiles, and missile guidance. After the war he served as executive secretary of the Research and Development Board in the Pentagon under Vannevar Bush and Karl Compton. In 1949 he became the first director of AEC's reactor development division. In 1955 he left the AEC staff and later that year became vice president of the research laboratories of General Motors Corporation, where he remained until 1969. He was chairman of the GAC the last four years of his term. He then chaired the Committee on Undersea Warfare of the National Research Council and retired in 1972.

Hafstad's research with the Carnegie Institution in the 1920s involved development of high-voltage vacuum tubes for the acceleration of nuclear particles; in 1931, he helped to engineer the first 1-MeV vacuum tube. He participated in the first precision measurements of the scattering of protons by protons, ultimately making possible evaluation of the magnitude of specific nuclear attractive forces. In 1939, working with his colleagues at Carnegie, Hafstad was able to produce one of the first experimental confirmations of the nuclear fission process postulated by Otto Hahn and Fritz Strassmann. This work predicted the delayed neutron emission from the uranium fission process and advanced nuclear-reactor-control research. Hafstad's work contributed to the study of wave propagation, atomic disintegration, artificial radioactivity, high-voltage techniques, and geophysics. He, like Fisk, possessed a sound knowledge and training in theoretical physics that carried over into the realm of engineering application.

DAROL K. FROMAN (April 1964–August 1966). Darol K. Froman earned a B.A. and M.S. at the University of Alberta and a Ph.D. in physics from the University of Chicago in 1930. From 1931 to 1941 he was a faculty member at Macdonald College of McGill University in Montreal, and he assumed a professorship at the University of Denver in 1941 where he directed the Mt. Evans High Altitude Laboratory. In late 1942 he became a group leader at the navy's Radio and Sound Laboratory in San Diego. About this time he also took the job of research associate with the University of Chicago Metallurgical Laboratory. In 1943 he began a twenty-year career of research with the Los Alamos Scientific Laboratory. There he moved from group leader (1943–1945) to division leader (1945–1948), assistant director of weapons development (1949–1951), and technical associate director (1951–1962).

Froman's research involved ultrasonics, x-rays, cosmic rays, electronics applied to nuclear physics, and nuclear reactors and reactor controls. He was the science director of the Eniwetok Atomic Weapons Tests of 1948 in the South Pacific. From 1955 to 1960 he was a member of the Science Advisory Committee on Ballistic Missiles for the secretary of defense. From 1963 to 1969, a period encompassing his GAC term, he served on the Science Directorate of the Douglas Aircraft Company. He ran his own consulting firm after he retired from employment with the Los Alamos lab in 1962.

EDWIN L. GOLDWASSER (September 1966–August 1972). Edwin L. Goldwasser took a B.A. at Harvard in 1940 and was a graduate student at Columbia University when his academic career was interrupted by World War II. From 1941 to 1945 he worked as a physicist with the navy Bureau of Ordnance, becoming a senior physicist of the 12th Naval District while serving at the navy yard at Mare Island, California (1943–1945). In 1946 he became an assistant professor of physics at the University of California at Berkeley, earning his Ph.D. in physics in 1950. In 1951 he began a long career of work with the University of Illinois at Urbana (1951–1967), moving through successive academic ranks to full professor. In 1967 he became deputy director of the Fermi Laboratory, serving in that capacity until 1978, when he returned to the University of Illinois to become chancellor of research and dean of the Graduate College.

Goldwasser spent much of the 1960s advising the National Research Council and the National Academy of Sciences in matters regarding high-energy accelerator physics. In 1962 and 1963, he served on the Ramsey panel, a joint PSAC-GAC advisory body that played an essential part in shaping the federal government's high-energy physics program. He served on the committee that ultimately chose the site of the Fermi lab. Very active in international organizations seeking exchange of knowledge on matters of elementary particle physics, Goldwasser's achievements have been in research of primary cosmic radiation, energy loss of charged particles, photoproduction of pi mesons, the interaction of strange particles, and electron and photon interactions.

JANE H. HALL (September 1966–August 1972). Jane H. Hall earned a B.S. (1937), an M.S. (1938), and a Ph.D. (1942) in physics from the University of Chicago. From 1944 through 1945 she worked as a senior supervisor for the Du Pont Company at Hanford, Washington. In 1945 she began a twenty-five-year period of employment at the Los Alamos Scientific Laboratory, rising to the position of laboratory associate director, where she pursued research on x-ray crystallography, x-ray medical research, neutron physics, reactor development, and cosmic rays. She retired from Los Alamos in 1970 and became a consultant, and in 1967 she joined the AEC Advisory Committee on Nuclear Materials and Safeguards.

HERBERT FRIEDMAN (August 1968–August 1974). Herbert Friedman earned a B.A. at Brooklyn College in 1936 and a Ph.D. in physics from the Johns Hopkins University in 1940. He soon after began a long career of employment with the Naval Research Laboratory, beginning as a physicist (1940–1943) and then heading the electron optics branch (1943–1958). In 1958 he was made superintendent of the Atmosphere and Astrophysics Division and in 1963 assumed the job of chief scientist at the laboratory's E. O. Hulbert Center for Space Research.

Friedman pioneered rocket development and satellite astronomy. In 1949 he began work on captured German V-2 rockets, which had been transported to White Sands, New Mexico. His rocket astronomy program obtained the first scientific proof that x-rays emanate from the sun. In 1956 his rocket-assisted experiments revealed that energy radiated as x-rays represents a major portion of the total energy output of a solar flare and can cause disturbances in the earth's ionosphere such as short-wave radio fade-out. In 1958 one of Friedman's rocket experiments, conducted from an aircraft carrier deck in the South Pacific during a solar eclipse, provided the first proof that x-radiation comes from the sun's corona (outer atmosphere) and that ultraviolet radiation comes from its chromosphere (inner atmosphere). He produced the first astronomical photographs made in x-ray wavelengths, discovered the hydrogen corona around the earth, and measured ultraviolet flares from early-type stars. His work in development of satellite instrumentation and radio astronomy contributed to the unmanned space exploration of the National Aeronautics and Space Administration (NASA).

Friedman served on many professional and governmental advisory bodies, among them the NASA Space Progress Advisory Committee

(1974–1977) and the executive committee of the Space Science Board of the National Academy of Sciences.

EVANS V. HAYWARD (October 1972–February 1975). Evans V. Hayward received a B.A. from Smith College in 1942 and an M.A. (1945) and Ph.D. (1947) in physics from the University of California at Berkeley. She worked as a physicist at Lawrence's Radiation Laboratory from 1947 to 1950. In 1950 she joined the National Bureau of Standards as a physicist employed at the Linac Laboratory and devoted most of her career to working with this lab. She has investigated the interactions of high-energy radiations with matter and has explored photonuclear reactions.

MICHAEL M. MAY (October 1972–September 1977). Michael M. May earned a B.A. at Whitman College (1944) and a Ph.D. in physics from the University of California at Berkeley in 1952. He worked as a research physicist at the Livermore National Laboratory in 1952 until he was offered a vice presidency with E. H. Plesset Associates in 1957. In 1960 he left this firm and returned to the Livermore lab where he advanced from research physicist (1960–1961) to division leader (1961–1962), associate director (1962–1964), lecturer in applied science (1964–1965), and then director (1965–1971). In 1972, accommodating his heavy travel demands, May was appointed research physicist and associate director-at-large at Livermore.

In 1974 May was appointed senior personal advisor to the secretary of defense for Strategic Arms Limitation Talks. He had previously served on the Defense Science Board of the Department of Defense (DOD). His research area specializations are in nuclear explosions, relativity, and heat and radiation.

WALTER H. ZINN (October 1972–February 1975). Walter H. Zinn earned a Ph.D. in physics from Columbia University in 1934 and then taught at City College of New York from 1932 to 1941. He assisted Fermi in developing the first self-sustained nuclear chain reaction. He was a pioneer in development of nuclear reactor technology and directed the University of Chicago Metallurgical Laboratory from 1942 to 1946 and the Argonne National Laboratory from 1945 to 1956. He was president of General Nuclear Engineering Company (1956–1964) and vice president of Combustion Engineering, Inc., a major U.S. reactor vendor (1959–1971). Not long after his retirement from Combustion Engineering, Zinn was appointed to the GAC.

Zinn is credited with major contributions to the study of neutrons.

He researched the basic problems of central station nuclear power in 1952 and designed several types of nuclear reactors, including a breeder reactor. He was undoubtedly a key advisor to the AEC on the planned Clinch River Breeder Reactor project during his period of GAC service.

RICHARD S. MORSE (September 1975–August 1976). Richard S. Morse did undergraduate work in physics at MIT. From 1935 to 1940 he worked for Eastman Kodak Company and from 1940 to 1959 served as president of the National Research Corporation. He was assistant secretary of the army from 1959 to 1961, a post that carried the designation of director of research. For a period, he served as chairman of the board for the air force Systems Command, technical advisor for the DOD Panel on Biological and Chemical Warfare, chairman of the Army Science Advisory Panel, and a member of the DOD Defense Science Board. From 1962 until 1972 he worked as a senior lecturer at MIT's Sloan School of Management and in 1972 became director of MIT's Development Foundation.

Morse has to be considered an applied rather than a theoretical physicist. He is an expert in high-vacuum technology, vacuum metallurgy, dehydration, evaporation of metals, vacuum pumps and gauges, and photo processes.

GERALD F. TAPE (September 1975–September 1977). Gerald F. Tape held a doctorate in nuclear physics but established his career in science administration. He studied and lectured at the University of Michigan from 1936 to 1939, taught at Cornell University for three years, and then joined the staff of the MIT Radiation Laboratory, then directed by DuBridge. He worked at MIT from 1942 to 1946, assumed an academic appointment with the physics department of the University of Illinois at Urbana (1946–1950), and served as deputy director of the Brookhaven National Laboratory from 1951 to 1962. He then advanced to the vice presidency and presidency of Associated Universities, Inc. (AUI), the contract operator of Brookhaven. From 1963 to 1969, Tape was an AEC commissioner. On leaving the Commission, he returned to his post as president of AUI.

Tape was known for his expertise in particle physics, accelerator development, reactor development, radioastronomy, and science administration. He preceded his ERDA GAC service with periods of service to the International Atomic Energy Agency (as the U.S. ambassador), the Defense Science Board, the Geneva IV Conference (as technical advisor), and the Atomic Industrial Forum.

GAC chemists

Six GAC members held postgraduate degrees in the discipline of chemistry. Chemists composed 20 percent of the total GAC basic science representatives and about 11 percent of total GAC life membership (Table 3.2). In some intervals of GAC operation (1950–1955 and 1957–1961), the number of chemists on the Committee closely matched or sometimes exceeded the number of physicists (Table 3.4). From 1947 to 1963, 22 percent of the GAC membership, or two of nine seats, were occupied by chemists.

Yet, by the end of 1964, chemists disappeared from GAC membership. As chemistry representation on the Committee declined (Table 3.3), chemical engineering representation correspondingly increased. The representation of chemists exceeded the representation of chemical engineers for each year from 1947 to 1961. In 1962 and 1963 each of these disciplines had only a single GAC representative, after 1964 no more chemists were appointed to the GAC while chemical engineers assumed increased representation, and from 1964 to 1969 a full third of the GAC comprised chemical engineers.

The decline of chemistry representation, a basic science discipline, and the rise of chemical engineering, an applied science discipline, affirms the theories regarding the displacement of basic science advisers by applied science advisers. Of course, Glenn T. Seaborg, a Nobel Prize winner in chemistry and an early GAC member, chaired the AEC from 1961 to 1971, so it may be argued that the appointment of chemists to the GAC was not considered essential in this period because a chemist was chairing the Commission itself.

There is a direct reference to the discipline of chemistry in an early GAC meeting. Chemists Eger V. Murphree and Willard F. Libby were in attendance at GAC Meeting 22 held in September 1950. Committee records disclose that the GAC discussed the problem of inadequate advertising of AEC chemistry research funding. The minutes recount, "Although fundamental research in chemistry has been encouraged, it appears that knowledge of the availability of funds for such projects is not yet sufficiently widespread to provide an adequate number of worthy projects."[13] This represents an example of Committee concern for AEC-funded chemical research. GAC advocacy of disciplinary interests was usually addressed more subtly.

While only six chemists served on the GAC, a small number compared with other fields, their impact on the work of both the AEC and the GAC was dramatic.

JAMES B. CONANT (December 1946–August 1952). James B. Conant earned an A.B. (1913) and a Ph.D. (1916) in chemistry from Harvard University. He remained with Harvard as professor of chemistry until 1933, when he began twenty years of service as president of Harvard. From 1941 to 1946 he worked with the National Defense Research Committee and served as deputy director of the OSRD. Working directly for Vannevar Bush at the OSRD, Conant helped to establish the Manhattan Project and was directly responsible for assigning to Oppenheimer the leadership of the atomic bomb research project. After World War II, Conant returned to full-time presidency duties at Harvard. From 1953 to 1955 he served as the U.S. high commissioner for Germany and then as U.S. ambassador to the Federal Republic of Germany (1955–1957).

Conant conducted research in organic chemistry with particular emphasis on free radicals, hemoglobin, superacid solutions, and chlorophyll and authored numerous textbooks that addressed experimental science. In addition, Conant had a keen interest in the problems of general education, particularly elementary and secondary education. He wrote and published extensively on the problems of teachers, students, and parents in the educational process, and from 1957 to 1962 he was supported by a Carnegie Corporation grant to study the education of American teachers.

GLENN T. SEABORG (December 1946–August 1950). Glenn T. Seaborg received an A.B. in 1934 from the University of California at Los Angeles and a Ph.D. in chemistry at the University of California at Berkeley in 1937. He remained at Berkeley as a research associate and rapidly rose to the rank of full professor. In December 1940 Seaborg and his Berkeley Radiation Laboratory associates bombarded uranium oxide with deuterons and succeeded in isolating chemically the unstable element-93 fraction of the resulting products. As predicted, this material decayed by emitting a beta particle to yield element 94, plutonium. Further research led to production of the isotope Pu-239, recognized as a potential source of nuclear energy. In 1942 Seaborg moved to the University of Chicago Metallurgical Laboratory in the hope that he could produce a sufficient quantity of the plutonium isotope for production of nuclear energy.

Seaborg discovered two more elements, element 95 (americium) and element 96 (curium). After 1945 Seaborg returned to Berkeley, and working with his colleagues, isolated six more new transuranium elements. He helped to identify over 100 isotopes distributed throughout the periodic table. For discoveries in the chemistry of transuranium elements, Seaborg and the physicist McMillan shared the 1951 Nobel Prize in chemistry. He has written extensively on the general subject of nuclear chemistry and nuclear physics.

Seaborg directed nuclear chemistry research at the Berkeley lab from 1946 to 1958 and again from 1972 to 1975. He served as chancellor of the University of California at Berkeley from 1958 to 1961 while retaining his post as associate director of the lab (1954–1961). In 1961 President Kennedy appointed Seaborg chairman of the AEC, a position he held for ten years, the longest period of service of any AEC chairman. He served on many advisory committees besides the GAC, among them the International Council of Scientific Unions (1946–1956), the Federal Council on Science and Technology (1961–1971), the Federal Radiation Council (1961–1971), the National Aeronautics and Space Council (1961–1971), and the Pacific Science Center Foundation Science Advisory Committee (1963–1977).

WILLARD F. LIBBY (August 1950–September 1954, May 1960–August 1962). Willard F. Libby earned a B.S. (1931) and a Ph.D. (1933) in chemistry from the University of California at Berkeley and taught at Berkeley until 1941. From 1941 to 1945 he worked in the War Research Division at Columbia University where he developed the gaseous-diffusion process for separating the isotopes of uranium, an essential step in the production of the atomic bomb. From 1945 to 1954, he was a professor of chemistry at the University of Chicago and the Institute of Nuclear Studies. Libby served as an AEC commissioner from 1954 to 1959; in this period he was employed as a research associate with the Carnegie Institution's Geophysics Laboratory. From 1959 to 1972 he was a member of the AEC Plowshare Advisory Committee and in 1959 became director of UCLA's Institute of Geophysics and Planetary Physics.

Libby conceived the method of radiocarbon dating that has enabled scientists to determine the absolute ages of organic materials (wood, charcoal, parchment, shells, skeletal remains) formed within the past 50,000 years. For this achievement he received the 1960 Nobel Prize in chemistry. Among his other accomplishments are the development of the atomic clock, contributions in radiochemistry, improvement in tracer techniques, and isotope tracer work.

EGER V. MURPHREE (August 1950–August 1956, April 1957–August 1958, October 1958–October 1962). Eger V. Murphree earned a B.S. (1920) and an M.S. (1921) in chemistry from the University of Kentucky. He held research positions at MIT and at Solvay Process Company in New York State. In the period 1926–1934 he directed the chemical engineering division and then the research department of Standard Oil Company of Louisiana. From 1937 until 1947 he occupied various senior executive positions with Esso Research and Engineering Company, in 1947 becoming president/director. During World War II, Murphree worked for the OSRD, helping to engineer some of the production plants required for generating the radioactive materials needed in fabrication of the atomic bomb.

Murphree had a great deal of knowledge and experience in distillation technology, heat transfer, oil processing, and industrial and military applications of atomic energy. He served as chairman of the Permanent Council of the World Petroleum Congress, was a member of a DOD Advisory Panel on Atomic Energy, and was special assistant to the secretary of defense for guided missiles (1956–1957). During his eleven years of GAC service, Murphree played a central role in virtually all committee deliberations.

JOHN C. WARNER (September 1952–August 1958, October 1958–August 1964). John C. Warner studied physical chemistry at Indiana University, earning his A.B. (1919), M.A. (1921), and Ph.D. (1923). He worked as a chemist in private industry in the 1920s; most of his career, however, was spent in academia. In 1926 he began a long association with the Carnegie Institute of Technology in Pittsburgh. There he became a professor of theoretical chemistry and professor of chemistry, headed the chemistry department (1938–1949), became dean of graduate studies (1945–1950), served as vice president (1949–1950), and in 1950 began a fifteen-year tenure as president of the Carnegie Institute of Technology. He worked for the Manhattan Project from 1943 to 1945 supervising research on chemistry and metallurgy of plutonium.

Warner had a very broad knowledge of the field of chemistry. His most important contributions concerned the kinetics of reactions in solution, including salts and medium effects. He researched the electrostatic contribution to activation energies, the thermodynamic properties of solutions, the rates and mechanism of corrosion, thermodynamics, and the acid-base properties of mixed solvents. He was also prolific in writing about educational and research administration, as well as scientific and technical education.

WARREN C. JOHNSON (October 1954–August 1960). Warren C. Johnson earned a B.A. from Kalamazoo College (1922), an M.A. from Clark University (1923), and a Ph.D. from Brown University (1925) with chemistry as his major field. He began a long career with the University of Chicago in 1927 where he became a professor of chemistry, chaired his department (1945–1955), served as associate dean of the division of physical science (1946–1955), and became dean (1955). From 1958 to 1967 he was the university's vice president in charge of special programs, and he became emeritus professor of chemistry and emeritus vice president of the university in 1967.

During World War II Johnson directed the chemical division of the Clinton Laboratories at Oak Ridge. He helped to establish the gaseous-diffusion plant works that were vital to production of the uranium products. His research areas included inorganic chemistry, liquid ammonia solutions, hydrides, and rare earths and rare earth elements.

Johnson was for many years an AEC consultant. He served as chairman of the GAC from 1956 to 1960, when his term expired. He also served on the DOD Defense Science Board from 1957 to 1960. In 1958 he became a member of the Oak Ridge Institute of Nuclear Studies. In 1960 he joined the Institute for Defense Analysis and in 1962 moved to Union Carbide Corporation. From 1963 to 1965 he served the Atomic Industrial Forum.

GAC mathematical physicists, mathematicians, and physical chemists

While physicists and chemists dominated representation of the basic sciences on the Committee, other basic sciences were represented. There were Committee members trained in mathematics, mathematical physics, and physical chemistry.

JOHN VON NEUMANN (February 1952–August 1954). John von Neumann, the only mathematician to serve on the GAC, studied at the University of Berlin and the Zurich Institute of Technology, where in 1925 he received a degree in chemical engineering. In 1926 the University of Budapest granted him a Ph.D. in mathematics. He briefly taught at the University of Hamburg before coming to the United States in 1930. He became a visiting professor at Princeton University in 1930 and a professor of mathematics at the Institute for Advanced Study in Princeton in 1933, spending most of his research career at the institute. Von Neumann spent intermittent periods of time conducting research at the Los Alamos Scientific Laboratory from 1943 until 1955 and at Oak Ridge National Laboratory from 1949 until 1954. During World War II, von Neumann did consulting work for the army, navy, and OSRD. His work on the lens principle of detonation conducted at the Los Alamos lab proved to be decisive in the development of the atomic bomb. In the postwar years, von Neumann provided advice on many aspects of national defense, including the development of intermediate and long-range ballistics missiles.

In 1928 von Neumann developed the theory of games and showed how it could be applied in a variety of social sciences. His work in set theory, the theory of continuous groups, ergodic theory, quantum theory, and operator theory contributed to the field of mathematics and to the application of mathematical techniques in numerous disciplines. He may best be remembered for his contributions to the development of computer theory and design. He and his colleagues at the institute designed and built MANIAC I, the first computer able to use a flexible stored program. In August 1954 he was appointed to the AEC.

EUGENE P. WIGNER (September 1952–January 1957, December 1959–August 1962, September 1962–May 1964). Eugene P. Wigner, the GAC's only mathematical physicist, was born in Budapest and educated at the Technische Hochschule in Berlin. His major field was chemical engineering and he took his doctorate in engineering. He held professorial posts at his alma mater from 1926 to 1933 and was an assistant professor at the University of Gottingen in 1927 and 1928. In 1930, at age twenty-eight, he became N. B. Ausserord Professor of theoretical physics at the Technische Hochschule.

Wigner emigrated to the United States in 1930 and assumed U.S. citizenship. From 1930 to 1936 he lectured in mathematics at Princeton University and then assumed a professorship of physics at the University of Wisconsin for two years. He returned to Princeton as the Thomas D. Jones Professor of Mathematical Physics with the university's Palmer Physics Laboratory. He continued his Princeton professorship from 1938 until 1971, when he assumed emeritus status.

During World War II Wigner took leave to work as director of theoretical studies at the University of Chicago Metallurgical Laboratory. He researched the problems of plutonium production, helped develop plans for a water-cooled atomic pile, advocated construction of a large-scale atomic pile for plutonium production, and developed engineering designs used by Du Pont Company in construction of an air-cooled atomic pile. In 1946 he became director of research and development at the Clinton Laboratories where he supervised design and construction of several new types of atomic reactors.[14]

Wigner applied group theory to quantum mechanics, researched the role of invariance and symmetry, particularly in quantum mechanics, and analyzed the rate of chemical reactions. He investigated nuclear structure and nuclear chain reaction, and his work in the structure of metals and metallic cohesion has been of great significance in reactor design. In 1963 he won the Nobel Prize in physics with his colleagues M. G. Mayer and J. H. D. Jensen. After his work on the GAC, he was Lorentz lecturer at the Institute of Lorentz at Leiden, West Germany, from 1957 to 1959. On returning to the United States, he was reappointed to the GAC. Wigner is one of those rare individuals who combines theoretical and experimental brilliance with exceptional engineering skills. Moreover, he is a science manager capable of supervising and coordinating the work of others.

KENNETH S. PITZER (October 1958–August 1964, July 1964–July 1965). Kenneth S. Pitzer, one of only two physical chemists to serve on the GAC, served two successive terms and was GAC chairman from 1960 to 1962. He received his B.S. from the California Institute of Technology (1935) and his Ph.D. from the University of California at Berkeley (1937). He joined the Berkeley faculty in 1937 and by 1945 became a professor of chemistry. From 1943 to 1944 he took leave to become technical director of the Maryland (War) Research Laboratories serving OSRD. He returned to Berkeley to become assistant dean (1947) and dean of the College of Chemistry (1951–1960). He became president and professor of chemistry at Rice University in 1961, spent 1968 to 1970 at Stanford University, and returned to a chemistry professorship at Berkeley in 1971. Pitzer was director of the division of research within the AEC from 1949 to 1951. He has long been a member of the board of trustees of the Rand Corporation. Among the organizations he has done consulting work for are the American Petroleum Institute (1947–1952), the National Academy of Sciences (1959–1962), the Carnegie Foundation for Advanced Teaching (1966–1970), and Owens-Illinois, Inc. (1966 on). He was director of the Federal Reserve Bank of Dallas from 1965 to 1968.

Pitzer's research achievements were in chemical thermodynamics, quantum theory, molecular spectroscopy, and statistical mechanics applied to chemistry. He was capable of offering the Committee both interdisciplinary and cross-disciplinary advice.

PHILIP H. ABELSON (June 1960–November 1963). Philip H. Abelson received a B.S. in chemistry in 1933 and an M.S. in physics in 1935 from what is now Washington State University. He then entered the University of California at Berkeley and, studying under Lawrence in the Berkeley Radiation Laboratory, received the Ph.D. in physics in 1939. As a graduate student he was the first American scientist to identify products of uranium fission, in 1939. Working with physicist McMillan, Abelson identified neptunium. From 1939 to 1941 he worked as an assistant physicist at the Carnegie Institution in Washington, D.C., and from 1941 to 1945 he worked at the Naval Research Laboratory. He devised a method for synthesizing purer uranium from uranium hexafluoride. He discovered that the uranium isotopes could be partially separated by liquid thermal diffusion. By progressively scaling up the process, Abelson's method became the basis for the design of the huge Oak Ridge gaseous-diffusion plant, which produced the enriched uranium in quantity that was indispensable to atomic bomb research.

In 1946, Abelson led a small group that prepared a feasibility report on the atomic submarine. The study set in progress the research and development work that eventually produced a nuclear reactor for submarine propulsion. From 1946 to 1953, he chaired the biophysics section of the Carnegie Institution's Department of Terrestrial Magnetism. In this period his work outlined the pathways of biosynthesis of amino acids in microorganisms. He then became director of the geophysical laboratory at Carnegie from 1953 to 1971. During research in that interval, he pioneered the study of organic geochemistry and identified original amino acids preserved in fossils and shells. This research contributed to the study of the origin of life. As editor of *Science* magazine and as a well-known lecturer and editorialist, Abelson has devoted much of his later life to studying the interaction of science and public policy. From 1971 to 1978 he was president of Carnegie.

Abelson served on the AEC Plowshare Advisory Committee (1959–1963), chaired the National Research Council's Radiation Cataract Committee (1949–1957), advised the biophysics and biophysical chemistry study section of the National Institute of Health, was a science counselor to the National Institute of Arthritis and Medical Disability (1960–1963), and served as a National Academy of Science council member (1978–1981).

Abelson's major contributions in nuclear physics and radioactive tracers, his investigation of the fission products of uranium, his experiments in the x-ray emissions of radioactive substances, and his work in paleobiochemistry, geochemistry, and biosynthesis in microorganisms have been highly regarded in the basic science research community. Like Pitzer, he could offer the Committee both interdisciplinary and cross-disciplinary advice.

The applied sciences

The applied sciences are associated with what is referred to as the professional estate. The professions, engineering and medicine in particular, "make tremendous use of the findings of the sciences, but they add something more: a purpose."[15] According to estate theory, "The engineer must translate a purpose into specified objectives, requirements, and criteria of performance — this is not a matter of pure science. It is a matter of engineering doctrine, which must be developed on the basis of scientific concepts, but it must also govern the allocation of resources—a kind of budget—to make the system work."[16]

Professions are intermediaries between abstract knowledge and political action. Engineers might be tempted to help their companies sell something fancier and more costly to the government. Nevertheless, as a professional, an engineer has an obligation to "standards of ethics and competence that his profession, not his employer, dictates."[17] While pure science can often ignore questions of purpose in order to be objective and precise, the professions cannot. Professional engineers take their purposes from the demands of their customers and employers, "as an engineer does in building a bridge."[18] One of the foremost contributions of professions is to help determine how the findings of basic research can be applied. They are judges of feasibility and cost who serve in the "retreat from abstraction."[19]

GAC chemical engineers

Of the GAC's fifty-five members, eighteen were educated and trained in applied science disciplines (Table 3.2). Among this group eight were trained in chemical engineering. While this was far fewer than the number of GAC members holding degrees in physics, chemical engineers had the second highest number of members on the Committee. Only in 1948 and 1949 was a chemical engineer not on the Committee. In any single GAC year, there was an average of one or two chemical engineers on the panel, most of whom were employed either by major private corporations or by AEC contract laboratories.

From 1965 to 1969 one-third of the GAC members were chemical engineers. This is evidence of the AEC's urgent need for applied research advice at a time when the Commission was making a concerted effort to promote the commercial viability and practical application of civilian nuclear electric power.

HOOD WORTHINGTON (December 1946–August 1948). Hood Worthington earned a B.S. (1924) and an M.S. (1925) in chemical engineering from MIT. From 1925 to 1935 he worked as a research chemical engineer in the chemistry department of Du Pont. From 1935 until 1943 he progressed through positions in the technical division of the engineering department and the nylon research section of the rayon department and became research supervisor. In 1943 he joined the technical division of the explosives department and from 1944 to 1945 worked as a chief supervisor. He supervised construction of the Hanford atomic fuels production plant, which Du Pont built and operated for the federal government during World War II.

After the war, Worthington became a process manager, assistant director of engineering research in the rayon department, and assistant director and then director of nylon research. In 1950 he reassumed an assistant director post in the atomic energy explosives department and from 1955 to 1963 directed that department. He helped to engineer one of the first power-generating nuclear reactors.[20] In 1957 he assumed directorship of the Atomic Industrial Forum. After 1964 he became a consulting engineer, and in 1965 he joined the AEC atomic safety and licensing panel.

WALTER G. WHITMAN (August 1950–August 1956). Walter G. Whitman, one of the two chemical engineers on the GAC who were full-time university employees, earned a B.S. (1917) and an M.S. (1920) from MIT in chemical engineering. He remained at MIT from 1920 to 1926 as an assistant professor, from 1922 to 1925 serving as assistant director of the research laboratory. Moving to employment with Standard Oil Company of Indiana in 1926, he began as a researcher and by 1931 was associate director. In 1934 he returned to MIT as professor of chemical engineering and later became head of the Department of Chemical Engineering. He remained at MIT and became an emeritus professor there in 1961. During World War II Whitman directed the basic chemistry division of the War Production Board and also chaired the Subcommittee on Aircraft Fuels and Lubricants for the National Advisory Committee on Aeronautics. In 1948 he headed the Lexington Project, a project dedicated to researching the feasibility of nuclear-powered flight (see Chapter 5). From 1951 to 1953 he chaired the Research and Development Board of the Department of Defense. In 1955 he served as secretary-general of the United Nations Conference on Peaceful Uses of Atomic Energy, and in 1960 he became a science advisor to the Department of State.

Whitman contributed to research of gas absorption, corrosion of metals, flow of heat, and petroleum engineering. He was especially knowledgeable in the field of aeronautical engineering and was also interested in the general problem of atomic energy's influence on world security and commerce. He retired in 1961.

ROBERT E. WILSON (October 1956–March 1960). Robert E. Wilson earned undergraduate degrees in chemical engineering from the College of Wooster (1914) and MIT (1916), joined the General Electric Company in 1916, and later worked as a research associate in the applied chemistry lab of MIT (1919–1922). In 1922 he began a long career with the Standard Oil Company of Indiana where he moved from assistant director of research, to vice president in charge of manufacturing and director and vice president in charge of research and development. From 1937 to 1944 he was president of the Pan-American Petroleum and Transport Company. He became chief executive officer and chairman of the board at Standard Oil of Indiana over the period 1945 to 1958 and in 1958 became chairman of the board for the American Oil Company.

Wilson made numerous contributions to both petroleum and nuclear research. He was thoroughly knowledgeable in petroleum refining, cracking, hydrocarbon synthesis, lubrication, and corrosion. He had an enduring interest in the impact that atomic energy would have on the mining and petroleum industry. After he left the GAC in March 1960 he served for five years on the AEC.

MANSON BENEDICT (October 1958–August 1968). Manson Benedict, like Whitman an MIT chemical engineer, graduated with a B.S. in chemistry from Cornell University (1928) and a Ph.D. in physical chemistry from MIT (1932). He became a research associate in geophysics at Harvard University (1936–1937). Benedict's early work yielded a key equation now used extensively to predict the distribution of hydrocarbons between vapor and liquid in high-pressure distillation processes. He worked as a research chemist at M. W. Kellogg Company from 1938 to 1943 and at its subsidiary firm, the Kellex Corporation, from 1942 to 1946. Working for this subsidiary, Benedict led the engineering group that completed development of the process for separating U-235 from its more abundant form, U-238. The group's calculations and designs were used by Kellex, under Benedict's supervision, to build the K-25 Gaseous Diffusion Plant at Oak Ridge. Completed in late 1945, some of the separated uranium that the plant yielded was used in the first atomic bomb. Benedict devised a practical procedure for separating U-235 from uranium hexafluoride, and he advanced research on thermodynamics of gases and isotope separation. He directed process development for Hydrocarbon Research, Inc., from 1946 to 1951. From 1951 until his retirement in 1971, he was employed as an MIT professor and headed the nuclear engineering department from 1958 to 1971.

In 1951 the AEC requested that Benedict set up an Operations Analysis Staff to determine the optimum combination of new gaseous-diffusion plants and plutonium production reactors that should be built to produce the maximum number of nuclear weapons for a given amount of money. The recommendations put forward by this body ultimately predicted the capacity of the Paducah, Kentucky, and Portsmouth,

Ohio, gaseous-diffusion plants as well as the production capacity of the Hanford and the Savannah River plutonium reactors. These plants produced enriched fuel for nuclear power plants.

Among Benedict's many consulting posts were science adviser (1951–1958) and director (1962–1967) for the National Research Corporation and director of the Burns and Roe Industrial Service Corporation (1978 on). He served with the Advisory Committee on Radiation Protection of the Atomic Industrial Forum, beginning in 1958. Benedict served on the GAC in a period in which his expertise in nuclear chemical technology was of great value to the AEC and he chaired the Committee from 1962 to 1964.

STEPHEN LAWROSKI (July 1964–August 1970). Stephen Lawroski earned the B.S. (1934), the M.S. (1939), and the Ph.D. (1943) from Pennsylvania State University. In 1943 he became a research chemical engineer at the Standard Oil Development Company of New Jersey. From 1944 to 1946 he worked at the University of Chicago's Metallurgical Laboratory as a Manhattan Project group leader. He trained personnel at the Clinton Laboratories in Oak Ridge from 1946 to 1947. Much of his professional career has been with the Argonne National Laboratory, where he directed the chemical engineering division (1947–1963), served as associate laboratory director (1963–1970), and worked as senior engineer (1970 on). From 1960 to 1966 he did consulting work for the U.S. Army Chemical Corps and in 1974 joined the National Research Council Advisory Committee on Reactor Safeguards. He was expert in separation processes for nuclear reactor fuels and conducted research and engineering studies of uranium ore purification, enrichment, and spent fuel reprocessing.

HOWARD G. VESPER (October 1965–February 1975). Howard G. Vesper graduated from the California Institute of Technology in 1922 and then joined the Standard Oil Company of California. He was vice president of Standard Oil of California during his nine years of GAC service and was an adviser to the Homestake Mining Company for many years. Vesper was recognized as a most capable executive and administrator, and during his GAC term he served for four years as chairman.

LOMBARD SQUIRES (August 1968–August 1974). Lombard Squires earned a Ph.D. in chemical engineering from the University of Illinois at Urbana. Squires, like Worthington, dedicated his career to working with Du Pont; he became assistant general manager and then manager of the atomic energy division. His work carried him into both the civilian and the defense areas of nuclear energy. In 1967 he joined the AEC Advisory Committee on Nuclear Materials and Safeguards. During his GAC service, Squires was also the chairman of the AEC Advisory Committee on Reactor Safeguards. He served as GAC chairman the final two years of his term.

HENRY R. LINDEN (September 1975–September 1977). Henry R. Linden was born in Vienna, came to the United States in 1939, and obtained citizenship in 1945. He earned a B.S. (1944) from the Georgia Institute of Technology, an M.A. (1947) from the Polytechnical Institute of Brooklyn, and a Ph.D. from the Illinois Institute of Technology (1952). From 1944 to 1947 he worked as a chemical engineer for Socony Vacuum Laboratories before joining the Institute for Gas Technology (now the Gas Research Institute) where he was employed from 1947 to 1978, moving from assistant research director to research director, executive vice president, and ultimately president and trustee (1974–1978). He held a concurrent appointment as an adjunct professor of chemical engineering and gas technology at the Illinois Institute of Technology.

Linden was the last chemical engineer to serve on the GAC, and his research expertise dovetailed well with the broadened energy responsibilities of the ERDA GAC (1975–1977). Linden's work included petrochemical research, synthetic fuels, and fossil fuel combustion and gasification. He held a number of U.S. and foreign patents in fuel technology and developed new processes for conversion of coal, oil shale, and petroleum into low-molecular paraffin hydrocarbons. He could thus speak authoritatively in a variety of nonnuclear energy research fields.

GAC electrical engineers

Electrical engineering was the second most heavily represented applied science on the GAC. Of the Committee's five electrical engineers, two were top research executives with American Telephone and Telegraph Company subsidiaries and another also had work experience with Bell Laboratories, one of the nation's premier corporate research laboratories. Much of the expertise of GAC electrical engineers was in the area of space science and defense-related research rather than in atomic energy directly. Only one of the five electrical engineer representatives served beyond 1959.

HARTLEY ROWE (December 1946–August 1950). Hartley Rowe earned a B.S. (1904) from Purdue University and took a job as electrical engineer for the Isthmian Canal Commission from 1904 to 1919. From 1926 to 1957

Rowe was employed by the United Fruit Company where he rose to posts of chief engineer, vice president, and director. During World War II, he worked as a division chief for the OSRD. In 1944 he was technical advisor to the Supreme Headquarters of the Allied Expeditionary Forces. Rowe worked at the Los Alamos Scientific Laboratory from November 1944 through most of 1945 where his industrial engineering experience was useful in development of the atomic bomb.

In 1957 Rowe became director, assistant to the president, and chairman of the board at Jackson and Moreland, Inc. Keenly interested in the civilian application of atomic explosives, he began his GAC term at age 64 (one of the first nine appointees) and was the most senior of his GAC colleagues. He was extremely knowledgeable in matters of isotope production.

OLIVER E. BUCKLEY (July 1948–August 1954). Oliver E. Buckley was trained in physics but embarked on a long and distinguished career as an electrical engineer. He earned a B.S. (1909) from Grinnell College and a Ph.D. (1914) from Cornell University. From 1914 to 1925 he was employed as a research physicist with Western Electric Company. He served with the army in Europe during World War I and in 1925 joined Bell Laboratories, moving from assistant research director (1927–1933) to research director (1933–1936), executive vice president (1936–1940), president (1940–1951), and chairman of the board (1951–1952).

During World War II he led the guided missile research division of the National Defense Research Committee. He invented the mercury vapor diffusion lamp, and he directed research and development of underwater cable technology for telephone and telegraph transmissions, particularly transoceanic and other submarine cables. Buckley's work on vacuum tubes helped advance both telephone and television technology. He also contributed to development of digital computer technology. In 1951 he chaired the science advisory committee of the Office of Defense Mobilization.

T. KEITH GLENNAN (October 1956–September 1958). After earning a B.S. (1927) at Yale University in electrical engineering, T. Keith Glennan began a unique career. He worked from 1927 to 1935 for Electric Research Productions, Inc., in New York. He then joined Paramount Pictures, Inc., from 1935 to 1941, rising to the position of studio manager. He did similar work for Samuel Goldwyn Studios in 1940 and 1941. During World War II Glennan directed the navy underwater sound lab in Columbia University's Division of War Research where he helped to improve sonar technology. Between 1945 and 1947, he served as an executive of the Ansco Corporation, a photographic company. He left this post to become president of Case Western Reserve University for the period 1947 to 1966.

In 1950 Glennan was appointed to the AEC and served two years. He was appointed to the GAC in 1956 but resigned from the Committee in 1958 when President Eisenhower chose him to be the first administrator of NASA. During his three years at NASA, Glennan supervised the progress of Project Mercury, America's first effort in manned space flight. In 1961 he became an executive with the Vega Airplane Corporation. He was president of Associated Universities, Inc. (1965–1968), was a Rand Corporation trustee (1962–1972), and served as U.S. ambassador to the International Atomic Energy Agency (1970–1973). Glennan's greatest achievements were in the realm of science and research administration. He was an authority in matters of nuclear propulsion of rockets, missiles, and satellites.

JAMES W. MCRAE (October 1958–February 1960). James W. McRae was a Canadian who received a B.S. (1933) from the University of British Columbia and later an M.S. (1934) and Ph.D. (1937) from the California Institute of Technology. He became a U.S. citizen in 1940. From 1937 to 1942 he was a member of the technical staff of Bell Laboratories, where he worked with Buckley. He then served in the army Signal Corps from 1942 to 1946.

After the war, McRae returned to Bell and led projects that perfected radio and television technology. He was director of radio and television research (1946–1947), director of electronic and television research (1947–1949), and director of transmission development and apparatus development (1949–1951). He was appointed vice president of Bell labs in 1951 and vice president of Western Electric and Sandia Corporation in 1953. Sandia was the contract operator of the Sandia Laboratory, a facility chiefly responsible for developing and maintaining the nation's nuclear weapons. McRae played a major role in engineering transoceanic radio transmitters, microwave and radar technology, and other electronic communications devices.

HUBERT HEFFNER (October 1972–February 1975). Hubert Heffner was the last electrical engineer appointed to the GAC. After serving in the army Signal Corps during World War II, he went on to earn a B.S. (1947), an M.S. (1949), and a Ph.D. (1952) in electrical engineering from Stanford University. Heffner was one of the first AEC fellows. He worked for Bell labs from 1952 to 1954 but devoted most of his career to work at Stanford University where he was professor of applied physics and electrical engineering (1954–1963), associate provost (1963–1967), and dean of research (1963–1967). In 1962 he chaired a DOD working group on microwave devices and in the 1970s he served on the DOD Defense Science Board's Cruise Missile Task Force. Heffner, like Glennan before him, assisted NASA in its pursuit of manned space science study (1965–1968). Shortly before his appointment to the GAC, Heffner had been deputy director of science and technology in the Executive Office of President Richard M. Nixon. His disciplinary research involved solid-state physics and quantum electronics, with specialized work in analysis of traveling wave tubes, electron beams, and microwave amplifiers.

GAC mechanical engineers

The three mechanical engineers of the GAC were not appointed until after 1963. They offered the AEC and ERDA first-hand advice regarding the problems and prospects of commercial nuclear power.

WILLIAM WEBSTER (March 1963–May 1972). William Webster's mechanical engineering education was obtained as a cadet with the U.S. Naval Academy. He chaired the AEC's Military Liaison Committee from 1948 to 1949.[21] Throughout his career he was deeply dedicated to promoting commercial nuclear power. In 1961 he became chairman of the New England Electric System; later he served as director and vice president of Connecticut Yankee Atomic Electric Company and then in 1967 became president and chief executive officer. This firm operates Connecticut Yankee Nuclear Power Station No. 1, which went into operation the same year Webster was appointed to the GAC. His service on the GAC provided a voice for electric utility companies that were building or planning to build nuclear power plants. He died in 1972 while still a GAC member.

ARTHUR G. HANSEN (September 1975–August 1976). Arthur G. Hansen became a mechanical engineer via his graduate training in mathematics. He took a B.S. (1946) and an M.S. (1948) from Purdue University and went on to complete a Ph.D. in mathematics from Case Western Reserve University in 1959. Hansen spent the 1950s as an aeronautical research scientist at Lewis Laboratory in Ohio. He later became head of the nucleonics section of the Cornell Aeronautical Laboratory, Inc. (1958–1959). He became a professor of mechanical engineering and department chair at the University of Michigan (1959–1966) and went on to a deanship and the presidency of the Georgia Institute of Technology (1966–1971). In 1971 he became president of Purdue University, a post he held during his short GAC term.

Hansen's research specializations included mechanics of viscous fluid flow and three-dimensional boundary-layer theory. He also made contributions to the study of partial differential equations and to pump design. Much of his applied research was of importance to aviation and to the transportation industry in general. Hansen served on the U.S. Department of Labor's Subcommittee on Professional Science and Technology Manpower beginning in 1971.

WILLIAM R. GOULD (September 1975–September 1977). William R. Gould, another Naval Academy mechanical engineering graduate, joined the ERDA GAC for its two years of operation. He earned a B.S. in 1942 from the University of Utah. Gould was a career employee of Southern California Edison Company, joining the firm in 1948 and working his way up through a variety of executive positions to become president in 1978. He was executive vice president of the company during his term of GAC service. Gould's company is majority owner and operator of San Onofre units 1 and 2 and has other nuclear facility investments as well. His research involves electric power generation, transmission, and distribution. He has been chairman of the board of the Fel Institute for Advanced Engineering and was U.S. committee president at the International Conference on Large High Voltage Electric Systems in 1973.

GAC metallurgists and civil engineers

CYRIL S. SMITH (December 1946–January 1952). Only one GAC member, Cyril S. Smith, was trained as a metallurgist. One of the most accomplished in his field, Smith was born and educated in England, emigrated to the United States, earned a doctorate of science in metallurgy from MIT (1926), and became a U.S. citizen in 1931. He worked for the American Brass Company for fifteen years and then became a division leader at Los Alamos Scientific Laboratory during World War II. He was director of the University of Chicago's Institute for the Study of Metals from 1946 to 1961. One of the first nine GAC members, he became Institute Professor at MIT (1961–1969) and was a Smithsonian Institution council member from 1966 to 1976.

Smith was an authority on the microstructure of polycrystalline metals, plutonium metallurgy, and the effect of explosive shock on metals. He also published extensively in the history of science and technology.

ROLF ELIASSEN (June 1970–February 1975). Rolf Eliassen, a civil sanitary engineer, received the B.S. (1932), M.S. (1933), and Ph.D. (1935) from MIT. In 1936 he went to work for Dorr Company of Chicago and Los

Angeles. He held an academic appointment at New York University during World War II and in 1949 began a long academic career with MIT where he rose to full professorship. In 1976 he left MIT to become an emeritus professor of environmental engineering at Stanford University. From 1961 on Eliassen held a concurrent post with Metcalf and Eddy Company, Inc., where he became a partner and senior vice president. This firm is engaged in numerous civil engineering projects, including nuclear power plant construction.

Eliassen was a consultant for the International Atomic Energy Agency (1957–1962), and he worked with the Office of Science and Technology in the Executive Office of the President in 1961. He is most noted for his achievements in researching various methods of water and wastewater treatment and is an expert in industrial and radioactive waste treatment processes, which made him a valuable advisor in GAC discussions concerning the major problem of high-level nuclear waste disposal. He resigned from GAC service in early 1975 as the AEC underwent dissolution.

The life and social sciences

The life or social science disciplines had no representative on the GAC until 1964, and only seven GAC members represented life or social science disciplines, about 13 percent of the total membership. No social scientists were ever appointed to the AEC GAC, and the two life scientists who were members were both physicians. The social sciences finally gained a modicum of representation when President Ford selected ERDA GAC members. Ford's appointments denoted an effort to comply with the provisions of the Federal Advisory Committee Act of 1972, which called for better balance in the representation of relevant interests on federal advisory committees. Although environmental, economic, labor, and public administrative expertise was added to the GAC, the final cohort of members was composed of people whose disciplines and work experience were tangentially related to nuclear energy.

AEC advisory committee life and social scientists

The life science disciplines had no representatives on the GAC until 1964. Two physicians served on the Committee. They helped the GAC and the AEC staff assess the medical and public health aspects of atomic energy by giving important information about the status of medical research in various domains of toxicology, pathology, industrial health, and environmental health.

JOHN C. BUGHER (May 1964–September 1970). The first life science appointee was John C. Bugher, a physician who specialized in pathology. He earned an A.B. (1921), an M.D. (1929), and an M.S. (1932) from the University of Michigan and continued work there as an instructor and then assistant professor of pathology in the medical school (1922–1937). He later joined the international health division of the Rockefeller Foundation where by 1955 he rose to the position of director of medical education and public health. He joined the AEC staff in 1951 as deputy director of biology and medicine and from 1952 to 1955 assumed the directorship of the division. Bugher also was a member of the Committee on Radiation Protection and the Committee on Atomic Casualties of the National Research Council. From 1960 to 1966 he directed the Puerto Rico Nuclear Centre. His research in clinical pathology often addressed the relationship of nuclear radiation to cancer in humans, and he frequently met with the GAC to address the problems of radioactive fallout from above-ground nuclear testing in the 1950s (see Chapter 7). Bugher served on the GAC from May 1964 until he died in September 1970.

JAMES H. STERNER (May 1971–August 1974). James H. Sterner was the second physician appointed to the Committee. He took a B.S. (1928) at Pennsylvania State University and an M.D. (1932) from Harvard University. From 1936 to 1949 he directed laboratory industrial medicine at Eastman Kodak in Rochester, New York, and from 1948 to 1961 worked as Kodak's associate medical director and then medical director. During World War II he was a medical consultant at the Holston Ordnance Works in Tennessee (1941–1945) and medical director at the Clinton Engineer Works of the Tennessee Eastman Company (1943–1945). A member of the interim medical advisory board of the Manhattan Project (1945–1947), he handled duties in the radiological safety section of the medical-legal board for the Operation Crossroads atomic tests in 1946. He was a visiting lecturer at Harvard Medical School from 1952 to 1956, did work for the National Cancer Institute (1957–1961) and the U.S. Public Health Service (1957–1961), and was a member of New York State General Advisory Committee on Atomic Energy (1958–1965). He was on the environmental health panel of the White House Office of Science and Technology from 1961 to 1965 and has been president of many prestigious health organizations.

When Sterner left Kodak in 1968, he became associate dean and professor of environmental and occupational health at the University of Texas School of Public Health. His chief research addressed clinical and experimental toxicology in industrial hygiene and environmental health.

ERDA GAC life scientists and social scientists

As the AEC underwent a bifurcation into ERDA and the Nuclear Regulatory Commission, the GAC was transferred to ERDA. Because ERDA was to be responsible for researching and promoting a wide variety of energy resources and technologies, the disciplines and interests associated with these concerns were taken into account by those who helped to select the members of the ERDA GAC.

At the suggestion of ERDA Administrator Robert C. Seamans, Jr., the six AEC GAC members whose terms had not expired resigned as a group, effective February 28, 1975. ERDA commenced operations on January 19, 1975, under the Energy Reorganization Act of 1974 (P.L. 93-438).[22] Using Seaman's nomination list, President Gerald R. Ford made nine simultaneous appointments to the GAC in September 1975. The disciplines and affiliations of those chosen reflected ERDA's broad-based energy clientele and exhibited a balance in the disciplinary composition of the Committee (Table 3.3): three physicists (basic science representatives), three engineers (applied science representatives), and three whose areas can be broadly classified within either the life sciences or the social sciences. Background information about the three physicists (May, Morse, and Tape) and the three engineers (Hansen, Gould, and Linden) was presented earlier in this chapter. Of the remaining appointees (Martin Ward, Charles J. Hitch, Ruth Patrick, James E. Connor, and Frank G. Zarb), each had a knowledge specialization that could be broadly interpreted as a life or social science.

MARTIN J. WARD (September 1975–August 1976, January 1977–September 1977). When appointed to the ERDA GAC, Martin J. Ward was general president of the 300,000-member United Association of Journeymen and Apprentices of the Plumbing and Pipefitting Industry of the United States and Canada and part of the executive council of the AFL-CIO. Members of this union build major projects, including nuclear power and coal power generating plants (Ward was a strong advocate of the coal slurry pipeline project). President Ford's appointment of Ward represents the only time organized labor secured a seat on the GAC. It is difficult to argue that Ward promoted any disciplinary interest, as he built his career through technical school education and union apprenticeship. He died in October 1982 while still serving as president of his union.

CHARLES J. HITCH (September 1975–September 1977). Charles J. Hitch chaired the ERDA GAC for its two years of operation. He received an undergraduate degree from the University of Arizona and his B.S. (1934)

and M.S. (1938) from Oxford University. He was a tutor and praelector at Queen's College of Oxford University from 1935 to 1948, and from 1941 to 1942, he worked as a staff economist for the U.S. Embassy in London. He worked for the War Production Board (1942–1943), served in the U.S. Army from 1943 to 1945, and was chief of the stabilizations controls division of the Office of War Mobilization and Reconversion (1945–1946). In 1948 he joined the Rand Corporation in California where he was employed until 1961. There he was chief of the economics division and later chairman of the research council. From 1961 to 1965 he was assistant secretary of defense under Defense Secretary Robert S. McNamara.

Hitch is an expert in operations research and resource economics. He is widely published in the areas of defense economics and environmental economics and was instrumental in advancing program plan budgeting in the defense department. When he left government employment in 1965 Hitch moved through senior administrative positions at the University of California at Berkeley until he was chosen president of that university in 1968. He has long been a professor of economics there. During his GAC term he was president of Resources for the Future in Washington, D.C.

RUTH PATRICK (September 1975–September 1977). Ruth Patrick earned her M.S. in 1931 and Ph.D. in 1934 from the University of Virginia in the field of botany. She began a long career with the Academy of Science in Philadelphia as a limnologist in 1939, becoming chairman of the board of the academy in 1973 and honorary board chairman in 1976. She held a concurrent academic appointment at the University of Pennsylvania beginning in 1952 and by 1970 had become a full professor. She has been a member of the board of directors of Du Pont and the Pennsylvania Power and Light Company.

Patrick was an authority in taxonomy, the ecology and physiology of diatoms (microscopic unicellular marine or fresh-water algae), limnology, and the biodynamic cycle of rivers. She served for a period on the Environmental Protection Agency's Science Advisory Board Executive Committee. She brought to the Committee a sensitivity toward environmental and ecological concerns, particularly those relating to the aquatic environment.

JAMES E. CONNOR (January 1977–September 1977). James E. Connor earned a Ph.D. in political science at Columbia University and for a time worked there as an assistant professor. He began his career as a White House fellow in 1968. He later worked in the Department of Commerce and for the Office of Equal Opportunity. In May 1972 he became director of the AEC Office of Planning and Analysis, a post that made him a special assistant to AEC Chairman James Schlesinger. By June 1973 Connor became President Ford's staff secretary and by January 1976, secretary of the cabinet.[23] Both of these jobs involved major public relations work for the president.

Connor, like Zarb, joined a major investment banking firm on his departure from government employment. During his GAC term he worked as assistant to the chairman of the board for First Boston Corporation, the sole subsidiary of First Boston, Inc., a holding company.[24] His expertise in the politics and administration of federal energy policy were his primary contributions to the work of the GAC.

President Ford's appointment of Connor in the waning hours of his term should also be understood as a token of appreciation for loyal service to his administration.

FRANK G. ZARB (January 1977–September 1977). Frank G. Zarb earned his M.S. in business administration from Adelphi University. Prior to his appointment, Zarb had been associate director of the Office of Management and Budget, director of the White House Energy Resources Council (1974), and then director of the Federal Energy Administration. He held this last post until President Ford left office in January 1977. When Zarb began his term of GAC service he worked for Shearson Hayden Stone, Inc., which became the parent company of American Express.[25] He was a vice president in charge of investment banking. As a federal executive Frank Zarb understood the politics and administration of energy policy, as well as the economic problems of energy policy.

His appointment by President Ford just before Ford left office, like Connor's, was in appreciation of Zarb's loyal service to the Ford administration.

Given the amazing magnitude and array of scientific and engineering accomplishments of GAC members, it is very difficult to offer generalizations about them as a group. There are, however, a few discernible patterns apparent in their knowledge specializations and work backgrounds.

In a very general sense, the work experience and knowledge specializations of Committee members corresponded to the history of atomic energy from 1947 to 1977. Physicists had the longest and most sustained period of representation on the GAC. Theoretical and experimental scientists dominated Committee membership from 1947 until the early 1960s. After 1964 the physicists became the exclusive representatives of basic science. Physicists appointed after 1964 were more closely associated with the administration of major AEC contract labs than were those appointed before 1964. Engineers, or applied scientists, always had a presence on the Committee, but it was not until the 1960s that the applied sciences came to occupy a major share of GAC seats. During the 1960s the engineering disciplines were called on to give the AEC extensive advice. Space science engineers as well as nuclear utility engineering executives began to secure appointments to the Committee in this decade. In the 1960s medicine finally gained GAC representation.

When the veterans of Manhattan Project work began to retire, the Committee recruited younger people whose careers did not always directly involve atomic energy. In the decade of the 1970s, particularly during the years of ERDA operation, there was a wide breadth in the knowledge specializations and work experience of GAC members compared with earlier eras. In this final period, energy policy administrators, an ecological scientist, a labor union official, and an economist secured appointments to the Committee.

4 Career path associations of GAC members

Significance of career histories

Many GAC members had mutual associations or shared experiences before their appointment to the Committee. These common experiences or affiliations of members must be considered as factors in their appointments to the GAC. Four specific variables are potential sources of pre-appointment interaction and common affiliations: education, wartime experiences, employment with the AEC, and service in White House science advising.

When examining education, several questions should be considered. What was the highest earned graduate degree of each GAC member? How many members earned their highest graduate degree from the same university? Is there evidence of overrepresentation of degree-holders from the same university, or the same groups of universities? Did members study in the same academic department? Did members serve as advisers and mentors to graduate students who became Committee members? By answering these questions inferences can be drawn about how elite or restricted the membership on the Committee was. Examining the educational histories of GAC members helps to determine whether the Committee became more, or less, exclusive in its recruitment of new members.

The second variable is the wartime experience of GAC members. How many GAC members worked in one or more of the Manhattan Project laboratories during World War II? Which labs? Did experience with the Manhattan Project constitute a necessary credential to being appointed to the GAC? Which members served in the Office of Scientific Research and Development (OSRD) or its subunit, the National Defense Research Committee (NDRC)?

A third variable in analyzing career paths involves employment with the AEC. How close was the GAC to the Commission? Was the Committee simply an ancillary body of scientific and technical experts who periodically advised the AEC but had few links to the Commission or to the AEC staff? Or had some, or many, members worked for the AEC or its staff before appointment? How many GAC members were later appointed to the Commission? Was the GAC a scientific and technical talent pool from which the AEC and the president could recruit AEC commissioners?

A fourth variable is the GAC's relationship with White House science advisers. When Eisenhower became president in 1953, the balance of scientific influence shifted away from the GAC toward the chairman of the AEC. An analysis of this period states: "The security hearings on Oppenheimer in 1954 marked the nadir of GAC. However, many of those same prominent scientists who had constituted SAC [Science Advisory Committee] and then belonged to the GAC reappeared phoenix-like in what later became the President's Science Advisory Committee [PSAC]."[1] The PSAC was abolished in January 1973. Did many early GAC members later join the PSAC? How many former PSAC members later joined the GAC? Were there overlaps in the membership of these committees?

These four general career path variables do not encompass all the possible points of interaction between those who would later serve on the GAC. Certainly there were other federal advisory committees on which GAC members served before and during their terms of GAC service, such as the Pentagon's Defense Science Board and the General Advisory Committee of the Arms Control and Disarmament Agency. Service on these and other advisory bodies may have established administrative and political contacts that helped to win appointment to the GAC. Interlocking advisory committee service of GAC members would be an indication of the breadth of their advisory influence, because such service allows interagency and interdepartmental interaction that increase the access and influence of an individual in governmental decision making. It is not possible, however, to examine exhaustively every single point of possible interaction among future GAC members. The four general variables of university education, wartime service, employment with the AEC, and presidential science advising can shed considerable light on the common associations and work experiences of GAC members.

Institutions of highest earned degrees

Identifying the highest earned degree of each GAC member by university and by region of university location is a valuable exercise (Table

4.1). A disproportionately large number of GAC members receiving academic degrees from the same university may be evidence of a clique or a form of academic nepotism in the selection of Committee members. The listing of universities by region identifies any regions that are under- or overrepresented on the GAC.

Table 4.1 lists only highest degree earned, in most cases the Ph.D. Most GAC members earned their doctorates from one university and their undergraduate and master's degrees from others; institutions conferring the lesser degrees are not listed.

Massachusetts Institute of Technology

The Massachusetts Institute of Technology (MIT) and the University of California at Berkeley had the largest number of graduates who went on to become GAC members. Eight graduates of each university were ultimately appointed to the Committee. Three members earned doctoral degrees from MIT in 1935; however, they studied in different disciplinary areas, and none served simultaneously on the Committee. James B. Fisk, a 1935 MIT graduate in physics, served on the GAC from 1952 to 1958. Two months after Fisk's term expired, Manson Benedict, a 1935 chemical engineering graduate, was appointed to the Committee. Benedict served until August 1968. In June 1970 Rolf Eliassen, a 1935 civil engineering graduate, was appointed to the Committee.

There was considerable overlap in the terms of the eight MIT graduates taken as a group. Cyril S. Smith and Hood Worthington served together on the GAC from January 1947 until August 1948. Smith and Walter G. Whitman served together from August 1950 until January 1952. Nine months after Smith left the Committee, Fisk was appointed to serve. Whitman and Fisk were both members from September 1952 until August 1956. Robert E. Wilson, another MIT graduate, was appointed to the GAC in October 1956 and served with fellow MIT alumnus Fisk until August 1958. In October 1958 Benedict joined Wilson on the Committee and from March 1960 until August 1968 was the only MIT graduate on the GAC. Eliassen was appointed in June 1970 and served until February 1975. In September 1975, MIT graduate Richard S. Morse was invited to join. The almost continuous service of MIT graduates on the Committee suggests that MIT graduates on the Committee may have strongly recommended other MIT graduates when there were seats to be filled.

University of California at Berkeley

The University of California at Berkeley (UC-Berkely) graduated an extraordinary number of outstanding theoretical and experimental scientists, due in great measure to the success and renown of Ernest O. Law-

Table 4.1. University of highest earned degree of each GAC member

University	Member	Degree[a]	Year
East			
Massachusetts Institute of Technology	C. S. Smith	Ph.D.	1926
	H. Worthington	M.S.	1925
	W. G. Whitman	M.S.	1920
	J. B. Fisk	Ph.D.	1935
	R. E. Wilson	B.S.	1916
	M. Benedict	Ph.D.	1935
	R. Eliassen	Ph.D.	1935
	R. S. Morse	S.B.	1933
Columbia University	I. I. Rabi	Ph.D.	1927
	N. F. Ramsey, Jr.	Ph.D.	1940
	W. H. Zinn	Ph.D.	1934
	J. E. Connor	Ph.D.	1968
Harvard University	J. R. Oppenheimer	A.B.	1925
	J. B. Conant	Ph.D.	1916
	J. H. Sterner	M.D.	1932
	C. J. Hitch[b]	B.A.	1931
Cornell University	O. E. Buckley	Ph.D.	1914
Brown University	W. C. Johnson	Ph.D.	1925
Princeton University	E. M. McMillan	Ph.D.	1932
Yale University	T. K. Glennan	B.S.	1927
Johns Hopkins University	L. R. Hafstad	Ph.D.	1933
	H. A. Friedman	Ph.D.	1940
U.S. Naval Academy	W. Webster	Naval Arch.	n.a.[c]
	W. R. Gould	Naval Arch.	n.a.[c]
Hofstra University	F. G. Zarb	M.A.	1961
Midwest and South			
University of Wisconsin	L. A. DuBridge	Ph.D.	1926
Purdue University	H. Rowe	B.S.	1904
	A. G. Hansen	Ph.D.	1970
Case Western Reserve University	A. G. Hansen	Ph.D.	1959
University of Kentucky	E. V. Murphree	M.S.	1921
Indiana University	J. C. Warner	Ph.D.	1923
University of Virginia	J. W. Beams	Ph.D.	1925
	R. Patrick	Ph.D.	1934
University of Chicago	D. K. Froman	Ph.D.	1930
	J. H. Hall	Ph.D.	1942
University of Michigan	J. C. Bugher	M.D.	1929
		M.S.	1932
	G. F. Tape	Ph.D.	1940
Pennsylvania State University	S. Lawroski	Ph.D.	1943
University of Illinois	L. Squires	Ph.D.	n.a.[c]
Illinois Institute of Technology	H. Linden	Ph.D.	1952
West			
University of California at Berkeley	G. T. Seaborg	Ph.D.	1937
	W. F. Libby	Ph.D.	1933
	K. S. Pitzer	Ph.D.	1937
	P. H. Abelson	Ph.D.	1939
	J. H. Williams	Ph.D.	1931
	E. L. Goldwasser	Ph.D.	1950
	E. V. Hayward	Ph.D.	1947
	M. M. May	Ph.D.	1952
California Institute of Technology	J. W. McRae	Ph.D.	1934
	H. G. Vesper	B.A.	1922
Stanford University	H. Heffner	Ph.D.	1952
Europe			
Gottingen University (Germany)	J. R. Oppenheimer	Ph.D.	1927
University of Pisa (Italy)	E. Fermi	Ph.D.	1922
Budapest University (Hungary)	J. von Neumann	Ph.D.	1926
Technische Hochschule (Germany)	E. P. Wigner	Ph.D.	1925
University of Leipzig (Germany)	E. Teller	Ph.D.	1930
Oxford University (England)	C. J. Hitch	M.A.	1938

[a]This list excludes honorary academic degrees, which exceed 200 for the fifty-five GAC members.

[b]See also European universities.

[c]Information was not available.

rence and his Berkeley Radiation Laboratory. Eight of these graduates served on the GAC, and all had earned doctoral degrees (compared with four of the eight MIT graduates). Two went on to win the Nobel Prize: Glenn T. Seaborg and Willard F. Libby. Each of the five UC-Berkeley alumni who earned doctorates in the 1930s had worked closely with Lawrence: Seaborg and Libby earned doctoral degrees in chemistry, Kenneth S. Pitzer and Philip H. Abelson in physical chemistry, and John H. Williams in physics. It is reasonable to conclude that these five knew each other, and at times two or more may have conducted joint research projects. Committee member Evans V. Hayward, a 1947 UC-Berkeley physics doctoral graduate, was another protege of Lawrence, as were Edwin L. Goldwasser and Michael M. May, who earned physics doctorates in the early 1950s.

Over the history of the GAC UC-Berkeley graduates were distinctive in several respects. The GAC operated from January 1947 until September 1977. With the exception of the period between September 1954 and October 1958, there was always at least one UC-Berkeley graduate on the Committee. There were twenty-six total years of UC-Berkeley representation on the Committee, which far exceeds the combined years of service for graduates of any other university. It is also remarkable that from November 1960 until August 1962, four of the Committee's nine members were UC-Berkeley doctorates: Abelson, Libby, Pitzer, and Williams. No other university, not even heavily represented MIT, ever had more than two graduates on the Committee at the same time.

Other universities

Two other universities had four graduates each as GAC members. Columbia University graduates Isidor I. Rabi, Norman F. Ramsey, Jr., Walter H. Zinn, and James E. Connor all served, but with little overlap in terms. Harvard University graduates J. Robert Oppenheimer, James B. Conant, James H. Sterner, and Charles J. Hitch were Committee members; Conant and Oppenheimer served together from January 1947 to August 1952. All other universities listed in Table 4.1 had only one or two graduates on the Committee.

The regional distribution of university degree data shows a very strong representation of eastern, particularly Ivy League, universities, dominated by MIT, Columbia, and Harvard. Only three western universities had graduates on the Committee; of the eleven graduates in this group, eight were from UC-Berkeley. Twelve GAC members earned their highest degree from a midwestern university. The University of Chicago, the University of Michigan, and Purdue University each had two graduates, and Pennsylvania State and Indiana universities, the Illinois Institute of Technology, and the universities of Illinois, Kentucky, Michigan, and Wisconsin each had one. The only southern university doctoral graduates to serve were Jesse W. Beams and Ruth Patrick, both of whom earned their doctorates from the University of Virginia.

In all, the fifty-five GAC members came from twenty-three U.S. universities and six European universities. University representation on the GAC, in terms of university of highest earned degree, does not exhibit a regional bias nearly as much as it reveals the domination of UC-Berkeley and MIT. Clearly, these two universities had outstanding scientific and engineering programs that produced graduates who were in high demand for advisory positions. The evidence also strongly suggests that GAC members who were graduates of UC-Berkeley or MIT proposed and promoted fellow graduates of their universities when nominations to the Committee were considered.

Wartime service

Many future GAC members were involved in government service during World War II, particularly at the Los Alamos Scientific Laboratory and other research laboratories. Still other arenas for association of scientists and engineers during the war were the OSRD and the NDRC.

Manhattan Project

Each of the first nine GAC appointees performed important work for the U.S. government in World War II.[2] All of the Committee's original members had served in some capacity with the mammoth Manhattan Engineer District (MED), or the Manhattan Project, a code name for the government's defense research and development program to build atomic bombs. The project, which represented the largest coordinated scientific research and development program ever undertaken by the United States up to that time, was an extraordinary assemblage of government, university, and corporate scientists and engineers.

Some Manhattan Project research centers were within university settings, such as Columbia University's War Research Division and the University of California's Berkeley Radiation Laboratory. Others were government laboratories operated under contract by universities, such as the University of California's Los Alamos Scientific Laboratory. The MED complex also included production facilities capable of supplying a variety of fission products and other necessary substances critical to atomic research, such as the Hanford Works in Washington State and the Clinton Laboratories near Oak Ridge, Tennessee. Major corporations and universities assisted in the construction and operation of these facilities.

It is no surprise that the first cohort of GAC members all had contributed in some way to the Manhattan Project. A $2.2 billion program with thirty-seven installations spread over nineteen states and Canada, with nearly 4,000 government workers and 37,800 contractor employees, the Manhattan Project attracted thousands of scientists and engineers.[3] The MED's administrative hierarchy included many of the nation's most outstanding scientists, as well as many great scientists who had emigrated from other countries. Questions arise: How many GAC members had worked in the Manhattan Project? Was Manhattan Project experience a long-standing prerequisite for appointment to the Committee? How many people who later became GAC members had common Manhattan Project work associations?

Los Alamos Scientific Laboratory

Twelve members (one-fifth) of the total GAC membership had worked at one time or another with the Los Alamos Scientific Laboratory during the war, among them: Oppenheimer, Smith, Rabi, Enrico Fermi, and Hartley Rowe (Table 4.2). Oppenheimer was the first director of the Los Alamos lab. Fermi performed extensive research on the atomic bomb project at Los Alamos, correctly estimating the yield that the Trinity test would produce. Rowe did industrial engineering work at Los Alamos, Rabi conducted much of his wartime research at MIT, but periodically visited Los Alamos as a consultant, and Smith was associate division leader in charge of metallurgy at the Los Alamos lab from 1943 to 1945.

The other seven GAC appointees with Los Alamos wartime experience were Williams, Ramsey, John von Neumann, Edward Teller, Edwin M. McMillan, Darol K. Froman, and Jane H. Hall. Von Neumann was an outstanding mathematician who conducted research at Los Alamos both during and after the war. He investigated the implosion method of A-bomb detonation with Seth Neddermeyer. Teller conducted wartime research first at Columbia University, then at the University of Chicago, and later at Los Alamos. He pursued work on the fission bomb, and with Fermi he estimated the yield and atmospheric effects of the anticipated blast. While at Los Alamos, Teller also was given some opportunity to research the fusion, or thermonuclear, bomb which he believed was a feasible and preferable alternative to the fission bomb.

McMillan, Williams, Froman, Hall, and Ramsey were research

Table 4.2. Manhattan Engineer District experience of GAC members

GAC Member	Years with MED	Position/Employer
	Los Alamos Scientific Laboratory	
J. R. Oppenheimer	1943–1945	Director
E. Fermi[a]	1944–1945	Consultant
I. I. Rabi[a]	1944–1945	Consultant
H. Rowe[a]	1944–1945	Consultant
C. S. Smith	1943–1945	Associate division director
J. von Neumann	1943–1955	Consultant
E. M. McMillan[a]	1943–1945	Researcher
E. Teller[a]	1943–1946	Physicist
J. H. Williams[a]	1943–1946	Group leader, physics
D. K. Froman[a]	1943–1945	Group leader
	1945–1948	Division leader
J. H. Hall[a]	1945–1946	Staff member
N. F. Ramsey, Jr.[a]	1943–1945	Group leader and associate division head
	University of Chicago and Metallurgical Laboratory	
E. Fermi[a]	1942–1945	Professor, physics
	1946–1954	Director, Institute for Nuclear Studies
G. T. Seaborg	1942–1946	Section chief
E. P. Wigner[a]	1942–1945	Guest scientist
E. Teller[a]	1942–1943, 1945	Researcher, Institute for Nuclear Studies
D. K. Froman[a]	1942–1943	Research associate
S. Lawroski	1944–1946	Group leader and assistant section chief
J. H. Hall[a]	1943–1944	Assistant
W. H. Zinn	1942–1946	Physicist
W. F. Libby[a]	1945–1959	Professor, Institute for Nuclear Studies
	Massachusetts Institute of Technology and Radiation Laboratory	
L. A. DuBridge	1940–1945	Director
I. I. Rabi[a]	1942–1945	Staff and associate director
W. G. Whitman	1934–1961	Professor and department head of chemical engineering
E. M. McMillan[a]	1940–1941	Researcher
N. F. Ramsey, Jr.[a]	1940–1942	Research associate and group leader
G. F. Tape	1942–1946	Staff member
	Columbia University and War Research Division	
E. Fermi[a]	1939–1942	Professor, physics
I. I. Rabi[a]	1945–1949	Professor and department chair, physics
W. F. Libby[a]	1941–1945	Chemist
T. K. Glennan	1942–1945	Director, U.S. Navy Underwater Sound Lab
E. Teller[a]	1941–1942	Professor, physics
N. F. Ramsey, Jr.[a]	1945–1947	Associate professor, physics
	Hanford Works, Washington State	
H. Worthington	1943–1946	Du Pont Company
J. H. Hall[a]	1944–1945	Consultant (Du Pont)
	Clinton Works, Oak Ridge, Tenn.	
M. Benedict	1943–1946	Kellex Corp.
W. C. Johnson	1943–1946	Director
J. H. Sterner	1943–1945	Industrial physician
E. P. Wigner[a]	1946–1947	Director of research and development
P. H. Abelson[a]	1944–1945	Consultant

Sources: *Who's Who in Science,* multiple volumes.
[a]Indicates multiple laboratory service and repeated name.
[b]Information was not available.

Table 4.2. *(continued)*

GAC Member	Years with MED	Position/Employer
Carnegie Institute; Johns Hopkins University (JHU); University of Maryland; and Naval Research Laboratory (NRL)		
P. H. Abelson[a]	1941–1945	NRL
L. R. Hafstad	1942–1947	JHU Applied Physics Lab
	1943–1945	Carnegie Institute
H. Friedman	1940–1958	Supervisor, NRL Electron Optics Branch
K. S. Pitzer	1943–1944	University of Maryland War Research Lab
Office of Scientific Research and Development (OSRD); National Defense Research Committee (NDRC)		
J. B. Conant	1941–1946	Deputy director, OSRD, and member, NDRC
L. A. DuBridge	1940–1945	NDRC
I. I. Rabi	1942–1945	Chairman, Vacuum Tube Committee, NDRC
H. Rowe	1940–1945	Chief, Division 12, OSRD
O. E. Buckley	n.a.[b]	Guided Missiles Division, NDRC
E. V. Murphree	1944	OSRD
J. von Neumann	1944–1945	OSRD
J. C. Warner	1943–1945	Research coordinator, OSRD
E. P. Wigner	1941–1942	Consultant, OSRD
J. W. Beams	1940–1945	NDRC
K. S. Pitzer	1943–1945	Director, Maryland research lab, OSRD
P. H. Abelson	1940–1942	NDRC
N. F. Ramsey, Jr.	1940–1945	NDRC
J. H. Williams	1942–1943	Official investigator, OSRD
L. R. Hafstad	1941–1946	NDRC
J. H. Sterner	1945–1947	Medical Advisory Board, OSRD

physicists of the Manhattan Project who worked at Los Alamos. McMillan started wartime work with the Berkeley lab and later became a researcher at Los Alamos from 1942 to 1945. From 1943 to 1946, Williams served as a group leader in the Physics Division at Los Alamos. Froman also worked at Los Alamos from 1943 to 1945, beginning as a group leader and then assuming the post of division leader.[4] Hall worked with the University of Chicago Metallurgical Laboratory from 1943 to 1944, and then served as a senior supervisor with the Du Pont Company at its Hanford facilities. It was not until 1945 that Hall joined the staff at Los Alamos.[5] Ramsey was a group leader and then a division head with the atomic energy project lab at Los Alamos from 1943 to 1945.

No other Manhattan Project facility yielded more future GAC members than the Los Alamos Scientific Laboratory. As war research progressed many labs and research facilities completed their primary assignments or were forced to suspend operations, and many of their scientists and engineers were transferred to Los Alamos to conduct research there. The Los Alamos lab began with only a modest staff in the early weeks of 1943, but as more and more effort and resources were directed to atomic bomb work there, it came to employ as many as 5000 workers, a significant number of them scientists and engineers.[6] These scientists and engineers constituted an immense talent pool and went on to assume key administrative and advisory positions with the government, including GAC membership.

Wartime Los Alamos associations no doubt affected the GAC's recruitment recommendations to the AEC and the president. GAC members were highly influential in deciding who would be nominated for appointment to the Committee, and they tended to recommend people they knew and had worked with before. Obviously, competent Los Alamos wartime service by young scientists and engineers had established their ability and trustworthiness, and the composition of the GAC heavily represented those with Los Alamos experience, such as Ramsey, Froman, and Hall.

Much of the work of the Los Alamos lab concerned defense research. Twelve of the GAC's fifty-five members had conducted defense-related research at Los Alamos, both during and after the war. The high representation of Los Alamos–experienced scientists on the GAC underscores the Committee influence of those working in defense-related fields.

Other wartime research institutes and laboratories

Also remarkable is the number of GAC members who worked at the University of Chicago Metallurgical Laboratory during the war. In January 1942 Arthur Compton, working with Vannevar Bush and Conant at OSRD, recognized that there would be "advantages in centralizing all work on producing uranium metal and separating element 94 from irradiated uranium."[7] However, total centralization was not practical given that so much was going on at so many different universities. Compton elected instead to concentrate only some of the project work. He organized the metallurgical lab and in so doing brought together Columbia University, Princeton University, and University of Chicago research groups.

Among Committee members with wartime research experience at the Metallurgical Laboratory were Fermi, Teller, Froman, and Hall. Eugene P. Wigner, Stephen Lawroski, Seaborg, Zinn, and Libby also conducted experiments there. The lab's atomic piles and other facilities "would allow scientists to examine experimentally the physics of a controlled fission chain reaction, something which had only been possible, so far, using theory. Secondly, it would be a source of the new fissionable element, plutonium."[8]

The MIT Radiation Laboratory was another key point of wartime interaction for scientists and engineers. This laboratory pursued a wide variety of research projects, many of which contributed to development of the atomic bomb. However, the MIT lab may best be remembered for its contributions in development of radar technology during the war. Lee A. DuBridge directed the MIT lab over the war years and relied on Rabi and Whitman for their senior expertise. McMillan, Ramsey, and Gerald F. Tape dedicated some of their wartime Manhattan Project service to work at the MIT lab.

The Columbia University War Research Division employed Fermi, Rabi, Libby, Teller, and Ramsey over various war years. Libby's work at Columbia pioneered research and development of the gaseous diffusion process for separating isotopes of uranium. From 1942 to 1945 T. Keith Glennan directed the navy's Underwater Sound Laboratory for this division, where sonar technology was dramatically improved.

A number of GAC members spent many of the war years working at the major production labs of the Manhattan Project. Among members who periodically worked at the Hanford Works near Richland, Washington, were Worthington and Hall. They both worked for Du Pont in helping to design and engineer the Hanford lab, Worthington as a chief supervisor and process manager and Hall as a senior supervisor.

Warren C. Johnson, Abelson, Benedict, and Sterner did important work at the Clinton Laboratories near Oak Ridge, Tennessee, during wartime years. Johnson directed the chemical division of the Clinton labs. Abelson and Benedict helped to devise and engineer the huge gaseous diffusion plant built at Oak Ridge. Sterner was employed as medical director of the Clinton labs' Holston Ordnance Works for Tennessee Eastman Company. Shortly after the war Wigner went to work at the Clinton labs as director of research and development.

There was often interaction and interchange among the major research institutes and laboratories located in the vicinity of Washington, D.C. Abelson and Herbert Friedman spent much of the war working at the Naval Research Laboratory. Pitzer conducted research at the University of Maryland War Research Laboratory from 1943 to 1944. Lawrence R. Hafstad began as a research physicist and later became director of the applied physics laboratory of the Johns Hopkins University during the war.

OSRD and NDRC

It is difficult to document how often Abelson, Friedman, Pitzer, and Hafstad interacted with each other during the war years. However, each participated in the work of elite presidential science advisory bodies, such as the OSRD and the NDRC during the war years, as did many other future GAC members. The NDRC was largely the product of

Bush's effort to organize American science for the prosecution of the war effort. While president of the Carnegie Institution in Washington, Bush had served on the National Advisory Committee for Aeronautics (NACA). When the war began in Europe, he approached Conant, then of Harvard, Frank B. Jewett of the National Academy of Sciences and president of Bell Laboratories, and his colleagues on NACA. He convinced them of the need to form a body comparable to the World War I Council of National Defense. President Franklin D. Roosevelt approved the NDRC plan in June 1940 and appointed Bush head of the committee, which included Conant, Karl T. Compton (MIT president), and Richard C. Tolman (high-level scientific adviser in the Roosevelt administration). The NDRC was to mobilize the scientific resources of the nation and was free to undertake research on its own.[9] "Bush felt that it would be appropriate to make the military aware of precisely what science and technology could provide and also make scientists aware of what the military required."[10] A civilian organization of scientists and engineers, the NDRC had as its initial line of research the development of radar.

After only a year of operation it became apparent that as "a research organization, the NDRC was not well adapted to fill the gap between research and procurement orders that engineers called development." Moreover, with a rank equal to that of the laboratories of the military services and NACA, it functioned as one of three research agencies and its advisories were not easily reconciled with those of the other agencies.[11] Consequently, Bush helped to draft the Executive Order of June 28, 1941, which established the much stronger Office of Scientific Research and Development. OSRD came into existence as an extension of NDRC and was linked to university and government research in a common effort for national security.[12] The NDRC continued operation within the OSRD.[13] Bush chaired the OSRD, Conant the NDRC. The OSRD was located in the Office of Emergency Management within the Executive Office of the President. Its funding was guaranteed by congressional appropriations independent of the military budget, but many of its top advisers were not on the government payroll. The OSRD issued a large number of contracts supporting university research that was beneficial to the government, particularly to the military.[14]

Sixteen future GAC members served at various times with OSRD, NDRC, or both during the war years. Foremost on this list is Conant, who occupied key presidential level advisory posts with NACA, NDRC, and OSRD. He assumed the chairmanship of the NDRC in June 1940 and concurrently served as deputy director of OSRD for most of the war. DuBridge and Rabi, both with NDRC, joined about thirty other scientists in organizing microwave radar research at MIT in November 1940. Five years later the lab had a staff of over 4000 and a budget in excess of $40 million[15] Service with these bodies was apparently a major credential considered in later appointment to the GAC.

As a division chief of OSRD, Rowe helped to supervise Manhattan Project work. He is credited with resolving many of the industrial engineering and procurement problems encountered at Los Alamos. Early in the war, Oliver E. Buckley advised the NDRC on the feasibility of large-scale uranium production for use in the war effort and the NDRC on matters regarding guided missile development. Eger V. Murphree helped to supervise the design, planning, construction, and operation of the Manhattan Project production plants. His Planning Board began operation in January 1942, assigned the task of determining whether the experimental methods used for separating uranium isotopes at Columbia and the University of Virginia could be used to construct a massive industrial production facility for isotope production. The board recognized the need to build an experimental centrifuge and an industrial-sized gaseous diffusion unit and also anticipated the need to design pilot plants to demonstrate the feasibility of various separation methods, acknowledging the need to secure adequate supplies of uranium oxide, hexafluoride, and other key materials. Murphree also supervised development of the S-1 electromagnetic separation facility at Oak Ridge as well as heavy-water pile development.[16]

During the course of the war von Neumann served as an adviser to the army, the navy, and the OSRD. A specialist in the study of armor-piercing projectiles, his knowledge of shock wave behavior proved to be invaluable in analysis of the implosion method of atomic bomb detonation at Los Alamos.[17] John C. Warner was an OSRD research coordinator for the Manhattan Project from 1943 to 1945 who worked at the Carnegie Institute of Technology in Pittsburgh. Wigner was among the first group of American scientists to recognize the need to initiate atomic weapons research. As a consultant to OSRD, Wigner worked at the University of Chicago Metallurgical Laboratory on the theory of chain reactions. He directed theoretical studies at the lab and researched the design and engineering of several atomic piles developed during the war, among them, the Clinton Laboratories pile.[18] Beams served on the NDRC before and after OSRD was established. His research offered the government a method for large-scale uranium isotope production. As a principal OSRD investigator Beams also directed ramjet and other military weapons projects. Pitzer was also a member of OSRD during his directorship of the University of Maryland's War Research Laboratory.

Abelson served on the NDRC from 1940 to 1942. His thermal diffusion research made possible the gigantic S-50 uranium enrichment facility at Oak Ridge.[19] Ramsey served on the NDRC from 1940 to 1945, first at the MIT Radiation Laboratory and then at Los Alamos. Williams was another OSRD official investigator who went on to serve at Los Alamos. A group leader within the Los Alamos Physics Division, he had studied fast neutrons at the University of Minnesota and later calculated plutonium neutron emission at Los Alamos.

Hafstad served on the NDRC from 1941 to 1946. His services to OSRD involved missiles and missile guidance research, ramjet engine development, and the fabrication of various forms of ordnance for the military. Sterner served the OSRD as a member of its medical advisory board. A physician experienced in pathology toxicology, Sterner spent most of the war working at the Holston Ordnance Works and Clinton Engineer Works in Tennessee. There he served as medical director for the Tennessee Eastman Company.

Both OSRD and NDRC had growing memberships during the war years, and work with these organizations brought together many who would later be appointed to the GAC. Service with OSRD or NDRC was most certainly evidence of scientific expertise recruited in behalf of the government: "The same individuals who are involved in cooperative research are often also providing advice. During World War II the advisory network was integrally connected with cooperation and research. Scientists served in an advisory capacity to win the war."[20] This modicum of advisory service continued after the war, not in the perpetuation of OSRD but through key federal advisory committees such as the AEC GAC. Sixteen people who had worked inside OSRD, NDRC, or both, eventually were appointed to the GAC. So many GAC members served with the OSRD and NDRC that it is clear such service was a major credential in recruitment and appointment to the Committee.

Several future GAC members spent the war years either as college students or in the uniformed military. May and Hayward were students at UC-Berkeley and Arthur G. Hansen at Purdue University. James W. MacRae and Hubert Heffner both served in the army Signal Corps, and Martin J. Ward served in the navy Seabees. Goldwasser was a navy physicist, and William R. Gould also served in the navy.

Some future GAC members were employed by business firms vital to the war effort, among them oil company executives Howard G. Vesper and Wilson. Others were Henry R. Linden of Socony Vacuum Laboratories, Buckley and Fisk of Bell labs, and William Webster of the New England Electric System. Two future GAC members, Frank G. Zarb and Connor, were children during the war years.

Relationships with the AEC

Many GAC members also served at some time on the AEC (Table 4.3). Simultaneous service on the GAC and the AEC was not permitted. A GAC member who was appointed an AEC commissioner would resign from the GAC. Sometimes long after leaving the Committee a former member would be appointed to the Commission, and in a few instances former AEC commissioners were appointed to the GAC. The AEC was composed of five members, appointed by the president and, unlike the GAC, subject to Senate confirmation. The president designated one of the five commissioners as chairman, while GAC members elected their own chairman. AEC commissioners were appointed for a five-year term or for the unexpired portion of a term.

GAC members Libby, von Neumann, Wilson, and Seaborg first served on the Committee and later were appointed to the AEC. Libby and Wilson were members of the GAC at the time they were informed of their impending appointment to the Commission. Libby was the only individual to resign from the GAC, join the AEC for a period of years, and then win reappointment to the GAC (soon after being awarded the Nobel Prize in chemistry in 1960). His stature in the scientific community and his willingness to serve the government may explain his multiple appointments to these elite groups.

Libby, von Neumann, and Wilson were picked to serve on the AEC by President Eisenhower. Wilson resigned from both the GAC and the board chairmanship of the American Oil Company shortly before he joined the Commission, and von Neumann was appointed to the Commission about seven months after his GAC term had expired. Almost eleven years after his GAC term had expired Glenn Seaborg, another Nobel laureate, was appointed to the AEC as chairman by President Kennedy. The only former GAC member to serve two full terms on the Commission, he was chairman of the AEC for both terms.

Table 4.3.   GAC members who served on the U.S. Atomic Energy Commission

Member	AEC Term of Office	GAC Term of Service
T. Keith Glennan	Oct. 2, 1950–Nov. 1, 1952	Oct. 26, 1956–Sept. 25, 1958
Willard F. Libby	Oct. 5, 1954–June 30, 1959	Aug. 7, 1950–Sept. 30, 1954
		May 26, 1960–Aug. 1, 1962
John von Neumann	Mar. 15, 1955–Feb. 8, 1957	Feb. 27, 1952–Aug. 1, 1954
John H. Williams	Aug. 13, 1959–June 30, 1960	Nov. 17, 1960–Apr. 17, 1966
Robert E. Wilson	Mar. 22, 1960–Jan. 31, 1964	Oct. 26, 1956–Mar. 22, 1960
Glenn T. Seaborg[a]	Mar. 1, 1960–Aug. 16, 1971	Dec. 12, 1946–Aug. 1, 1950
Gerald F. Tape	July 15, 1963–Apr. 30, 1969	Sept. 24, 1975–Sept. 30, 1977

Source: U.S. Department of Energy 1982, pp. 93–94.
[a]Served as chairman of the AEC for this period (two terms).

Four former AEC commissioners were later appointed to the GAC: Libby, Glennan, Williams, and Tape. Libby served on the GAC, then the Commission, and then the GAC again. Tape is particularly notable as a commissioner because of the strong interest he took in the work of the GAC. Some have suggested that his appointment, as well as the appointment of May, to the ERDA GAC was an effort to provide continuity in the Committee's transition from the AEC to ERDA.

Five GAC members worked for the AEC staff prior to their Committee appointments: Fisk, Pitzer, Benedict, Hafstad, and Bugher. Fisk was the first director of the Division of Research (1947–1948). He was followed by Pitzer, who directed this division from 1948 to 1951. Fisk was appointed to the GAC in 1952, Pitzer in 1958. Benedict established the Operations Analysis Staff Office in 1951. As former administrators of the research division, these three men had inside knowledge of early AEC operations, which no doubt strengthened the work of the GAC in the 1950s and 1960s.

Hafstad and Bugher had longer periods of employment on the AEC staff than any other GAC members. Hafstad was the first director of AEC reactor development, a position he held from February 1949 until December 1954. He concurrently occupied the post of director of the AEC Division of Engineering from June 1951 until August 1954.[21] He was appointed to the GAC in September 1962 and served until August 1968, where his expertise in reactor engineering was undoubtedly a valuable asset.

Bugher directed the AEC Division of Biology and Medicine from July 1952 until September 1958.[22] A physician and pathologist, he was much experienced in studying the effects of radiation on humans. He was appointed to the GAC in May 1964, was reappointed in August 1968, and served until his death in September 1970. Bugher's expertise was essential in GAC oversight of the AEC risk-assessment studies of nuclear reactor operation.

Webster chaired the Department of Defense Military Liaison Committee of the AEC from 1948 through 1949. A successful utility executive and former military official, he was appointed to the GAC by President John F. Kennedy in 1963.

Clearly these thirteen GAC members were not the only Committee members to have worked in some capacity with AEC staff. Many future members at some time worked closely with the AEC as consultants or while employed by an AEC contract laboratory.

Presidential science advisory committees

Science Advisory Committee to the Office of Defense Mobilization

The GAC was only one of a number of sources of scientific advice available to the government after 1946. The Science Advisory Committee (SAC) was established in April 1951 to advise the Office of Defense Mobilization (ODM) in the Executive Office of the President and furnished scientific and technical advice to Presidents Truman and Eisenhower.[23] Buckley, a GAC member at the time, chaired SAC until 1952. DuBridge, who had just completed a term of GAC service, succeeded Buckley as SAC chairman in 1952, and Rabi replaced DuBridge as chairman in 1957. Rabi had then just completed more than seven and a half years of GAC service, four as GAC chairman.

Under DuBridge, the SAC became involved in scientific and technical problems, especially those associated with the military. The Korean War compelled the Committee to address problems of military technology. In 1953 the SAC moved forward on recommendations prepared by a special defense advisory committee chaired by von Neumann, who was a member of the GAC at the time. The von Neumann committee called for development of intercontinental ballistic missiles, more jet-propelled military aircraft, and nuclear-powered submarines capable of launching ballistic missiles.[24] In 1957, the SAC staff was used by the Gaither committee in preparation of a report that called for strengthened U.S. security, particularly against the danger of strategic nuclear attack. The Gaither Report advocated stepped-up civil defense and triggered the fallout shelter craze in American society. Both Rabi and Fisk had worked on the Gaither Report. At the time Fisk was also a member of the GAC and must have been well aware of the problems of radioactive fallout from above-ground nuclear testing (see Chapter 7).

President's Science Advisory Committee

In 1958, as the nation entered a space race with the Soviet Union, the system of presidential science advice was completely reorganized. President Eisenhower created the position of White House science advisor. In order to institutionalize science advice within the Office of the President, the science advisor was to chair a President's Science Advisory Committee (PSAC), which he would impanel with presidential approval. This transformation abolished SAC-ODM, and its responsibilities were transferred to the science advisor and the PSAC; Rabi resigned from his chairmanship of SAC and James R. Killian became chairman of the PSAC.[25]

The PSAC consisted of one chairman, one deputy, and sixteen other regular members who were rotated, usually every four years. Turnover in PSAC membership was gradual. The original PSAC was a relatively homogeneous group consisting mostly of physical scientists concerned with a limited number of problems, with a staff that possessed wartime experience.[26] In the Eisenhower years, about two-thirds of the PSAC's work dealt with national security. In 1962 the Office of Science and Technology was created to serve the president, also chaired by the science advisor.[27]

The PSAC operated from 1958 until 1973. Through the decade of the 1960s the PSAC garnered more attention and publicity than did the GAC. However, the White House science advisor and the PSAC encountered frequent periods of political turbulence and controversy, which the GAC largely escaped. Many studies of the PSAC indicate that its influence was both a function of how it was used by the science advisor and how the science advisor himself was perceived by the president. President Eisenhower's science advisor, George B. Kistiakowsky, apparently had a good relationship with the president, and he, as well as the PSAC, were frequently consulted. Jerome Weisner, President Kennedy's science advisor, was also reported to have worked affably and independently with the president. When Kistiakowsky and Weisner expressed views contrary to those of their president they were rarely subject to reprimand.

However, the science advisor and the PSAC were not the only sources of science advice in the White House. In the early 1960s the PSAC began to encounter serious competition from the Defense Department's military advisory committees, which were markedly improved under Defense Secretary Robert S. McNamara.[28]

The PSAC's status deteriorated dramatically during the years President Johnson held office: "When Lyndon Johnson became president, a watershed was crossed in terms of science advice and the presidency."[29] In both the Johnson and Nixon administrations, the science advisor was excluded from the inner circle of presidential advisers.

In February 1964, under the leadership of Donald F. Hornig, the PSAC began to expand in size and it broadened its base of expertise to include persons from as yet unrepresented disciplines and sectors of the general public. It simultaneously began to address new scientific and technical issues, acting on its own initiative. The PSAC frequently found itself blocked, however, by political constraints and bureaucratic warfare.[30] When it began to come into regular conflict with the president's military advisers, the committee's recommendations came to be perceived as disruptive and at times disloyal.[31]

As President Lyndon B. Johnson became increasingly preoccupied with issues relating to defense and the Vietnam War, he came to believe that the PSAC was little more than an insular scientific elite that spoke for an academic community opposed to the war. He did not view the PSAC as a source of options but as a source of criticism. Johnson had long been an advocate of the supersonic transport (SST) but found that his science advisor and many PSAC members opposed SST development. In 1967, Johnson and McNamara endorsed the light "sentinel" antiballistic missile (ABM) system, but Richard Garwin and Hans A. Bethe of the PSAC opposed the ABM proposal in the spring of 1968.[32] This and other controversies drove a wedge between Johnson and his science advisers.

When President Richard M. Nixon came to office in 1969 he too came to distrust and disparage the PSAC. In 1973 Nixon disbanded the committee but retained the science advisor. Nixon's Bureau of the Budget came to believe that the science advisor and the PSAC were self-interest advocates who were assuming too much independence within the Executive Office.[33] Some PSAC members believed that the resources of science and technology were not being directed toward social problems within the United States. When members openly criticized the Nixon administration, White House officials concluded that the PSAC was expendable.

There was considerable parallel operation of the PSAC and the GAC during the 1960s. In a sense, by impaneling joint PSAC-GAC committees over those years, the advisory influence of the GAC was amplified. This was particularly true in regard to the government's high-energy physics program (see Chapter 9).

GAC members on presidential science advisory bodies

Of the fifty-five members of the GAC, fourteen served on a president's science advisory committee (Table 4.4). Oppenheimer served on the SAC-ODM from 1951 to 1954 and was GAC chairman from 1947 to 1952. Conant, DuBridge, Rabi, Buckley, Whitman, and Fisk also had overlapping GAC and SAC-ODM terms, which highlights the great prestige accorded these scientists and engineers. Concurrent committee service enabled them to convey vital scientific and political information between the presidential science advisory level and the departmental GAC level. For example, GAC analysis of AEC programs could be carried forward into SAC-ODM deliberations, and presidential-level initiatives disclosed in SAC-ODM meetings could be introduced in GAC meetings.

The high point of SAC-ODM and GAC membership overlap occurred in the early 1950s. Friedman was the only person to serve simulta-

Table 4.4.   GAC members who served on the PSAC and/or the SAC-ODM

Member	Years of GAC Service	Years of PSAC or SAC-ODM Service
J. R. Oppenheimer[a]	1947–1952	1951–1954 (SAC-ODM)
J. B. Conant[a]	1947–1952	1951–1953 (SAC-ODM)
L. A. DuBridge[a]	1947–1952	1951–1956 (SAC-ODM)
		1969–1973 (PSAC)
I. I. Rabi[a]	1947–1956	1952–1958 (SAC-ODM)
		1958–1960 (PSAC)
G. T. Seaborg	1947–1950	1959–1961 (PSAC)
C. S. Smith	1947–1952	1959 (PSAC)
O. E. Buckley[a]	1948–1954	1951–1955 (SAC-ODM)
W. G. Whitman[a]	1950–1956	1951–1955 (SAC-ODM)
J. B. Fisk[a]	1952–1958	1951–1958 (SAC-ODM)
		1958–1960 (PSAC)
K. S. Pitzer	1958–1965	1965–1968 (PSAC)
W. Webster	1963–1972	1951 (SAC-ODM)
H. Friedman[b]	1968–1974	1970–1973 (PSAC)
W. H. Zinn	1972–1975	1960–1962 (PSAC)
G. F. Tape	1975–1977	1969–1973 (PSAC)

Sources: SAC-ODM and PSAC data from Golden 1980, pp. viii–ix; GAC data from the AEC records of Anthony A. Tomei (AEC/ERDA, retired).
[a]Indicates overlapping GAC and SAC-ODM membership.
[b]Indicates overlapping GAC and PSAC membership.

neously on the PSAC and the GAC (1970–1973). As a specialist in physics and astronomy and as chief scientist at the E. O. Hulbert Center for Space Research, he was called on to advise on rocket development, satellite astronomy, astrophysics, and other space research matters. Some of his research involved nuclear propulsion of spacecraft, which placed him between the work of the AEC and NASA.

Most of those who served on the SAC-ODM first served as members of the GAC. GAC experience may have been a key consideration or qualification in appointment to the SAC-ODM. In three cases, service on the SAC-ODM or the PSAC preceded appointment to the GAC. Webster, an early member of the Defense Department military liaison committee to the AEC, served on the SAC-ODM in 1951; twelve years later he was appointed to the GAC. Soon after resigning as director of the Argonne National Laboratory, Zinn was appointed to the PSAC, and ten years later he was appointed by President Nixon to the GAC. After Tape's term of service on the AEC in 1969, he was appointed to the PSAC. Two years after the PSAC was disbanded, President Gerald R. Ford appointed him to the ERDA GAC. These appointments suggest that in the 1960s and 1970s the GAC absorbed several individuals who were already well established in the realm of federal science advice.

DuBridge, when serving as science advisor to President Nixon, was accused of acting as a lobbyist for university scientists by officials of the Budget Bureau.[34] He also drafted a report critical of the SST program that Nixon supported. For these and other reasons, DuBridge was replaced as science advisor in 1970. Pitzer completed more than six years of GAC service and then was immediately appointed to the PSAC in 1965. Equally important, Seaborg served a three-year period on the PSAC and was plucked from the committee by President Kennedy in 1961 to chair the AEC.

GAC members of the 1950s seem to have stood a far better chance of moving to key presidential science advisory positions than did GAC members of the 1960s and 1970s (Table 4.4). Of the twenty-six people appointed to the GAC up to October 1958, ten went on to appointments with either the SAC-ODM or the PSAC. Of the twenty-nine people appointed to the GAC after October 1958, only one subsequently went on to PSAC membership. Appointment to the problem-plagued PSAC of the late 1960s and early 1970s, however, was not as highly prized as appointment in the Eisenhower and Kennedy eras.

In the group analysis of GAC members, four general variables were considered: university of graduate education, wartime service, working experience with the AEC, and service with presidential science advisory committees.

Were there identifiable concentrations of GAC members who earned their highest academic degree from the same university? Over the full GAC history there was an extraordinarily high concentration of UC-Berkeley and MIT graduates who served as members. The sustained and almost serial representation of MIT graduates on the committee suggests that at least one GAC seat was always reserved for an MIT graduate. UC-Berkeley graduates also served on the Committee for extended periods. In the early 1960s four of the GAC's nine members were UC-Berkeley doctorates, which indicates that UC-Berkeley graduates already serving on the Committee were highly successful in promoting the appointment of other UC-Berkeley graduates. An overwhelming number of GAC members with UC-Berkeley doctorates had studied under Lawrence at the Berkeley Radiation Laboratory.

There was a considerable number of Ivy League university graduates on the GAC, but a great many GAC members had earned their highest graduate degree from a midwestern university. Twenty-three U.S. universities and six European universities made up the list of institutions graduating individuals who would ultimately be appointed to the GAC.

Although this indicates significant breadth in the representation of universities, nevertheless the number of UC-Berkeley and MIT graduates on the GAC was disproportionately large.

Review of the wartime activities of GAC members revealed that thirty-five of the Committee's fifty-five members had worked in some capacity for the Manhattan Project. Of this number, twelve worked at the Los Alamos Scientific Laboratory during the latter years of the war. The shared wartime experience of the many hundreds of scientists and engineers who worked at Los Alamos seems to have created a comradeship that continued long after the end of the war. Veterans of Manhattan Project work at the University of Chicago Metallurgical Laboratory, the MIT Radiation Laboratory, and the Columbia University War Research Division were also heavily represented on the GAC, but none of these institutions yielded as many members as did the Los Alamos lab. Sixteen GAC members had worked in some capacity for the OSRD or NDRC. Clearly, service with a Manhattan Project laboratory or with OSRD and NDRC was an important, if not decisive, credential considered in the GAC appointments process.

Four GAC members were subsequently appointed to the AEC. Seaborg was appointed AEC chairman, and Libby went from the GAC to the AEC and then back to the GAC. Three former commissioners were appointed to the GAC after their AEC periods of service. This was evidence of an interchange of AEC commissioners and GAC members. However, it is apparent that previous GAC service was not in any respect a prerequisite for appointment to the Commission. Most GAC members who were later appointed to the Commission won their AEC appointments in the 1950s and early 1960s. Those former commissioners who won appointment to the GAC were generally appointed in the 1970s. Four GAC members had worked in an administrative capacity with the AEC before they were appointed to the Committee. While a fraction of the GAC membership did serve at some time as either a commissioner or staff member with the AEC, in a general sense most GAC members do not have employment histories of long and frequent work experience with the AEC.

More remarkable is the number of GAC members who served with presidential science advisory bodies. Six of the first nine GAC members served either with the SAC-ODM or with its later counterpart, the PSAC. Oppenheimer, Conant, DuBridge, Rabi, Buckley, Whitman, and Fisk served GAC terms that overlapped some of their terms of service on the SAC-ODM, and Friedman's term encompassed all three years of his term on the PSAC. Five GAC members served on SAC-ODM, six on the PSAC, and three served first on the SAC-ODM and then on the PSAC.

Buckley, DuBridge, and Rabi each held positions at various times in which they served as the president's science advisor. A great many former GAC members served on presidential science advisory bodies; movement was usually from the GAC to the PSAC. Several joint PSAC-GAC panels were formed in the 1960s, the Ramsey panel foremost among them, to consider special science policy problems. Virtually all those who served on the GAC were politically established enough to be tapped for service as presidential advisers. A great many GAC members had served in some capacity as a presidential-level science adviser before their appointment to the Committee. This is particularly true if service with the presidential-level OSRD and NDRC of World War II is included.

Although the organizational points of interaction among individuals later appointed to the GAC were many, their university graduate education, Manhattan Project experience, and previous experience as government advisers were clearly of paramount importance in their appointment to the Committee.

5 The GAC and the great atomic energy laboratories

MORE TIME AND EFFORT WAS DEVOTED by the GAC to oversight of the great atomic energy laboratories than to any other single concern. There are two general reasons for this preoccupation: the centrality of AEC contract laboratories in fulfillment of nearly all major AEC functions and the associations that nearly all GAC members had with the laboratories themselves.

At the end of World War II, the U.S. government owned most of the existing equipment for nuclear research and development. Even more significant, the government employed directly or indirectly most of the nation's nuclear scientists and held a virtual monopoly on "a national treasure of knowledge."[1] The chief repository of this scientific expertise and physical plant was the laboratory system of the former Manhattan Project.[2]

When the U.S. Army Corps of Engineers transferred ownership and control of its extensive network of atomic energy research facilities to the civilian-run AEC on January 1, 1947, the Commission inherited a decentralized, poorly coordinated collection of contractor-operated government facilities. The AEC decided that it was inadvisable to staff these laboratories with federal government employees. Instead, the Commission elected to operate these labs as government-owned, contractor-operated (GOCO) facilities. Under this arrangement, each lab is owned and funded by the government but is managed and staffed by a private contractor. This policy came as a perpetuation of the basic wartime policy of the Manhattan Project.[3] Some see the system as one in which the AEC became a kind of "holding company" for the expertise and capabilities in its field facilities.[4] Contracting with a few of the nation's largest and best-qualified companies and universities seemed to be the most expeditious and effective way to design, develop, and produce the atomic

114

bomb.[5] Contractors for the labs came in the form of major private corporations, large prestigious universities, or alliances of major universities incorporated to form contractor organizations.

The AEC, with GAC guidance, moved to convert its applied-research, military-oriented laboratories into sophisticated, multipurpose laboratories. Together, the AEC and the GAC advocated greater federal support for basic research, much of it to be conducted by or through these laboratories. Basic research in high-energy physics, pursued under the Office of Naval Research (ONR) up to that time, was to be continued under joint ONR-AEC sponsorship. Ultimately, the AEC assumed virtually complete control over this area; much of the research entailed the construction and operation of various types of particle accelerators, and these facilities were often huge, complex, and extremely expensive.[6]

In the 1947 budget year, the AEC approved thirteen contracts totaling about $60 million. About half this money went to the Oak Ridge Laboratory (called the Clinton Laboratories at the time). The Argonne National Laboratory received $11 million and the Berkeley Radiation Laboratory and Brookhaven National Laboratory each was awarded $6 million.[7] By the time the AEC was dissolved in 1975, the federal appropriation for AEC's programs totaled nearly *$60 billion,* and the major part of this money funded the AEC contract laboratories.

There have been only a limited number of major AEC lab contractors. Since the end of the war, the University of California has been the contract operator of the Berkeley Radiation Laboratory, the Los Alamos Scientific Laboratory, and after 1952 the Livermore National Laboratory. The University of Chicago has been the long-standing operator of the Argonne National Laboratory. A consortium of nine eastern universities incorporated as Associated Universities, Inc., has directed the Brookhaven National Laboratory under contract. The Enrico Fermi Laboratory has been run by a consortium of universities incorporated as the Universities Research Association. This lab, which operates one of the nation's largest particle accelerator facilities, has been in operation since 1972. Some major AEC labs have been run by industry rather than by universities. Union Carbide Nuclear Company has managed the Oak Ridge National Laboratory. The Hanford Works in Washington State were originally built by Du Pont Company during the war and from 1946 to 1964 were managed by the General Electric Company. Today a variety of contractors, foremost among them the Battelle Memorial Institute, manage facilities of the original Hanford Works. The Sandia National Laboratory became independent of the Los Alamos lab in 1949 and has been managed by Sandia Corporation, a subsidiary of American Telephone and Telegraph's Western Electric Company. (See Appendix B

for an overview of the ten AEC contract laboratories that were frequently the subject of GAC meetings and discussions, the nine labs
mentioned above plus the smaller Ames Laboratory of Iowa State University.)

Many GAC members had established their early careers through
education and work experience at one or more of the Manhattan Project
laboratory facilities in World War II. To appreciate why the GAC devoted so much time and effort to laboratory matters, a consideration of
the wartime environment of the Los Alamos lab is necessary. In testimony before the AEC's hearing board in 1954, J. Robert Oppenheimer
recalled his role in establishing the Los Alamos laboratory: "We needed a
central laboratory . . . where people could talk freely with each other,
where theoretical ideas and experimental findings could affect each
other, where the waste and frustration and error of many compartmentalized experimental studies could be eliminated, where we could begin
to come to grips with chemical, metallurgical, engineering, and ordnance
problems that have so far received no consideration."[8]

Oppenheimer explained that to make the laboratory a success, he
needed to recruit scientists and engineers willing to work there for the
duration of the war. Their family lives would be under a severe hardship
given the primitive conditions of the facility's living quarters, and due to
travel restrictions and other military impositions. "In order to bring
responsible scientists to Los Alamos, I had to rely on their sense of
interest, urgency, and feasibility of the Los Alamos mission."[9]

Oppenheimer added that after the war ended there was still a national need for major central laboratories like Los Alamos, but it was
more difficult to convince members of the scientific community to join
and work for such facilities without the sense of urgency apparent
during the war. He claimed that development, testing, and ultimate deployment of the atomic bomb had basically fulfilled the Los Alamos
mission.[10] Hans A. Bethe expressed a belief held by many Los Alamos
scientists at the end of the war:

> We all felt that, like the soldiers, we had done our duty and that
> we deserved to return to the type of work that we had chosen as our
> life's career, the pursuit of science and teaching. The older ones
> among us (at Los Alamos) felt a heavy responsibility to our teach-
> ing. Wartime had shown that this country had a very short supply of
> competent scientists, and Los Alamos was one of the best examples.
> The young scientists whose careers had been interrupted by the war
> wanted to get training under the G.I. Bill of Rights. The largest
> graduate schools in physics before the war had about fifty graduate
> students; now this number jumped to a hundred and, in some uni-
> versities, to over two hundred.[11]

Oppenheimer understood the need to sustain and invigorate the laboratories of the former Manhattan Project. He remarked that during his six-year chairmanship of the GAC much of the work involved encouraging and supporting the activities of the major installations of the AEC.[12] Oppenheimer said that the GAC helped the Los Alamos lab gain permission to conduct timely atomic weapons tests. He also indicated that the committee "encouraged and supported building up the laboratory of Sandia, whose principal purpose is the integration of the atomic warhead with the weapons system in which it would be used."[13] More than half of the fifty-five people who served on the GAC had worked in some capacity for the Manhattan Project, and most of these Manhattan Project veterans worked at the Los Alamos lab. Therefore, a great many GAC members had a special affinity for Los Alamos, or for other major government laboratories, as a result of their wartime research experiences. It is claimed that "most of the influential university scientists were effectively coopted by their personal involvement in some aspect of the national laboratories or by the involvement of their institutions with the AEC. Anyone who was anyone in nuclear physics was associated with the laboratories in some way."[14]

From its inception in 1947 until its termination in 1977, the GAC worked assiduously to ensure that the major laboratories were thriving and fruitful research institutions. At virtually every meeting of the Committee, the agenda contained items that either directly or indirectly involved or affected the laboratories. The GAC regularly made reviews and recommendations involving the AEC, and later ERDA, laboratories. At Meeting 38 held January 8, 1954, the Committee declared: "We believe that the general objective should be to make the laboratories as productive and efficient as possible. To this end, people should feel content to work in the environment the laboratories afford. There should be a minimum of difficulties about salaries, retirement, housing, community affairs, and above all the threat of congressional cuts in appropriations affecting the support of research."[15]

This quotation is by no means unique. The Committee delved into nearly every facet of laboratory operation, and often members exhibited well-meant paternalism toward various laboratories. It was customary for the GAC to conduct two of its quarterly meetings each year at AEC laboratories. AEC lab directors were frequently invited to testify and participate in GAC meetings, whether the meetings were held in the field or at AEC headquarters. The Committee utilized individual members or subcommittee teams as field research agents in order to investigate the progress and problems of laboratory-based research. The work of the GAC reveals the history of the AEC's major research laboratories.

The labs and manufacturing facilities of the Manhattan Project employed approximately 40,000 people at the time the AEC assumed control. But the labyrinth of former Manhattan Project institutions and offices were, at that time, devoid of coherent central management. Laboratory capabilities were further attenuated because leading atomic scientists who had worked on the atomic bomb and on other wartime projects were streaming back to their prewar employers or were finding new positions outside of AEC lab employment. This left the major laboratories in disarray.[16] It was the job of the AEC to revive the laboratories, and the GAC shouldered major advisory responsibilities in this undertaking.

The GAC's effort to assist in the resuscitation of AEC laboratories after World War II was evident in the following exchange. At Meeting 2 in February 1947, one discussion involved whether the AEC should give priority to reactor development or to atomic weapons. According to the minutes of the meeting, Enrico Fermi offered a comment that was typical of the Committee's high regard for and vigilance toward the AEC labs: "It was [Fermi's] own feeling that weapons were more important at this time in regard to the international situation, and that one should not risk loss of strength in the field of weapon production development and research. It is more important to make Los Alamos healthy than to develop reactors."[17]

Recruitment of scientists and engineers

Part of rebuilding and expanding the great labs of the former Manhattan Project involved recruiting promising scientists and engineers to work at AEC laboratory facilities, and the GAC shared in this task. In Meeting 2 discussion, Oppenheimer responded to Fermi's support of weapons development at Los Alamos by offering his own view, one that reflected his concern for the Los Alamos lab he had directed during the war: "It is conceivable that because of the prejudice against weapons among our colleagues, it might be wiser to steer clear of this subject and not ask to have the super bomb pushed at Los Alamos. Perhaps a really brave reactor program at Los Alamos would provide the new blood and incentive which would be successful."[18]

The lengths to which the GAC went to revive the Los Alamos lab are apparent in this summation of deliberations at Meeting 2: "Practically all aspects of the Los Alamos situation were examined: lack of adequate theoretical strength, the quality of the present direction of the laboratory, the degree of achievement of the past year, the merits of a different location, the community problems which exist there, and the possibility of stimulation of Los Alamos by a directive to develop a reactor or to concentrate on thermo-nuclear explosives."[19]

The GAC agreed that its members should assist in recruiting personnel for the Los Alamos lab. Recruitment of personnel for the major AEC laboratories became a long-standing secondary function of the GAC. This GAC recruitment obligation was explicitly stated at the same GAC meeting. The minutes indicate, "It arose in regard to strengthening Los Alamos and in the question of how much active work would be required from the Committee members as individuals. It was recognized that working on weapons was a psychological deterrent to obtaining personnel, and that the General Advisory Committee had an obligation to decrease this feeling among scientists. Adequate and attractive salaries were also suggested as an aid in emphasizing the importance attached to this work."[20]

As well as offering scientific and technical advice to the AEC, many Committee members devoted time to encouraging colleagues and graduate students to consider embarking on a career with an AEC lab. As preeminent scientists and engineers holding major positions in universities or corporations, GAC members attracted a coterie of young, ambitious, emulative researchers to their sides. GAC members directing leading scientific organizations or serving as editors of the foremost scientific and technical journals could use their personal influence to attract the country's best scientific talent to AEC laboratories. In fact, during Meeting 2 of early 1947 Oppenheimer actually recommended that "GAC members might spend six weeks at Los Alamos."[21] Recommendations and references supplied by GAC members most certainly carried weight in AEC lab hiring decisions.

Recruiting scientists and engineers to work at the labs on secret, defense-related research was especially important to the AEC. AEC secrecy restrictions, however, were often a disincentive to potential research applicants. Scientists and engineers were well aware that if they accepted jobs involving secret research, they might not be able to make public their discoveries or technical contributions and thus be precluded from winning scientific credit and recognition of their achievements. Given the concern many young scientists and engineers had about dedicating their research careers to weapons-related work, it was utterly sensible for the AEC to operate its research and development labs as multipurpose facilities in which scientists would not be permanently mortgaged to weapons research and testing. Sam Cohen, chief developer of the neutron bomb and a longtime Los Alamos scientist, commented that it was beneficial to have nonmilitary lines of research available at

Los Alamos so that scientists and technicians would not be perpetually committed to weapons work and could move back and forth between military and nonmilitary research.[22]

Another critical personnel problem confronting the AEC labs in the years after World War II was the shortage of highly trained and educated scientists and technicians able to research the atomic energy field in general. At Meeting 2, Isidor I. Rabi pointed out that the AEC faced a grave problem involving personnel shortages and research policy. Anticipating the conflict that the AEC labs were about to encounter, Rabi stated, "It will be difficult for various government agencies to avoid detrimental competition arising from their desire to take part in atomic energy activities."[23] Over the years, through AEC support to graduate education in various nuclear science fields, the AEC purchase of scientific equipment and facilities for universities and research institutes, and the in-lab training and education provided at AEC facilities, the number of scientists and engineers qualified to work at the labs increased. But for many years, the fierce competition among the labs for qualified researchers made it difficult for the AEC and the GAC to approve the establishment of new labs, which might siphon off scarce scientific and technical talent from existing labs.

Sometimes the GAC was asked to denounce statements or comments in the public media, which made it difficult to attract scientists to work on major AEC lab projects. At Meeting 28 in December 1951, the renowned physicist Harold C. Urey spoke before the GAC. He said he "deplored the effect of public statements that useful atomic power is a long way in the future." Urey insisted that "the atomic power effort be encouraged and that young men be attracted into it."[24]

In order to attract the scientific and technical talent produced by major U.S. universities, the AEC organized the working environment of many of its labs to simulate an academic environment. According to a noted authority on the U.S. scientific community, the pursuit of science is a nonhierarchical activity; the best scientists either personally prefer, or are instructed by their "guilds" to prefer, the university's combination of research, teaching, and undisciplined administration, and in order to recruit the best scientific and technical minds, the "government took them on their own terms."[25] The AEC encouraged relatively unconstrained research lab administration and often encouraged lab scientists and engineers to maintain academic appointments that would allow them periodically to return to classroom instruction. Because the labs were operated by contractors rather than by civil servants, they were "much more attractive to academic scientists and engineers." This had the added benefit of building a long-term partnership between government and the scientific community.[26]

A portion of each AEC research laboratory was dedicated to matters of pure or basic research, that is, to research with no short-term, practical application. This also helped to create the academic environment of the university and increase the standing of the laboratory in the scientific community. Numerous advances flowed from the cross-fertilization of pure and applied scientific efforts. If pure research or nonmilitary or unclassified lines of research generated scholarly publication, it was beneficial to the AEC lab: "Without significant publications, the Laboratory's reputation cannot be kept at a sufficiently high level and the Laboratory's ability in recruiting and keeping outstanding people will suffer."[27]

Overseeing the laboratories

The GAC periodically evaluated the performance of major AEC contract laboratories for the Commission. The deliberations of Meeting 38 reveal standard GAC operating practices in this regard. The session, which convened on January 8, 1954, involved a lengthy review of the AEC laboratories. In his letter to the AEC about the session, GAC Chairman Rabi indicated, "For the past several months the committee has been considering the competence of the AEC laboratories as research organizations." He commented, "They are of good standard, though not in all instances excellent, and are in one or two instances in particular fields definitely below the standard we believe should be maintained."[28]

Rabi's letter went on to present seven formal recommendations. Most of these proposals reflected the Committee's vexation about management, personnel policy, and working conditions at the major AEC laboratories and were indicative of the panel's desire to keep the labs flexible, dynamic, and progressive.[29] Following are these recommendations (in abbreviated form).

1. The Commission should reiterate and restate its support of basic fundamental research in general fields of interest to the atomic energy program.

2. Employment transfer among the laboratories and the production facilities should be facilitated. The transient period in the atomic energy business is over, and normal university and industry procedures should

be applied. One laboratory should feel free to offer an employee in another laboratory a better position or the same position at a higher salary. The one restriction that should be left is that any offer that is to be made should be discussed with the director of the laboratory in which the individual is employed.

3. There should be annual reviews of employees on salaries, assignments, and positions.

4. New employees should be made to recognize that tenure is not automatic.

5. The laboratories should make transient housing available for summer visits of scientists.

6. The laboratories should use sabbaticals or extended leaves for employees.

7. Laboratory directors should meet once a year without AEC staff present.

These recommendations demonstrated the depth of GAC involvement with the workings of the laboratories. The Committee behaved at times almost as a management consultant for the AEC and was not reluctant to voice criticism of laboratory practices and procedures that members believed impeded the progress of scientific and technical research. Many GAC advisories on matters of lab management were not well received by lab directors; nevertheless, the directors must have understood that the GAC was serving a useful function for AEC officials.

The personnel transfer issue was one that the GAC had addressed five months earlier at Meeting 36 when Willard F. Libby had advocated an exchange of personnel among the national laboratories to prevent stagnation. He maintained that all such transfers should be subject to the approval of the respective directors. Libby even called for more frequent turnover in the directorship of each AEC lab, suggesting an automatic rotation system for lab directors.

Laboratory secrecy and security

In his Meeting 36 plea for increased interlab employee mobility, Libby spoke about another recurring controversy when he remarked, "In general the security fences between laboratories should be made more penetrable."[30] The GAC regularly confronted problems posed by AEC laboratory research pursued under the restrictions of official secrecy. Committee members often argued that classification restrictions were too frequently imposed and that as a result the pursuit of scientific and technical research was being unnecessarily impeded. On a number of occasions the Committee discussed whether some AEC labs should adopt a laboratorywide policy prohibiting any scientific research project that required security classification restriction. In other words, these labs would minimize, or eliminate completely, all classified research work in progress and would take on no new projects if they entailed security restrictions.

In the Pitzer report of 1949 (named for its principal author, AEC Research Division Director Kenneth S. Pitzer), the GAC Research Subcommittee addressed the problem of classified research. The report explored the question of whether the Brookhaven and Berkeley labs should be run exclusively as unclassified research labs, and several GAC members advised that a declassification policy be adopted by each AEC lab. Also, members agreed that the Brookhaven and Berkeley labs were the most appropriate facilities to convert to wholly unclassified research status.[31]

Fourteen months later, Pitzer returned to the GAC with reactions to the unclassified lab proposal. He read a letter from Ernest O. Lawrence, then director of the Berkeley Radiation Laboratory. Lawrence argued that "it would be undesirable to operate Berkeley in such a fashion." Pitzer added, "Dr. Lawrence would like to feel that there was always an area at Berkeley in which classified work could be done."[32] As for Brookhaven, Pitzer said his survey revealed that "the chief classified area there is the reactor." After reviewing the argument for unclassified status, Pitzer voiced his own reservations to the Committee. Pitzer believed the AEC should be able to use Brookhaven and Berkeley for classified work. Because a very large number of AEC projects entailed either complete or partial classification restrictions, Pitzer feared that by forswearing all secret research Brookhaven's role in AEC's research programs would be severely curtailed and the lab would "have no part in the programmatic, classified work of the Commission."[33] Since very early in its history, however, Brookhaven officials have indeed avoided classified research projects, electing to host research work unfettered by government secrecy restrictions. Berkeley, on the other hand, has continued to allow classified research at its laboratory facility.

Security issues were again discussed at Meeting 35 in May 1953. GAC Chairman Rabi told the group that laboratory directors were infuriated because employees at their laboratories who were assigned to highly classified research projects had personnel dossiers that were declared off-limits to lab director inspection. Rabi said this was intolerable overzealousness on the part of government security officials and insisted that the director of each AEC laboratory should at least have the right to examine a worker's dossier in nonclassified areas of work.[34] Rabi and other Committee members claimed that security clearance responsibility was becoming completely divorced from laboratory operating and management groups. Lab directors were chief operations authorities who, in the opinion of GAC members, were being hampered in the management and coordination of research projects by the intrusion and interference of security officials.

The GAC regretted that official secrecy tended to isolate projects within specific AEC labs. At Meeting 43 in December 1954, Eugene P. Wigner declared that projects pursued at AEC laboratories were all too often highly compartmentalized and subject to many unnecessary classification restrictions. He referred specifically to Project Sherwood, a long-term research enterprise that explored the feasibility of controlled nuclear fusion. He insisted that "most existing technical information on Project Sherwood does not need to be classified" and remarked to AEC officials attending the session, "Do not conceal the existence of the project."[35]

To Wigner, the "air of mystery" surrounding the project was a deterrent to the participation of scientists in the fusion reactor research program. He was still making the same plea a year and a half later. In a letter report of Meeting 50, GAC Chairman Rabi informed AEC Chairman Lewis L. Strauss that Wigner had convincingly argued that the weight of opinion among scientists engaged in Project Sherwood research was to declassify the project. Rabi also referred to an official document (unidentified) that indicated "a sincere willingness on Russia's part to cooperate in declassification and publication of work in this field."[36]

On this and on many other occasions GAC members fought what they believed were overly stringent security restrictions. Holding top security clearances themselves, GAC members were able to spotlight areas of research that they believed were being hampered by oppressive classification. It was not unusual for GAC members to argue that they themselves could more appropriately judge whether a research endeavor's public disclosure posed a threat to national security than could the government's official censors.

Laboratory funding

The government had to create organizations with sophisticated, expensive capabilities and with large aggregations of facilities, equipment, and highly skilled personnel in order to pursue research and development in atomic energy. Once established, according to one scholar of science policy, these organizations develop their own dominant elites and their own areas of special expertise: "The desire for autonomy is particularly strong in technical organizations, because of the nature of the R&D process itself and the degree of specialized knowledge required to manage it effectively. Because of the costliness of their capabilities, large laboratories are especially sensitive to budget issues and to policy issues which might affect their budget levels. They seek influence over these matters in order to protect their interests."[37]

The GAC regularly and routinely heard presentations from the AEC staff regarding budget requests submitted by the laboratories and often commented on these requests. Sometimes the GAC identified seemingly imprudent lab spending requests and occasionally identified requests that represented a duplication of research effort. The GAC was more likely, however, to comment on the probable impact of budget reductions at the labs when the AEC or the Bureau of the Budget proposed to curtail lab funding. The Committee, through its reports to the AEC, sometimes won reinstatement of funds cut from certain lab program requests, but it was not always successful in restoring funding despite its considerable scientific prestige and political leverage.

Typical of GAC lab-budget-related meetings was Meeting 15 of July 1949. AEC Division of Research Director Pitzer presented the Committee with a breakdown of the expenditures for research at the Argonne, Brookhaven, Oak Ridge, Berkeley, and Ames labs. The GAC discussed the figures and examined the objectives and status of each. During this review members were alarmed to find that research support in a national laboratory amounted to about $30,000 per year per worker, approximately twice as expensive as similar research costs at universities. Members were informed that large overhead expenses made necessary by high construction costs and classification of work at the AEC labs accounted for this disparity.[38]

Pitzer was back before the Committee a year later again discussing money matters, saying, "The original formulation of the budget for 1950 caused some concern because of the implied drastic cut in research funds." Pitzer explained that this problem had been corrected and the AEC research division activities were now "adjusted to an over-all 9% cut in funds."[39] He reassured the Committee that the AEC would not let funding lapse for contractors of joint ONR-AEC projects as the transition from joint operation to full AEC project assumption took place. The GAC had been concerned that research in high-energy physics conducted at the joint facilities might suffer a serious setback if, in the transition, funding previously provided by ONR was not made up. Disciplinary concerns were clearly at stake in this matter. The physicists of the GAC were highly protective of the research facilities ONR had established and did not want to see the expensive instruments built and managed by the ONR put in jeopardy by financial exigencies.

More overt GAC lobbying for funds can be found in the deliberations of Meeting 26 in May 1951. At this time, Rabi expressed his view on AEC basic research funding, commenting that the AEC figures he was reviewing for basic research were "not right dollarwise, but should be increased, possibly doubled."[40]

Over the thirty-year existence of the GAC, many sessions were the scene of debates and discussions of laboratory budgets. Some particular AEC projects were the responsibility of specific AEC labs. For example, Alvin Weinberg, director of the Oak Ridge lab for many years, regularly testified before the GAC to promote the Aircraft Nuclear Propulsion (ANP) project (Oak Ridge was the lead research lab for the ANP project). Weinberg realized that the health of his lab was dependent to a great degree on continued funding for ANP research. Consequently, not only the lab budgets in the aggregate but project budgets as well were important to lab directors, particularly if the labs conducted most or all of the work on these projects, because, as a House report pointed out, "each laboratory budget is not a separate line item in the [AEC or] ERDA budget, but a composite of several allocations determined by negotiations between program offices and the laboratory. The laboratories report programmatically to the offices for which they work. Institutionally, they report to the [AEC or] ERDA administrator through an assistant administrator for field operations."[41]

The GAC members had an abiding interest in budgetary issues. They understood that money fueled research advances at the labs. In the competition for research funding, the major AEC labs were often pitted against one another. In some instances, the GAC behaved as a referee; it ensured that the fight was fair and that the competitor most likely to produce the scientific and technical work the AEC desired secured the necessary funding.

In a seminal article about the federal budgetary process, political scientists Peter B. Natchez and Irvin C. Bupp used the AEC as their object of budgetary and policy analysis. They concluded:

> National priorities are not set by administrators with national constituencies; they are set at the operating levels of federal bureaus—by program directors sensitive to their own clienteles. National priorities are established by bureaucratic entrepreneurship in

a process which settles priorities without anyone being aware of them. . . . Programs prosper because energetic division directors successfully build political support to withstand continuous attacks upon a program's resource base by competing claims.[42]

The GAC was privy to both project manager and division manager budget requests. As a statutory advisory committee organizationally bonded to the uppermost Commission level, the GAC could review the entire sweep of AEC divisions, offices, projects, and labs in its deliberations. This placed the Committee in the thick of the division director (and project director) entrepreneurship activities. In explaining the gradual and regularized spending increases for the AEC high-energy physics program, as well as for the AEC Sherwood program, it has been maintained that the "constant level of prosperity is an indicator of stable political support, not of the operation of some 'budgetary constant.' "[43] The GAC was one source of political support for these programs, particularly in the case of high-energy physics.

Project Sherwood is a good example of the GAC's role in project assessment and budget formulation. In 1962 AEC Division of Research Director Paul McDaniel asked the GAC to conduct a review of the entire Sherwood program. Philip H. Abelson led the GAC subcommittee that assumed this task. By August 1962, the subcommittee rendered its findings, praising the Livermore mirror program but advising that no new large machines be funded until extensive preliminary work had been done on simpler devices. The group recommended, "As long as such cheap, interesting, and straightforward experiments are available for elucidating Toy Top behavior, the committee cannot endorse proceeding with the expensive Toy Top 2-X program."[44] The GAC fully endorsed the Abelson group recommendations and insisted that the commissioners implement them. The Division of Research disagreed with the GAC recommendations and attempted to convince the commissioners that the Abelson group report was inadequate and incomplete. The Commission overruled the GAC recommendation, which had called for a stop in construction of the Toy Top 2-X, but some other GAC findings so alarmed the commissioners that they demanded a thorough programwide review of Sherwood by 1965. At that time a stop-or-go decision on the entire controlled thermonuclear effort would be made.[45]

The Sherwood case is just one of many examples of the GAC exerting influence in the determination of AEC policy and program priorities. The Committee did not always advocate economies; in periods of relatively generous funding the GAC helped the AEC direct the infusion of fiscal resources to the most promising scientific projects, most of them directed by the AEC labs with a substantial amount of corporate and university subcontracting. In periods of AEC budget funding reductions, however, the GAC helped the AEC apportion financial sacrifice in a manner the Committee believed was reasonable or likely to cause the least disruption of scientific and technical work at the labs. Sometimes the members exploited their prerogative as advisees by simply opposing all budget cuts rather than assisting in the selection of organizational or project victims.

The GAC faced an awkward advisory predicament at Meeting 35 in May 1953. After having listened to AEC Chairman Gordon E. Dean recite a litany of Budget Bureau funding reduction proposals, the Committee explored the wisdom of the budget cuts the bureau was asking the president to make. Libby compared the proposed $4.6 million cut in the physical research budget with the $5 million reduction in spending on the Brookhaven Bevatron, which was under construction. He suggested, "If there was a choice, he would choose to cut the bevatron." Committee member John C. Warner agreed with Libby on this point. GAC Chairman Rabi argued against cutting funding for the bevatron "on the ground that research is more flexible, while the other would be closing a door." He also cautioned, "The GAC should not weaken the position of any research item and should fight very strongly for both."[46]

Careful transcriptions of GAC meetings were kept and summarized for circulation to AEC officials. AEC personnel could often discern which projects were of questionable value in the minds of Committee members, sometimes even when the Committee itself took no official stand, as in the case above. Advisory committee members are sometimes unaware that their offhand or informal comments made at meetings can yield unintentional or unanticipated consequences in the decision making of the host agency. For example, after this May 1953 meeting, the GAC recording secretary added a parenthetical comment to the minutes: "Committee seemed to agree that if a cut was needed, CR&D breeder project should go."[47] This observation regarding an informal consensus may have given AEC officials the scientific advice they needed to choose which project to cut back. Not long after this session, the proposed cut in the "CR&D part of the fast breeder program" was ratified by the Bureau of the Budget.[48]

While AEC laboratory directors hoped that the GAC might lobby in defense of their individual budgets, the Commission wanted the GAC to help shield the entire agency from proposed budget reductions. During Meeting 35 in May 1953, AEC Commissioner Henry D. Smyth "begged the GAC to supply definitive examples of items in the physical research budgets of preceding years which resulted in [dollar] savings."[49] The AEC was obviously under pressure to prove that spending on physical research was both cost effective and likely to produce future dollar savings in the government's applied research and development programs. Taken aback by this request, GAC members did suggest a few examples for Smyth. Warner and Oliver E. Buckley said it was unfair to ask for practical applications so soon. However, Libby confidently volunteered to supply the commissioner with at least six examples within a week.[50]

Program managers at headquarters may have appreciated that vested interests in a laboratory could cause that laboratory to go off in directions that were not intended by the program manager. The degree of trust and autonomy a program manager invests in a lab "is a function of how competent the manager believes the laboratory personnel are to make correct technical decisions and whether the manager believes the laboratory will make choices according to the interests of the program or according to its own (divergent) interests."[51] The GAC was an instrument through which AEC and ERDA program managers could gauge both a laboratory's scientific and technical competence and its level of blatant self-promotion.

Visitor use of laboratories

While it may seem to be a relatively inconsequential issue, the matter of visitor policy at major AEC laboratories was often a source of controversy in GAC meetings. Most AEC research laboratories provided opportunities for scientists employed by outside universities or private corporations to use laboratory facilities, usually accomplished by scheduling a period of lab visitation for those scientists or engineers whose formal applications were approved. Besides gaining access to unique and expensive capital facilities that employers could not provide, the visitor was also likely to be given office space, special technical assistance, temporary lab-based housing, and other resources.

Visiting scientists were often in competition with full-time AEC lab researchers to secure machine time. Test reactors, particle accelerators, and other major pieces of scientific equipment operated by the lab were often scheduled for use virtually 100% of the time. The question became, Who would get to use a device, for what period of time, and for what particular purpose? The matter of lab visitation rights remains a key concern of the scientific and engineering research community. Some of the most momentous scientific breakthroughs have been made by visiting scientists conducting research at a government laboratory, as the physical and personnel resources of an AEC lab were used for purposes set forth by the visitor. However, this sometimes complicated or delayed fulfillment of other lab research projects and missions. Furthermore, visitors challenged lab directors in the sense that directors, aided by their lab-based proposal review committees, had to select worthy visitor research projects from what was invariably a large number of visitor proposals. The directors had to choose between denying lab access to a large number of irate applicants and alienating full-time lab researchers by limiting their access to vital equipment.

At Meeting 47 in December 1955, the GAC met with the five AEC commissioners, the AEC general manager, and the directors of the Ames, Argonne, Berkeley, Brookhaven, Livermore, Los Alamos, and Oak Ridge laboratories.[52] The group devoted considerable attention to the matter of laboratory visitors. Leland J. Haworth, representing Brookhaven, declared, "Government should make available unique facilities to visiting scientists, whether at National Labs or not." To this, GAC Chairman Rabi asked whether or not visiting scientists posed inconveniences for the laboratories. Haworth replied that visitors do indeed cause inconveniences and that visitors may not enable the lab to "maximize total research accomplishment." He posed the question, "Does a visitor deserve special privileges because he or she is a visitor?" and asked what the balance should be between the number of in-house laboratory staff and the number of laboratory visitors. Lab Director Weinberg and John Swartout, representing the Oak Ridge lab, contributed their views on this point. Swartout claimed, "The visitors from industry are the real problem." Weinberg commented that visiting scientists posed "no real problem" in the laboratory's pursuit of basic research. Rabi responded that Oak Ridge did not yet have to face the problem of competition between visitors and staff for available facilities.[53] This may have been because Oak Ridge had major production, rather than expensive research, facilities in place at that time. Moreover, extensive military research conducted there precluded civilian visitations to many areas of the lab complex.

This exchange illustrates how the GAC routinely delved into even the most minute aspects of laboratory management. At the same time, the Committee functioned as a kind of special appeals board used by lab directors, either directly or indirectly, to express a grievance or special request to the AEC. Meetings with the directors of the major AEC labs often helped to promote coordination and consistency in research laboratory affairs. By examining issues such as visitor policies, the GAC could uncover and constructively address the common or shared problems of the directors. At Meeting 2 in February 1947, Rabi expressed the opinion that the various Commission laboratories "were not pulling together, and that in some way an attempt to improve their spirit and actual cooperation should be made."[54]

At least once a year the GAC made it a point to meet with AEC laboratory directors as a group. In many cases, the session with the directors would be closed to attendance by AEC officials and staff in order to give the directors a chance to express private concerns in a candid and informal environment away from the scrutiny of AEC administrators. On such occasions, the directors could concede mistakes, express personal or professional concerns off the record, and seek the wisdom and counsel of GAC members and fellow lab directors, to the benefit of both the AEC and the U.S. scientific research community.

Patent policy

Another seemingly mundane issue regularly cropped up at GAC meetings over its thirty-year history. The Committee frequently wrestled with the topic of patent restrictions and how they should or should not be applied at the AEC laboratories. In a session held in May 1953, two GAC members from the corporate research world complained that the patent provisions of the Atomic Energy Act of 1946 were onerous. Eger V. Murphree, director of Esso Research and Engineering Company, and Buckley, president of Bell Telephone Laboratories, argued that the AEC patent restrictions imposed on their firms were often counterproductive and unnecessary.[55]

Patent restrictions applied to scientific and technical inventions produced at AEC laboratories often prohibited private firms, including the lab's own industrial contractor operator, from securing proprietary rights and commercial gain. AEC patent restrictions were imposed on the products of work generated by individuals pursuing research at the AEC lab even when those individuals were employed by a corporation or university outside the lab.

Patent and copyright regulations involve more than minor disagreements between government labs and private sector firms. Whenever the federal government subsidizes private research and development, stipulations take effect that often prevent the recipient of the funding from assuming even limited ownership of inventions or innovations. For many years industry has waged protracted battles with government over what business executives claim to be overbearing, unfair, and obstructive government patent restrictions. Many corporate officials contend that these restrictions ultimately discourage private participation in federally subsidized research and development endeavors.

This claim was evident in a criticism put forward by Murphree in December 1955. He told the GAC, "Because of patent restrictions, industry will tend to avoid the National Laboratories when facilities are available elsewhere."[56] Almost twenty years later, the GAC was still attacking the problems posed by patent policy. During an October 1976 meeting, the ERDA research grant program came up on the agenda. Heading the list of questions was, What effect would patent restrictions have upon the progress of various ERDA research projects? The Committee advised that the criteria used to determine whether a project should be assigned to a national laboratory, a privately operated government contract lab, a private firm, a university, or some combination of sponsors, must take into account the possible effect of patent restrictions on the research organization.[57]

Two years later, as ERDA promoted the commercialization of its energy research projects, the GAC spent time examining waiver applications to ERDA patent policy.[58] Regardless of the legal nature of patent and copyright disputes, GAC scientists and engineers regularly offered their observations and advice on government patent restrictions. In each instance, what a member had to say about patent policy was usually a function of his or her employer affiliation. Members working for corporations usually were interested in the matter of patent policy because it was so central to their firm's calculations in deciding whether to apply for, or join in, federally subsidized research projects.

Public versus private research

Disputes about government patent restrictions were symptomatic of broader conflicts between industrial and government-sponsored research. Periodically, the GAC was caught in conflicts between directors of corporate research institutions and of AEC laboratories.

In a speech before fellow executives of the U.S. atomic power industry on November 17, 1959, Chauncey Starr, at that time general manager of the Atomic International Division and vice president of North American Aviation, Inc., made a provocative accusation:

> By continuing to develop the national laboratories the government has in fact "nationalized" nuclear technology and throttled the industry. . . . The national laboratories (should be) confined to "providing the new scientific and engineering information needed to advance the art" and federal engineering, research, and development funds (should be) placed in the hands of industry.[59]

Most atomic energy industry executives of the period probably agreed with Starr's claim. They perceived the AEC labs as rivals in the research and development of civilian nuclear power technology and as competitors for federal funds. Only three representatives of nuclear industry ever secured appointment to the GAC: Walter H. Zinn, William Webster, and William R. Gould. Shortly after his retirement from the employ of reactor vendor Combustion Engineering, Inc., Zinn was appointed to the GAC in 1972 by President Richard M. Nixon. He had been Enrico Fermi's student and assistant at the University of Chicago at the time Fermi's group created the first controlled nuclear chain reaction and went on to head the Argonne lab and in 1956 assumed the presidency of General Nuclear Engineering Company. Webster, who was appointed by President John F. Kennedy in 1962 and served until 1972, joined as an employee of the New England Electric System and during his term assumed a senior position with Connecticut Yankee Atomic Electric Company, an operator of several nuclear power facilities. Gould was appointed to the ERDA GAC by President Gerald R. Ford in 1975. He held an executive position with Southern California Edison Company, a huge utility with expansive nuclear operations. Although Webster and Gould worked for electric utilities, not reactor vendor companies, each on occasion expressed a private sector position in GAC debates about public versus private research.

Corporate executives of firms that were AEC laboratory contractors (e.g., Union Carbide, General Electric, or Western Electric Corporation) were ambivalent toward the issue of public versus private research. In one sense, the AEC contract labs were adversaries of private atomic energy corporations. Yet private corporations that managed major AEC research labs occupied both public and private research worlds. Contractor firms had controlled access to the latest scientific discoveries and inventions produced within their government-funded labs. Their scientific and technical employees were often assigned to the contract lab, which gave them valuable insight and special training and enabled them to team up with full-time lab researchers in scientific and technical projects. Running an AEC lab under contract gave the operating firm a privileged position; it allowed the company to occupy a key intersection of public and private research interaction. Some claim that there should be great "fear of a system in which the government will pay all of the costs of a series of expensive programs each of which will be contracted out to the private corporations and managed in their private interests."[60]

Meeting 47 in December 1955 was the scene of an exchange demonstrating that the concerns Starr later expressed in 1959 were not groundless. Norris E. Bradbury, director of the Los Alamos lab, commented about how nuclear power technology could be advanced, remarking to the Committee, "It is unwise to assume that industry could be relied on to do what is needed." Standard Oil of New Jersey President Murphree responded, "It depends on the incentive to industry."[61]

Also present at this meeting was Oak Ridge Director Weinberg, who joined the debate and insisted, "If development of nuclear energy is . . . of deep public interest and is to be an instrument of national policy, then there is no alternative to government responsibility. . . . One can't afford to let it take a course determined by the internal economic situation. . . . The government can do it better, and the government needs to be in control in order to be able to bargain with this merchandise. He ended with a note of warning: "Industry with government support provides a different approach from industry alone."[62]

As one of the few GAC members working for private industry, Murphree felt compelled to offer a counterargument. He articulated a position that would be endorsed by the American nuclear industry for many years to come; Murphree "believed the fields deserving emphasis would change as industry comes into the picture and develops fields on a profit motive. When this happens, the laboratories should shift emphasis. They should always be working on the longer range problems."[63]

This debate reflects the ideological disagreements that sometimes emerged between those working in private industry research and those working in the domain of public scientific research. GAC members often found themselves arbitrating disputes between private firms working to gain a commercial advantage and government labs working to maintain control and funding of their research and development endeavors. AEC lab officials resisted surrendering their lines of research, or their developed products, to private industry. Correspondingly, major private corporate officials resented the fact that the AEC labs could take on high-risk technical projects underwritten by the resources of the U.S. Treasury. Even more aggravating to industry was the tendency of AEC labs to stake out commercially promising scientific and technical areas in a way that effectively screened out private exploitation. The AEC was often forced to decide when its subsidized research and development work served a public interest requiring public control and ownership and when it was mature enough to no longer require public underwriting but instead warranted pay-as-you-go commercial advancement by private industry.

In an assessment of the history of AEC nuclear reactor research, it has been stated that "the laboratories have been a centrifugal force in reactor development, promoting their own ideas and seeking support for them. The Commission, particularly since the mid-1960s, has been the limiting agent, time and again seeking to focus laboratory efforts on what it regarded as the most promising avenues of development."[64] This may well be true, but it is also true that the private nuclear power industry has benefited immensely from the huge public investment in nuclear research and development underwritten by the taxpayer and expended through AEC lab research, with commensurate subcontracting to nuclear firms. The Atomic Energy Act of 1946 declared, "Development and utilization of atomic energy shall be directed toward . . . strengthening free competition among private enterprises so far as practicable."[65] This authority, as well as the powers conferred by the Atomic Energy Act of 1954, invited AEC promotion of private nuclear industry. The labs were conduits for AEC subsidization of private nuclear power interests and were at the same time competitors of nuclear power interests in the fight to secure control of research projects and funding from the Commission.

Oak Ridge and the nuclear airplane

The GAC regularly evaluated the progress of scientific and technical project work conducted at the AEC labs. Among the many lab-directed research projects addressed by the Committee over its history was Aircraft Nuclear Propulsion, a controversial and relatively expensive project to build a nuclear reactor–powered jet aircraft. ANP was long pursued by the Oak Ridge National Laboratory with extensive subcontracting to aviation industry firms. The AEC–Oak Ridge role fundamentally involved development and testing of the reactor power plant for the aircraft. The air force directed development through its own research labs and with major defense contractors. Much of the air force work addressed the design and engineering of the plane's engines as well as development of an appropriate airframe for the craft.

To appreciate why and how such a project was undertaken, a short history of ANP is necessary.[66] ANP was the brainstorm of Colonel Donald J. Keirn. During World War II, he worked as a jet engine expert at Wright Field in Ohio. In 1944, he wrote President Franklin D. Roosevelt's top science adviser, Vannevar Bush, to ask if it were possible for the Manhattan Project to undertake reactor development that could be used in aircraft propulsion.[67] Pressed by many other wartime problems, Bush rejected Keirn's idea. However, after the war the nuclear plane concept was revived by a group of senior air force officers, a number of researchers at the navy's Bureau of Aeronautics, and a contingent of aircraft engine manufacturers.

In these early years, the project was designated Nuclear Energy for Propulsion of Aircraft (NEPA). In 1948, the Joint Committee on Atomic Energy (JCAE) and the AEC put 40 MIT scientists and engineers to work on exploring the feasibility of atomic-powered flight, under the Lexington Project. Leading this effort was Massachusetts Institute of Technology Chemical Engineering Department Head and Professor Walter G. Whitman. The Lexington group determined in its 1948 report that NEPA progress would depend on major breakthroughs in new metals and development of more powerful chemical fuels. The group indicated that it could take fifteen years of development work, costing as much as a billion dollars, before a nuclear-powered airplane could be made operational.[68] This cost prediction proved to be remarkably accurate.

Whitman was appointed to the GAC in August 1950 and served a full six-year term on the Committee. The nuclear airplane was researched and technically refined at Oak Ridge during this period. Consequently, Whitman's Lexington group experience prepared him to advise the AEC authoritatively on the matter of the nuclear plane. Committee member James B. Fisk, working as AEC research division director in 1947, was an early NEPA project director.[69] He was appointed to the GAC in September 1952 and served until August 1958. Fisk, like Whitman, had a special knowledge of the nuclear airplane project that added weight to his advisories on the project in GAC meetings of the mid-1950s.

According to the official history of the AEC, the GAC was "never enthusiastic over aircraft nuclear propulsion." From the beginning, "It was clear that NEPA was to be the domain of engineers, not nuclear physicists, and that the chief concern was engines and equipment, not nuclear reactors."[70] In 1948, Oppenheimer and James B. Conant had attacked the nuclear plane project in testimony before the Department of Defense (DOD) Research and Development Board as too expensive and too technologically questionable to warrant a major investment of AEC reactor research budget funds. A year earlier, Conant had told Keirn that "NEPA should be exclusively an AEC Project, and that the Air Force should not be involved in it."[71] Despite the reservations and objections of Conant and Oppenheimer, the nuclear plane project lumbered into the decade of the 1950s. Over the course of its development history, ANP cost the federal government an estimated $1 billion. The AEC and the air force had pushed the nuclear plane research forward, however, before air force leaders furnished a full military rationale for nuclear-powered warplanes.[72]

Weinberg promoted the plane reactor project, which had been assigned to his lab. By January 1951, Oak Ridge had finished much of the ANP reactor design work. The early design work called for a nuclear-powered supersonic bomber to be completed in the 1960s. Many expected that because the reactor could operate many weeks or even months before needing refueling, the plane could stay airborne for extremely long time periods while attacking enemy targets. A writer for *Flying* magazine said, "It will revolutionize flight with its unlimited range and endurance. On less than one pound of uranium, an A-plane will be able to fly 100,000 miles. In the future it can eliminate our need for a worldwide chain of military air bases."[73]

Unfortunately, just as Oak Ridge design work was off the drawing boards, an air force committee directed by F. Wheeler Loomis determined that existing nuclear plane research proposed too long a development time scale. The Loomis committee opposed development of a new airframe for the reactor-powered plane and instead called for fast development of a reactor that could be encased in the body of the existing B-52 airframe to provide subsonic bomber flight. Lawrence R. Hafstad, AEC engineering division director in this period, agreed with the Loomis committee recommendations, as did air force research and development officials. Consequently, the old NEPA project died in April 1951 to be replaced by a drive to produce ANP. Thus, the first project explored the creation of a new reactor and a new type of airframe, while the second project required a new reactor and modification of an existing jet bomber but not a wholly new airframe.[74] In 1952, a Joint Office of Aircraft Nuclear Propulsion was set up to coordinate the AEC–air force effort to develop the plane.[75] Major General Keirn, the project's original promoter, was named director of the ANP program.

In spite of turnover in membership through the 1950s, the GAC as a body was either opposed to or ambivalent to the ANP program. Members acknowledged the great technical challenges facing the project, but they grew intolerant of the very high cost of the program, in terms of demands made on both reactor research budgets and the nation's scientific and technical talent pool. In September 1953 Edward Teller, usually an ardent proponent of atomic energy applications, "indicated he was dubious as to whether an atomic plane could be built."[76] Several GAC members apparently suspected that the project was a major boondoggle for aircraft engine manufacturing companies. For example, in September 1955, Wigner wrote GAC Chairman Rabi a letter criticizing the Pratt and Whitney jet engine company's ANP project work. Wigner complained that too much work had already been assigned to the firm and the company could not be trusted to meet its obligations.[77] Pratt and Whitney Division of United Aircraft Company had been assigned the job

of designing and engineering the indirect cycle approach to nuclear propulsion while General Electric worked on the direct cycle approach.[78]
The AEC and Pratt and Whitney had had a long-running argument
about provisions of the air force contract with the company.

About the same time Wigner drafted his letter, the GAC was told
that the navy was contemplating construction of a nuclear-powered seaplane. The navy's Louis H. Roddis, Jr., informed the Committee that
the navy was circulating a plan to develop a new aircraft nuclear reactor
for the envisioned seaplane. This plan was apparently initiated before
being fully authorized by the DOD. Presumably, the Pratt and Whitney
and the General Electric aircraft reactors being built under ANP did not
meet the navy's nuclear seaplane specifications. In the course of this
briefing, Committee member Edwin M. McMillan jokingly remarked,
"It would be sensible to fly one nuclear airplane before getting deluged
with orders."[79] The atomic seaplane proposal was symptomatic of the
interservice rivalry between the air force and the navy in their competition for atomic hardware. A senior air force official had claimed, "A
nuclear-powered water-based aircraft may become an effective bomber
suitable for the Air Force's wartime strategic bombing mission."[80] The
navy atomic seaplane was the navy's reply to this observation. The nuclear-powered seaplane proposal was ultimately quashed by President
Dwight D. Eisenhower, but not before several million dollars had been
expended by the navy in preliminary design contract work.[81]

In January 1957, during a GAC meeting convened at Oak Ridge,
Weinberg and his staff briefed the Committee on the progress of ANP
work. Weinberg commented, "The main problem of nuclear flight is the
problem of obtaining adequate thrust with sufficient low weight."[82] Over
the years, costly contracts had been drawn up with a number of firms in
an attempt to fashion a reactor containment vessel composed of light but
strong ceramic materials. The aircraft reactor, like all reactors operated
in proximity to humans, had to have adequate shielding to protect the
flight crew as well as maintenance personnel.[83] Developing lightweight
and durable reactor shielding proved to be no easy task. An added com-
plication was the danger a hot reactor would pose in the event of a crash.
The atomic scientists, who understood this danger better than any other
group, advised that nuclear planes not be flown over populated areas.[84]

By November 1957, GAC collective patience with aircraft nuclear
power was exhausted. In a letter to AEC Chairman Strauss, GAC Chairman Warren C. Johnson summarized the Committee's position. When
notified that "work may be directed toward an actual nuclear powered
flight based on easily foreseeable technology," the Committee re-

sponded: "We believe that such an airplane will not serve any objective purpose and will be very expensive. Considering the great urgency of several other programs, and considering the budgetary situation, we feel that to plan such a flight is unwise. Most particularly we feel that one should not justify such a flight on the basis of propaganda designed to counter the Russian successes in the satellite field."[85]

When the Soviet Union launched Sputnik on October 4, 1957, the JCAE, led by Representative Melvin Price, exhorted President Eisenhower to "put a flying test-bed with a nuclear power plant into the air as soon as possible." Both the air force and the AEC agreed that the atomic plane was an important "means of increasing American scientific prestige."[86] Apparently, sufficient ANP work had been done so that a plane carrying an operating nuclear reactor in its fuselage could be test-flown by the air force in 1960.[87] The quote suggests that the air force had proposed flying the nuclear plane as a direct U.S. response to the internationally recognized Soviet launch of the first earth-orbiting satellite, Sputnik.

Despite the full Committee rejection of the atomic plane project work in 1957, members of the GAC Reactors Subcommittee issued a statement in 1958 that suggested their willingness to cooperate in advancement of the General Electric direct cycle A-plane approach: "If the Defense Department is in favor of proceeding with this system, then the Reactors Subcommittee recommends that the necessary steps be taken to develop the XMA power plants by General Electric and that these steps include provision for flight testing and demonstration of these propulsion systems as proposed by General Electric and Convair."[88]

The GAC continued to grapple with problems of ANP research until the whole project was canceled by Secretary of Defense Robert S. McNamara in 1961. McNamara told Congress that a nuclear aircraft would "expel some small fraction of radiofission products into the atmosphere, creating an important public relations problem if not an actual physical hazard."[89] The GAC's major reservations about the project stemmed from what members believed were its engineering infeasibility, contamination risks in deployment, extremely high dollar costs, and insatiable demand for scientific and technical manpower. To the GAC, the nuclear-powered airplane was simply not worth the resources the federal government was pouring into it. Libby best summed up the matter: "The scientists did not sabotage the nuclear plane; they simply couldn't build it." A writer on this period observed, "What he meant was not that a plane could not have been developed, but that scientists and engineers working on the program could not have built the kind of plane the new

(Kennedy) Administration felt it could 'buy' in 1961, given its projected costs, technical limitations, and the existence of alternative means of securing the nation's defenses."[90]

The biggest battles over the nuclear plane were fought within the DOD, where uniformed and civilian personnel wrangled over how the plane would be designed, how it could be used, and which branch of the service would get to use it. The AEC and its Oak Ridge lab were profoundly affected by the frequent changes and modifications made in ANP work. Each time the DOD issued new objectives and specifications for the plane, the AEC had to go about refashioning the plane's reactor accordingly. By 1958 more than $600 million had been spent, but the United States was not much closer to an aircraft reactor than it had been in the summer of 1953. Both contractors could suggest military applications for the reactors they were developing, "but in almost every case," according to a history of the AEC, "new designs of conventional aircraft offered superior performance at an earlier date."[91]

The GAC became embroiled in ANP disputes because the AEC had to craft the reactor that would be the power plant of the nuclear plane. The Committee fully appreciated the risks and dangers of a nuclear plane, and some of its members had researched the feasibility of atomic-powered flight years earlier. Although not wholly impartial analysts of the ANP program, the members during the ANP era had no vested interest in perpetuating the ANP program merely to sustain Oak Ridge scientific and technical work on the plane's reactor power plant. However, the Committee continued to provide scientific and technical advisement needed to engineer the nuclear plane even after the group had expressed disapproval of the whole nuclear-powered-plane concept.

There was a strong bond and mutual interdependence between the laboratories and the AEC/ERDA. The laboratories were depended on for initiatives in program development, which gave them leverage over the agency and provided opportunities for them to shape policy according to their own interests.[92] On the other hand, the laboratories were almost abjectly dependent on the AEC and ERDA to provide the political, administrative, and budgetary support needed to realize their scientific and technical objectives. Between these two groups was the GAC, which helped broker agreements between laboratory officials and AEC/

ERDA administrators. While Committee members were not without their own personal interests, these interests did not usually coincide with those of laboratory entrepreneurs or AEC/ERDA bureaucratic officials. Most members understood and appreciated the interdependence of the federal government's research and development effort, and they determined what the implications of certain lines of scientific and technical research might mean for other areas of government-supported research and development. Since resources were scarce and often not sufficiently augmented, resources that one lab or one program received were resources withdrawn from, or unavailable to, other labs or programs. Committee members were continually sensitive, as well, to the role AEC lab research played in the advancement of knowledge, particularly in the fields of their own expertise.

The wartime lab experience of most GAC members, particularly of those serving on the Committee in the 1940s and 1950s, gave them a first-hand appreciation of the problems at the great labs. The breadth of lab representation on the Committee, as well as the neutral third-party position most members held in advising on lab matters, enabled the GAC to evaluate the full array of laboratories on both an individual- and collective-laboratory basis; the Committee was not a republican institution through which each member advanced the cause of a single lab or lab contractor. On a few occasions, an individual laboratory's interests were evident in the pleadings of a member (see Chapter 9), but impartiality usually prevailed at each meeting.

It may appear rather strange for the Committee to have agonized over laboratory matters such as recruitment of scientific and technical personnel, budgeting for programs, visitor policy, relations with private corporations, and even the effect of security restrictions on research. Yet, these managerial concerns were as strategically important to the Committee as were other questions: What is to be the future of high-energy physics? Should the government go forward with crash development of a hydrogen bomb? What dangers are posed by above-ground thermonuclear testing? To the GAC, laboratory affairs were not trivial matters of "micromanagement." Members realized that all these seemingly mundane program and managerial affairs together established the capability of the AEC and its labs to fulfill assigned missions and to take on new ones.

6 The GAC and the Project Super controversy: The thermonuclear bomb

THE MOST IMPORTANT MEETINGS of the AEC GAC were those held in the fall of 1949. At this time the Committee was asked whether the federal government should undertake an accelerated program for development of the thermonuclear, or hydrogen, bomb.[1]

The theoretical possibility that a thermonuclear bomb could be developed was recognized by Enrico Fermi and Edward Teller in 1942. The possibility of using thermonuclear reactions was researched by Teller, J. Robert Oppenheimer, Fermi, Hans A. Bethe, and others during the war, at which time most physicists, including Oppenheimer and Fermi, considered a thermonuclear weapon only a long-range possibility.[2] Teller, however, remained steadfast in his belief that a thermonuclear weapon could be perfected earlier if sufficient scientific and technical resources were put to the task. At his insistence, he was given the opportunity to devote some of his research at Los Alamos to theoretical studies of a thermonuclear weapon that became known as the "Super." After the conclusion of World War II, Teller continued to devote himself to and press for thermonuclear development. It was not until 1951 that breakthroughs in design concepts by Teller, Stanislaw M. Ulam, and others and confirmed by computer calculations, made a thermonuclear bomb truly technically feasible.[3]

The Soviet atomic bomb

On September 22, 1949, the GAC opened Meeting 16 at the AEC Washington headquarters. Present over the course of sessions conducted from September 22 to 24 were AEC Commissioners Gordon E. Dean, Sumner T. Pike, Lewis L. Strauss, and Henry D. Smyth. Also present were AEC General Manager Carroll L. Wilson, Los Alamos Director

Norris E. Bradbury, and Alvin Graves, a Los Alamos scientist directing atomic bomb–testing activities.

The first day's sessions were taken up by relatively routine matters. However, during the next day, the AEC's Information Division rushed to the Committee a copy of a presidential statement issued that morning. President Harry S. Truman had announced, "We have evidence that within recent weeks an atomic explosion occurred in the U.S.S.R."[4] Therefore, most GAC members and the AEC commissioners learned of the public announcement of the Soviet detonation at the same time. However, the announcement probably was no surprise to Oppenheimer, Commissioner Pike, and AEC General Manager Wilson. Each had been part of a special committee impaneled under the chairmanship of Vannevar Bush to examine evidence of measurable radioactivity collected by the air force's Long Range Detection System. The samples were detected by a WB-29 weather reconnaissance plane on patrol from Japan to Alaska in late August.[5]

President Truman's statement also indicated that ever since 1945 it had been officially recognized that "no single nation could in fact have a monopoly of atomic weapons." The president declared, "There is substantial agreement that foreign research can come abreast of our theoretical knowledge in time."[6] The Soviet atomic bomb had been exploded August 29, 1949, in Asia near Semipalatinsk. The bomb, which came to be known as Joe 1 (for Soviet Premier Josef Stalin), provided a political stimulus for approving and accelerating the superbomb program.[7]

The assembled group spent a considerable amount of time assessing and discussing the implications of the successful Soviet atomic test; the meeting had originally been scheduled to run two days, but the GAC added a third day. The only detailed document written as a result of this meeting was the secretary's minutes. The Committee members said they were unable to offer formal recommendations or observations on the matter of the Soviet atomic bomb, stating that "it was inadvisable to submit a formal report of this Meeting, but [they] would, however, report informally at this time."[8] When the group concluded their analysis of the implications of this international event, Commissioner Pike remarked that he hoped the AEC could call on members of the GAC "should unforeseen developments arise before the next regular GAC meeting." The Committee agreed to continue to oblige the AEC.

Project Super

At the request of the Commission, the GAC convened Meeting 17 at Washington headquarters on October 28, 1949. Over the three-day period all GAC members were present with the exception of Glenn T. Seaborg, who was in Sweden. Before the meeting, Seaborg had been apprised of the meeting agenda, and in a letter to Oppenheimer, he cautiously and reluctantly expressed his approval of Project Super, code name for the project to develop a superbomb, the thermonuclear bomb.[9] Seaborg was the only GAC member to endorse the superbomb project at that time, and his approval was qualified with numerous reservations. The Seaborg letter stated, "Although I deplore the prospects of our country putting a tremendous effort into this, I must confess that I have been unable to come to the conclusion that we should not. . . . My present feeling would perhaps be best summarized by saying that I would have to hear some good arguments before I could take on sufficient courage to recommend not going towards such a program."[10]

That GAC meeting, perhaps more than any other, involved a remarkable array of scientific, diplomatic, and military dignitaries. For example, George F. Kennan, then counselor of the Department of State and an adviser to Secretary of State Dean G. Acheson, briefed the Committee on the world situation. An experienced and noted authority on the Soviet Union, Kennan fielded a variety of questions that pertained to the Soviet atomic bomb program. Oppenheimer, Fermi, Isidor I. Rabi, Oliver E. Buckley, Lee A. DuBridge, and Cyril S. Smith listened attentively and asked questions. Kennan spoke with the group for about forty-five minutes.[11]

In writing on the matter, Kennan claimed that prior to the Soviet detonation he had insisted, "If the Russians come into possession of it [the atomic bomb], then it had to be viewed as a suicidal weapon, devoid of rational application in warfare; in which case we ought to seek its earliest possible elimination from all national arsenals."[12] He declared that he was never asked to take an official position on the development of atomic weapons in the postwar era "until shortly after the first Soviet detonation of a nuclear device became known, in 1949." He wrote, "It was soon after this that the question arose whether our government should proceed to the development of the hydrogen bomb. I was then just completing a three-year period of service as director of the Policy Planning Staff of the State Department; and I placed my views on this subject before Secretary of State Dean G. Acheson in a paper of January 1950."[13]

In his January 1950 paper, Kennan argued for renunciation of the first use of the superbomb and of nuclear weapons in general. He insisted that the U.S. public position should be that "we deplore the existence and abhor the use of these weapons; that we have no intention of initiating their use against anyone; that we would use them only with the greatest of reluctance and only if this were forced upon us by methods of warfare used against us or our allies."[14] According to Kennan, his views on this subject were not well received by the secretary of state or by other government officials, "except (by) Robert Oppenheimer, who joined me (for somewhat different reasons) in trying to persuade our government to pause at this particular brink."[15]

Hartley Rowe, who had been absent during the session with Kennan, arrived as the Committee went on to listen to physicists Bethe and Robert Serber discuss the range of alternatives available to the AEC in atomic weapons development. Bethe was a professor at Cornell University and Serber a professor and researcher at the Berkeley Radiation Laboratory. Both had done extensive theoretical work on atomic weapons. Bethe personally opposed the thermonuclear bomb, but at this meeting he "confined his remarks to the technical feasibility of the Super."[16] The opening-day session was adjourned by the dinner hour.

When the Committee reconvened at 9:30 A.M. on Saturday, October 29, Oppenheimer, Buckley, DuBridge, Fermi, Rabi, Rowe, Smith, James B. Conant, John H. Manley (secretary), and Anthony A. Tomei (administrative assistant) were present. At 10:00 A.M. AEC Commissioners David E. Lilienthal, Dean, Smyth, and Strauss entered the meeting with AEC General Manager Wilson, and Deputy Manager Carleton Shugg. AEC's director of production, director of reactor development, general counsel and executive officer of the program council also joined the meeting. Soon thereafter the director of biology and medicine, the director of military application, and the director of research joined the group. At this time Tomei was excused, but Manley remained and recorded Committee deliberations. The general minutes indicate that the assembly discussed the superbomb program.[17]

At 11:00 A.M., the GAC met with the Joint Chiefs of Staff, chaired by General Omar N. Bradley. General John E. Hull represented the army, General Lauris Norstad the air force, and Admiral William S. Parsons the navy. Also present were members of the DOD Military Liaison Committee to the AEC: Robert LeBaron, chairman, and General Alvin R. Luedecke, executive secretary. The four commissioners, the AEC general manager, and the AEC director of military application were also still in attendance. The group assessed the military implications of Project Super and the general matter of present and future AEC weapons work. The military, at the time, even then was uncertain as to how a thermonuclear bomb could be incorporated into an order of battle and doubtful of its value. One notation in meeting records revealed that General Bradley stated, "The principal advantage of the Super would be psychological."[18] In other words, a nation that possessed the thermonuclear bomb in its arsenal of weapons could instill dread fear of massive retaliation in the minds of enemies who might contemplate attack. At 12:30 P.M., the session with the military contingent was concluded.

In one study of the superbomb decision, the claim was made that the Joint Chiefs of Staff "had not expected the Soviet Union to detonate a fission weapon until 1952." The Soviet atomic bomb had made a two-way atomic war feasible. Defense officials had to confront the fact that "the Soviet Union would have the ability to mobilize from inside its own frontiers enough military power to accomplish what had heretofore been beyond the means of any single foreign nation: the capacity to strike a mortal blow at the American continent."[19]

At 2:10 P.M. of that day the Committee, along with the AEC commissioners, listened to a briefing given by the intelligence staff provided by AEC Deputy Director of Intelligence Malcolm C. Henderson, who supplied information on Russian activities known to his office. Henderson concluded his remarks at 3:30 P.M., and the session continued, with the four AEC commissioners still present, until 5:00 P.M.[20] During the afternoon session Fermi gave a technical summary of the prospects for the weapon. He was reported to have said that the chances of successfully building a deliverable weapon with such a program were "little better than even."[21] An evening session ran from 8:15 to 10:10 P.M., at which time GAC members agreed to prepare drafts of specific positions on Project Super at the next day's sessions.

By this time, Committee members began to assume individual positions on the matter of Project Super. The Committee had listened to testimony furnished by an elite corps of scientific, diplomatic, and military officials. Members had read a large assortment of classified papers and documents. The GAC was now prepared to announce its recommendations on Project Super. According to one account, when Oppenheimer canvassed the members for their individual opinions it became clear that they had a variety of technical, political, and moral reasons for opposing crash development of the project.[22]

On the morning of Sunday, October 30, the Committee decided to prepare a general report to fulfill its technical advisory responsibility, plus two supplemental statements on policy to the AEC. Oppenheimer summarized the views of the Committee before all five AEC commissioners (Lilienthal, Dean, Pike, Smyth, and Strauss) and the general manager and general counsel. Records disclose,

> During this portion of this Session, the Committee agreed that the Commission should feel free to use as it wished the reports and written views it would receive from the Committee. It was the implication of this action that the members of the GAC would not discuss

the Committee's views until freed to do so by action of the Commission. In addition it was agreed that each member would avoid discussion of his personal opinion at least for a period of one week, the initial day of the proposed Los Alamos conference. This was done in order to assure the maximum freedom of action to the Commission in the matters under discussion. . . . It was agreed that in view of the nature of the documents they should bear a Top Secret classification.[23]

A draft of what would become the foundation of the majority group GAC statement was written by Conant, with the assistance of Manley. Oppenheimer, Buckley, DuBridge, Smith, and Rowe conducted a careful line-by-line editing of the Conant draft. Entitled, "An Opinion on the Development of the 'Super,' " it is reproduced below:[24]

[October 30, 1949]

We have been asked by the Commission whether or not they should immediately initiate an "all-out" effort to develop a weapon whose energy release is 100 to 1000 times greater and whose destructive power in terms of area of damage is 20 to 100 times greater than those of the present atomic bomb. We recommend strongly against such action.

We base our recommendation on our belief that the extreme dangers to mankind inherent in the proposal wholly outweigh any military advantage that could come from this development. Let it be clearly realized that this is a super weapon; it is in a totally different category from an atomic bomb. The reason for developing such super bombs would be to have the capacity to devastate a vast area with a single bomb. Its use would involve a decision to slaughter a vast number of civilians. We are alarmed as to the possible global effects of the radioactivity generated by the explosion of a few super bombs of conceivable magnitude. If super bombs will work at all, there is no inherent limit in the destructive power that may be attained with them. Therefore, a super bomb might become a weapon of genocide.

The existence of such a weapon in our armory would have far-reaching effects on world opinion: reasonable people the world over would realize that the existence of a weapon of this type whose power of destruction is essentially unlimited represents a threat to the future of the human race which is intolerable. Thus we believe that the psychological effect of the weapon in our hands would be adverse to our interest.

We believe a super bomb should never be produced. Mankind would be far better off not to have a demonstration of the feasibility of such a weapon until the present climate of world opinion changes.

It is by no means certain that the weapon can be developed at all and by no means certain that the Russians will produce one within a decade. To the argument that the Russians may succeed in developing this weapon, we would reply that our undertaking it will not prove a deterrent to them. Should they use the weapon against us, reprisals by our large stock of atomic bombs would be comparably effective to the use of a super.

In determining not to proceed to develop the super bomb, we see a unique opportunity of providing by example some limitations on the totality of war and thus of limiting the fear and arousing the hopes of mankind.

JAMES B. CONANT
HARTLEY ROWE
CYRIL STANLEY SMITH
LEE A. DUBRIDGE
OLIVER E. BUCKLEY
J. R. OPPENHEIMER

This statement was remarkable in several respects. Oppenheimer, Conant, Rowe, and Smith had all made essential contributions to the development of the first atomic bombs as members of the Manhattan Project. As postwar government scientific advisers, Oppenheimer, Conant, Rowe, Smith, and other GAC colleagues had worked in earnest to help build the nation's stockpile of atomic weapons and to perfect new generations of these weapons. As early as February 1947, Oppenheimer had exhorted the group, and the Commission itself, to make atomic weapons a top priority. He said at that time, "The making of atomic weapons is something to which we are now committed."[25] Notwithstanding, the magnitude of destruction that could be produced by a thermonuclear bomb so alarmed GAC members that most perceived the weapon as qualitatively different from then-conventional atomic bombs. The atomic, or fission, bombs of the era had tactical and strategic military value in the minds of these scientists because they believed that the destructive effects of these weapons were geographically confined and ecologically absorbable in some set time period. According to GAC Secretary and physicist Manley, nature provides limits to what can be done with a fission weapon. The maximum explosive power of a fission weapon is approximately 500 kilotons. In "booster" enhancement experiments, the upper limit of fission weapon destructiveness was found to be not much above 500 kilotons.[26] They believed that this could not be assumed in the case of thermonuclear weapons, so tremendous would be the power; the thermonuclear bomb's blast and radioactive effects would make it "a weapon of genocide."[27] To GAC members, this bomb represented an intolerable threat to the human race, even posing the possibility of human extinction.

According to Manley, they understood that there was virtually no limit to the destructive power thermonuclear weapons might be built to attain. Consequently, a move from fission to thermonuclear weapons was a move to a position from which there was no fixed outer boundary of weapon destructive power.

Use of the word *genocide* was wholly appropriate. It has been contended: "Hitler's attempt to extinguish the Jewish people is the closest thing to a precursor of the extinction of the species that history contains. . . . The connection between genocide and extinction is further suggested by the fact that what the superpowers *intend* to do if a holocaust breaks out . . . is to commit genocide against one another—to erase the other side as a culture and as a people from the face of the earth."[28] GAC scientists recognized this possibility in 1949, a full three years before the United States successfully detonated the first thermonuclear bomb.

This majority statement discounted the value of the "psychological effects" of superbomb possession. Contrary to General Bradley's remark that the weapon had psychological value for its possessor, the statement concluded that it would be a major liability in U.S. foreign policy and international relations.

The second supplemental statement was presented by Rabi and Fermi as the minority opinion. They hoped that the nations of the world would join the United States in a pledge to renounce development of the superbomb. Tied as it was to international controls and agreements, the Rabi-Fermi position did not represent a blanket rejection of the envisioned weapon as did the majority group statement. If other nations refused to pledge that they would not develop a thermonuclear bomb, "presumably they (Rabi and Fermi) would then reluctantly favor development of the Super."[29] Following is the full text of the Rabi-Fermi supplemental statement:[30]

[October 30, 1949]

A decision on the proposal that an all-out effort be undertaken for the development of the "Super" cannot in our opinion be separated from considerations of broad national policy. A weapon like the "Super" is only an advantage when its energy release is from 100–1000 times greater than that of ordinary atomic bombs. The area of destruction therefore would run from 150 to approximately 1000 square miles or more.

Necessarily, such a weapon goes far beyond any military objective and enters the range of very great natural catastrophes. By its very nature it cannot be confined to a military objective but becomes a weapon which in practical effect is almost one of genocide.

It is clear that the use of such a weapon cannot be justified on any ethical ground which gives a human being a certain individuality and dignity even if he happens to be a resident of an enemy country.

It is evident to us that this would be the view of peoples in their countries. Its use would put the United States in a bad moral position relative to the peoples of the world.

Any postwar situation resulting from such a weapon would leave unresolvable enmities for generations. A desirable peace cannot come from such an inhuman application of force. The postwar problems would dwarf the problems which confront us at present.

The application of this weapon with the consequent great release of radioactivity would have results unforeseeable at present, but would certainly render large areas unfit for habitation for long periods of time.

The fact that no limits exist to the destructiveness of this weapon makes its very existence and the knowledge of its construction a danger to humanity as a whole. It is necessarily an evil thing considered in any light.

For these reasons we believe it important for the President of the United States to tell the American public, and the world, that we think it wrong on fundamental ethical principles to initiate a program of development of such a weapon. At the same time it would be appropriate to invite the nations of the world to join us in a solemn pledge not to proceed in the development or construction of weapons of this category. If such a pledge were accepted even without control machinery, it appears highly probable that an advanced stage of development leading to a test by another power could be detected by available means. Furthermore, we have in our possession, in our stockpile of atomic bombs, the means for adequate "military" retaliation for the production or use of a "Super."

E. FERMI
I. I. RABI

Rabi recalled that he and Fermi intended to "couple American forbearance with a Soviet pledge to do the same. He said that he (and others on the GAC) saw the 'super question' as providing an excellent opportunity to rekindle interest in the international control of nuclear arms, not just the super alone."[31] Oppenheimer and Rabi had been, in effect, the original inventors of the plan for nuclear arms control that later became known as the Baruch plan.[32]

Both the Rabi-Fermi statement and the Oppenheimer–majority group statement were written in an outspoken manner. Both statements followed similar lines of reasoning; both expressed moral indignation about the implications of the superbomb. Both statements were sensitive to matters of public opinion and to the general international ramifications that would stem from development and deployment of the device. Both letters professed philosophical and political positions that superseded the scientific and technical dimensions of weapon development.

Did these pleas to the conscience of humanity mean that these GAC scientists would withhold scientific and technical advice on the project? Not necessarily. The Committee felt obliged to offer advice, just as on myriad matters of atomic weapons technology in the past. Records show that accompanying these statements was the GAC chairman's meeting report to the AEC, also dated October 30, 1949. A portion of this declassified report (compiled from two sources) follows.

> The General Advisory Committee has considered at great length the question of whether to pursue with high priority the development of the super bomb. No member of the Committee was willing to endorse this proposal. The reasons for our views leading to this conclusion stem in large part from the technical nature of the super and of the work necessary to establish it as a weapon. We therefore transmit "an elementary" account of these matters.
>
> The basic principle of design of the super bomb is the ignition of the thermonuclear DD reaction by use of a fission bomb, and of high temperatures, pressure, and neutron densities which accompany it. In overwhelming probability, tritium is required as an intermediary, more easily ignited than the deuterium itself and, in turn, capable of igniting the deuterium. The steps which need to be taken if the super bomb is to become a reality include:
>
> 1. The provision of tritium in amounts perhaps of several [deleted] per unit.
> 2. Further theoretical studies and criticisms aimed at reducing the very great uncertainties still inherent in the behavior of this weapon under extreme conditions of temperature, pressure, and flow.
> 3. The engineering of designs which may on theoretical grounds appear hopeful, particularly with regard to the [deleted] problems presented.
> 4. Carefully instrumented test programs to determine whether the deuterium-tritium mixture will be ignited by the fission bomb . . . [33]
>
> It is notable that there appears to be no experimental approach short of actual test which will substantially add to our conviction that a given model will work or will not work, and it is also notable that because of the unsymmetric and extremely unfamiliar conditions obtaining, some considerable doubt will surely remain as to the soundness of theoretical anticipation. Thus we are faced with a development which cannot be carried to the point of conviction without the actual construction and demonstration of the essential elements of the weapon in question. This does not mean that further theoretical studies would be without avail. It does mean that they could not be decisive. A final point that needs to be stressed is that many tests may be required before a workable model has been evolved or before it has been established beyond reasonable doubt that no such model can be evolved. Although we are not able to give

a specific probability rating for any given model, we believe that an imaginative and concerted attack on the problem has a better than even chance of producing the weapon within five years.[34]

The GAC estimation was correct because on November 1, 1952, almost precisely three years after this report was submitted, the United States detonated the first thermonuclear bomb.

Oppenheimer's formal report to AEC Chairman Lilienthal continued with a warning about the destructive power of the bomb. He cautioned,

> A second characteristic of the super bomb is that once the problem of initiation has been solved, there is no limit to the explosive power of the bomb itself except that imposed by requirements of delivery. This is because one can continue to add deuterium — an essentially cheap material — to make larger and larger explosions, the energy release and radioactive products of which are both proportional to the amount of deuterium itself. Taking into account the probable limitations of carriers likely to be available for the delivery of such a weapon, it has generally been estimated that the weapon would have an explosive effect some hundreds of times that of present fission bombs. This would correspond to a damage area of the order of hundreds of square miles, to thermal radiation effects extending over a comparable area, and to very grave contamination problems which can easily be made more acute, and may possibly be rendered less acute, by surrounding the deuterium with uranium or other material. It needs to be borne in mind that for delivery by ship, submarine, or other such carrier, the limitations here outlined no longer apply and that the weapon is from a technical point of view without limitation with regard to the damage that it can inflict.[35]

It is apparent from this passage that Oppenheimer was attempting to stress not only the stupendous increase in destructive power of the new weapon but also the feasibility of its transport, perhaps through concealment or stealth, to a target. In the next portion of the report, Oppenheimer indicated that the Committee considered the bomb an inappropriate weapon for tactical use against enemy military installations. The report stated,

> It is clear that the use of this weapon would bring about the destruction of innumerable human lives; it is not a weapon which can be used exclusively for the destruction of material installations of military or semi-military purposes. Its use therefore carries much further than the atomic bomb itself the policy of exterminating civilian populations. It is of course true that super bombs which are not as big as those here contemplated could be made, provided the initiating mechanism works. In this case, however, there appears to be

no chance of their being an economical alternative to fission weapons themselves. It is clearly impossible with the vagueness of design and the uncertainty as to performance as we have them at present to give anything like a cost estimate of the super. If one uses the strict criteria of damage area per dollar and if one accepts the limitations on air carrier capacity likely to obtain in the years immediately ahead, it appears uncertain to us whether the super will be cheaper or more expensive than the fission bomb.[36]

The anticipated huge investment of public money and scientific manpower required to make a thermonuclear bomb was of great concern to GAC members. Oppenheimer's comment about the uncertain cost estimates of Project Super and his reference to a crude cost-benefit comparison of conventional atomic bombs with superbombs reveal some of the concern the Committee had about the cost of the project. Conant, in particular, was concerned over Project Super's capacity to redirect and voraciously consume scarce scientific and technical resources to the detriment of other projects. At the time, he was quoted as saying that he disapproved of the project if it "would disrupt weapon development at Los Alamos."[37] The GAC understood that the manufacture of tritium for the project would mean foregoing the manufacturing of plutonium for fission bombs. In addition, the defense science talents of the nation were largely committed to existing fission weapons projects: "Scientists put to work on the Super would be scientists not available to work on the new fission weapons. A more intensive effort to make an H-bomb would, in short, involve costs to the nation's A-bomb program."[38]

In the closing section of the report on Meeting 17, Oppenheimer expressed the Committee's key concerns about Project Super, and he asked that the AEC declassify some of the information about the superbomb and issue a public statement on the matter:

> Although the members of the Advisory Committee are not unanimous in their proposals as to what should be done with regard to the super bomb, there are certain elements of unanimity among us. We all hope that by one means or another, the development of these weapons can be avoided. We are all reluctant to see the United States take the initiative in precipitating this development. We are all agreed that it would be wrong at the present moment to commit ourselves to an all-out effort toward its development.
> We are somewhat divided as to the nature of the commitment not to develop this weapon. The majority feel that this should be an unqualified commitment. Others feel that it should be conditional on the response of the Soviet government to a proposal to renounce such development. The Committee recommends that enough be declassified about the super bomb so that a public statement of policy can be made at this time. Such a statement might in our opinion

point to the use of deuterium as the principal source of energy. It need not discuss initiating mechanisms nor the role which we believe tritium will play. It should explain that the weapon cannot be explored without developing it and proof-firing it. In one form or another the statement should express our desire not to make this development. It should explain the scale and general nature of the destruction which its use would entail. It should make clear that there are no known or foreseen nonmilitary applications of this development.[39]

Eventually, both the U.S. and Soviet governments would try to find nonmilitary applications of thermonuclear explosions in their respective peaceful nuclear explosives programs (see Chapter 8). Neither country, however, progressed beyond the test-shot phase, and both programs were ultimately discontinued.

In retrospect, GAC members must have anticipated tremendous pressures in their decision to oppose Project Super. The first successful detonation of an atomic device by the Soviet Union, announced only weeks before Meeting 17 (October 1949), was evidence that the United States no longer held a monopoly in atomic weapons. Moreover, the Joint Committee on Atomic Energy (JCAE), the AEC's congressional watchdog, strongly advocated development of the superbomb. Senator Brian McMahon, chairman of the Joint Committee, was quoted as saying, "In my judgment, a failure to press ahead with the hydrogen bomb might well mean unconditional surrendering in advance by the United States to alien forces of evil." He argued, "If we let the Russians get the super first, catastrophe becomes all but certain, whereas if we get it first, there exists a chance of saving ourselves. Total power in the hands of total evil will equal destruction."[40] The only JCAE member to express public reservations about the weapon was New York State Congressman W. Sterling Cole.[41] Both Secretary of Defense Louis Johnson and, to a degree Secretary of State Acheson, supported development of the weapon at the time.[42]

The Joint Chiefs of Staff favored development of Project Super but initially opposed a crash program as the means to make it a reality. They concluded, "If the Soviets were to come into sole possession of such a weapon, the position of the United States would be intolerable," and in commenting on the moral issues raised by the GAC, they said that one weapon is no more moral than another.[43]

In a letter he had written to Conant only about three weeks before GAC Meeting 17, Oppenheimer commented,

> What concerns me is really not the technical problem. I am not
> sure the miserable thing will work, nor that it can be gotten to the

target except by oxcart. It seems likely to me even further to worsen the unbalance of our war plans. What does worry me is that this thing appears to have caught the imagination both of the Congressional and military people, as the answer to the problem posed by the Russians' advance. It would be folly to oppose the exploration of this weapon. We have always known it had to be done, though it appears to be singularly proof against any form of experimental approach. But that we become committed to it as the way to save the country and the peace appears to me full of dangers.[44]

Oppenheimer's plea to open AEC declassifiable material on Project Super to the public would have given the Committee's moral and ethical reservations about the weapon a wider audience: "They obviously felt very strongly that such momentous decisions affecting all mankind should not be made by a tiny elite in-group exclusively privy to all of the relevant facts, even though in this case they were themselves included in it."[45]

When AEC Chairman Lilienthal received the official GAC Meeting 17 report and the two supplemental directives, he expressed satisfaction. Both Lilienthal and Commissioner Smyth agreed that Project Super should be rejected.[46] Lilienthal believed that U.S. reliance on nuclear weapons should not be the cornerstone of national defense. He thought that a crash program on the superbomb would forever transform American foreign policy in a way that would inexorably move the country into fighting a war with weapons of mass destruction.[47] Lilienthal wanted a full review of U.S. strategic doctrine to be undertaken before a decision to approve the weapon was made.[48] Commissioner Dean disagreed with the unilateral "renounce and announce" position of the GAC majority report. He concurred with Fermi and Rabi that the president should use regular secret diplomatic channels with the Kremlin to negotiate some form of international control and disarmament. Commissioner Pike was uncertain about whether to approve or reject the project.

Commissioner Strauss, a naval reserve rear admiral who would be appointed AEC chairman by President Dwight D. Eisenhower in 1953, drafted his own statement on the matter in a letter to President Truman (November 25, 1949). Strauss declared,

I believe that the United States must be as completely armed as any possible enemy. From this it follows that I believe it unwise to renounce, unilaterally, any weapon which an enemy can reasonably be expected to possess. I recommend that the President direct the Atomic Energy Commission to proceed with development of the thermonuclear bomb, at highest priority subject only to the judgment of the Department of Defense as to its value as a weapon, and of the advice of the Department of State as to the diplomatic conse-

quences of its unilateral renunciation or its possession. In the event
that you may be interested, my reasoning is appended in a memorandum.[49]

Strauss put forward the following eight premises for justifying development of the superbomb.

1. The production of such a weapon appears to be feasible (i.e.,
   better than a 50–50 chance).
2. Recent accomplishments by the Russians indicate that the production of a thermonuclear weapon is within their technical competence.
3. A government of atheists is not likely to be dissuaded from producing the weapon on "moral" grounds. ("Reason and experience
   both forbid us to expect that national morality can prevail in [the
   absence] of religious principle." G. Washington, September 17,
   1796.)
4. The possibility of producing the thermonuclear weapon was suggested more than six years ago, and considerable theoretical
   work has been done which may be known to the Soviets — the
   principle has certainly been known to them.
5. The time in which the development of this weapon can be perfected is perhaps of the order of two years, so that a Russian
   enterprise started some years ago may be well along to completion.
6. It is the historic policy of the United States not to have its forces
   less well armed than those of any other country (viz., the 5:5:3
   naval ratio, etc. etc.).
7. Unlike the atomic bomb which has certain limitations, the proposed weapon may be tactically employed against a mobilized
   army over an area of the size ordinarily occupied by such a force.
8. The Commission's letter of November 9th to the President mentioned the "possibility that the radioactivity released by a small
   number (perhaps ten) of these bombs would pollute the earth's
   atmosphere to a dangerous extent." Studies requested by the
   Commission have since indicated that the number of such
   weapons necessary to pollute the earth's atmosphere would run
   into many hundreds. Atmospheric pollution is a consequence of
   present atomic bombs if used in quantity.[50]

Strauss argued in his memorandum that the danger in the weapon
resided not in its physical nature but in human behavior. He feared that
unilateral renunciation of the weapon by the United States could result
in its unilateral possession by the Soviet Union. Strauss dismissed the
claim that a thermonuclear bomb could not be confined to tactical military use. He said, "The weapon may be critically useful against a large
enemy force both as a weapon of offense and as a defensive measure to
prevent landings on our own shores."[51]

Commissioner Strauss further argued that there was considerable hypocrisy in the position of several GAC members who opposed Project Super. He wrote,

> I am impressed with the arguments which have been made to the effect that this is a weapon of mass destruction on an unprecedented scale. So, however, was the atomic bomb when it was first envisaged and when the National Academy of Sciences in its report of November 6, 1941, referred to it as "of superlatively destructive power." Also on June 16, 1945, the Scientific Panel of the Interim Committee on Nuclear Power, comprising some of the present members of the General Advisory Committee, reported to the Secretary of War, "We believe the subject of thermonuclear reactions among light nuclei is one of the most important that needs study. There is a reasonable presumption that with skillful research and development, fission bombs can be used to initiate the reactions of deuterium, tritium, and possibly other light nuclei. If this can be accomplished, the energy release of explosive units can be increased by a factor of 1000 or more over that of presently contemplated fission bombs." This statement was preceded by the recommendation, "Certainly we would wish to see work carried out on the problems mentioned below."
>
> Obviously the current atomic bomb as well as the proposed thermonuclear weapon are horrible to contemplate. All war is horrible. Until, however, some means is found of eliminating war, I cannot agree with those of my colleagues who feel that an announcement should be made by the President to the effect that the development of the thermonuclear weapon will not be undertaken by the United States at this time.[52]

Strauss could not comprehend why the GAC would endorse the "booster program" to improve the efficiency of nuclear bombs and simultaneously oppose development of a thermonuclear bomb.[53] In 1949, there were two thermonuclear programs under way at Los Alamos. "One of these was the so-called booster program, which had as its main practical objective improving the efficiency of fission bombs. The other was the 'super' program, which had as its objective producing a weapon having a power at least a thousand times greater than that of the standard nuclear bomb."[54] The GAC strongly supported the booster program as being potentially very useful. Strauss saw little difference between the booster program and Project Super. In other words, the GAC had not made clear to him why they had such strong moral objections to the thermonuclear bomb but no similar objections to improvements in the new fission weapons that would be yielded by the booster program.[55]

Senator McMahon, chairman of the JCAE, followed similar lines of reasoning. During this time period McMahon had toured the Los Alamos Scientific Laboratory where he was briefed by Teller, one of Project Super's most strident advocates. McMahon returned to Washington determined to get the project approved. He could see "no moral dividing line . . . between a big explosion which causes heavy damage and many smaller explosions causing equal or still greater damage."[56] McMahon's dogmatic advocacy of the superbomb did not escape the notice of President Truman.

To help him determine whether or not to approve the superbomb initiative, President Truman relied on a special working group of the National Security Council. Formed on November 10, 1949, this group had as members Secretary of Defense Johnson, Secretary of State Acheson, and AEC Chairman Lilienthal. However, since Johnson supported a stepped-up thermonuclear program and Lilienthal opposed it, there was little incentive for the group to meet until Acheson had formulated a position.[57]

Meanwhile, Meeting 18 of the GAC was held on December 2 and 3, 1949, in Washington. This time all members of the GAC were present, including Seaborg. During one meeting session Oppenheimer informed the five AEC commissioners that no GAC member wished to retreat from the position he had taken at the October 30 meeting. Moreover, several members wanted to explain through individual letters additional reasons for opposing Project Super. Rowe's letter to the AEC intimated that the superbomb might lull the public into a false sense of security. He also contended that superbomb project work might involve a breach of security that could furnish the Soviet Union with information needed to produce their own thermonuclear bomb. It was during this month that the Alger Hiss spy trial resulted in a conviction.

In January 1950, only four days before President Truman issued his statement approving Project Super, Klaus Fuchs, one of the British team at Los Alamos during the war and one of the participants in a spring 1946 conference concerning Project Super, "confessed that he had engaged in espionage on behalf of the U.S.S.R. between 1942 and 1949."[58] Three days after the public disclosure, the GAC met in special session and concluded that Fuchs could have communicated a great deal of information to the Soviet government. The Committee's findings on the matter were directed immediately to the National Security Council for its January 31 meeting, but some think the Fuchs issue did not affect the Truman H-bomb decision.[59] Teller and Lawrence addressed the Joint Committee on Atomic Energy (JCAE) very soon after the announcement of Fuchs's arrest. They insisted that the U.S. fission and thermonuclear research programs that had been conducted up to that time were completely compromised by the information Fuchs could have passed on to the Soviet Union. They insisted that there was no choice now but to pursue Project Super as rapidly as possible. The JCAE met with President Truman the same day as the Teller-Lawrence hearing and reportedly urged the president to overrule the GAC recommendation against the project.[60]

The Joint Chiefs of Staff reviewed the GAC advisories on the matter of the superbomb, but they insisted that Project Super was a vital deterrent to Soviet aggression, that the commitment of additional material and manpower resources to the project in a measured way would not dislocate the nation's defense effort, and that the United States had to assert its moral and physical leadership by developing the most effective weapons against Communist aggression.[61] Moreover, General Bradley felt compelled to offer his own opinion on the moral arguments surrounding the weapon. In a letter to Defense Secretary Johnson (January 13, 1950), Bradley declared, "It [is] folly to argue in war that one weapon [is] more moral than another."[62] Bradley apparently chose to overlook the internationally acknowledged immorality of the use of chemical and biological weapons in warfare.

Bradley was not alone in his rebuke of GAC advisories on the morality of the weapon. During a January 1950 meeting of the JCAE, Senator McMahon criticized Oppenheimer and his GAC colleagues because "they had gone far beyond their area of competence in opposing the Super on moral and political grounds and for that transgression they would suffer in the judgment of history."[63] As more and more information about the superbomb was leaked to the press, the JCAE and the Pentagon urged President Truman to approve the project.

The debate over Project Super had progressed from a dispassionate review of a scientific and theoretical concept to a cataclysmic moral and ethical dilemma. But the question was ultimately decided on the narrow and somewhat expedient grounds that it was militarily and diplomatically valuable to a major segment of the defense community. The Departments of State and Defense review of the superbomb proposal, which became NSC-68, called for approval of a stepped-up thermonuclear research and development program, but it did not actually address the issues of "nuclear strategy" raised by the GAC and others.[64] Proponents of the weapon believed it to be a way in which the United States could maintain a lead over the Soviet atomic program at a time when the United States had lost its monopoly on fission weapons. There were those who believed that the Soviet Union might actually develop a thermonuclear bomb before the United States. The leaders of the armed services insisted that to both maintain effective deterrence against attack and ensure victory if a war had to be fought, the military would need the most powerful weapons that could be secured.[65]

During Meeting 19 on January 31, 1950, Oppenheimer was handed a presidential press release, which he read to the Committee. President Truman had announced,

> It is part of my responsibility as Commander-in-Chief of the armed forces to see to it that our country is able to defend itself against any possible aggressor. Accordingly, I have directed the Atomic Energy Commission to continue its work on all forms of atomic weapons, including the so-called hydrogen or super-bomb. Like all other work in the field of atomic weapons, it is being and will be carried forward on a basis consistent with the over-all objectives of our program for peace and security. This we shall continue to do until a satisfactory plan for international control of atomic energy is achieved. We shall also continue to examine all those factors that affect our program for peace and this country's security.[66]

It has been argued that Secretary of State Acheson exerted a decisive influence on the outcome of the superbomb discussion. President Truman believed Acheson and those who assisted him on the NSC working group when they claimed that the Russians were not interested in serious negotiations to control atomic weapon development.[67] Acheson and Secretary of Defense Johnson called for a determination of the feasibility of Project Super, to which Truman agreed. According to one account, when Truman looked over the NSC working group paper, Lilienthal began to make one final plea against development of the weapon. The president cut him off, saying, "We have no other course." With this, Truman initialed the recommendation to show his approval, and the meeting ended. It had lasted seven minutes.[68] On February 24, 1950, however, the Joint Chiefs of Staff, with Johnson's assent, requested "an all-out development of hydrogen bombs and means for their production and delivery."[69] On March 10 the president approved the request and set in progress construction of the Savannah River production reactors.

Two years and nine months after the issuance of President Truman's January announcement, the United States successfully detonated the first thermonuclear bomb, code-named Mike, at Eniwetok Atoll in the western Pacific. It was a ten-megaton blast, which, as predicted, was more than five hundred times more powerful than the Hiroshima bomb, a bomb that had killed a hundred thousand people seven years before. Only three years after Mike, the Soviet Union exploded a somewhat smaller thermonuclear bomb in central Asia.[70]

Aftermath of Project Super

The Project Super controversy had many ramifications. Some former AEC officials have argued that the period of Project Super deliberations marked the high-water point of GAC advice and influence. Presumably, the Committee never again enjoyed the stature and authority of expertise that it had enjoyed from 1947 to 1949. Clearly, the advisory career of Oppenheimer began a descent after, and perhaps to some degree as a result of, the issue. However, it is difficult to argue that the GAC became relatively ineffectual over the twenty-seven years to follow, because it continued to advise the AEC as it had in the past.

When the AEC suspended Oppenheimer's security clearance at the end of 1953, reference was made to his opposition to the thermonuclear bomb project in 1949. AEC officials alleged that his condemnation of the superbomb had constituted questionable loyalty. In retrospect, the claim was groundless; his impassioned statement opposing the bomb, in the mind of any reasonable person, cannot be considered an act of disloyalty. In the months following Truman's decision to proceed with Project Super, Oppenheimer and the GAC assisted the AEC in developing the weapon. He chaired the GAC up to Meeting 31 in June 1952.[71] His presidential appointment expired one month later, and his security clearance was permanently terminated in June 1954.

In a December 1953 letter to Oppenheimer explaining why his security clearance was being suspended, AEC General Manager K. D. Nichols wrote,

> It was further reported that you departed from your proper role as an adviser to the Commission by causing the distribution separately and in private, to top personnel at Los Alamos of the majority and minority reports of the General Advisory Committee on development of the hydrogen bomb for the purpose of trying to turn such top personnel against the development of the hydrogen bomb. It was further reported that you were instrumental in persuading other outstanding scientists not to work on the hydrogen-bomb project, and that the opposition to the hydrogen bomb, of which you are the most experienced, most powerful, and most effective member, has definitely slowed down its development.[72]

Oppenheimer's GAC colleagues spoke in his behalf at the hearing. Conant, Rowe, and Buckley, each cosigners of the majority position statement, testified in support of Oppenheimer, helping to rebut Nichols's claim. Fermi, Rabi, and Manley also testified for Oppenheimer's case. Teller was the only witness who left the impression that Oppenheimer impeded the progress of Project Super. The quoted accusation, which was damaging to Oppenheimer's case, was false. The record supports Manley's claim that Oppenheimer did not circulate the GAC report on the thermonuclear bomb. Before Senator McMahon of the JCAE traveled to the Los Alamos Scientific Laboratory in mid-November 1949, the AEC had sent the senator copies of the GAC's October 1949 reports on the superbomb. "And so," according to an account of the Oppenheimer case, "in order that key members of the Los Alamos staff would be as informed as the Senator, the AEC General Manager [Carroll L. Wilson] called John Manley, an associate director at the Los Alamos laboratory and secretary to the GAC, and asked him to show the same report to a select number of Los Alamos officials. Manley carried out the instructions."[73]

In response to a Truman directive regarding thermonuclear weapons, GAC records of late 1951 disclose that the Committee replied, "Were the Committee called on to advise the President as to an appropriate directive, it would recommend the most rapid development of a thermonuclear capability. It had no evidence that the President had any other point in mind."[74]

Why did Oppenheimer and sitting GAC members who had opposed Project Super nevertheless go on offering advice that facilitated the weapon's creation? Scientific and technical advisers may be wise in not opposing administration policies too vehemently, either in private or in public, because such actions tend to undermine public support for science and science education.[75] Members of the GAC must have concluded that once the president made a decision, the debate was over and further dissent would have been improper or disloyal.

In another sense, the Project Super controversy was symptomatic of the dangers posed by trusting an elite group of political, scientific, and military persons to advise in conditions of nearly complete secrecy on an issue that even at the time was recognized to have enormous national and global implications. It is particularly unfortunate that the position statements, submitted as supplemental directives to the AEC by members of the GAC, were not made public at the time they were written but instead kept classified for nearly thirty years.

The GAC statements on Project Super refute the accusation that atomic scientists in positions of trust and responsibility were utterly indifferent and dispassionate about the moral and ethical ramifications of the products of their work. What does seem curious is the moral and ethical distinction members of the Committee drew between the atomic, or fission, bomb used in World War II and the thermonuclear bomb envisioned in 1949. Theoretical calculations made between 1947 and 1949 and the progress being made in scaled-up fission bomb tests in this period led GAC members to reason that thermonuclear bombs were qualitatively different from conventional atomic bombs. They reacted with horror to the conclusion that there was no upper limit to the scale of devastation superbombs could cause, short of global annihilation. Fission bombs did not, in their minds, pose the same dangers or moral dilemmas. Fission bombs were created when a war was under way, but at the time of their deliberations on Project Super, GAC members expected thermonuclear bombs to be developed under peacetime conditions. To them, there was no justification for devising such destructive weapons when the country seemed not to be under a threat of massive attack.

In opposition to the Oppenheimer-GAC position were a multitude of scientific and politico-military experts, with Teller at the forefront. Teller, who would later be appointed to the GAC and who at the time was pursuing thermonuclear-related research at Los Alamos, did not subscribe to the view that scientists must take responsibility for the dangerous tools they constructed.[76] He has stated: "If scientists consider themselves an elite with responsibility for the world resting on their shoulders, they should no longer be scientists. . . . I cannot be responsible for all the consequences of my actions. No one ever is. To believe in such a comprehensive responsibility would be akin to believing in one's own omnipotence."[77] To Teller it was not the scientist's job to decide whether a thermonuclear bomb should be constructed, whether it should be used, or how it should be used. This responsibility rested with the American people and their chosen representatives.[78]

The permanent members of the Los Alamos staff reacted negatively to the GAC report on Project Super: "The GAC report seemed to say: As long as you people work very hard and diligently to make a better bomb, you are doing a fine job; but if you succeed in making real progress toward another kind of nuclear explosion, you are doing something immoral."[79] The Los Alamos scientists were angered by this allegation, and they became even more devoted to researching the bomb. Bethe remembers, "I visited Los Alamos around April 1, 1950, and tried to defend the point of view of the GAC in their decision of October 1949. I encountered almost universal hostility. The entire Laboratory seemed enthusiastic about the project."[80] To many people, once the world entered the nuclear age with the detonation of the Hiroshima and Nagasaki fission bombs, there would be no turning back and no disinvention of the technology even if the scale of devastation attainable by future nuclear weapons assumed apocalyptic dimensions.

As if they were indeed nuclear oracles, the GAC members had the vision and wisdom to recognize that the United States and the Soviet Union could, if they desired, step away from a nuclear weapons arms race. While the general belief is that the nuclear arms race started with the first fission bombs, many scientists in the postwar defense establishment consider the true nuclear arms race to have begun with development of thermonuclear, not fission, weapons. Nevertheless, when the U.S. government was advised by the GAC that forswearing development of the thermonuclear bomb might allow mankind to escape the totality of war in global terms, the Committee's recommendations went unheeded.

A new lab for Project Super

Once President Truman approved Project Super research, the defense science community had to reorganize and adjust to the demands the project would make. In the years between Truman's approval of the project and the successful detonation of the first thermonuclear bomb, there were frequent disputes over where and how research on the weapon should be done. At the heart of these disputes was Teller, the physicist who pioneered theoretical research of the thermonuclear bomb.

Teller became increasingly dissatisfied with the progress of Project Super research conducted at the Los Alamos Scientific Laboratory in the late 1940s and in 1950. He and a number of his associates came to believe that the Los Alamos lab was an inhospitable site for the project's development. According to Bethe, Teller demanded as a condition for his staying that Los Alamos pursue superbomb research on a large scale, or plan for twelve fission bomb tests a year. Bethe claimed that these were unrealistic demands in the postwar years from 1946 to 1950.[81] Teller left Los Alamos in October 1951 and returned to the University of Chicago adamant in his view that a completely new weapons laboratory was needed to research and develop a thermonuclear device in a manner to his liking.[82]

There were those who assumed that Oppenheimer's opposition to Project Super in 1949 meant that he would, for years after, discourage other scientists from working on the hydrogen bomb. They made Oppenheimer the scapegoat for a variety of scientific and managerial problems impeding thermonuclear weapon development. In the period spanning 1951 and early 1952, Strauss maintained that he, Atomic Energy Commissioner Thomas E. Murray, Willard F. Libby, and Berkeley Dean Kenneth S. Pitzer believed that Oppenheimer was responsible for delaying approval of the second weapons lab, the lab that Teller argued was essential to the superbomb program.[83]

The GAC was drawn into the debate surrounding a proposal for a new weapons laboratory. At Meeting 27 in October 1951, Los Alamos Director Bradbury convinced the GAC that a second weapons laboratory was not necessary. He feared that a new lab would bleed Los Alamos of scientific and technical talent, which was in short supply. A new lab would also be a competitor in budgetary politics.

When Teller learned that the Committee had not approved the new lab proposal he was incensed and was reported as "frankly emotional and intuitive" in arguing his case for a new laboratory.[84] A month after Bradbury's meeting with the GAC, Teller met Oppenheimer at Princeton. He told the GAC chairman that Los Alamos was poorly organized for, and only weakly committed to, development of Project Super. He declared that the GAC had been wrong in failing to endorse the proposal for a second laboratory and asked Oppenheimer for, and was given, permission to address the GAC at its 1951 year-end meeting.

Teller met with the GAC on the morning of December 13 at AEC Washington headquarters. He said: "The [Los Alamos] Laboratory staff has become a group of experts, with both the good and bad implications of that term. . . . Its working characteristic is to set itself a sequence of limited objectives."[85] He maintained that this type of laboratory was not suited to, or indeed able to, explore fully the very great possibility of thermonuclear weapons.

Teller argued that interest in the thermonuclear program was low among physicists because the nation was "not in a hot war and because of unexpected rebuffs from the (Los Alamos) Laboratory." Assuring the GAC that he was confident that competent scientists could be recruited to the program if there were the prospect of a new, flexible laboratory, Teller indicated that the structure of the Los Alamos lab had become somewhat rigid and was not conducive to the success of a forward-looking development group.[86]

Teller then described to the Committee the type of laboratory he believed could do the job. He thought the new lab's main interest should be in thermonuclear weapon development and in development of other types of nuclear bombs, but he believed that research at the new lab should be purely scientific. Presumably he did not want the new lab to take on production or industrial responsibilities. Teller envisioned that the lab would have a relatively small staff of 300 technical people, which would be augmented by scientists assigned to the lab under short-term appointments. In the ensuing discussion, Rabi disagreed and estimated that a staff of 1500 or more was a more realistic approximation for the lab Teller anticipated.[87]

Teller exhorted the Committee to act quickly on the matter in view of alleged Soviet advances in thermonuclear research and development. Aware of the paternalistic affection many GAC members had for the Los Alamos lab, Teller sought to reassure the Committee that a new lab would not bring about its degeneration: "Dr. Teller said it would probably have been a mistake to do this [set up a new lab] earlier than 1950 because Los Alamos progress would have been impeded. However, it is urgent now because thermonuclear developments have been unnecessarily slow; the Russians may have advanced more rapidly."[88]

Teller warned the committee not to wait until the first U.S. thermonuclear bomb test before approving the new lab proposal. He reasoned that if the initial test was successful a mood of complacence among scientists might result and they might conclude that a new lab was not needed. If initial tests were failures, on the other hand, he expected that there would be support for creation of a new lab but test failures would make it difficult to recruit scientific talent at the new facility.

Teller suggested the following plans for the new laboratory. It should establish a close relationship with Los Alamos but have a separate and distinct administration. It should rely on the Los Alamos GMX and J Divisions for explosives and tests; the test divisions might be shared by the two labs. The new lab should be staffed by recruiting from outside Los Alamos.[89] Teller told the GAC that concentrating all thermonuclear development in one location, Los Alamos, was a mistake and suggested that the new lab be located at the AEC Nevada test facilities or in some other location distant from Los Alamos. He boldly proposed that a planning group for the lab be created and even suggested who should serve in the group: Fermi, Pitzer, Manson Benedict, Frederick Seitz, John Wheeler, and Wendell Latimer.

Committee members had listened attentively to Teller's speech. In the discussion that followed, Oppenheimer asserted that Teller's proposal "would not go at all unless it went fast." T. Keith Glennan, an AEC commissioner attending the meeting, explained that he had no quarrel with the objectives of the proposal but questioned its methodology. AEC Commissioner Smyth added his own reservations and claimed that the proposal might not be feasible.[90]

Later in the meeting, before the GAC had to make a recommendation on the second lab proposal, Oppenheimer summarized Teller's case for the Committee. Repeating Teller's claim that Los Alamos works from test to test, he noted that Teller considered this wasteful, frustrating, and evidence of a failure to engage in long-range planning. He indicated that Teller thought Los Alamos had not changed its organization since 1943.

As the father of the Los Alamos lab, Oppenheimer may well have been offended by many of Teller's criticisms. However, Oppenheimer was reportedly polite and deferential toward Teller and seemed to sympathize with some of Teller's concerns. At the close of his summary Oppenheimer expressed his personal belief that some new situation was needed through which "Dr. Teller's contributions will be as great as possible."[91] He added that if the new lab proposal was approved, Teller should not be burdened with the administrative duties of directing the lab. Oppenheimer did not want Teller's scientific work in the new laboratory to be impeded by mundane administrative obligations.

The GAC did not want to offend either Teller or Bradbury. After agonizing over possible options to resolve the dispute, the Committee identified what members believed was an appropriate compromise. They advocated creation of a new division at Los Alamos rather than establishment of a completely new lab. The new division would handle broad, long-range assignments and would be insulated from other immediate demands of the greater laboratory. In addition, the new division would be led by someone acceptable to both Bradbury and Teller.[92]

This compromise position was referred to as the intermediate proposal. When the Committee pondered the proposal, Los Alamos sympathizers were able to make their case. Rabi declared, "The proposed step was only part of what needed to be done at Los Alamos, and that it should not be taken in such a way that Los Alamos was confronted with a piece of paper presenting a division in which the Laboratory had had no part, but rather that a group should first talk over the proposal with the Los Alamos people in a most friendly and sympathetic way."[93]

Darol K. Froman of the Los Alamos lab and Brigadier General Kenneth E. Fields of the AEC Military Applications Division both advised the Committee to reject Teller's new lab proposal. Froman argued that if approved the new lab would create administrative disarray and would lead to interlab competition for scarce talent. GAC member Libby expressed sympathy with Froman's concern that the large requirements for trained manpower at the new lab would create problems.[94] Then Fields explained that recent changes made at Los Alamos had created favorable conditions for establishing the new division called for in the intermediate proposal. He presented a comprehensive study of the Los Alamos work load and insisted that previous impositions made on atomic weapon testing and production work at Los Alamos were being alleviated by the delegation of much of this work to new facilities in Sandia, New Mexico, Kansas City, Missouri, and Burlington, Iowa.[95]

The GAC adopted the intermediate option, avoiding the elaborate and expensive problems of siting and building a second weapons lab. The Committee believed that this course of action would not harm Los Alamos, whereas a new laboratory might cause "general havoc" at Los Alamos. This recommendation was not to be an irreversible step; the new division could be moved to a new site if events or conditions justified such an action.[96]

In this exchange Teller had lost a battle but eventually won the war. Months after failing to win AEC and GAC endorsement of his second lab proposal, he joined forces with Ernest O. Lawrence and Herbert F. York; Teller and his allies were able to convince the secretary of the air force, several other top Pentagon officials, and Secretary of State Dean Acheson that a new weapons laboratory should be organized.

This effort represented a major end run around the AEC and posed a threat to the agency's monopoly control of the government's atomic weapon research and development work. Consequently, the AEC and the GAC reconsidered the second weapons lab proposal and approved it before the Department of Defense lab initiative progressed further. Operated under contract by the University of California, the new facility was to be located on the grounds of UC-Berkeley's Mark I accelerator. In the accord reached with the AEC, Livermore sponsors negotiated an arrangement with Bradbury that promised peaceful cooperation between the Livermore and Los Alamos laboratories. The new Livermore lab was officially established in July 1952 and by September of the same year Teller was again proceeding with Project Super research, this time at Livermore. He began with a staff of 123 scientific and technical personnel, but within only two years Livermore's staff grew to more than 1000.[97]

After major theoretical breakthroughs by Teller and Ulam, scientists at both Los Alamos and Livermore cooperated to achieve the successful test of the thermonuclear bomb (often referred to as the hydrogen bomb) on October 31, 1952. GAC proceedings on the second-laboratory issue, which occurred in 1951, reveal the Committee's constant efforts to protect the Los Alamos program while simultaneously arbitrating disagreements among the leaders of the defense science community. Teller was undoubtedly pleased that a second weapons lab was created; however, Livermore had no role in development of the first H-bomb test series and had its first successful test in 1955.

Project Super was one of the greatest tests of the GAC. The decision on whether to approve a crash program to develop a superbomb pulled the Committee into uncustomary political, moral, and ethical domains. Each GAC member at this time must have been reminded of the moral and ethical debate that surrounded the decision to use the atomic bomb during the war.[98] The majority and minority supplemental statements submitted to the AEC in October 1949 articulated the critical issues in this decision.

GAC members, and others who shared their reservations about the implications of the thermonuclear bomb, considered development of the Soviet Union's atomic bomb to be a crossroads in history and recognized that a nuclear arms race was about to begin. Because the superbomb appeared to be both expensive and difficult to make, because it would undercut new fission bomb work in progress, because it had as yet undetermined military utility, and because its destructive power would be catastrophically immense, the group reasoned that the weapon should not be developed. If the United States renounced thermonuclear bomb development the country could gain "considerable moral prestige at very little cost."[99] They hoped that the American renunciation example, the technical uncertainty associated with the weapon's development, and the device's drain on national economic and technical resources would convince the Soviet government not to pursue its own thermonuclear bomb program.

It serves no purpose to speculate on how history might have been changed if the United States had decided unilaterally not to develop thermonuclear weapons. What is important is that a group of the nation's most outstanding scientists and engineers clearly understood and anticipated many of the ramifications of successful development of a thermonuclear weapon in a period when such a device was only a theoretical possibility. The group understood that if the United States went ahead with superbomb development, the Soviet Union would have no choice but to do the same. They were confident that the current U.S. stockpile of fission bombs was so much larger than that of the Soviet Union that U.S. national security would not be jeopardized by suspending superbomb development, or better yet, by seeking an international agreement to prohibit thermonuclear weapon development.

In interpreting the prescient and evocative words of the GAC in terms of today's situation, it should be understood that many of the reservations that members had about the weapon stemmed from its technical uncertainty, high cost, and questionable means of delivery to an enemy target. Bethe has argued that the members' skepticism regarding the technical feasibility of the classical superbomb proved to be justified.[100] The GAC did not object to development of new and more powerful fission bombs; in fact, there is no record that the Committee ever collectively opposed superbomb development before the fall of 1949. Moreover, there is no evidence from Committee records that members ever manifested their 1949 opposition to Project Super in the years following President Truman's approval of the project. Once Teller and Ulam had achieved their remarkable theoretical breakthroughs in the spring of 1951, the GAC enthusiastically endorsed thermonuclear research. In June 1951 Oppenheimer was quoted as saying, "If this had been the technical proposal in 1949, [the GAC] would have never opposed the development."[101] He described Teller's new development as "technically so sweet that you could not argue about that" and told Teller, "You go ahead and do it and you argue about what to do about it only after you have had your technical success."[102] This remark stands in striking contrast to Oppenheimer's position on Project Super in 1949. Some may interpret this to mean that his October 1949 reservations about the project were not so much based on moral and ethical issues as on the scientific and technical problems he knew had to be resolved. Others may interpret it as an enthusiastic compliment to the genius of the Teller-Ulam research achievement, one that does not deny the moralistic sentiments expressed in the GAC statements of 1949.

The GAC's review of the second-laboratory proposal makes it clear that the members' reluctance to support Teller's proposal was a result of fears that a competing lab would hurt the Los Alamos lab. The Committee's intermediate option was an attempt to satisfy most of Teller's demands without alienating Bradbury and his Los Alamos staff, not an attempt to impede Project Super; on the contrary, the hope was that a satisfactory working relationship would facilitate superbomb work.

The GAC's recommendations against Project Super required considerable courage on the part of Committee members. The statements stand as evidence that scientists and engineers engaged in defense-related research can appreciate and anticipate the moral and ethical implications surrounding the use of the products of their research. The Committee's warning that the superbomb was a weapon of genocide should be heeded by those governments armed today with thermonuclear weapons. It would be bitterly ironic if a government that reviled the genocidal atrocities of Nazi Germany either intentionally, or accidentally, destroyed an enemy by use of thermonuclear weapons.

7 The GAC and Project Gabriel: Radioactive fallout

FROM THE DAY THE FIRST ATOMIC BOMB was successfully detonated at the Trinity site in New Mexico, scientists were captivated by the unique and unexplained phenomena produced by the blasts. While the defense establishment was interested in the tactical and strategic military potential of atomic weapons, the scientific establishment was intrigued by the scientific anomalies that accompanied each atomic explosion. At Meeting 2, GAC members acknowledged that the behavior of the atomic weapons fired up to that time could not be "accurately predicted in advance." During this February 1947 meeting, members agreed that much more testing was necessary. Lee A. DuBridge warned that there was a need for "thorough and adequate preparation since a test would be a major undertaking in personnel, time, and money, and would involve physical and political dangers."[1] It became apparent, as above-ground atomic testing proceeded, that each explosion had considerable potential effects far beyond the point of detonation.

The AEC's investigation of the problem of large-scale contamination from the explosions of many atomic bombs was called Project Gabriel. Throughout the 1950s, the GAC examined and critiqued numerous aspects of Project Gabriel. Relying heavily on the field work of its subcommittees, the Committee analyzed a vast number of AEC studies and reports concerning the deposition of radionuclides produced in above-ground atomic detonations. How the GAC grappled with the many unknowns surrounding the dangers of radioactive fallout illustrates the style of Committee deliberations and the global experimental nature of each atomic and thermonuclear blast in that era. Moreover, the Committee's advisories about atomic fallout reveal the nature of judgments by the physical scientists and engineers who served on the GAC in a time period when the world public grew increasingly concerned about the dangers and unknowns of fallout. GAC advice and recommendations on this matter, of course, were rendered under conditions of strict official secrecy. It is also significant that few of the GAC members who considered Gabriel and problems of fallout had been on the original committee.

In detonations greater than 100 kilotons, part of the fallout produced by the blast does not fall to the ground in the vicinity of the explosion but instead rises high into the troposphere and then into the stratosphere where it circulates around the earth. Over months or years, the radioactive material descends, contaminating the whole surface of the globe with radiation doses that are, of course, far weaker than those produced near the blast zone. The potential for global catastrophe was publicly acknowledged years before detonation of the first thermonuclear bomb. In contemplating the effects of a thermonuclear bomb explosion, Albert Einstein said in 1950, "Radioactive poisoning of the atmosphere and hence annihilation of any life on earth has been brought within the range of technical possibilities."[2]

The problem of fallout

GAC Meeting 36 was called to order in Washington, D.C., on August 17, 1953. The Committee devoted a great deal of attention to Project Gabriel.[3] Willard F. Libby briefed fellow members about a Rand Corporation study, RM-1128-AEC, Project Sunshine. The Rand study was made available to the AEC eleven days before Meeting 36.[4]

Libby told the panel that, like earlier Gabriel studies, Project Sunshine concluded, "The main global hazard is the ultimate ingestion of fission product strontium-90." The study determined that strontium-90 (Sr-90) was an abundant fission product and bone seeker. "[The] hazard is the development of bone cancer."[5] Author Jonathan Schell offers further clarification of the dangers:

> Two of the most harmful radioactive isotopes present in the fallout are strontium-90 (with a half-life of twenty-eight years) and cesium-137 (with a half-life of thirty years). They are taken up into the food chain through the roots of plants or through direct ingestion by animals, and contaminate the environment from within. Strontium-90 happens to resemble calcium in its chemical composition, and therefore finds its way into the human diet through dairy products and is eventually deposited by the body in the bones, where it is thought to cause bone cancer. Every person in the world now has in his bones a measurable deposit of strontium-90 traceable to the fallout from atmospheric nuclear testing.[6]

According to Libby, Project Sunshine had determined that, because of the nature of the fission precursors, "It is believed that Sr-90 (Strontium-90) will probably plate out on the particles present in the explosion cloud; and, hence, when the particles fall out, the strontium is absorbed in water and uptaken in plants."[7] Libby outlined the fundamental assumptions of the Sunshine Model:

1. That all of the Sr-90 is uniformly distributed over the surface of the globe.
2. That there is no atmospheric storage mechanism which will permit Sr-90 to decay significantly before it is deposited on the surface.
3. That the deposited material is completely available for incorporation into the biosphere.
4. That the bones of an individual growing in an environment having a given ratio of Sr-90 to natural strontium will contain Sr-90 and natural strontium in the same ratio (no isotopic fractionation).
5. That the amount of agriculturally available natural strontium per acre is 60 pounds.
6. That the normal U.S. adult contains 0.7 gram of strontium in his bones.
7. That one microcurie of Sr-90 per adult individual is the maximum amount which can be retained safely in the body.[8]

The prevailing estimate was that one kiloton of fission explosive yielded one gram of Sr-90. In the detonation of the first U.S. thermonuclear bomb an explosive power of 10,400 kilotons, or 10.4 megatons, had been unleashed. In the early 1950s many scientists suspected that this and other atomic explosions set off by the United States, the Soviet Union, and the United Kingdom posed a serious problem for humankind and for global ecology. Some began to ask what the maximum tolerable dosage of Sr-90 might be that the world population could safely absorb from the environment? In other words, how many nuclear explosions of some total magnitude would it take to reach a catastrophic threshold?

Incredible as it may seem, the Project Sunshine study postulated an answer to this question. The GAC was told "that the *minimum* [fission] bomb yield required to bring the population of the world up to maximum tolerable amount of contained Sr-90 is *25,000 megatons*. This is believed to be a firm lower limit, on the ground that the quantitative assumptions were made on the pessimistic side."[9]

Libby reported that an earlier Gabriel estimate indicated the number lay in the interval from 20,000 to 90,000 megatons. From 1945 to 1963, the AEC reported that 310 nuclear explosions were conducted by the United States. This figure includes the wartime atomic bombs as well as a small number of underground contained nuclear blasts. U.S. nuclear weapons tests in this period totaled 263. The first and second thermonuclear bombs were detonated by the United States in 1952. From 1953 until the signing of the Partial Test Ban Treaty of 1963, there were 231 announced U.S. nuclear weapons tests.[10] The vast majority of these 231 tests were probably detonations of thermonuclear devices of multimegaton yield.

Correspondingly, the Soviet Union conducted, according to the AEC, at least 126 nuclear test detonations from 1949 through 1963. Like the United States, the vast majority of Soviet tests (about 120) were carried out after successful development of a thermonuclear bomb. Consequently, the bulk of Soviet testing in the late 1950s and early 1960s were of the thermonuclear type capable of multimegaton explosive power. In one test, the Soviet Union was said to have detonated a 60-megaton nuclear device.[11] Moreover, between 1952 and 1963 the United Kingdom carried out twenty-three nuclear tests and France another seven. Given the frequency and magnitude of the above-ground nuclear testing conducted by the United States, the Soviet Union, and other nations, the 20,000-megaton danger threshold estimated in Gabriel calculations could have been met and exceeded at some future date if above-ground nuclear testing had not been prohibited.

The question remained, How much Sr-90 could be safely cumulated in the biosphere (how many megatons of explosive power could be produced over years of tests) before the Sr-90 danger threshold was met or exceeded? The estimate of 25,000 megatons was based on an extrapolation of the amount of Sr-90 dispersed by these explosions and the cumulative effect of probable exposure for any single human being. Uncertainty existed, however, as to precisely how much Sr-90 it would take to trigger the onset of bone cancer. The GAC was told, "The tolerable figure of one microcurie of Sr-90 per person was arrived at by the International Commission on Radiological Protection and is based on radium experience. One microcurie of Sr-90 (0.54 Mev betas) was taken as biologically equivalent to one-tenth microcurie of radium (6 Mev alphas). Carcinogen effects are observed with radium at one microcurie per human. (Secretary's note: How valid the quantitative figure for Sr-90 is, and just what significance should be attached to it seem at present unclear.)"[12]

In his diary recounting his experiences as President Eisenhower's scientific and technical advisor, George B. Kistiakowsky wrote, "Since we know virtually nothing about the danger of low-intensity radiation, we might as well agree that the average population dose from man-made radiation should be no greater than that which the population already receives from natural causes; and that any individual in that population shouldn't be exposed to more than three times that amount, the latter figure, of course, totally arbitrary."[13] Kistiakowsky made this entry on April 13, 1960, nearly seven years after Meeting 36 (August 1953). Throughout the decade of the 1950s, and virtually up through the time of the 1963 Partial Test Ban Treaty, scientists and physicians apparently could not prove with scientific and medical certainty that exposure to the infinitesimal quantities of atomic bomb–generated radionuclides measurable then posed a significant risk to human health.

A year and a half before Meeting 36, the GAC listened to a report on the probable physiological effects of large-scale radioactive contamination. The report was presented by the government's top anatomical and forensic pathologist, Dr. Shields Warren, a physician and professor of pathology at Harvard Medical School from 1925 to 1965 and director of the AEC's Division of Biology and Medicine from 1947 to 1952. A pioneer in the study of the somatic effects of exposure to atomic radiation, Warren directed the Cancer Research Institute of the New England Deaconess Hospital from 1951 to 1968. Moreover, Warren had been chief of the naval medical team that visited Hiroshima and Nagasaki immediately after the Japanese surrender in order to examine casualties of the atomic bomb raids.[14]

Dr. Warren told the GAC that "the conclusion had been reached that to explode 10 (to the 5th) nominal atomic bombs would render large portions of the earth's surface uninhabitable because of the alpha radioactivity in the air. This would be dispersed in a band about 30 (degrees) wide in the northern hemisphere; little would be exchanged between hemispheres.[15] Since the explosive power of atomic bombs was discussed in kiloton units at this time, a 10^5 bomb total, using the generally accepted figure of 20-kiloton yield per fission bomb, would yield 2000 megatons, or the equivalent of the explosive power of two billion tons of TNT.

Warren said that his estimate was reasonably sound and conservative in terms of the order of magnitude, but he warned that even one-tenth his original estimate might produce serious fallout. He added that besides major global atmospheric contamination, there was the problem of the local hazard of external radiation from the cloud after a burst. Consequently, in the period when South Pacific and Nevada above-ground atomic testing began to move swiftly forward, AEC officials and their science advisers had been alerted to the possible health dangers that local or regional fallout posed to downwind populations. Warren offered another foreboding when he told the AEC and the Committee that much more research had to be done on the ingestion of Sr-90 from crops grown on contaminated soil.[16]

Many of the points that Warren raised in 1951 resurfaced in GAC Meeting 36 in 1953. At the time, the United States had publicly acknowledged conducting forty-three atomic test detonations, excluding the wartime Hiroshima and Nagasaki explosions. The Soviet Union and the United Kingdom each had begun above-ground testing in earnest. By August 1953, official sources reported that the Soviet Union had exploded five atomic devices, while the United Kingdom had conducted one nuclear test. In late 1952 and early 1953 the United States fired the first and second thermonuclear devices.[17] These thermonuclear bombs produced lofting effects reported to be beyond any of the norms encountered in previous atomic bomb blasts. Radioactive materials were lifted into, and circulated about, the stratosphere.

Those serving on the GAC in this period identified the unknowns, examined the dangers, and sometimes proposed solutions in their advisories to the AEC on atomic testing. In one exchange, Eugene P. Wigner, a professor of mathematical physics, debated the dangers posed by inhaling radioactive particulate matter with John C. Bugher, a physician-pathologist serving as AEC chief of biology and medicine. Wigner claimed that if radiation originated from one point, it was more likely to start cancer than if it was distributed uniformly, on account of the high radiation density near the source. Consequently, distance from the blast zone would be inversely related to the probability that exposure to bomb fallout would produce cancer in humans. Bugher challenged Wigner's claim, saying, "There exist no unequivocal data on this question . . . it is very hard to study experimentally since human subjects cannot be used." He declared, "At the moment the data do not support the idea that particles are more dangerous than at an evenly distributed source."[18] In responding to Bugher, Wigner asked for data on tests with mice but was told that no such information was yet available.

Again, it is useful to consider the remarks of Kistiakowsky on this subject, even though they were written seven years after this meeting. In a diary entry of May 13, 1960, he recounted a discussion by members of the White House–level Federal Radiation Council, a body that he chaired at the time: "At issue was the reference to a linear relation between dose and effect, which as I still believe is entirely unnecessary for the definition of the current radiation guidelines since they are pulled out of thin air without any knowledge on which to base them."[19] From this it can be inferred that research of the type Wigner had demanded in

1953 was as yet still inconclusive or incomplete seven years later.

Wigner's inquiry at Meeting 36 about the pattern of fallout deposition and measured concentration levels was immediately relevant. U.S. tests in Nevada and Utah, as well as those conducted in the South Pacific, produced fallout carried hundreds or thousands of miles from the point of detonation. Moreover, Soviet atomic explosions in the Arctic yielded tremendous volumes of radionuclides, which were then carried across vast areas of the Arctic polar reaches and North America by prevailing wind patterns.

Arnold Kramish, a former AEC staff physicist (1947–1951) and a researcher with Rand Corporation, the consulting firm conducting much of the Project Gabriel research for the AEC, attended Meeting 36. He joined in the Wigner-Bugher exchange, explaining to the Committee, "There are considerable fluctuations in fallout density in the U.S., by a factor of about 100."[20] Walter G. Whitman of the GAC observed that arable land might have a greater-than-average fallout, since it tended to receive more rain and was likely to be near nuclear attack target areas.

As the Committee pondered the problem of counteracting human exposure to radioactive fallout, the minutes reveal that "it was . . . suggested that there may be a possibility of prophylactic control of the Sr-90 hazard by feeding people more strontium."[21] The reasoning behind this proposal was that ingestion of natural (nonradioactive) strontium and perhaps additional quantities of calcium, may allow people to reduce or mitigate their absorption of the radioactive strontium contained in fallout; the hope was that extra natural strontium would serve to screen out radioactive strontium, both forms of which are deposited in the skeleton.

Underscoring the high level of medical uncertainty surrounding the problem of fallout, Kramish stressed the need to gather more accurate information on the scientific parameters of the Project Sunshine calculations. He remarked, "It appears possible to obtain very valuable data on many of the integral features of the problem by instituting a world-wide sampling program for Sr-90, since the amount which has already been released (about 10 kilograms) is probably sufficient to be detectable in samples of inert and biological materials throughout the world. In addition, data are required on the natural strontium content of soils, waters, and biological materials."[22]

Project Sunshine researchers asked for a major sampling program and a pilot project. Plans called for sampling six global areas. Regions mentioned as possible sampling test sites were Utah ("a heavy fallout area"), Kansas ("a grain area"), England, Japan, and a South American country.[23] Subsequent records indicate that the AEC did institute an international testing program, although sampling sites may not have been located precisely in the above areas.[24]

Toward the close of Meeting 36, the Committee recommended that the AEC launch "a parallel biomedical effort on the carcinogenic action of ingested or inhaled radioactive materials . . . closely coordinated with the sampling program."[25] GAC members wanted this effort to determine how the particulate material was formed, how best to collect particulates to ensure that smaller particulate matter was not overlooked, and how to improve fallout predictions.

At one point, the Committee examined empirical data that measured the prevalence of Sr-90 in the United States (Table 7.1). Libby explained that it was "very convenient to determine the Sr-90 by milking it for the short-lived yttrium daughter and counting the yttrium."[26] He said this work was being performed by Dr. Merril Eisenbud of the AEC, Dr. J. Laurence Kulp at Columbia University, and by Libby's own group at the University of Chicago laboratory facilities.

The "rib from a Harvard man" listed in Table 7.1 was a human rib extracted through a surgical operation and then later examined. The "Harvard man" reference may have been a somewhat ghoulish attempt at humor by research scientists. The rib and the reference to the stillborn infant indicates that means were apparently available as early as 1953 to gather Sr-90 samples from human beings. In his review of these findings, Libby indicated that the Sr-90 measured in the Chicago baby was "presumably accumulated mainly in the last two or three months of gestation, (and) corresponds to about $\frac{1}{1000}$th of the tolerance figure."[27] What is important is that the measurement of Sr-90 uptake measured in these human samples denoted the likely rate of uptake by the general sampling area population and to a degree by the continental population of North America. Obviously there could not be a perfect correspondence between amounts detected in these human samples and amounts absorbed

Table 7.1. **Strontium-90 sampling data presented to the GAC at Meeting 36, August 17–19, 1953**

Sample and Source	Strontium-90 Activity
Stillborn fullterm baby, Chicago	128 ± d/min or 3.6 d/min−g Ca
Rib from a Harvard man	.8 d/min−g Ca
Filtered seawater, Santa Monica, Calif.	Less than 22 ± 8d/min−80 liters
Clam shells, Long Island, N.Y.	.04 d/min−g Ca
Wisconsin cheese (1 month old)	3 ± 0.3 d/min−g Ca
Wisconsin cat bone (2 years old)	4 ± 0.4 d/min−g Ca
Montana cat (6 months old, fed on milk from range cows)	10 ± 0.1 d/min−g Ca
Soil from Lamont, N.Y.	24 ± 2 d/min−g Ca

Note: d = disintegrations.

into the bones of people living in that time, but the human samples were used to approximate how much Sr-90 was being absorbed into the skeletal structure of people living in North America. Since no place on the North American continent escaped atomic fallout in the period, no person living on the continent could have escaped exposure. (It is noteworthy that Project Teacup tests conducted February 23, 1955, resulted in Chicago registering on March 1, 1955, the highest Geiger counter readings ever measured from the atmosphere. In the same period, New York City's readings of radioactivity in the air were four times higher than normal.[28])

Eight months later at Meeting 39, held in late March and early April of 1954, Libby made a follow-up report to the GAC, presenting new data on the worldwide distribution of Sr-90. He disclosed that stillborn Chicago and Utah babies contained "about 0.15 to 0.20 units," with one unit representing $\frac{1}{1000}$th of the tolerance ratio of Sr-90 to calcium. Stillborn babies from India measured 0.05 units, much less than the U.S. figures. Libby went on to say that teeth extracted from New England adults and teeth removed from adult Londoners had no detectable traces of Sr-90. Wisconsin cheeses contained about ten times more units of Sr-90 than the stillborn Chicago infant, while European cheeses measured slightly lower in Sr-90 content than Wisconsin cheeses. Wisconsin calves were reported to register one to two units of Sr-90.[29] The references to milk, cheese, and calves were used to gauge Sr-90 content in dairy products. People were ingesting Sr-90 as they consumed the dairy products of cows that had grazed on grass on which radionuclides had been deposited.

The findings shown in Table 7.1 demonstrate that under Project Sunshine the AEC had launched a concerted effort to monitor the distribution of Sr-90 in the biosphere. Nevertheless, Libby and other scientists complained about the unavailability of human samples. Libby had suggested to the Committee at Meeting 36 that because "stillborn babies are often turned over to the physician for disposal, (they) might be a practical source" of information about human exposures.[30]

Data from fallout victims

There were, on several occasions, accidental human exposures to radioactive particulate matter that enabled scientists to gather physiological data concerning the effects on humans. From March 1 through May 14, 1954, the U.S. government exploded six thermonuclear bombs in the Castle series of test detonations. These tests were conducted in the Bikini

Islands. One shot, code-named Bravo, was a 15-megaton ground detonation that produced a cloud height of about 110,000 feet.[31] In his comments about the detonation, researcher Jonathan Schell wrote,

> On one of the few occasions when local fallout was generated by a test explosion in the multi-megaton range, the fifteen-megaton bomb tested on Bikini Atoll, which was exploded seven feet above the surface of a coral reef, "caused substantial contamination over an area of more than seven thousand square miles." . . .
> Perhaps the second big surprise was the extent of harmful fallout; this came to light in the fifteen-megaton test at Bikini in 1954, when, to the amazement of the designers of the test, fallout began to descend on Marshall Islanders and on American servicemen manning weather stations on atolls at supposedly safe distances from the explosion.[32]

In a short announcement, the *New York Times* reported on March 25, 1954, that a U.S. hydrogen bomb blast had "astonished" scientists. Congressman Chet Holifield of the Joint Committee on Atomic Energy (JCAE), who apparently witnessed the test, described the explosion as "so far beyond what was predicted that you might say it was out of control."[33] Five days earlier, the *Times* disclosed that the JCAE wanted to know why 315 people were permitted close enough to the blast area to be exposed to radiation. The article revealed, "Japanese fishermen [of the *Lucky Dragon*] 80 miles away, just outside the hazard zone, were seriously burned in a shower of nuclear ashes. Twenty-eight American technicians and 264 natives on the islands more than 100 miles away from the flashpoint were exposed to milder radiation. The blast was three to four times greater than expected and was 600 to 700 times more powerful than the Hiroshima bomb which killed 60,000 people."[34]

Oliver E. Buckley, James B. Fisk, Eger V. Murphree, Isidor I. Rabi, John von Neumann, John C. Warner, Whitman, and Wigner were present at Meeting 40, held in late May 1954. At this time Herbert Scoville, Jr., reported to the GAC on the Bravo test and on the Castle series of explosions. Scoville, who held a doctorate in physical chemistry and had worked as a senior scientist at Los Alamos under an AEC contract (1946–48), was technical director of Armed Forces Special Weapons Projects from 1948 to 1955, and it was in this capacity that he spoke before the GAC.[35]

While the code name of the specific shot was deleted in classification review by the government, declassified GAC minutes report that the following remarks by Scoville referred to the 15-megaton Bikini test: "Dr. Scoville described the general fallout pattern [deleted]. From available data it appears that in an area of over 5,000 square miles of ocean, a dose of 500r (r2 rads) would have been obtained in the first 50 hours from shot time; and in an area of over 1,000 square miles, a dose of 2000r would have been obtained in the first 50 hours. It was pointed out that the natives on the island of Rongerik received 150r before being evacuated."[36] In this shot residents of Rongerik, Rongelap, Ailinginal, and Utirik islands were exposed to fallout that ranged from 14 to 175 roentgens (200 roentgens was normally considered the minimum fatal dose).[37] No islander died immediately, but all those exposed suffered radiation burns, loss of hair, and seriously reduced blood counts.

The Rongerik Atoll is located 124 miles (or 200 kilometers) from the Bikini Atoll test site and 372 miles (or 600 kilometers) from the Eniwetok Atoll site.[38] These islands are all part of the Marshall Islands, a U.S. trust territory during this testing period. Through recent lawsuits against the U.S. government, Marshall Islanders have won partial compensation for the medical costs for treatment of cancer that they allege was contracted as a result of the U.S. above-ground testing conducted in the Marshalls twenty-five to thirty-five years ago.[39] The medical analysis of islanders and others exposed to radiation in the vicinity of some of the tests were a source of human sampling in studies of the effects of nuclear fallout.

U.S. medical personnel assisted in the treatment of the twenty-three Japanese fishermen of the *Lucky Dragon*. Most of these fishermen suffered serious radiation burns, and one, Aikichi Kuboyama, died September 24, 1954. The United States formally apologized for the incident and paid $2 million in reparations for the loss of Japanese life and property.[40]

After listening to the Scoville briefing, the Committee reviewed several aspects of the worldwide, long-range fallout problem. The group was informed by von Neumann, "The Sunshine Studies indicated that about 10,000 megatons seemed to be the limit with a concept of 'tolerance' that may be too strict."[41] As mentioned previously, in August 1953, less than a year before this meeting, the Committee had been told that 25,000 megatons was possibly the maximum tolerable threshold of cumulated detonations, above which human health was imperiled.

During Meeting 40, the Committee assessed the potential use of fallout as a weapon itself. Fisk asserted that the GAC should "point out their interest in fallout studies from both offensive and defensive points of view."[42] In other words, it might be feasible to assault the population of an enemy country not by direct nuclear bombardment but by distant atomic detonations, perhaps even in the attacking country. These detonations might loft enough radioactive material into the upper atmosphere that, carried by prevailing winds, the radionuclide deposition would be lethal to people of the enemy country. The GAC might well have been warning the AEC that such a threat would be posed to the North American continent by Soviet testing in the Arctic regions of the Soviet Union.

Public relations and atomic fallout

During Meeting 40 the GAC complimented the AEC staff for their work in researching fallout, dosage, and rates of decay. At this time the GAC performed a public relations service for the AEC in the matter of atomic fallout: "The members agreed with Mr. Whitman's suggestion that the Commission get out some authoritative information on the fallout problem as soon as possible. All agreed that an incorrect statement could cause trouble but that periodic public statements on fallout effects, similar to Mr. Strauss' statement on the Castle tests, would be very helpful."[43]

At Meeting 51 in late October 1956, the GAC members were Fisk, Warner, Wigner, Jesse W. Beams, Warren C. Johnson, Edwin M. McMillan, T. Keith Glennan, Edward Teller, and Robert E. Wilson. This group also took up the issue of public relations problems regarding atomic fallout. During one session, the GAC decided that, as a result of a briefing they had been given on Project Sunshine and due to recent articles in the public press, the Committee would prepare a public statement. The statement was touted as something "which described in qualitative, although factual, terms the present situation regarding radiation exposures from weapons test activities."[44]

When public concern about the dangers of radioactive fallout escalated in the mid-1950s, there emerged a sizable political constituency advocating a complete termination of U.S. above-ground atomic testing. *Newsweek* magazine declared in October 1954, "The question, 'how dangerous is fallout,' is potentially the most dangerous gap in modern man's scientific knowledge." *Time* magazine concurred in this view, commenting, "Without additional information, it would be impossible to estimate how many H-explosions (in tests or in war) would be necessary to do damage to the whole earth."[45] While negotiations moved forward with the United Kingdom and the Soviet Union on a proposed cessation of above-ground nuclear detonations, the AEC queried the GAC for an opinion on how such an agreement might affect the future ability of the United States to develop and test nuclear weapons. This matter and concerns about atomic fallout were central in GAC Meeting 58 held in early May 1958 at AEC Washington headquarters.

Beams, Fisk, Glennan, Johnson, McMillan, Murphree, Teller, Warner, and Wilson were still on the GAC at the time of Meeting 58. In formal terms, the AEC asked the GAC whether the U.S. weapons program would be detrimentally affected if atomic testing were confined to underground detonations. The GAC devoted two half-day sessions to this question, and their deliberations culminated in the following response:

> The General Advisory Committee feels that the country is approaching a crisis with regard to the continuation of atomic tests on anything like the present scale. While most of the widely disseminated arguments against further tests are exaggerated and unsound, there is widespread uneasiness in the country over the prospect of constantly increasing radioactive fallout, and even many sincere scientists share this feeling. The statements of the President (Eisenhower) regarding a possible change of policy after the completion of the present series of tests (Hardtack series) make it important in our unanimous opinion that a statement should be issued before the end of the present series, indicating that hereafter we are willing to restrict tests so that future fallout will be sharply reduced.[46]

The GAC statement went on to suggest what the AEC should and should not concede in the test ban negotiations:

> In our opinion the least concession which the Commission could offer with prospect of winning over a substantial part of the sincere opposition would be to say that hereafter the great bulk of our tests would be carried out underground, with no fallout production, and that tests in the atmosphere would be limited so that the maximum fission yield from the tests of the free nations in any year would not exceed a megaton providing the Russians agreed to a similar limitation. If they did so, and our allies cooperated, we would reduce the addition to potential fallout to between 10% and 20% of the average annual addition resulting from the tests made during the past four years. What is more important, in view of the rate of radioactive decay, etc., we would *actually not increase the total amount of potential radioactive fallout beyond that prevailing this summer.*
> Admittedly the policing of this agreement would not be easy, but an international inspection agency could be created which could determine compliance fairly accurately for each side. And, as a matter of fact, such a policy would penalize us so little that we might continue it for some time even if Russia did not cooperate. Actually, the only tests of any size and importance which now appear could not be carried out underground would be in connection with the development of anti-missiles and some "Plowshare" tests.
> While a majority of the Committee recommends that the first proposal be the one made, it would be possible to go still further if necessary and eliminate all above-ground testing for a period of say,

two years. This would make it much harder to develop anti-missiles. It would prevent tests on some peaceful uses such as "ditch-digger" unless special exceptions were made for them, possibly under international inspection. Such an agreement could not be readily policed, especially on small weapons, and would probably be evaded by the Russians unless there were extensive policing inside Russia, but it would practically eliminate any addition to fallout during the period the agreement was effective.

The Committee is unanimously agreed that to go any further than this in the restriction of testing would seriously endanger the security of the United States.[47]

This statement made it obvious that the GAC was going far beyond simply offering scientific advice devoid of political or social content. Members felt compelled to offer their observations on international relations and Soviet military policy. However, the nature of the question posed by the AEC, and the coincidence of political and diplomatic affairs with scientific and technical aspects of atomic testing, seemed to warrant the GAC response.

Yet only a year later, the GAC issued a rare public statement on the problem of fallout. Disseminated as a "Statement by the General Advisory Committee to the U.S. Atomic Energy Commission," it was reproduced in its entirety in the June 1959 issue of *Bulletin of the Atomic Scientists*. Portions of this statement follow:

We find that the Atomic Energy Commission has released all significant fallout data to other agencies and to the public. Certain information as to the estimated yield of various weapon tests and certain other factors bearing on the radioactive content of the upper atmosphere have defense implications which require classification, but the significant information on actual fallout throughout the free world that the AEC has developed has been released.

The principal result of later information has been to *reduce* somewhat the earlier estimates of *future* fallout of debris which has been injected into the stratosphere near the Equator by U.S. and U.K. tests. The debris injected last autumn by USSR tests into the stratosphere in the more northerly latitudes has been falling out quite rapidly and is largely confined to the Northern Hemisphere.

A reasonable estimate of the amount of fission products that has been injected into the stratosphere by all nuclear tests is 65 megatons (TNT equivalent) of fission energy. This corresponds to about 100 pounds of strontium-90 in the entire stratosphere. It is estimated that fully 50 per cent (50 pounds) of this strontium-90 has already fallen out. This means that half of the total strontium-90 injected into the stratosphere still remains there.

The present state of knowledge does not permit a full evaluation of the biological effects of fallout. However, in order to place the hazard of fallout in proper perspective, it should be pointed out

that the amount of total body external radiation resulting from fallout to date, together with future fallout in any part of the world
from previous weapons tests, is:

(a) less than 5 per cent as much as the average exposure to
cosmic rays and other background radiation;

(b) less than 5 per cent of the estimated average radiation exposure of the American public to X-rays for medical purposes.

It is interesting to note that human beings have lived for many
generations in parts of the world which have five times or more the
background radiation normal to the United States, or more than one
hundred times the average amount of radiation from fallout in the
United States.

In regard to internal effects of strontium-90 due to ingestion,
the amount of strontium-90 which has been found in food and water
is less of a hazard than the amount of radium normally present in
public drinking water supply in certain places in the United States,
and in public use for many decades.

We feel that the Commission should assume this responsibility
(keeping the public informed of the facts). It should be clearly explained to the public that weapons tests have been an essential part
of our effort to prevent the occurrence of nuclear war.[48]

The GAC statement was signed by Beams, Manson Benedict, James
W. McRae, Murphree, Kenneth S. Pitzer, Warner, Wilson, Johnson, and
Wigner, who signed as consultant. An editor of the *Bulletin* identified
only as E. R., appended the following comment to the report:

The key sentence of the above statement of the authoritative
General Advisory Committee of the AEC is the last one (as shown
above). The statement shows clearly and concisely how the biological dangers of nuclear weapons test [*sic*] appear to those convinced
that American leadership in the nuclear arms race is the most important guarantee against the occurrence of nuclear war. The statement
undoubtedly will be criticized from two sides: (1) by those who
consider the most important aspect of the biological problem not
the relative smallness of the test consequences compared to natural
background radiation or exposure to medical X-rays, but the large
absolute number of malignancies, damage, and genetic deficiencies
which are likely to be produced (which the statement does not attempt to estimate), and (2) by those who believe that the most promising way to prevent nuclear war lies not in winning the arms race,
but slowing down and ultimately reversing it; and see in the cessation of weapons tests the first step in this direction. These opinions
probably are shared also by many — perhaps all — authors of the
statement; the disagreement consists mainly in the relative emphasis
laid on the two aspects of the biological situation and of the political
strategy. This is an important fact for the public, confused by apparent wide disagreements between equally well-qualified groups of
scientists, to understand.[49]

In a subsequent issue of *Bulletin of the Atomic Scientists* there appeared a point-by-point criticism of the GAC report, written by Ralph E. Lapp. A key assertion was made by Lapp: "So far as the GAC statement is concerned, the important thing is that the appropriate studies have not been concluded—they are hardly begun."[50]

After protracted negotiations, the United States, the United Kingdom, and the Union of Soviet Socialist Republics signed a treaty in August 1963 banning nuclear weapon tests in the atmosphere, in outer space, and underwater. Although this eliminated atmospheric tests and their radioactive fallout, it "exerted virtually no effect on the nuclear arms race, because it allowed unlimited underground testing, and this has since been extensively practiced by the superpowers."[51]

The nature of GAC deliberations often reflected the scientific and technical disciplines of GAC members. When the GAC reviewed and debated the public health implications or risks posed by fallout generated from atmospheric bomb tests in the 1950s, no physicians or life scientists served on the Committee. Admittedly, the GAC could, and sometimes did, consult AEC medical experts such as Bugher and Warren. However, the essential nature of Committee transactions on the matter of fallout reflect a disciplinary parochiality. As physical scientists and engineers, GAC members were not qualified to advise on the human health and ecological ramifications of Sr-90 deposition or on radionuclide deposition effects in general. Still, the GAC did furnish advice and make recommendations on above-ground testing and atomic fallout, unconstrained by the narrowness of disciplinary representation at that time.[52]

The GAC members, in Meetings 36 through 57, did not seem overly concerned about the implications of Project Gabriel and Project Sunshine findings. In a sense, the decade of deliberations on the problem of radioactive fallout was a period of, at best, limited insight and, at worst, base ignorance in identifying the physiological and ecological risks and dangers of above-ground nuclear testing. Although medical and environmental science in the 1950s was ill equipped and unprepared to assess the dangers of atomic fallout, physical scientists and engineers who were generally promoters of ambitious testing programs of fission and thermonuclear bombs were concurrently furnishing the AEC with advice on the effects of radiation exposure to humans and on matters pertaining to bone cancer. The proposal that as a prophylactic measure humans should ingest large quantities of natural strontium to combat the absorption of radioactive strontium into the bones of the skeleton ignores the question as to whether atomic tests that pose a danger requiring such a dramatic response should be conducted at all.

Furthermore, some find it appalling that the GAC spent so much time and effort attempting to identify for the government a "safe" limit for contamination of the earth's atmosphere by atomic testing at a time when testing was actually being conducted. The identification of an upper limit of megatonnage in atomic testing also had as an implicit goal the determination of the point at which the total cumulation of radionuclides in the atmosphere from testing by the Soviet Union, the United Kingdom, and other countries might impinge on the amount of atomic testing the United States could safely conduct.[53]

Yet in the context of the period in which the GAC was advising on fallout, the ongoing Cold War between the United States and the Soviet Union created a climate in which major government officials could not comfortably advocate or publicly propose unilateral restrictions on U.S. nuclear testing. None of those appointed to the GAC during the AEC chairmanships of Strauss (1953–1958) or McCone (1958–1961) had been opponents of nuclear weapons testing. In that era, a scientist or engineer who advocated a unilateral cessation of, or even major restrictions on, nuclear weapons testing would not be considered for GAC membership. Those serving on the Committee who contemplated moderation in weapons testing may have been intimidated by what happened to many people in the McCarthy era, a time when the House Committee on Un-American Activities launched numerous investigations of individuals who worked for or advised the government in some capacity. The highly publicized ordeal of J. Robert Oppenheimer in 1954 may have made GAC members wary of offering opinions that could be construed as obstructive or disloyal.

From 1953 to 1958, the GAC endorsed and facilitated numerous AEC thermonuclear detonations. The Committee periodically raised a caution flag about the problem of radioactive fallout dispersed in this nuclear testing, but the usual concern was how to alleviate and measure the effects of fallout. Advocating suspension of above-ground tests due to the dangers posed to downwind populations was not a position taken by GAC members until very late in the decade. It is ironic that the AEC and the GAC could not scientifically and medically identify the dangerous effects of fallout without continued above-ground atomic testing.

In the statement publicly issued by the GAC in May 1959, the Committee offered the people of the world reassurance that atomic fallout was only a very small hazard. Providing curious correlations of risk, the statement was criticized by a number of established figures in the scientific community. In a sense, the Committee sought to allay public fears while above-ground testing continued, protecting the Commission from what GAC members believed was unfair, unscientific, and sensationalized press accounts of the dangers of fallout. The 1959 public statement of the GAC stands in stark contrast to the classified advisory that was put forward by the Committee in May 1958.

It is remarkable that scientists and engineers serving on the GAC in the period 1953 to 1959 did not recognize the limits of their own knowledge in an area that demanded the utmost prudence. The seductive atmosphere of high-powered deliberations carried out under conditions of maximum secrecy, however, may have encouraged GAC scientists and engineers to treat atomic fallout as a kind of ongoing global experiment. In December 1954, Eugene Rabinowich, editor of *Bulletin of the Atomic Scientists* "blamed the AEC for its excessive secrecy about a problem which may end in a slow but irreparable decay of the human race."[54] Libby had long argued, unsuccessfully, for the gathering of fallout data on a national and worldwide scale on open, unclassified blasts. The AEC chose to maintain Gabriel as a classified project in order not to arouse public alarm.[55]

The GAC fallout advisories carry a message: it is the cardinal responsibility of a free society to ensure that secret scientific and technical bodies are not trusted to advise or influence matters that, given the magnitude of their possible consequences, deserve a full and open public hearing. The AEC classified fallout information was assessed by the GAC as restricted data. The material could not be published "without undue risk to the common defense and security." This secrecy prevented the American public from learning more about a problem that posed a threat to the health, welfare, and security of this and other nations. The shroud of official secrecy may have helped to hide the government's uncertainty and ignorance in the realm of radioactive contamination.

The GAC and Project Plowshare: Peaceful use of nuclear explosives

PROJECT PLOWSHARE WAS THE NAME given to an AEC program to investigate possible nonmilitary uses for nuclear explosives. Plowshare was an offshoot of President Dwight D. Eisenhower's Atoms for Peace proposal. In a speech delivered on December 8, 1953, President Eisenhower declared, "This greatest of destructive forces can be developed into a great boon for the benefit of all mankind."[1] After World War II and through the 1950s many scientists, engineers, and government officials shared a vision of a nuclear utopia. Nuclear power was expected to propel aircraft, trains, naval vessels, commercial ships, rockets, and even military vehicles.[2] Atomic energy would be used to alter crops genetically and preserve grains, meats, and fish. Nuclear reactors were envisioned that would generate huge quantities of cheap electricity.[3]

This scientific fascination with potential applications of atomic energy spawned a wide variety of military and civilian AEC research and development contracts, some of which were successful and many of which were not. For many advocates of nuclear technology, mechanical applications were not enough. There were those who believed that the power yielded by the thermonuclear bomb itself could have peaceful applications. Nuclear swords were to be transformed into plowshares that would excavate new harbors and canals, cut gorges through mountain ridges, and blast open valuable mineral deposits.[4]

The idea for Plowshare originated at the Lawrence Livermore National Laboratory of the University of California in 1956, and a classified symposium thereon was held in February 1957 at the behest of the Livermore lab. The Plowshare concept developed in response to concerns resulting from the 1956 Suez crisis: "The original notion was to use nuclear explosives to excavate a sea-level canal through Israel."[5] By June 1957, the AEC approved the Livermore plan and established Plowshare as a full-fledged program.[6] By 1961, the AEC had formed a Division of Peaceful Nuclear Explosives, thus giving the program an institutional identity within the Commission's office hierarchy. Over the course of the program, scientists at the Livermore lab assumed a key role in the formulation and implementation of Plowshare tests for the AEC.

The peaceful application of nuclear explosives was not possible until the thermonuclear, or hydrogen, bomb was developed and successfully detonated. The earlier fission (atomic) bombs were too expensive and released too much radiation, but the cost and radiation problems of thermonuclear explosions seemed to be of manageable proportions. Unlike fission devices, these explosions could be tailored to reduce radiation effects.[7]

The Plowshare program received federal budget funding from 1957 to 1978.[8] Why did such a high-risk, controversial application of atomic energy intrigue the scientific community of the 1950s and 1960s? Why was Plowshare such a long-lived program? What did its advocates expect it to achieve? Who and what interests were responsible for promoting Plowshare and what were their motives in doing so? What role did the GAC assume in its development and oversight? What were the reasons for the decline and eventual termination of the project?

This chapter addresses four separate test projects concocted for Plowshare: Project Chariot, Project Carryall, Project Gnome, and the Atlantic-Pacific Interoceanic Canal Project. Of these, only Project Gnome was carried through to the point of an actual thermonuclear explosion. By examining these Plowshare projects, it is possible to identify the major purposes of the program. There were at least four objectives embodied in Project Plowshare, each with an associated set of interest groups: (1) national security and defense, (2) scientific advancement, (3) public works, and (4) commercial gain. In addition, two distinct types of Plowshare detonations were planned, which were to serve explicit and tangible purposes, such as natural resource exploitation, transportation, and storage or disposal of nuclear wastes.

The history of Plowshare can be characterized as a process of "policy termination."[9] In this process, programs undergo a process of delegitimation. Termination does not result from a single administrative or political action but is instead the result of a long series of events and actions that culminate in the quiet cancellation of an endeavor.

Throughout the project history the GAC was regularly briefed and consulted about planned, as well as detonated, Plowshare experiments. Occasionally the Committee would offer comment or make an inquiry about the projects. In 1971 the GAC produced a complete report on Plowshare for the AEC. The Committee was not a major source of

Plowshare criticism but instead acted as a helpful and sometimes promotive observer.

Interests and objectives in Project Plowshare

First and perhaps foremost, Project Plowshare was thoroughly intertwined with the issue of national security and defense. The AEC's first underground nuclear test, code-named Rainier, was performed September 19, 1957. Conducted at the Nevada test site located at Frenchman's Flat, Rainier was a 1.7-kiloton blast detonated in a cave drilled 2000 feet into the side of a mountain. The test was of immense military significance because it proved that nuclear tests could be conducted without producing radioactive fallout.[10] At the same time, Rainier opened the way to underground nuclear detonations for civilian purposes under Project Plowshare. The AEC's biannual report to Congress in 1957 openly acknowledged that Rainier, a military test, had civilian value.[11]

Glenn T. Seaborg, who served as AEC chairman from 1961 to 1971, has alleged that many military and national security interests perceived Plowshare as a way to escape the restrictions that might be imposed by a comprehensive test ban treaty prohibiting all forms of military nuclear bomb testing.[12] In the late 1950s and early 1960s, advocates of a test ban recognized that Plowshare could provide such a means for evading restrictions against military testing, as could the Soviet Union's peaceful nuclear explosives program. While neither the United States nor the Soviet Union would officially admit that they might exploit their peaceful nuclear programs in this fashion, each side was suspicious of the other. Seaborg indicates that Soviet Premier Nikita Khrushchev opposed any test ban treaty that permitted peaceful nuclear explosions, apparently with the assumption that Plowshare-type projects could be resurrected at some future time when a system of joint international control and supervision had been established.[13] Although military and national security interests embraced Plowshare when the possibility of a comprehensive ban on weapons testing appeared a possibility, as it turned out the Partial Test Ban Treaty of 1963 prohibited atmospheric, surface, and underwater detonations of nuclear devices but not underground testing. Several military nuclear "shots" (AEC term for detonations) had Plowshare "add-on" experiments. Conversely, the seismic analysis of many Plowshare shots assisted the Advanced Research Projects Agency of the Department of Defense (DOD) in testing technologies that could be used in the verification of atomic testing by other nations.[14]

Scientific advancement was a second major objective of Project

Plowshare. Nuclear explosions were, and still remain, objects of scientific curiosity. The 1950s and to a lesser extent the 1960s were a period of scientific exuberance. In 1945, the general public and its political representatives observed the effects of the first atomic bomb and were in awe of the accomplishments of the scientific and engineering community. Theoretical scientists who had helped create the atomic bomb, like J. Robert Oppenheimer, Edward Teller, and Enrico Fermi, were in great demand for their advice and counsel after World War II. The scientific community itself, to the extent it can be characterized collectively, saw much to be learned through the exploration and application of atomic energy in a variety of forms. Admittedly, not all scientists were advocates of Plowshare, but many believed that there was much to be discovered through Plowshare testing. Many nuclear experiments could only be performed outside the laboratory through an actual detonation.

In the defense-related detonation of a thermonuclear bomb in 1952 code-named Mike, two new transuranic elements were identified and named einsteinium and fermium. This led scientists to conclude that the large neutron flux produced in thermonuclear explosions might create "rare transplutonium isotopes and, possibly, new elements by instantaneous multiple neutron capture" if the device were encased in specific kinds of materials.[15]

The AEC reported in 1958 that government-supported scientists were contemplating the use of nuclear explosives as a way to produce large quantities of radioisotopes: "This might be accomplished by placing various materials around the device to be detonated in containing media so as to effect changes in the materials through nuclear reaction."[16] Each of the four Plowshare projects examined in this chapter was of high potential scientific value. Consequently, the scientific research community, including physicists, chemists, geologists, and biologists, was a source of advocacy as well as caution in Plowshare's history.

Many of the interested scientists worked for major AEC contract laboratories, such as Livermore and the Los Alamos Scientific Laboratory. Scientists from the Bureau of Mines, Geological Survey, Weather Bureau, and other agencies were also intrigued by Plowshare's potential scientific value. At least four Plowshare scientific symposia were held in the United States between 1957 and 1969. These were attended by as many as 500 to 700 people on each occasion and were usually cosponsored by the AEC, by major AEC laboratories, and by prestigious scientific and engineering societies.

A third major objective of Project Plowshare was the public works potential of nuclear explosions. Nuclear blasts intended to reshape natural surface formations were given the formal name *geographic engi-*

neering. Nuclear devices used for explosive power could redirect rivers, gouge out (or excavate) water impoundments, carve out canals, cut canyons out of mountains for road and railroad building, and dredge harbors where none had existed. Seaborg professed that Plowshare nuclear blasts could dig a harbor at Point Barrow, Alaska; excavate a channel across the Aleutian Islands; deepen the Bering Strait; and accomplish other engineering feats previously beyond human capacity.[17] One remark attributed to Plowshare advocate Edward Teller illustrates the visionary expectations of some American scientists; as well as advocating the use of nuclear explosives in building a second Atlantic-Pacific interoceanic canal, Teller envisioned using nuclear explosives to close the Straits of Gibraltar, "which would supposedly cause the Mediterranean to rise and freshen to the point that it could be used to irrigate the Sahara."[18] (The Gibraltar scheme would, however, have inundated Mediterranean sea-level cities, particularly Venice.)

One organization that had a keen interest in Plowshare's public works potential was the U.S. Army Corps of Engineers. The AEC maintained that one of the ultimate objectives of Plowshare was to make possible safe nuclear explosive construction techniques that the Corps of Engineers could use in civil works projects.[19] Legislators were enticed by the monumental constituency benefits that might stem from a project serving home states or districts. Seaborg indicated that many members of the U.S. Congress Joint Committee on Atomic Energy (JCAE) were ardent supporters of Plowshare.[20]

Commercial gain was a fourth major objective of Plowshare. Nuclear explosives could revolutionize major, grand-scale, private construction enterprises. Nuclear explosives could be employed in natural resource exploitation, perhaps facilitating oil and natural gas exploration and drilling. Underground nuclear blasts could advance mining of low-grade ore by stripping overburden materials. In a 1968 speech, Congressman Craig Hosmer of the JCAE called Plowshare "the pot of gold." He insisted that this newly invented pump would make it possible to extract $14 billion of gold, $50 billion of natural gas, and $1,000 billion of oil, oil shale, and copper, silver, molybdenum, and other metals. He even warned gold speculators that Plowshare might produce a glut that would collapse gold prices.[21]

Kennecott Copper Corporation, the Continental Oil Company (Conoco), El Paso Natural Gas Company, CER Geonuclear Corporation, the Austral Oil Company, and other firms joined into formal cooperative agreements with the AEC for either mining or oil and natural gas extraction experiments. The AEC even posted charges that industry would have to pay in order to have the AEC detonate Plowshare explosives in commercial ventures. A 2-megaton Plowshare thermonuclear explosive cost $600,000 in 1964. This price included AEC arming and firing services as well as the explosive itself.[22]

Besides revolutionizing mining for hydrocarbons and valuable ores and minerals, nuclear explosives were assumed to be useful in many other commercial ventures. For example, many public and private officials believed that underground cavities formed by nuclear detonations might serve as safe repositories for the vast quantities of high-level nuclear waste produced by civilian, as well as defense, nuclear reactors. Such a use of nuclear explosives, if successful, could benefit commercial nuclear power.[23]

Types of Plowshare detonations

The original Plowshare enterprise began with studies of the use of nuclear explosives in excavation work, but it was not long before Plowshare researchers recognized the potential value of contained underground detonations as well. In either case, the explosive is emplaced at the bottom of a large-diameter drill hole. If an excavation is desired, the emplacement hole is relatively shallow and the blast fractures overlying material and excavates that material through subsidence. By varying the depth of emplacement, wider or deeper craters can be formed. For a contained blast, the emplacement hole is deeper; the explosion creates a chimney of crushed and jumbled rock, but the fractures do not reach the surface. Within the chimney the porosity is very high, equal to the volume of the cavity created by the blast. If a detonation occurs at an intermediate depth so that a porous chimney of broken rock just reaches the surface, a sink is formed. However, here sink blasts are categorized with excavation, rather than contained, blasts because surface effects are produced and because sink blasts were closely associated with water storage and surface impoundments.

Contained blasts versus excavation blasts are an important distinction, dividing Plowshare detonations actually carried out from those that were studied, perhaps planned, but never actually fired. Beginning with Project Gnome, the first nonmilitary detonation of a nuclear device, the AEC pursued a long series of contained underground thermonuclear explosions. While there were a number of nuclear excavation tests conducted in Nevada and elsewhere, there is no evidence that a Plowshare detonation was ever used in an actual civil or commercial construction project.

The Chariot, Carryall, and Interoceanic Canal excavation projects were seriously investigated and researched by the AEC in conjunction with other parties but were never actually pursued to the point at which a thermonuclear bomb was detonated at the scene of each construction enterprise.

Purposes of peaceful nuclear explosions

Peaceful nuclear explosions were envisioned to serve three major purposes: natural resource exploitation, transportation enterprises, and storage or waste disposal structures or devices.

Natural resource exploitation

Natural resource exploitation seemed to have a wide array of possible applications. For example, by fracturing aquifers through nuclear detonations, large quantities of potable water might be obtained. Special measures, however, would have to be imposed to prevent contamination of this water by radiation, or by substances produced by the blast, that could pollute the water. Contained blasts were expected to be the method used to fracture an aquifer.

Natural resource exploitation also involved the potential mining of low-grade ores, an alternative to conventional deep mine and strip mine practices. A contained blast could open up ore deposits through block excavation or leaching, while an excavation blast could strip the overburden from low-grade ores. In 1967, the AEC completed a feasibility study that opened the way for Kennecott Copper to submit a proposal to the AEC and the Department of the Interior (DOI). Designated Project Sloop, the proposal was fashioned into a plan to explode a 26-kiloton thermonuclear charge 1200 feet underground at a site on Kennecott property near Safford, Arizona.[24] The shot was expected to make 10 million pounds of copper recoverable through leaching techniques. The AEC called the radioactive contamination of copper in the project "a manageable problem."[25]

Most significant, natural resource exploitation included the mining of hydrocarbons, using nuclear blasts to unlock natural gas or oil reserves through retorting. Such blasts could also produce the fractures needed for in situ recovery of oil shale. Moreover, nuclear charges could heat rocks to temperatures that might make possible the recovery of fluids from tar sands.

Early in 1959, a symposium was held at the Lawrence Berkeley Radiation Laboratory to consider the possibility that Plowshare's thermonuclear explosions could be used to recover oil from shale. Among the conference participants were officials from the AEC, the Bureau of Mines, scientists from the Berkeley lab, representatives from some three or four dozen industrial companies, and many of the leading geologists and oil scientists of the country. In an article published in *Bulletin of the Atomic Scientists,* renowned chemist Willard F. Libby (at that time an AEC commissioner) reported that he and other conferees pondered ways in which nuclear explosives could be used in mining oil and gas:

> A principal question was what would happen if we were to detonate, say, 300-kilotons of nuclear explosive in the Green River oil shale deposit in Colorado. We would expect the result to be crushed and broken shale containing 20 to 40 million barrels of oil. Gas and oil would be produced from the organic matter by the thermal energy of the explosion. The actual quantities of the products would depend upon the temperature history of the shales surrounding the explosion, the grade of the shale, and other factors. The Piccance Creek Basin of northwestern Colorado was suggested as being particularly appropriate for a test explosion of .10-kiloton. If one-half the energy released by the device were utilized in heating shale to 900 degrees (F), this would be enough to produce about 10 million cubic feet of gas and 15,000 barrels of oil.[26]

Libby went on to caution that substantial quantities of radioactive fission products might become trapped in the rock, thereby impeding efforts to extract natural gas and oil that could be safely consumed. However, conference participants and Libby himself advocated continued Plowshare test detonations of the type then envisioned. Libby added that the atomic weapons test cessation proposals being discussed in Geneva at that time should exclude nonmilitary applications of nuclear explosions. Seaborg, who served as chairman of the AEC before, during, and long after the approval of the 1963 Test Ban Treaty, chronicled the effort made to exempt Plowshare detonations from the Test Ban Treaty negotiated between the United States and the Soviet Union.[27] He specifically referred to his hope that Plowshare projects could succeed in extracting oil from shales. At Meeting 95, held in February 1966, an AEC official informed the Committee about a plan to have nations that did not sign the test ban treaty use Plowshare explosives. The AEC was then discussing with the White House and the State Department a proposal "to send a team to the United Arab Republic to learn about a project in which it was interested, and possibly render assistance."[28]

The Partial Test Ban Treaty of 1963 seriously impeded Plowshare excavation blasts because it prohibited the release of radioactive materials that would migrate across international borders, as excavation detonations might. Treaty provisions specified an absolute ban on dispersal of radioactivity over borders; therefore, signatories promised that peaceful nuclear detonations that pollute the atmosphere with even minute quantities of radioactivity would not be conducted. Because contained nuclear detonations deep underground have little or no surface or atmospheric discharges of radioactivity, the treaty was not a major obstacle to this kind of Plowshare detonation.

In 1967, for example, plans were made to carry out the contained blast that Libby said was proposed as theory in 1959. CER Geonuclear, on behalf of eighteen oil companies, proposed an experiment with AEC and the DOI. Code-named Project Bronco, the plan called for explosion of a 50-kiloton thermonuclear device in the Piccance Creek Basin 25 miles west of Rifle, Colorado. The device was to be emplaced at a 3350-foot depth and was expected to open up 1.3 million tons of oil shale to extraction operations that would yield 750,000 barrels of oil.[29] The Bronco shot program never was carried to detonation, although several Plowshare mining and gas extraction nuclear devices were fired in the years after 1963.

As late as 1973, the AEC was contemplating two more mining-related nuclear experiments. From the inception of Plowshare the AEC had kept the GAC informed about the plans and progress of each Plowshare experiment, and the Committee regularly volunteered advice about Plowshare activities. Teller, one of Plowshare's founders and leading advocates, served on the GAC from 1956 to 1958. The minutes of GAC Meeting 123 for February 15, 1973, indicate that the Committee again addressed Plowshare. GAC Chairman Howard G. Vesper, an executive of Standard Oil of California, asked the Committee to comment on the reduction in spending for Plowshare contained in the AEC's fiscal year 1974 budget. Vesper lamented the cuts and praised Plowshare. He mentioned a 1972 GAC review of the project, which concluded, "It has potential for increasing critical energy supplies in a reasonable time schedule."[30] Lombard Squires of Du Pont Company, a firm with a long history in the field of atomic energy, suggested that the AEC proceed with two planned Plowshare shots: Rio Blanco and Wagon Wheel. But he added that the program might be impractical thereafter. Stanford University's Hubert Heffner believed that Plowshare had reached a point where industry should pursue it, along with government.

James H. Sterner of the University of Texas suggested that the AEC should be prepared to undertake the nuclear explosions, but he doubted that "any geographical area" would submit to such events. To this, Livermore Laboratory's Michael M. May responded, "Local personages support AEC programs whenever they are informed in a straightforward manner." May stated that opposition was usually from organized groups residing elsewhere. He also argued that industry could not develop the nuclear devices, that funds cut from Plowshare should be restored, and that Plowshare was "an excellent bargaining chip in negotiations with oil- and gas-rich nations." Vesper agreed with May. On the matter of local test impact of underground thermonuclear bomb detonations, Vesper said, "The public need expect some inconvenience if it is to secure its energy requirements."[31]

Vesper then asked if anyone on the Committee objected to recommending that Plowshare device development be adequately funded. Squires answered affirmatively but suggested that the AEC explore possible private industry funding of the project. May observed that industry was not certain it could legally engage in the project, and moreover, security restrictions would prevent industry from knowing exactly what it was buying by its participation. The GAC ended the discussion of Plowshare at this 1973 meeting by noting that the Committee had, in its 1972 report, endorsed the project as a possible way to create repositories for long-term storage of nuclear wastes.[32]

Storage and waste disposal structures

Plowshare proponents believed that nuclear explosives could be used to create underground water reservoirs and storage caverns or could facilitate construction of dams, spillways, or drainage craters. Excavation or sink blasts would be the methods for creating the necessary surface structures or formations. Contained blasts or sink blasts might be employed to fashion underground reservoirs or storage caverns. Water storage problems included contamination, leakage, and slope stability. For a number of years the Bureau of Mines, the Geological Survey, and other federal agencies investigated nuclear explosives as an instrument in water supply programs. In 1968, the governor of Arizona approached the Interior Department with a plan to engage in cooperative studies "of the feasibility of applying nuclear explosions to water resource management in his State." This proposal, dubbed Project Aquarius, was not pursued beyond the research stage.[33]

An additional proposal that received scientific and industry attention for many years was the creation of storage caverns for natural gas. In the mid-1960s the AEC and the Columbia Gas System Service Corporation pursued Project Ketch, a proposal that originally called for the discharge of a 24-kiloton nuclear explosive at a depth of 3000 feet in impermeable shale at a site twelve miles southwest of Renovo, Pennsylvania. The cavity created was expected to store 465 million cubic feet of natural gas under high pressure.[34] The concept was technically feasible but was hampered by economic obstacles that did not make it a profit-maximizing choice. Gas line companies find it economical to store excess gas during the summer months so they can meet increased demands in winter months. Because producing areas are usually far from major consuming areas, it is important for the natural gas industry to store gas close to the areas of consumption. This meant that nuclear caverns made to store natural gas should ideally be sited near the large eastern gas-consuming market. This reasoning was apparent in the Pennsylvania location of Project Ketch, but location factors soon led to complications that called the whole concept of nuclear caverns into question. The problems of detonating underground nuclear devices in a densely populated region containing numerous buildings and structures, such as at Renovo or at many other eastern region sites, were more serious than the problems encountered in the use of nonnuclear alternatives. For example, natural underground caverns might be used despite their relatively great distance from eastern markets. Also, given the limited dimensions needed for storage caverns, conventional explosives proved to be preferable to nuclear ones.

Of all the potential storage purposes, nuclear caverns created for long-term storage of toxic wastes or radioactive effluents received the most sustained attention. This matter came up as late as GAC Meeting 120 on May 24, 1972. Then, AEC researchers discussed with the Committee how Plowshare explosions could be used to create long-term underground storage cavities for high-level nuclear wastes and toxic wastes.[35]

Transportation

The third and most controversial category of Plowshare's major purposes was that of transportation. According to the AEC, Plowshare had civil engineering applications because "large volumes of earth and rock can be moved or broken" by "nuclear explosives at costs below those of conventional methods."[36] The Commission's 1958 report to Congress mentioned nuclear explosives for use in digging harbors and canals, clearing navigation hazards, and a variety of other transportation-related tasks.

Besides the transportation projects discussed below, thought was given to several others. In 1964, the AEC cooperated with the Tennessee-Tombigbee Waterway Development Authority, the Army Corps of Engineers, and other agencies in a Plowshare-related plan. These agencies evaluated "the technical feasibility of using nuclear explosives to excavate approximately 3 miles of the 'divide cut' through low hills in the northeast corner of Mississippi (the highest terrain) on the proposed waterway."[37] Ultimately, nuclear explosives were deemed inappropriate for this canal project. Also in 1969, the Australian government engaged the AEC in the study of a project to develop a harbor at Cape Keraudren through nuclear excavation. This project was abruptly canceled when the mining company that initiated the scheme withdrew from the venture.[38]

The key problem of using nuclear explosives in transportation projects is that every detonation must be the excavation type. This means that the thermonuclear devices would have surface and atmospheric effects that would pose hazards in the form of ground shocks, air blasts, and radioactive fallout. In the case of an air blast, waves set up from a near-surface explosion not only would move outward from the explosion but might also be reflected from, and amplified by, layers in the atmosphere, producing effects several hundred miles away from the explosion epicenter. Ground shock would come from the earthquakelike tremors that result from the underground detonation of large explosive charges. The magnitude of ground shock is a function of both depth of implant and the natural geology of the site. In excavation detonations, fallout can be distributed over an area of several hundred square miles or more. Finally, excavation-type detonations would involve release of highly radioactive isotopes including strontium-90 and cesium-137.[39] As a result, excavation detonations usually would require the evacuation of population and reinforcement of buildings and structures.

From the inception of Plowshare until its termination, constant efforts were made to reduce the amount of radioactivity generated in each nuclear explosion. For example, the Palanquin nuclear test explosion in 1965 was designed to study how emplacement techniques might reduce radioactivity release. The Commission expressed disappointment with this test, as it would with many others, because the results revealed more released radioactivity than expected.[40]

Four Plowshare case studies

The four projects discussed in this chapter illustrate the range of purposes envisioned for Project Plowshare, the interest groups that supported it, the kinds of blasts planned (if not executed), and the problems encountered. Project Gnome was an underground blast intended to answer a number of questions, some scientific and some commercial. Project Chariot was to excavate a new Alaska harbor, thus opening another region for mineral resource development. Project Carryall, a combined road/railway transportation project, was to carve a ravine out of a southern California mountain range. The Atlantic-Pacific Interoceanic Canal Project, the largest and most controversial enterprise, investigated the possible use of nuclear devices to dig a second isthmian canal in Central America. It was expected to have political, military, and commercial implications. Of these four projects, only Gnome was carried to the point of thermonuclear explosion.

In all, Plowshare experiments resulted in thirty thermonuclear explosions. There were five Plowshare blasts before the October 10, 1963, approval of the Partial Test Ban Treaty: one in 1961 (the Gnome experiment), three in 1962, and one more in early 1963. In the period 1963 to 1968, after the treaty restrictions went into effect, there were twenty-three more Plowshare detonations: one in late 1963, six in 1964, one in 1965, four in 1966, three in 1967, and eight in 1968 (which includes five devices separately used in the Project Buggy test).[41] There were at least two more Plowshare detonations after 1968, Rulison in 1969 and Rio Blanco in 1973.

Project Gnome

Project Gnome was one of the first Plowshare program experiments. Preliminary Gnome feasibility studies began before 1958. In 1960, the plan called for detonation of a 10-kiloton explosive at a depth of 1200 feet.[42] However, by 1961 this was scaled back to a 5-kiloton explosive. Gnome would be used to study the production and recovery of heat and isotopes produced in a contained nuclear explosion.[43]

AEC officials believed that the energy stored as heat in the nuclear cavity might be released in a controlled manner by use of transfer agents such as water, carbon dioxide, or nitrogen. The energy recovered from this heat could be used "industrially or in the production of electric power."[44] In a sense, the heat recovered from the contained blast was expected to be harnessed for power production as a type of nuclear power plant.

Project Gnome enabled AEC-supported laboratories, such as Livermore, Los Alamos, and Brookhaven, to conduct neutron experiments that were "either impossible or extremely difficult to perform" with then-conventional laboratory techniques.[45] In a related sense, the AEC looked on Project Gnome as an economical alternative for producing synthetic isotopes. Economical isotope production had important implications for national defense and security because it could facilitate production and fabrication of nuclear warheads of various types.

When Gnome was exploded in New Mexico in December 1961, the ground surface heaved upward, producing a permanent two-foot bulge. The explosion, however, did not reach the surface. Radioactive steam produced from heated water in the underground salt was vented to the air above the site through a shaft. Maximum readings of 10,000 roentgen per hour detected in downwind monitoring caused the AEC to close several public roads near the site.[46]

When President John F. Kennedy approved the Gnome shot in October 1961, he stated that it was "a further example of this country's desire to turn the power of the atom to man's welfare rather than his destruction."[47] Project Gnome was to open the way to a succession of contained nuclear explosions in the 1960s. The large underground cavity created by the Gnome blast was opened to press tours by the AEC. Project Gnome findings revealed that production of electric power from nuclear-generated salt cavities was economically uncompetitive with alternative electric power production technologies.[48]

At Meeting 78 in January 1962, the GAC heard John S. Kelly, Director of the Division of Peaceful Nuclear Explosives, review the outcomes and findings of the Gnome detonation.[49] The Committee followed with interest this and other Plowshare experiments.

Project Chariot

In 1958, the AEC announced that it was pursuing a detailed investigation to determine whether nuclear explosives could be used to excavate a harbor in northwestern Alaska between Cape Seppings and Cape Thompson, an area located north of the Arctic Circle. The Commission insisted that a harbor in this region was necessary in order to make possible the development of its mineral resources.[50] Its survey estimated costs, collected physical and economic data, and evaluated safety factors. The AEC also notified the national governments of Canada and the Soviet Union about this project, called Project Chariot, and about the Alaska harbor studies that would be conducted prior to the detonations.

Project Chariot bioenvironmental and engineering field surveys were conducted in 1959. The Fish and Wildlife Service, the Weather Bureau, the Public Health Service, the Army Corps of Engineers, and scientists from several universities performed much of this work.[51] Two years later Project Chariot research continued, but the AEC had not yet received authorization to explode a nuclear device. Nevertheless, the Commission had formulated the project's civil engineering plan, which called for simultaneous detonation of four 20-kiloton explosives and one 200-kiloton nuclear explosive. The smaller charges were to be buried at a depth of 400 feet and the large charge at 800 feet. These explosives were to create a channel 900 feet wide and 2000 feet long with a 200-foot maximum depth. The large nuclear fulmination would excavate an 1800-foot-diameter, 400-foot-deep turning basin that would link the channel created by the smaller nuclear charges to the ocean.[52]

By 1962, the AEC's environmental studies of Project Chariot's predicted effects concluded that harm to Eskimos and to the Alaskan environment was "exceedingly remote."[53] Despite years of research, however, the AEC was never granted permission by the president to detonate a nuclear explosive at the Chariot site. The project was bypassed as the AEC pursued numerous nuclear excavation detonations at the AEC Nevada test site to perfect nuclear explosives. The first Project Buggy, for example, yielded information about what would happen if five nuclear explosives were detonated simultaneously to produce a ditch. There was also an estimated 100-kiloton shot in hard rock, another nuclear shot in sandstone, and a multiple-charge shot in hard rock with varying surface terrain.[54]

A major reason why Chariot was abandoned stemmed from the prohibitions imposed by the 1963 Partial Test Ban Treaty, which banned detonations that produce debris or fallout that could not be contained within the borders of the nation exploding the mechanism. There was little assurance that fallout produced by the Chariot explosions could be completely confined to the United States. By 1963, Project Chariot was postponed indefinitely and the AEC began returning the test site land to the public domain.[55]

While Project Chariot may seem to have been of little consequence, it laid the foundation for numerous domestic U.S. nuclear excavation tests. Because of the attendant risks of the Chariot detonations, AEC scientists did not favor firing the proposed detonations as part of a research program. Instead, they wanted the Chariot blasts to be based on predictable, routine, and safe pretesting. Project Chariot coexisted with, and to a degree set the stage for, the most ambitious Plowshare proposal, the nuclear excavation for a second isthmian canal in Central America.

Project Carryall

Project Carryall was a highly controversial nuclear excavation proposal. In 1963, executives of the Santa Fe Railway asked AEC officials about the feasibility of using nuclear explosives to effect a cut through the Bristol Mountains north of Amboy, California. This site was in the southeastern portion of the state at a point equidistant between Barstow and Needles. The railroad expected that the project would shorten travel time, reduce fuel consumption, and preclude construction of a long, more expensive tunnel.[56]

Soon after the Santa Fe Railway made its proposal, it was joined by the California Division of Highways, which was converting Highway 66 into Interstate 40 at the time. The relocation plan called for a northern, higher, and straighter route, which the Carryall Project cut could provide. Both the railroad and the highway authorities could use the 350-foot-deep cut to be created by the blast.[57]

A Carryall feasibility study was completed in late 1963 by a study group composed of staff members from the AEC San Francisco Operations Office, the Lawrence Livermore lab, the Santa Fe Railway, and the California Division of Highways. The proposed pass, which was to be about 10,000 feet long, would involve cuts up to 350 feet deep and would dig out about 60 million cubic yards of rock. The study concluded that the project was technically feasible.[58]

Project Carryall was not realized "because it ran afoul of the time schedule for completion of the Interstate Highway System."[59] By 1965, the AEC reported that Carryall was largely defunct.[60] The Carryall proposal would have been of more economic gain to the railroad.[61] The project involved a curious assortment of public and private parties who were encouraged by the AEC to explore the feasibility of atomic explosives in civil construction.

The Atlantic-Pacific Interoceanic Canal Project

Why was a second Central American interoceanic canal considered desirable? A second, and deeper, canal could accommodate more and larger vessels. It would presumably be less vulnerable to military attack, particularly a sea-level canal with no lock systems. The second canal, as envisioned, was also expected to be simpler and cheaper to run. Proponents argued that routing a new canal through Panama might even reduce political tensions between Panama and the United States.[62]

Plowshare and the second isthmian canal involved three overlapping domains. First, diplomatic and political decisions preceded and paralleled research of the proposed project. Second, domestic U.S. nuclear excavation experimentation conducted by the AEC was planned to determine how nuclear explosives might be used in the canal's construction. Third, the Canal Study Commission was to assess the feasibility of nuclear excavation in the canal project.

The story begins in the diplomatic and political realm. At the Second International Conference on Peaceful Uses of Nuclear Energy held in Geneva in 1958, Edward Teller contended that Plowshare could help to dig a sea-level canal across Panama.[63] Two years later, George B. Kistiakowsky, President Eisenhower's science advisor at the time, made the following entry in his diary: "From a remark of the President, I gather he intends to address the UN General Assembly and at that time (September) announce that we are going ahead with the Plowshare program for digging a second Atlantic-Pacific canal through Mexico, which has agreed to the project. It was obvious that both the President and the Vice-President think Plowshare is terribly important." Kistiakowsky's entry has a subscript disclosing that President Eisenhower had been "premature" in his reference to a canal through Mexico, "which had not formally agreed to this project."[64]

In 1962, legislation was introduced in Congress to authorize the Panama Canal Company to conduct surveys of possible routes for the construction of a sea-level, transisthmian canal. This was welcomed by the AEC, which was continuing to study nuclear excavation tests that could serve the canal project.[65] In September 1964, Public Law 88-609 was enacted. This measure authorized the president to appoint a five-member commission to investigate and study the feasibility of, and the most suitable site for, the building of a sea-level canal connecting the Atlantic and Pacific oceans. This commission was to determine the best means of constructing the canal, "whether by conventional or nuclear excavation, and the estimated cost of each."[66] It was not until April 18, 1965, that President Johnson made the five appointments to the Canal Study Commission. By this time, the three preferred routes were the present Canal Zone, the Darien region of Panama east of Panama City, and northwestern Colombia along the border of Panama. Permission to conduct on-site surveys of route 17 (Sasardi-Morti) in the Darien region and of route 25 (Atrato-Truando) through Colombia was secured by the United States from Panama and Colombia, respectively, in 1966.[67]

In anticipation of the use of nuclear explosives in excavating a new interoceanic canal, the AEC planned a series of tests at its western facilities. The largest by far, called Project Sedan, was a 100-kiloton detonation 635 feet below a central Nevada site. The crater formed was 1280 feet deep. This test occurred in July 1962, before the successful negotiation of the Partial Test Ban Treaty. A second 100-kiloton cratering experiment was deferred and later scaled back as a result of limitations imposed by the 1963 treaty.[68]

Ratification of the treaty forced the AEC to move to nuclear detonations smaller than Project Sedan and therefore less likely to release radioactive matter to the atmosphere.[69] The AEC concluded from an analysis of the results of Project Sulky in 1964 that, with the proper design, excavation experiments could be carried out without releasing radioactive debris beyond national boundaries.[70] Nevertheless, the U.S. Kiwi Transient Nuclear Test in January 1965, which involved the destruction of a reactor, yielded fallout that went over the U.S. border and so triggered official objection by the Soviet Union.[71]

In February 1966, at the only GAC meeting convened outside the continental United States (Meeting 95 in Mayaguez, Puerto Rico), the full GAC and the AEC commissioners listened to Kelly, director of the Nuclear Explosives Division, review the AEC's Atlantic-Pacific Canal studies.[72]

By 1966, the AEC initiated Project Cabriolet, a nuclear excavation test specifically tailored to determine the feasibility of using nuclear explosives in building a sea-level canal across the Pan-American Isthmus. Cabriolet, a 2.5-kiloton device, was detonated in January 1968. It was 40 times smaller than the Project Sedan detonation but nonetheless produced a crater 120 feet deep and 360 feet in diameter.[73] Another project, termed Buggy, was one of the first nuclear row charge experiments. It too was detonated in 1968. The five nuclear charges, spaced 150 feet apart and 150 feet underground, produced a channel 300 feet wide, 900 feet long, and 80 feet deep.[74] The Commission announced that some radioactivity migrated from the site of each of these tests, but no further details were given.

While AEC field researchers continued to gather data about the two proposed route areas in Central America, and as the agency continued to assess the results of its Nevada tests, the Commission announced that cratering experiments demonstrated "that nuclear excavation of a sea-level canal is a possible means of constructing such a waterway."[75]

In its recommendations, the Canal Study Commission's 1970 report offered a contrary view. If route 17, the Sasardi-Morti route, had been selected as the canal site, it would have required breaking through a "backbone-like ridge that reaches 1,100 feet in elevation at one point."[76] Cuts of this magnitude had never been attempted. The study commission calculated that route 17 would require 250 separate nuclear excavation charges, which would yield a cumulative 120 megatons of explosive power. This would have been accomplished with the firing of 30 salvos of varying yields over at least a three-year period. The largest salvo would have had a yield of 11 megatons of TNT equivalent.[77] Route 17 nuclear excavation across Panama would have affected 6,500 square miles, and an estimated 43,000 inhabitants would have had to be evacuated for a period of months. The effects of ground shock and air blast might be felt as far as 300 miles away, with glass breakage and masonry damage extending from Panama City to the Colombian border.

A similar continental divide cut would be required for route 25, the Atrato-Truando route across northwestern Colombia. About 150 individual nuclear charges would have to be fired in twenty-one-row salvos over a three-year period. The largest salvo would be 13 megatons and the total explosive power of all the route 25 nuclear detonations was predicted to be 120 megatons, about the same as for route 17. Geographic and demographic differences existed for each route. Route 25 in Colombia was expected to affect 3100 square miles, which encompassed approximately 10,000 inhabitants. As in the route 17 plan, these people would need to be evacuated for many months.[78] Route 17 affected a far larger area and more than four times as many people.

Nuclear explosives were to excavate only a fraction of each canal route. Nevertheless, the ground motions and radioactive fallout produced would have had serious implications for the host country. According to an article in the *Scientific American,* the cumulative nuclear explosive energy released in canal excavation "would be twenty times the cumulative amount of explosives used in all previous wars combined."[79] The Canal Study Commission reported that many scientists around the world were alarmed about the radioactivity that would be released to the environment in such nuclear excavation.

In advising against the use of nuclear explosives, the study commission discussed all three overlapping domains involved in this project. The body concluded that the Partial Test Ban Treaty of 1963 would need to be modified to permit major nuclear excavation projects because "there seems to be no possibility of excavating an Isthmian canal with nuclear explosives without transport of some radioactive material across territorial boundaries."[80] Moreover, the study group's 1970 report indicated that each prospective host country opposed nuclear canal excavation even more vehemently than in 1964.

The study commission also referred to serious economic dislocations envisaged for each route by nuclear excavation. For example, route 17 would have an impact on large numbers of Choco and Cuna Indians, who have strong cultural attachments to their lands. Route 25, while affecting far fewer people, also would uproot Choco Indians in northwestern Colombia. Moreover, routes 17 and 25 would drain financial resources and economic opportunity away from the existing Panama Canal Zone.

The Canal Study Commission disclosed that the AEC had only been able to conduct three U.S.-based nuclear excavation test shots, instead of the planned minimum of six. Throughout the 1960s, the Plowshare testing grew increasingly controversial. Consequently, Congress declined to furnish all of the funds needed to prepare each canal-related test. Presidents Kennedy, Lyndon B. Johnson, and Richard M. Nixon were not always forthcoming in granting prompt permission to fire each Plowshare excavation shot. Eventually, AEC Chairman Seaborg recommended to the study commission that because "the AEC had not been able to do all of the experiments required to make a determination of the feasibility of using nuclear explosions" in canal excavation, "any decision in the near future to construct a sea-level canal would have to be made without reliance on nuclear excavation."[81]

In the end, nuclear excavation of a second canal was deemed to be a premature use of the technology. The Canal Study Commission's technical associates strongly advised against nuclear canal building on the grounds that appropriate techniques for such an enterprise would not be available within the next ten years.[82]

The new canal proposal itself was abandoned when the United States and Panama entered into a long process of negotiation that ultimately resulted in the transfer of the Panama Canal Zone to the Republic of Panama in the administration of President James E. Carter. What had sustained nuclear excavation Plowshare in the 1960s was the hope and belief that this new instrument of civil engineering would prove its value in construction of a second great Pan-American canal.

The decline of Plowshare

The demise of Plowshare was hastened by the emergence of the U.S. environmental movement. This was intimated in the AEC's 1970 report: "Along with the growing concern for environment, there have been an increasing number of indications of public uneasiness about nuclear testing and particularly about high-yield nuclear testing and Plowshare excavation experiments. Because these matters had become worrisome to the public, a considerable bioenvironmental study program has grown up in the past years and this program was intensified during 1970."[83] What this statement omitted was that the Plowshare underground nuclear testing also fostered public fears and consternation.

The political implications of this public concern were felt all the way to the White House. By 1970, all AEC plans for nuclear testing were subject to review by the National Security Council's Undersecretaries Committee. Furthermore, the Council on Environmental Quality, a statutory executive office, examined all Plowshare testing plans for compliance with the National Environmental Policy Act of 1969 (NEPA). Environmental impact statements were to be prepared for each planned Plowshare explosion.[84]

The AEC became highly vulnerable to accusations by public interest science organizations that full public disclosures about planned Plowshare detonations were not being made. As more information about each was released, more of the public became concerned. Civilian use of nuclear explosives in Plowshare could no longer proceed as elite or concealed policymaking. Though NEPA could not force the declassification of Plowshare thermonuclear technical data that described how the devices themselves functioned, the possible on-site and off-site consequences of a Plowshare explosion were more easily subject to public disclosure through the legally mandated environmental impact statements required under NEPA.

The AEC's final official mention of Plowshare as an operating program came in its 1974 report to Congress. Reference was made to the Gasbuggy detonation of 1967 and the Rulison blast of 1969. Each of these were gas stimulation experiments. The Commission also reported that it was continuing to assess the results of its 1973 Rio Blanco underground thermonuclear explosion. Rio Blanco proved to be the final detonation of a nuclear device for Project Plowshare; the mixed results and public controversy produced by this experiment in northwestern Colorado helped close the door on the use of nuclear explosives as instruments to be used "in augmenting the Nation's energy resources."[85] Kennecott continued analyzing the potential feasibility of a Project Wagon Wheel detonation, but the firm never approached the government with a request to cosponsor the project through an actual blast.

In the mid-1970s the AEC itself underwent a transformation that preceded its bifurcation into the Nuclear Regulatory Commission and the Energy Research and Development Administration. In this final phase, the AEC moved its applied technology projects away from peaceful nuclear testing and toward "environmental research, energy storage and transmission systems, synthetic fuels and non-nuclear energy."[86] But the AEC did not carry Plowshare into an era of renewable energy, energy conservation, and environmental sensitivity. In 1971, the Commission had participated in a joint government-industry feasibility study that concluded, "There is no technical reason why electricity cannot be produced from geothermal energy sources with the aid of nuclear explosives."[87] Yet, this and other creative attempts to move Plowshare into alternative energy schemes were unsuccessful. The firms that stood the most to gain from Plowshare concluded that political and regulatory restrictions, as well as legal liability for explosion effects, were too costly to warrant sponsorship of commercial thermonuclear detonations.

Plowshare was, in a sense, two separate programs. One was for nuclear excavation projects applied to grand-scale civil engineering ven-

tures, the other for contained underground blasting to serve parties interested in mining, underground natural gas storage, and long-term
storage of toxic and radioactive materials. Both programs were intertwined with civilian and national security–related experiments. Given
the heavy security that (justifiably) surrounded AEC use of thermonuclear devices, and given fears of nuclear terrorism as well as nuclear
proliferation, even Plowshare's most strident supporters never expected
the project to give private industry a thermonuclear explosive device.

Project Plowshare captured the imagination of many scientists,
engineers, and elected political officials. Many expected Plowshare to be
a tool of geographic or planetary engineering. The excavation-type
Plowshare projects failed to meet political and diplomatic restrictions,
however, due to the surface and atmospheric effects in nuclear detonations. Efforts to downsize excavation blasts to comply with restrictions
of the Partial Test Ban Treaty moved nuclear explosives into a range in
which more economical conventional explosives were the preferred alternative. At the same time, the environmental movement expressed
criticism of Plowshare's ecological effects. It became difficult to win
approval for any major public works construction projects, and those
planning nuclear excavation faced a heavy barrage of public and private
criticism.

Contained-blast Plowshare projects seem to have been exhaustively
researched, particularly for mining potential. Major oil and natural gas
companies, as well as a huge copper mining firm, pursued tests and
feasibility studies with the AEC up to and through actual AEC-directed
underground nuclear detonations. Yet the cost of removing radioactive
contaminants from oil, natural gas, copper, water, or other substances of
commercial value made nuclear fracturing or nuclear caverns a poor,
high-risk business investment. If business was to become a copartner in
the use of nuclear explosives, as originally envisioned, new and extraordinary responsibilities would have to be shouldered. The federal government provided no insurance against damage claims by third parties affected by Plowshare blasts. The Price-Anderson Act of 1957 had placed
a ceiling on the liability of electric utilities operating nuclear power
plants that provided protection against damage claims of more than
$580 million, making possible the private insurability of nuclear power
plant operations. But no such shield or insurance umbrella protected
private firms sponsoring Plowshare detonations. If a thermonuclear explosion sponsored by a private company went awry and damaged the
lives or property of third parties, that firm would be fully exposed to
ensuing damage claims, a risk few firms were willing to assume.

The Plowshare projects were forced to deal with the problem of political and legal accountability; the excavation-type projects failed to meet the restrictions of international relations in a political realm, and the contained-blast projects failed to prove practical and profitable in an economic realm. While the U.S. government was held increasingly accountable for the international consequences of nuclear excavation shots, the AEC and its industrial copartners were held increasingly accountable under property, negligence, and environmental protection laws for any deleterious effects produced in contained nuclear explosions. Despite significant technical advances in the design of thermonuclear devices, Plowshare nuclear explosions could not be engineered to meet constantly tightening sets of restrictions.

Over the years, the GAC behaved more as an advocate than a critic or reviewer of Plowshare projects. Teller, an original architect of Plowshare, hoped to see the thermonuclear bomb converted to peaceful uses, such as geographic engineering and mining. In the period 1956 to 1972, the Committee's engineers were more vocal about Plowshare than were its theoretical scientists. Committee members employed by corporate research labs pressed for Plowshare progress more than did members working at universities. Moreover, because Livermore and Los Alamos were leading laboratories in Plowshare experimentation, GAC members associated with them understandably lobbied hard for continuation of Plowshare work.

Many programs and policies can fend off termination efforts if those committed to the program have a great intellectual reluctance to see it end, if there is a high degree of institutional endurance that keeps a policy moving forward, if the organization implementing the policy is able to make dynamic and defensive organizational adjustments, if an antitermination coalition can be forged to block threatened termination actions, if a body of law or other legal obstacles prevent dissolution of a program, and if there are considerable sunk costs in a program.[88] Plowshare failed on virtually all these counts. The scientific community, one of the program's staunchest supporters at the beginning, gradually lost interest in using thermonuclear explosives to pursue scientific experiments. The AEC Division of Peaceful Nuclear Explosives lost funding and personnel over the years and so there was not a strong internal group of AEC officials fighting to save Plowshare in the 1970s. The 1974 dissolution of the AEC thrust the program into ERDA, a multiple-mission energy agency that relegated atomic energy programs to a somewhat diminished position. The effort to use Plowshare in geothermal energy research represented a feeble attempt at defensive adjustment against proposed termination. There were no antitermination coalitions fighting to save Plowshare in the 1970s because the business community became disenchanted with Plowshare and its marginal commercial benefits. The defense establishment did not need Plowshare because the military could have its underground tests conducted by the AEC, ERDA, or the Department of Energy unencumbered by major treaty restrictions. The JCAE, an early and longtime source of Plowshare protection and promotion, itself was disbanded in the mid-1970s. Plowshare had no firm basis in federal statutes, other than those promoting the general application of atomic energy for civilian uses in the Atomic Energy Act of 1954. Because Plowshare progressed as a research and development project pursued by AEC contract lab staff members who could be easily detailed to other project work and because Plowshare did not rely on or generate major physical facilities, there were few sunk costs that the government would lose if the program were canceled. The official termination of Plowshare came as a budget decision of the Congress, a decision unopposed by the president.

The story of Project Plowshare is one of sustained and futile scientific and engineering optimism in the face of a world public becoming increasingly intolerant of such nuclear ventures. The base of nuclear energy's constituency and private clientele support eroded significantly in the 1970s, and Plowshare proved too marginal to maintain. The termination of Plowshare was the reluctant admission that a nuclear utopia was not imminent.

The GAC and the great accelerator debates

Academic science advising

Universities, colleges, and academic research institutes discover and disseminate knowledge. They own and operate elaborate physical equipment and facilities, and more important, they retain highly educated faculties and staffs. Institutions of higher education create environments that facilitate experimentation in the pursuit of pure and applied research. Some of this research produces tangible end products that are of immediate practical value; much, however, yields intangible products that are often of little or no immediate utility but may be vital in the advancement of knowledge. Some products of basic university science research are not at first appreciated for their potential impact; only through subsequent scientific and technical research can pure research achieve practical value.

Institutions of higher education train the people who ultimately become the scientific and technical staffs of private industry, government research laboratories, and universities and colleges themselves. Therefore, university scientists and engineers, as well as the universities themselves, have long been perceived by government officials as an essential national resource. Federal agencies with technoscientific missions and programs are manifestly dependent on institutions of higher education, particularly institutions with established programs of learning in the physical sciences and engineering.

As prototypical technoscientific federal agencies, the AEC and ERDA and their lineal descendent, the Department of Energy (DOE), have maintained close ties with the academic physical science and engineering communities and regularly furnish these agencies with professional advice or information. Federal administrative officials commonly believe that university researchers provide relatively unbiased reviews of proposed scientific and technical projects.[1] University scientists and engineers are thought to be motivated by the goals of their knowledge disciplines and enjoined by the ethics of their professions. They are commonly assumed to be dispassionate, objective, and selfless.

Over the last century this view of academic objectivity has become less tenable as scientific research conducted on university campuses has been pursued under conditions increasingly associated with government objectives. In the last century land grant colleges and private universities were drawn into the public policy process of the national government because in the absence of a professional, career, public bureaucracy, academic institutions served as a "main reservoir of expertise on which politicians could draw for advice."[2] Government became more solicitous of this academic assistance and more generous in paying for it, and thus university and college researchers became more and more dependent on the government's financial support. Universities have multiple sources of support, however, which have prevented their total subservience to government-funded programs. Nevertheless, in this century a state of interdependence has evolved among university academic scientific and technical interests and the interests of federal technoscientific agencies.

Few would dispute the claim that the paramount source of basic scientific research in the United States has been, and continues to be, the university. The federal government has used the products of basic scientific research to develop and promote countless public and private applications. President Franklin D. Roosevelt's science advisor, Vannevar Bush, once declared, "As a matter of public policy the government should support basic research without regard to its application."[3] Since World War II federal government support of basic research has been substantial and at times extremely generous. The level of federal subsidization of university basic research has fluctuated dramatically over the period, but university scientists have become accustomed to competing for a share of federal research funding. This relationship has raised doubt about whether university scientists who are grant applicants can maintain a high degree of detachment and independence in their transactions with the federal administrators who manage the flow of this federal support.[4]

University scientists and engineers have come to behave much like other clientele groups who benefit from government social and economic programs; they lobby the government to support and expand the scientific and technical programs administered by the technoscientific agencies. The National Academy of Sciences and its associated divisions have a long history of assessing, promoting, or criticizing various lines of government-supported scientific and technical research. Since World War II the Federation of American Scientists has become a politically active professional scientific organization with a small but active membership, most from universities.[5] The American Association for the Advancement of Science has been another platform from which university science interests articulate their concerns and desires to the government and to the public. In recent years, the Union of Concerned Scientists has emerged as a formidable manifestation of public-spirited science lobbying. It too has a large contingent of university-based scientists and engineers as members. These and other scientific or engineering professional organizations have, at times, promoted self-serving objectives. Some scientists, including university scientists, have used their professional platform base to promise "technological miracles" in order to obtain government funds for basic research.[6]

A carefully chosen citizens' advisory committee or board composed of representatives of an agency's outside constituencies enables the constituency to bring its needs and demands to the attention of the agency. It also furnishes a form of public representation to the agency that helps redistribute authority to reduce or undercut executive and legislative domination.[7] In other words, advisory committees can be a source of legitimacy for agency initiatives. Agency officials can use such committees as a base for building supportive external coalitions for its actions, even when the agency does not yet have executive or legislative approval for planned actions. Moreover, the agency can claim to be responsive to public concerns when it responds to the needs and demands brought to it through its advisory committees. Scientific and technical advisory bodies convey the added advantage of knowledgeably dealing with esoteric and specialized subject matter that is often incomprehensible to executive and legislative officials. Agency leaders acting on the recommendations of advisory committees composed of elite groups of scientific and engineering authorities can claim to be addressing professional scientific and technical issues that higher authorities are ill equipped to take up.

The general question is, How did the GAC communicate university science interests to the federal government? This chapter chronicles several instances when the GAC operated as an arena for the articulation of university science interests. What these examples reveal is that the AEC actively used the Committee to help fashion, refine, and sometimes improve its relationship with U.S. universities and colleges. In addition, the GAC furnished guidance to the AEC in disputes that emerged between AEC contract labs and major universities. The Committee also was influential in helping the AEC decide whether a certain line of research should be assigned to university-based scientists or to AEC laboratory scientists. Such matters have been pivotal in charting the course of numerous U.S. research and development programs.

In matters of academic affairs, GAC recommendations were dramatically affected by the knowledge disciplines of the Committee's members. The GAC, much like other scientific advisory committees, was a vehicle through which scientists and engineers working outside of government could help chart the futures of their knowledge disciplines. This was possible because government subsidization of scientific and technical lines of inquiry, as well as government purchase of expensive instruments vital to these lines of inquiry, was often decisive in determining the progress of scientific and engineering disciplines. The scientific discipline most heavily represented on the GAC was physics, and the physicists on the Committee understood well that the health and progress of present and future physics research would be fundamentally determined by the resources and technology supplied by the federal government.

AEC and ERDA research funding to universities

AEC/ERDA research sponsorship was divided into three general categories: project research, support of university research labs, and national and multiprogram laboratories. Project research furnished individual scientists or groups of scientists working at various colleges or universities with government support for their projects and experiments. Sometimes this assistance carried with it an equipment budget that allowed the grant-sponsoring organization to keep scientific instruments after the government research project was completed. It was customary for this type of aid to be distributed to a very large assortment of universities, colleges, and academic research institutes. Sometimes the requests for proposals circulated by the AEC or ERDA allowed researchers working at corporate research facilities to compete for project research funding. In 1964, annual assistance in project grant research ranged from $10,000 to $50,000 for each recipient.[8] This funding level increased to the $100,000–$200,000 range in the 1970s, but there were many exceptions above or below these amounts. For many university scientists and engineers, the project research grant has been the chief medium of interaction with the AEC or ERDA.

The second general funding category was the support of research laboratories located on university campuses. The Berkeley Radiation Laboratory, which flourished under AEC support after 1946, set the precedent of the campus big-science laboratory underwritten heavily by government funding. It was understood that a major government-subsidized research laboratory on campus represented a dramatic departure from "the traditional pattern of academic research built around a professor and a few graduate students."[9] Universities establishing big-science labs were dependent on a continuous flow of federal financial support because the cost of operating these facilities often greatly exceeded the university's ability to pay. For decades these government-subsidized campus research labs have helped to train the scientists and engineers needed by both the private sector and the federal government.

Government particle accelerator installations were in this second category. The Stanford Linear Accelerator, for example, was almost entirely paid for by AEC budget funding. Today the facility continues to receive support for its operations from the DOE. Particle accelerators have been made available to scientists of a sponsoring university as well as to scientists from other universities. Besides training scientific and technical manpower, accelerator research facilities have made possible significant scientific advances. Discovery of a variety of subatomic particles has been made through research experiments conducted at university-based or university-operated particle accelerators. A decision as to which university's accelerator proposal would be approved was of fundamental importance to the universities competing for the facilities and to the high-energy physics research community as a whole, as well.

The third funding category encompasses operation of the national laboratories and multiprogram laboratories. Lesser multiprogram labs as well as the national labs have affected the interests of specific universities or groups of universities (see Chapter 5). The University of California, the University of Chicago, and Iowa State University, among others, have been contract operators of AEC/ERDA laboratories. Brookhaven National Laboratory and the Enrico Fermi Laboratory have been managed by separate university consortium groups incorporated to form a contractor organization. Universities and colleges have banded together to create nonprofit corporations or associations to govern and regulate scientific access to major AEC/ERDA laboratory facilities.

Associated Midwest Universities, for example, in cooperation with the University of Chicago, arranged researcher access to the Argonne National Laboratory and its sophisticated technical facilities. This association was formed in the 1950s by thirty-three institutions of higher education. Since then university and college membership increased, and the organization was renamed the Argonne Universities Association (apparently a weak organization with little influence over the Argonne facilities, it disbanded about 1980). Similarly, the Oak Ridge Institute of Nuclear Studies, Inc., established in the late 1940s, began with forty member universities. Operating as Oak Ridge Associated Universities

(ORAU) today, the organization regulates the use of visitor machine time at Oak Ridge National Laboratory and facilitates researcher interaction with government lab officials. ORAU institutional membership has ballooned well beyond its original group of forty.[10]

The AEC/ERDA laboratories have offered graduate and postgraduate research opportunities to students and faculty of both U.S. and foreign universities. The ebb and flow of scientific and engineering researchers between universities and the AEC/ERDA labs works to the advantage of each institutional group and has fundamentally affected scientific research both inside and outside the United States.

University representation on the GAC

Individuals employed at universities who serve on the GAC cannot be characterized as an undifferentiated bloc. Some GAC members working at universities were presidents or senior administrative officials at their institutions, such as Lee A. DuBridge, James B. Conant, John C. Warner, Warren C. Johnson, T. Keith Glennan, Kenneth S. Pitzer, John H. Williams, Arthur G. Hansen, and Richard S. Morse.[11] Others were professors who held academic appointments at the time of their GAC service, as in the case of Enrico Fermi, Isidor I. Rabi, Glenn T. Seaborg, Willard F. Libby, Walter G. Whitman, Eugene P. Wigner, Jesse W. Beams, Edwin M. McMillan, Edward Teller, Manson Benedict, Norman F. Ramsey, Jr., Rolf Eliassen, James H. Sterner, and Hubert Heffner. Many who held academic appointments later ascended to high administrative posts at their universities, becoming deans, department heads, and university research institute directors or faculty.

A special category of academic representation exists in the case of research institutes quite independent of universities, such as the Carnegie Institution of Washington and the Institute for Advanced Study at Princeton. During their years of GAC service, Philip H. Abelson worked for the former and J. Robert Oppenheimer and John von Neumann for the latter. Both institutes function as elite research and quasi-academic organizations sometimes engaged in grant-supported work. Other institutes are segments of universities, such as the Institute for Nuclear Studies (which employed Fermi and Libby) and the Institute for the Study of Metals (directed by Cyril S. Smith), both part of the University of Chicago. The Academy of Natural Science is tied to the University of Pennsylvania; both institutions concurrently employed Ruth Patrick during her GAC term. The Gas Research Institute has links to Illinois Institute of Technology, and both employed Henry R. Linden at the time of his GAC service.

Further complicating analysis of academic representation is the fact that several GAC members held academic appointments with universities when in fact they pursued most of their work with AEC/ERDA-funded labs operated under contract by their universities. For example, Seaborg held an executive post in the Berkeley lab and a UC-Berkeley academic appointment at the same time. Similarly, in the years of his GAC service, Teller was associate director of the Lawrence Livermore National Laboratory and was concurrently a UC-Berkeley professor of physics. Those employed directly and exclusively by a laboratory operated under contract by a university may well have spoken for the interests of their contractor universities. Darol K. Froman and Jane H. Hall of Los Alamos and Michael M. May of Livermore could well have spoken on behalf of the University of California. Similarly, Stephen Lawroski of Argonne could have worked for the interests of the University of Chicago.

University representation on the GAC, therefore, flowed from a number of sources. Affiliation with a specific university did not necessarily mean that the GAC member acted as a spokesman or delegate for that university. In fact, GAC members usually voluntarily abstained from participating in discussions directly involving their universities. Some GAC members, however, did engage in special pleading for their universities. The question of any possible "conflict of interest" in Committee recommendations is difficult to assess in cases where members had only indirect links to a university or to a university contract lab.

Over the years, the GAC addressed a broad spectrum of issues that affected the universities and research institutes. The Committee regularly reviewed AEC budget requests for university-based research and often made an effort to spotlight what members believed was underfunding.[12] For example, the Committee occasionally took up the matter of AEC research reactors for universities and colleges, and at Meeting 29 in February 1952, the University of Chicago's Johnson criticized the AEC as well as the universities for failing to be more aggressive in securing research reactors. He explained that these reactors were necessary "to fill research needs at the universities and the needs of the AEC for wider training in reactor techniques."[13]

The particle accelerator controversy

The field of high-energy physics

High-energy physics, which is the study of the ultimate constituents of matter and the interactions of forces among them, is of tremendous scientific interest and has attracted to its study "some of the best and most creative scientists in the country."[14] Discoveries in the field have often led to increased international scientific prestige, as illustrated by the many high-energy physicists who have won Nobel Prizes.

In more specific terms, according to a 1965 Joint Committee on Atomic Energy (JCAE) report to Congress:

> High energy physics research is concerned with the experimental study of elementary particles and with the theoretical analysis of the properties and interactions of these particles. This research offers the promise of acquiring an understanding of the fundamental forces which control the behavior of the particles within the atomic nuclei, and is directed toward obtaining a more complete knowledge of the nature and behavior of the basic constituents of the physical universe. Investigations are carried out chiefly in experiments employing intense and well-controlled primary, secondary, or tertiary beams of elementary particles—the basic elements of matter—produced by high energy accelerators. Experimental studies in the recent past have resulted in a broader understanding of the significant phenomena which occur within the domain of elementary particles.[15]

The study of elementary particle physics seeks the unifying concepts that underlie and determine the principles of physics and provide the ultimate basis for all natural science, according to the physics community, who thus assert the overriding importance of this scientific discipline.

In order to pursue experimentation at ever-higher energy levels, however, increasingly larger and more powerful particle accelerators had to be built, which required ever-larger sums of money. The AEC assumed dominant responsibility in managing and funding the federal government's high-energy physics research program. To successfully manage this program government officials had to determine the level of physics research that the government could support to "further the quest for knowledge" and to assure maintenance of national leadership.[16] They also had to measure the effect of the program on the overall development of scientific education and on the distribution of government-supported university research programs. Moreover, the economic effects of the distribution of federal research funds to various areas of the country had to be considered, as well as the coordination of the program with other federal research programs.

Particle accelerators as research instruments

High-energy particle accelerators are machines that accelerate particles to energies greater than 1 Bev/nucleon. The unit of energy is the charge on the electron times the voltage, or electron volts (ev); energies of a billion electron volts are labeled "Bev" in the United States and "GeV" in Europe.[17] An accelerator propels electrically charged particles to high kinetic energies. For nuclear research, electrons, protons, deuterons, and alpha particles can be accelerated to nearly the speed of light. Types of accelerators include the cyclotron, linear accelerator, synchrotron, and synchrocyclotron. Most U.S. accelerators larger than 1 Bev are either synchrotrons or linear accelerators.[18]

Table 9.1 lists the accelerators built or under construction in the United States in the mid-1960s. There were no new multi-Bev accelerators added to the list between 1965 and 1977, so this is an accurate display of the U.S. particle accelerator inventory for the years of GAC operation.

There are many important scientific considerations in the use of particle accelerators, foremost among them the kind of particle or particles the machine can accelerate and the maximum energy production level the machine can achieve: "Although other factors are significant, the most important factor in the cost and utility of an accelerator is the energy to which the particles are accelerated."[19] Physicists are drawn to using the most powerful machine available to conduct experiments on the particles they seek to investigate or identify. However, dramatic increases in the power of the machine from 1 Bev to ever-higher multi-Bev ranges results in a geometric increase in costs, such that machines in the range above 100 Bev cost several hundred million dollars to construct and many millions each year to operate. As the size and complexity of each new accelerator increases, cost limitations mean that only very few new machines can be constructed. Once constructed, the competition among scientists seeking to use the machine is usually fierce. Older, less powerful machines tend to experience a decline in user demand when newer, more powerful machines become available.

This creates a dynamic situation in which fewer and fewer accelerator proposals can be approved for construction by the government, while the gains to the operator and the local economy of a chosen accelerator site area become immense. Selecting which accelerator project to approve is a matter of high-stakes technoscientific politics.

No issue was more likely to peak GAC interest than the matter of AEC-funded particle accelerators. If there was a high probability that a university rather than an AEC/ERDA lab would obtain a new accelerator, major universities inevitably became locked in heated competition to secure it. Sometimes major universities individually competed for an accelerator, and other times alliances were formed by regional groups of

Table 9.1. Accelerators with energies greater than 1 Bev operating in the United States

Location	Name	Particle	Energy (Bev)[a]	Completion Date
Brookhaven National Laboratory	Cosmotron	Proton	3.0	1952
Princeton	Princeton–U. of Penn. accelerator	Proton	3.0	1963
Lawrence Radiation Laboratory	Bevatron	Proton	6.2	1954–1963[b]
Argonne National Laboratory	Zero-gradient synchrotron	Proton	12.5	1963
Brookhaven National Laboratory	Alternating-gradient synchrotron	Proton	33.0	1960
Stanford	Mark III	Electron	1.2	1950 and 1964[b]
Cal Tech	Synchrotron	Electron	1.5	1952 and 1962[b]
Cornell	Synchrotron	Electron	2.2	1955
Cambridge	CEA[c]	Electron	6.0	1962
Cornell	Synchrotron	Electron	10.0	1968
Stanford	SLAC 1[d]	Electron	20.0	1966
Fermi Lab	National accelerator laboratory	Proton	200.0	1972

Source: U.S. Congress, Joint Committee on Atomic Energy 1965, p. 44.
Note: The Fermi Lab entry, added as an update, appears as only a planned and unsited project in the source above.
[a] Bev = billion volts of electric power as of 1964.
[b] Date of last major improvement project.
[c] CEA = Cambridge Electron Accelerator.
[d] SLAC 1 = Stanford Linear Accelerator Center 1.

universities to compete. On the other hand, if there was a question as to whether an accelerator should go to a university or to an AEC laboratory, the labs and the universities would come into conflict. If a lab or labs competing for the machine were operated under contract by a university or a university group, those at the contractor universities worked to have the machine built at their lab.

The GAC, universities, and particle accelerators

It became customary for the AEC to obtain the opinions of outside scientific advisers so as "to get as good a technical judgment of the value of a particular program, so that decisions as to priorities" could be made confidently.[20] The GAC members were for many years a source of advice on high-energy physics for the AEC and, to a degree, for the White House and other federal agencies.

In 1953 and 1954, the universities and the great AEC labs clashed over the matter of planning for new particle accelerators. Much of the debate on this subject occurred among participants in GAC meetings. Ultimately, the recommendations put forward by the GAC as a result of these meetings helped to establish a standing AEC policy of many years. The procedures that emerged from this policy have been carried on with few changes by ERDA and today by the DOE.

During their review of the AEC research program in February 1953, GAC members unanimously agreed that a much broader AEC research program was permissible under the provisions of the Atomic Energy Act of 1946. This broadened interpretation was used by the Committee to argue for increased federal funding to build new, larger, and more powerful particle accelerators. The group recognized that these mammoth scientific instruments made possible more ambitious experiments in high-energy physics and in related fields of inquiry. At that time members agreed to assist AEC Research Division officials in "selling" a particle accelerator construction program. To generate public support for this initiative, the Committee suggested that the AEC staff prepare a public study modeled on an existing article, "Why Build Accelerators?"[21]

In 1965 the AEC had presented the JCAE with the following list of benefits provided by advances made in high-energy physics research using particle accelerators. This list was used for many years to justify expanded high-energy physics research endeavors:

> Accelerator technology, beginning with the earliest cyclotrons, has produced some ideas and stimulated inventions useful in other areas of science and industry. High-power transmitting tubes were developed in the late thirties in conjunction with the cyclotron. The early impetus to the development of the klystrons arose from the

desire to build a linear accelerator. The Van de Graaff electrostatic generator, now widely used in radiology and radiography as well as nuclear physics, was developed by physicists as a particle accelerator. More recently, the alternating gradient principle, discovered by high-energy accelerator physicists, has been applied in electron tubes in the communications industry. There have been some particularly direct contributions of high-energy research to the national strength. These are the developments in particle and photon production and detection techniques which are necessary for both military and civilian nuclear technology, for the study of the upper atmosphere and of space, and for use in biology and medicine. Some examples of such developments have been the Cerenkov counters, spark chambers, improved vacuum pumps, ion sources, magnet designs, photomultiplier and image-intensifier designs, improved fast electronics systems, and automated devices for pattern recognition and data encoding and analysis.[22]

One of the most heated debates developed in 1953 over whether to fund a new particle accelerator at Harvard University or at Brookhaven National Laboratory. There were proposals from institutions located in other regions as well. Midwest Universities Research Association wanted to build an accelerator situated near the University of Wisconsin campus at Madison. The University of Chicago wanted an accelerator built at its Argonne laboratory. Plans were put forward for an accelerator at Princeton University in New Jersey.

According to a study of federal science and technology policy, "The importance of a particular technological choice is due not only to the nature of the technology chosen, but also to the fact that such choices utilize scarce resources and, therefore, close off alternative options."[23] This assertion applies to the case of AEC particle accelerators. GAC members completed a review of the technical differences of the university versus the national laboratory accelerator plans, knowing that government resources to pay for these expensive projects were very limited and every proposal could not be approved. The decision to select one project over another, however, might close off alternative research options; therefore, such decisions would be critical in shaping the future of high-energy physics. They knew that American physics research, which depended on particle accelerator technology, would be profoundly affected by their recommendations and by the AEC's subsequent actions on those recommendations. Another important issue was also involved. If AEC labs rather than major universities were to obtain most or all of the new accelerators, federal administrators and laboratory executives would be able to guide and influence the progress of high-energy physics research. University officials also were aware that if new accelerators went to off-campus AEC contract labs, the university research community's access to the machines would be regulated and restricted by government lab officials; in effect, AEC lab-based accelerators would pull physics researchers away from the campuses and toward the national labs, an arrangement that would not only sustain the intellectual vitality of AEC labs that secured accelerators but would also ensure that the accelerator use was more closely tied to research priorities of the federal technoscientific agencies.

The accelerator debates of 1953–1954

Promising the advancement of science in high-energy research proved to be considerably easier than determining which accelerator project proposals would be approved. In the August 1953 sessions of Meeting 36, the AEC basic research budget was again a topic of discussion. This time the issue of accelerators triggered a heated exchange. Members understood that a choice had to be made between approving construction of a new particle accelerator proposed by Harvard University and approving a project to build a somewhat larger accelerator at the Brookhaven National Laboratory (BNL). Presumably, a number of Boston-area universities and colleges would share in use of the Harvard machine; the Harvard plan itself was often referred to as the Cambridge proposal. The Brookhaven lab, operated under a contract by Associated Universities, Inc. (AUI), and located on eastern Long Island, also planned to make its machine available to university visitors in the region. The driving distance between Boston and Brookhaven is only about 250 miles, and it made little sense to build two very expensive machines in such close proximity.

Understanding the ties that GAC members had with institutions seeking approval of their accelerator proposals is essential in analyzing the Committee's handling of these high-energy physics issues. Rabi, who chaired the GAC from October 1952 until July 1956, was a professor at Columbia University, one of nine universities on the board of directors of AUI. Whitman, who served on the GAC from August 1950 until August 1956, was a professor at MIT. Wigner, of Princeton University, served on the GAC from August 1952 until January 1957. MIT and Princeton were also on the AUI board of directors. Other Committee members employed by universities in the period 1953–1954 included Libby, Johnson, Warner, Beams, and McMillan. In this period Libby and Johnson worked for the University of Chicago. Warner was president of the Carnegie Institute of Technology in Pittsburgh. Beams was a professor and department chair at the University of Virginia during his GAC tenure and also served on the Board of the Oak Ridge Institute for Nuclear Studies. McMillan was a professor at the University of California who concurrently held the position of associate director of the Berkeley lab.

Corporation-affiliated GAC members in the period 1953–1954 included Oliver E. Buckley, Eger V. Murphree, and James B. Fisk. Buckley and Fisk were senior executives of the Bell Telephone Laboratories. Murphree became president of Esso Research and Engineering Company in 1947 and retained this position during his terms on the GAC. Because corporate-affiliated members did not have a vested interest in particle accelerator research, they often arbitrated debates between the university interests.

In the debate surrounding the Brookhaven and Harvard accelerator proposals at Meeting 36 in August 1953, Chairman Rabi led the discussion. At one point he remarked: "BNL (Brookhaven National Laboratory) represents a $50–100 million investment and its usefulness depends on its possessing the best that there is in unique facilities. To build an accelerator of this size at a university instead of at Brookhaven would tend to make Brookhaven obsolescent and curtail its usefulness in its primary function."[24] Rabi went on to question both the motives and needs of universities that were seeking large accelerator facilities. In the presence of several AEC commissioners and his GAC colleagues, he asserted: "There is a strong tendency for some people in the universities to want to build big machines rather than conduct research on the scale appropriate for their university campuses. Machines of this sort are not a necessary element in student training and indeed may not provide a good environment for the student. It is up to the Commission to see that the National Laboratories have the best facilities that can be made. Such a facility on a campus does not work as a National Laboratory and creates grave problems within the institution.[25]

Warner, president of Carnegie Institute of Technology in Pittsburgh, agreed with Rabi and offered his own comment: "It is a mistake to put these big machines on the campus. It is difficult to see any really strong advantage in having a university department run such a facility; it is in no way a normal extension of the functions of a university department. Conversely, it is very important to utilize the momentum which has been built up at Brookhaven.[26] During this exchange, Buckley argued that putting an accelerator at Cambridge would weaken Brookhaven, arguing "People would not go to BNL who otherwise would do so." Rabi claimed that Cambridge, the home of Harvard and MIT, was "already loaded with research facilities."[27]

Whitman, professor and head of MIT's Department of Chemical Engineering, defended the Harvard proposal. Although MIT was on the board of directors of AUI, Brookhaven's contract operator, the proximity of MIT to Harvard and the close interrelationship of these universities would allow Harvard to share the use of its proposed accelerator with MIT. Harvard University had no representative on the GAC at the time of the debate and would not until Ramsey joined the Committee in November 1960.

Rabi recommended that the Committee rank the BNL accelerator first, a midwest group accelerator second, and the Harvard accelerator third. All members of the GAC, including Whitman, eventually agreed that only the BNL accelerator should be given priority funding. The AEC endorsed the GAC recommendation and the Brookhaven accelerator—or the alternating-gradient synchrotron (AGS), as it was called—was completed and put in operation in 1960.[28] In this dispute Brookhaven won and Harvard lost, but more important, the foundation was set for justifying the siting of accelerators at the national laboratories rather than on university campuses.

Continuing accelerator conflicts

A year after Meeting 36, the fight over whether accelerators should go to universities or to AEC laboratories erupted again. By late 1954, however, there had been considerable turnover in GAC membership. Libby had resigned, and the terms of Buckley and von Neumann had expired. Lewis L. Strauss had been appointed AEC chairman in July 1953 by President Dwight D. Eisenhower. On the recommendation of Strauss and the other four AEC commissioners, Eisenhower appointed Beams, Johnson, and McMillan to the GAC, all in October 1954. Beams and McMillan were physicists and Johnson a chemist. Each understood the significance of particle accelerators in high-energy physics research, recognizing that particle physics could fundamentally shape the essential character of many, if not all, of the physical sciences.

After reviewing a report prepared by the GAC research subcommittee, the full Committee agreed that construction of higher-powered accelerators was necessary for "the progress and health of physics." Yet there was still disagreement and division on the matter of university-based accelerators. An observation was made that "the effect of such large facilities on the universities, if placed there, is a serious matter."[29]

At this time the Committee became embroiled in what came to be known as the MURA controversy. In an effort to gain approval for a particle accelerator project in the midwest, the University of Illinois, Indiana University, the University of Minnesota, and the University of Wisconsin banded together to form the Midwest Universities Research Association (MURA).[30] Researchers at these institutions believed at the time that the eastern and western regions of the country possessed the most sophisticated and expensive high-energy physics research facilities, with the midwest far behind. MURA spokesmen argued that they were the object of regional discrimination by the East Coast and West Coast university science communities. The MURA plan called for construction of a high-intensity accelerator to be built at a site not far from the campus of the University of Wisconsin.

At this time also the University of Chicago sought an AEC accelerator for its Argonne National Laboratory (ANL). MURA researchers disliked the prospect of having to gain access to an Argonne accelerator through the University of Chicago, strongly preferring a university-based accelerator facility devoted to the research interests of their own faculties. There was also the recognition that a huge accelerator facility held out the potential for local and regional economic growth. These facilities were grand-scale construction enterprises that would eventually draw university, government, and corporate scientists from the nation and the world.[31] MURA university people, of course, preferred a site adjacent to one of their own member institutions.

During this period, no MURA-affiliated university had a representative on the Committee. The University of Chicago, however, was represented by Johnson, who served as vice president in charge of special science projects from 1958 to 1967.

Because the Princeton–University of Pennsylvania accelerator proposal was among those being considered at Meeting 42 in November 1954, Princeton's Wigner excused himself from discussion of the proposals so as to avoid a possible conflict of interest. As the meeting progressed, Whitman suggested that the Princeton and Cambridge (Harvard) proposals be held in abeyance until the Argonne-MURA matter was resolved. He expressed his hope that an agreement could be reached between Argonne and the MURA group without further delay. McMillan disagreed and recommended that the Harvard and MURA proposals be considered together. Arguing that both proposals deserved further technical study, McMillan added that he was not sufficiently well informed to give definitive advice in the Argonne-MURA controversy. Beams also voiced his uncertainty regarding the Argonne-MURA matter.

Despite the fact that his university's contract lab was a central party in the issue, Johnson joined in the discussion. He began by admitting that he could not be completely objective, but he commented that the national laboratories had to be made strong: "If Argonne does not get a big accelerator which will attract and stimulate people, it is likely to fail as a National Laboratory."[32] He also remarked that he hoped to see the Argonne problem settled before deciding about individual university proposals, such as Harvard's and Princeton's. Johnson's expressed position on this matter constituted special pleading for Argonne's interests, which could be interpreted as a conflict of interest.[33] His suggestion that the MURA group settle for sharing in use of an accelerator built for Argonne was directly contrary to the MURA position. There was no MURA spokesman on the GAC at the time to challenge Johnson's claims.

Johnson found an ally in Warner, who said that he hoped the "ANL (Argonne National Laboratory) imbroglio" could be settled within six months. Fisk also endorsed Johnson's position, counseling, "It would be a mistake at this time to have these items in the budget for single groups, since it would prejudice the chance of a machine at Argonne." He recommended that "a sum of money be budgeted to give the Argonne (accelerator) a strong go-ahead."[34]

On the afternoon of November 4, 1954, Chairman Rabi summarized the GAC consensus on accelerators. He declared that the GAC would like the AEC to formulate "a more complete general policy on accelerators at universities and at the National Laboratories." He asked, "If large accelerators are to go on university campuses, how will these be handled—on the basis of the individual university or as facilities for community groups?"[35] The reference to community groups denotes the common practice of shared use of research facilities by scientists from colleges and universities in the vicinity of the accelerator. This includes researchers from universities or colleges who have formed a consortium organization to govern access and use of the machine. In other words, Rabi's question can be interpreted as, Should the university securing an AEC accelerator be responsible for determining its use, or should the accelerator be dedicated to the work planned for it by a university "cooperative" of some kind?

Rabi then moved on to the MURA controversy. He asserted, "We should make a definite recommendation that the Commission proceed to solve the Midwest situation in the direction of budgeting a machine for the Argonne National Laboratory." He maintained that the GAC saw little difference between the MURA and the Harvard proposal and argued: "[To approve Harvard's proposal] would give MURA ground for pressing its own proposal, which would interfere with Argonne. Action should be delayed until a policy is formulated and until some decision is made with respect to MURA."[36]

MURA's quest to obtain an accelerator for its use, exclusive of Argonne, would continue for almost twelve more years. By 1962, MURA researchers had invented designs for a fixed-field alternating-gradient synchrotron that "at fairly high cost, enabled the acceleration of a larger number of protons than the conventional synchrotron."[37]

This was a completely new technique for particle acceleration. MURA people hoped that the boldness and innovation of the new accelerator design would finally win federal government approval for construction of the accelerator they had long sought. For a period, it appeared that MURA might actually succeed.

In 1963, the Ramsey panel, a joint PSAC-GAC group, was directed to examine the government's high-energy physics program. Asked to present a program "with some indication of priorities from a technical standpoint," the panel considered several proposals for major new or expanded particle accelerator projects. AEC officials, predisposed to support the project at the time, asked the panel for its comments on the MURA proposal. The panel's response was that the "MURA accelerator was extremely valuable and should be undertaken if its construction would not significantly delay that of higher energy machines." In other words, the proposed higher-energy proton and electron accelerators that the panel reviewed and ranked in order of priority were more important than the MURA accelerator. Relaying the panel's qualified support of the MURA plan, in the fall of 1963 the AEC asked the Bureau of the Budget to approve the new accelerator. "At the same time," according to another source, "a number of midwestern congressmen wrote letters to the President supporting the accelerator, and articles appeared in the newspaper discussing it. One or two congressmen also wrote opposing the accelerator because they felt the program of the accelerator at Argonne Laboratory near Chicago might be harmed if the MURA accelerator were built."[38]

After President John F. Kennedy assumed office in 1961, hopes ran high that he might approve the MURA proposal as a favor to powerful midwestern congressmen. However, when President Kennedy was assassinated in 1963 and Vice President Lyndon B. Johnson assumed the presidency, President Johnson quashed the MURA proposal and advised MURA universities to enter into an indirect comanagerial arrangement with the University of Chicago in order to operate Argonne's new accelerator. Left with no alternative, MURA universities complied with Johnson's request.[39] As related by another source: "For budgetary reasons, President Johnson decided not to construct the MURA accelerator. He considered the effect on the overall federal budget and how much of that budget he was willing to put into basic science. Given the priorities within science as a whole, he did not feel that he could propose to Congress the construction of this new, expensive facility. Accordingly, the final step in the successful authorization of an accelerator, discussion and approval by the Congress, did not occur.[40] Johnson had other reasons for rejecting the MURA plan. He had built his career promoting the progress and development of the U.S. space program. Since space-related research was the foremost scientific issue on his mind, he tended to perceive the MURA machine as a nonessential project that diverted scientific resources and talent away from the central scientific and technical challenge of space exploration.[41]

The history of the MURA controversy illustrates the high-stakes politics of particle accelerator decision making. Each time a newer type or higher-powered accelerator was proposed, operators of existing accelerators feared that their machines would fall into disuse or would no longer represent the state of the art. As these machines increased dramatically in cost, decision making was no longer left to the subsystem authorities of the AEC and their advisers. Instead the Bureau of the Budget, and the President himself, entered into this technoscientific realm.

Policies for university accelerator use

In deliberations on other university accelerator proposals the Committee confronted other, very different problems. At Meeting 42 in November 1954, some GAC members argued that the AEC was imposing unacceptable conditions on certain universities seeking approval of their particle accelerator proposals. McMillan, a research scientist and administrator at the Berkeley lab, claimed that Princeton was being coerced into becoming a national laboratory by making that a condition for approval of its proposal. He said that was wrong and suggested that action on the Princeton proposal be deferred until final decisions were made on the Harvard and midwestern proposals.[42] Reacting to the success of the pro-Argonne group, McMillan declared that if the Argonne proposal could be budgeted, then so could the Harvard proposal. The GAC was unmoved.

Those attending understood that some kind of accommodation to universities and university groups would be essential. Esso research executive Murphree summarized some of the debate and put forward a recommendation regarding accelerator location. He described the issue as a matter of policy, asking, "How far does one go in placing big machines at individual universities? The policy might be to set up the larger machines on a regional basis, and the intermediate sizes on a community basis. The Committee might recommend that the AEC produce a policy paper for its consideration."[43] McMillan continued his argument at Meeting 43 in December 1954. He again objected to the idea of compelling a university to "take on a National Laboratory flavor as a condition for having a machine."[44] He claimed that the strings and complications accompanying national laboratory designation would be obnoxious, and that rules of that kind were an insult to the institution. Therefore, although a university might be fortunate enough to win government approval of its accelerator proposal, the conditions of acceptance imposed on that university might be objectionable. McMillan's point was well taken. Officials of those few universities with an on-campus national laboratory have sometimes discovered that the facility is run more in conformity with national program objectives than with university objectives and interests. Murphree suggested that the AEC claim the right to "designate a certain fraction of the machine's use to other universities."[45] He also advised that the AEC should in fact exercise this right.

The GAC was quite receptive to Murphree's joint-participation proposal. This approach had several advantages. First, it made easier any justification to build accelerators at the national laboratories rather than at particular universities. If accelerators were owned and operated by AEC contract labs, it would be more difficult for the president or Congress to transfer the government's high-energy physics research program to another agency. In this period, considerable attention was given to a proposal that would transfer high-energy physics from the AEC to the National Science Foundation, or possibly to a new federal science department. If the instruments needed to conduct high-energy physics experiments were an integral part of the AEC national laboratory complex, it would be difficult to turn them over to another agency. However, campus-based accelerators could be transferred to another federal agency with fewer organizational and managerial complications.

Second, giving accelerators to the AEC national laboratories would help to alleviate interuniversity competition for accelerators. By opening AEC lab–based accelerators to use by regional consortiums of universities and colleges, more scientists from more universities could acquire at least some machine-use time. Speaking as highly placed university administrators, Warner and Johnson said that joint-participation conditions and arrangements would be quite acceptable.[46] The joint-participation proposal was eventually approved and became a common operating norm at AEC particle accelerator facilities. A third advantage of the approach became apparent once joint-participation procedures had taken hold. Many officials of the AEC contract research laboratories had built cooperative links with universities located in their area or region. T. H. Johnson of the AEC staff told the GAC at Meeting 47 in December 1955 that the Oak Ridge National Laboratory had strengthened southern universities through research contracts and joint participation in use of the Oak Ridge facilities.[47]

The joint-participation system of accelerator use emerged, to a great degree, from GAC recommendations to the AEC. This system helped to bring about a shift of basic research in high-energy physics away from the university campus to the AEC contract laboratories. The Committee's handling of accelerator project issues in this period revealed the GAC's predisposition toward advancing the interests of the major AEC labs. Because some GAC members represented different universities and because these universities stood to gain or lose in the assignment of accelerators to specific universities, there was a tendency on the part of many members to protect their university and laboratory vested interests. The conflicts that ensued made it difficult for the GAC to give priority to one university's proposal over another's. Carefully allotting accelerators to AEC contract labs (e.g., Argonne, Brookhaven, Oak Ridge) with the proviso that the facilities be open to joint use by regional university and college scientific researchers proved to be a satisfactory compromise. Nevertheless, this promised to give the national laboratories immense scientific power. McMillan complained that the national laboratories were being given monopoly control of essential research instruments such as accelerators, which, he alleged, would confound university science research through delay and inefficiency. He saw no good reason why individual universities or university groups should be "cut out in accelerator location debates."[48] This ongoing controversy is one that cannot be resolved as long as the federal government continues to heavily subsidize research in the nuclear sciences, and as long as the universities and national laboratories continue to compete for funding as well as use of expensive research technology.

The diminished GAC role in accelerator location

In matters of high-energy physics research and the use of particle accelerators, the GAC exercised peak influence in the early 1950s. In the years that followed, individual GAC members were assigned to serve as representatives on other formal panels and committees that advised on matters of high-energy physics and on the need for new particle accelerator facilities and technology.

For example, Rabi, while a member of the GAC, served with Williams and Ramsey on the National Science Foundation's Advisory Panel on Ultrahigh Energy Accelerators in 1954. Williams and Ramsey would become GAC members in 1960. The report filed by this panel emphasized that the cost of high-energy physics research was becoming too great for universities and research institutions to support from their own funds.[49] Two years later, Rabi and Williams helped prepare another report as members of NSF's Advisory Panel on High Energy Accelerators.

In 1958 a long period of interaction with the president's science advisor and the PSAC began. Known as the Piore panel, named for Chairman (and IBM Research Director) Emanuel Piore, the joint PSAC-GAC group was composed of five members. GAC representatives to this group were Beams and McMillan. The chief responsibility of the Piore panel of 1958, and later 1960, was "to examine the question of building the Stanford linear (accelerator) within the context of the whole field of high-energy physics and to make recommendations."[50] The initial Piore panel recommended against building higher-energy machines because, they contended, not enough experience had been gathered with lower-energy accelerators and the high cost would not be justified. The Piore panel reconvened in 1960 with Beams, McMillan, and Wigner representing the GAC. This group, using new scientific evidence, strongly supported construction of a two-mile-long, 20-billion-electron-volt linear accelerator at Stanford University. President Eisenhower personally made the decision to build the Stanford accelerator. A study of this issue asserts, "The AEC saw clearly that this $100 million machine could not be justified solely in terms of its own mission but only on the basis of a broader national interest."[51] Consequently, high-energy physics rose to the status of a national research program, no longer charted only by academic theoreticians and no longer a minor vestige of AEC program responsibility.

In 1963 the Ramsey panel, another joint PSAC-GAC panel, was formed. It had ten members, four of them GAC members: Ramsey, who was chairman, and Abelson, Williams, and Edwin L. Goldwasser. Owen Chamberlain of the UC-Berkeley, Murray Gell-Mann of the California Institute of Technology, T. D. Lee of Columbia University, W. K. H. Panofsky of the Stanford Linear Accelerator Center, E. M. Purcell of Harvard University, and Frederick Seitz of the National Academy of Sciences were the other panel members. Like the Piore panels that preceded it, the Ramsey panel was asked to advise on the relative balance between funds for new construction and for accelerators already in operation, on the relative needs for university laboratories and national laboratories, on new accelerators and experimental concepts, and on the prospect for joint international cooperation with the European Organization for Nuclear Research (CERN) in Geneva.[52] Among the many comments and recommendations of the panel was an insistence that the distinction between "university accelerators" and "national accelerators" is minimal. Since large accelerators represent significant capital investments of public funds, the panel concluded that new large accelerators should be open to competent scientists or groups of scientists without regard to their affiliations but rather in accord with the scientific merit of their proposals.[53]

This observation made it apparent that accelerators, whether at university or at national laboratory sites, would be operated in accord with national high-energy physics research program interests. Use of the devices would not be exclusively determined by either a university or a national lab. The degree to which research physicists could determine use of the accelerators was a function of the power they could use in influencing the many authorities regulating access to the machines and providing the resources necessary to conduct experimentation. The pursuit of high-energy physics research was becoming highly bureaucratized and subject to increasingly demanding conditions of disciplinary self-regulation.

Political scientist Robert H. Salisbury identified self-regulation as a category of public policy. In self-regulation, limits are set on what people can do, but "the group itself is authorized to set these limits." In allocative policies the benefits are distributed in some fashion by government officials. However, in structural policies, units are created and guidelines are developed to govern future allocations of benefits.[54] In the late 1940s and early 1950s the politics of high-energy physics research were distributive or allocative in the sense that agency officials, the Bureau of the Budget, and the JCAE, with some advisory input from groups such as the GAC, routinely reviewed and approved proposals for experimental facilities paid for by the government but used and consumed by universities and national laboratories. In those rare periods when federal basic research funding was generous, the GAC had no difficulty in helping the AEC identify worthy accelerator research proposals. However, when particle physics became the center of attention for the physics community and had to be researched through use of increasingly large, complex, and expensive scientific instruments, the era of distributive policy in basic science research ended. Thereafter, decisions to approve or reject proposals to build new high-energy accelerators involved controversial redistributive issues; winners succeeded at the losers' expense, but the winners themselves were no longer free to use their accelerators as they pleased.

Accelerators, whether built at a university campus or on the grounds of a national laboratory, were to be subject to considerably more regulation than had been the case before. It was some satisfaction to the physics community that they would play a central role in determining and regulating use of these devices. The guidelines and the judgment of the scientific merits of a user's proposal, however, were made by boards and panels of physicists working in government or on special review panels. Acquiring accelerators and acquiring accelerator research time continue to be a challenge as new self-regulatory structures are imposed.

The GAC always took a special interest in the federal government's high-energy physics research program. The many physicists who served on the GAC over its history recognized that the recommendations put forward by the Committee could conceivably shape the future of the entire field. Universities have a special interest in basic research and continue to be the nation's chief source of basic research and development. Before physics research required use of high-energy particle accelerators, academic interests on the campus helped to determine the course and progress of physics research. However, with the ascendance of high-energy particle physics research, universities grew to depend on federal support in the purchase of accelerators and related technology.

In addition, universities entered into competition with AEC contract laboratories in their quest to obtain accelerator facilities. It soon became clear that the cost of newer, higher-powered accelerators would severely limit the number of new accelerators that could be built and operated. The GAC occupied a central position in the transformation of high-energy physics from a relatively private, deliberative, campus-based academic research activity to an activity that became highly competitive, considerably more bureaucratic, and increasingly subject to the regulation of disciplinary peers or superiors. As the program became much more costly, new accelerators seemed to gravitate to national laboratories rather than to universities, with the Stanford accelerator a notable exception.

The GAC played a key role in encouraging the practice of cooperative or shared use of AEC lab accelerators by outside, university user-groups. More important, the Committee continually emphasized the importance of high-energy physics to the AEC, even when Commission officials began to complain that high-energy physics research was diverting the agency from its primary mission, the development of nuclear reactor technology. The Committee was a formidable lobbying force; the members were experts with almost unquestioned intellectual authority who often apprised the government of high-energy physics research achievements of other nations, particularly the Soviet Union. The GAC often stressed that the nation's scientific prestige in the world was dependent on continued advance of U.S. particle physics work.

The issue of official secrecy is ever present in GAC matters. In the field of high-energy physics, however, official secrecy is not a major issue because little work in this field has been subject to classification by the government. In the first year of AEC operation, Oppenheimer exhorted the AEC not to attempt to classify basic nuclear research, saying, "We feel very strongly that it is a prejudice to security and will in the end thoroughly corrode it and is a very great violence to the good that the Commission can do in the cultivation of science not to take advantage of the existence of openness where it is possible, and I feel this even to the point of saying that where the predominant character in the given job is non-secret, the secret stuff must not be allowed to force a wrong kind of classification on the non-secret work."[55]

The GAC helped to ensure that high-energy physics research was unfettered by classification restrictions. Meeting under conditions of secrecy themselves, however, GAC members have a mixed record in objectivity. While some members voluntarily withdrew from discussions of proposals submitted by their home university or by a laboratory operated by their university so as to avoid a possible conflict of interest, other members did not. There were several instances of special pleading by GAC members, but not all of it was necessarily predicated on self-interest.

GAC advice regarding high-energy physics research continued through the Committee's history of operation, but it seems to have exercised the greatest influence in the early 1950s. After the late 1950s, certain select GAC members were regularly invited to serve on joint PSAC-GAC high-energy physics advisory panels, but the full GAC itself gradually lost advisory powers in this realm. One fact bears repeating: A chief reason why so many physicists served on the GAC was because high-energy physics researchers are so thoroughly dependent on federal resources to build, maintain, and operate their chief research instruments. Service on the GAC afforded an opportunity to guide the government in cultivation of this scientific discipline.

10 The life cycle of an elite scientific advisory committee

The early GAC, 1947–1963

In reviewing the history of the GAC, the following comment is appropriate: "Science has achieved its great power by insisting on defining for itself the problems it proposes to solve, and by refusing to take on problems merely because some outside source considers them important."[1] To a great degree this statement characterized the mode of early GAC operation. From 1947 to 1963 Committee membership included the pioneers of atomic energy—physicists, chemists, mathematicians, chemical engineers, and others who were acclaimed authorities in the world of university, corporate, and government research, including a succession of Nobel laureates.

The GAC was not a part-time technical consulting group operating at the beck and call of the AEC but a highly independent panel entrusted to provide "advice on major matters of policy."[2] The panel's level of expertise made it the AEC's chief repository of scientific and technical knowledge. So authoritative were the recommendations of the early GAC that the group functioned as a scientific directorate, although one devoid of authority to issue direct administrative orders.

The GAC of the late 1940s and early 1950s shouldered scientific and technical responsibilities that afforded the Atomic Energy Commissioners "increased flexibility and greater opportunity to concentrate on basic policy matters."[3] After the AEC recruited larger numbers of qualified scientific and technical personnel, perfected its organization and operations, and acquired experience in the management of its programs, the GAC's guidance and expertise became less essential.

Many early GAC members were held in very high public regard. Everyone of the Committee's first nine members had done important work in the huge wartime Manhattan Project. A remarkable number of them had worked at the Los Alamos Scientific Laboratory during the war, and many had also worked in the Office of Scientific Research and Development or were part of the National Defense Research Committee. Public personalities and science celebrities in their own right, most of these people were regularly interviewed by the press. Their ability to influence public opinion accorded them some degree of leverage in securing what they needed from government, or in getting government to address problems they believed were important. Because all GAC members were established and successful in their careers and professions, they could afford to be independent and sometimes brutally frank in advising the AEC.

The AEC sometimes exploited the celebrity and stature of GAC members for public relations purposes. The AEC enlisted the help of the GAC, for example, to address the issue of atomic fallout. Having been briefed by the AEC staff about the growing public concern and panic about radioactive contamination of the environment from above-ground nuclear testing, the GAC responded by issuing a prepared statement intended to help the AEC confront public pressure.

Besides public relations duties the early GAC played a major role in helping the AEC recruit scientific and technical personnel for its contract laboratories. Since many GAC members were leaders of university, corporate, or government research facilities, they easily attracted many of the nation's talented scientists and engineers to AEC facilities. Because many who served on the Committee periodically continued to conduct research at one or more of the AEC's contract laboratories, talented graduate students and research assistants often had the opportunity to accompany their mentors on trips to the AEC research labs. GAC members understood that the progress of defense science work required a regular infusion of young, dedicated, competent researchers. Often by their own example members encouraged others to engage in research work, frequently conducted under conditions of official secrecy, at the major AEC laboratories. This recruitment service was particularly critical in the years when the AEC was trying to revive the Los Alamos lab and when it was attempting to reignite operations at Oak Ridge National Laboratory and the Hanford Works, as well as at other research laboratories.

The GAC devoted considerable time and effort to the problem of fission material production. In the late 1940s and 1950s, the production of radioactive isotopes (essential in the development of materials used in fission and thermonuclear bombs, as well as in other basic and applied scientific research) in quantity was complex, difficult, and expensive.

The industrial facilities that produced these substances were not always reliable. There were a variety of methods that could be used, each with varying degrees of success, in the extraction of radioactive isotopes from primary elemental materials. Many of the early GAC members had developed or engineered these processes and methods, and their advice on the matter of isotope production was invaluable to the AEC. The design and planning of production facilities in the Oak Ridge, Hanford, and Savannah River national laboratories were influenced by GAC recommendations to the AEC. The GAC supervised and followed the progress of a whole generation of test reactors, and several scaled-up reactors were designed to produce plutonium and other vital substances in their operation.

Central among GAC concerns, along with manpower and materials production, was the entire matter of scientific project management. The GAC was often used by the Commission as an instrument of program evaluation. The full Committee regularly held meetings at various AEC contract labs; more often, GAC subcommittees would engage in field research for the full Committee. The information gathered at the AEC labs became the basis for determining the progress, or lack of progress, in various program and project areas. The early GAC (more so than its later counterparts) was never reluctant to criticize poor lab administration or bad science. Although it might be assumed that the leaders of the major AEC contract labs would be wary of the GAC, Committee records disclose that in meeting after meeting lab officials welcomed the chance to state their cases before the Committee. At least once a year a regular private meeting was held with all of the lab directors, who used the GAC as a powerful ally when they petitioned the AEC for project support or money.

The GAC tracked the progress of Project Super in the postwar years just as it had followed the other AEC projects and missions. The Committee did not take a stand against that project until the fall of 1949, at which time eight members went on record opposing a program of "crash development" for a thermonuclear bomb. Appended to their official technical advisory were two extraordinary supplemental statements. In an unprecedented manner, Committee members expressed moral and political opposition to this project, calling it a weapon of genocide. In this period, shortly after the Soviet Union's first successful atom bomb explosion, the GAC was under great pressure from military and national security interests to endorse a dramatically accelerated program of thermonuclear weapon development. Several members of the Joint Committee on Atomic Energy (JCAE), a powerful pro–Project Super pressure group, were openly critical of the GAC's rejection of the initiative. The political impact of the GAC's anti–Project Super recommendation was further undermined by the Klaus Fuchs espionage case and by the strident opposition of AEC Commissioner Lewis L. Strauss. Secretary of State Dean G. Acheson and Secretary of Defense Louis Johnson also were critical of the GAC position.

President Harry S. Truman disregarded the GAC recommendation and approved Project Super in early 1950. The Committee's opposition to the project produced considerable future fallout. The 1954 Security Hearings into the Oppenheimer case delved extensively into his expressed opposition to the project in 1949. In the years following 1949, however, no member of the GAC, not even Oppenheimer, acted to impede the progress of thermonuclear research; if anything, the Committee promoted the research in virtually every respect. The failure of the GAC to endorse a crash program of thermonuclear bomb development in 1949 did not mark the end of the Committee's major advisory role in government, as some have claimed.

In no area was the early GAC more influential than in high-energy physics. The GAC helped to shape the entire AEC high-energy physics program. The Committee regularly reviewed particle accelerator proposals prepared by major universities, university groups, and AEC contract laboratories and often became the central arena in which proposals were debated and ranked, usually with the AEC commissioners and key staff present. By the late 1950s and early 1960s the Committee lost the influence it had once held in this area. Nonetheless, many of the Committee's physicists were recruited to serve on joint PSAC-GAC panels assigned the task of reviewing the federal government's complete high-energy physics program. In this area, more than almost any other, GAC physicists played an active and sometimes dominant role.

The Committee also made many contributions in the development of nuclear power. The GAC Reactor Subcommittee frequently traveled to laboratories in even the remotest locations to monitor the progress of various reactor prototypes that were being engineered. The GAC played only a peripheral role in the naval reactor program promoted by Admiral Hyman Rickover, but it was active in supervising a variety of other experimental reactor projects for the Commission, such as the nuclear-powered airplane, the nuclear reactor–powered rocket, and peaceful uses of thermonuclear explosives. The GAC recommended against development of the nuclear plane but generally endorsed, with limitations, the Plowshare program.

By 1959 the GAC faced some competition from the newly constituted President's Science Advisory Committee. In that year Commonwealth Edison's Dresden Unit 1 prototype nuclear reactor went into operation on the outskirts of Chicago, and a year later Connecticut Yankee Atomic Electric Company loaded fuel and began generating power in Massachusetts.[4] This began a wave of nuclear power plant construction and experimentation by a number of the nation's largest electric utilities. In 1962, AEC Chairman Glenn T. Seaborg announced, "We conclude that nuclear power is on the threshold of economic competitiveness and can soon be made competitive in areas consuming a significant fraction of the nation's electrical energy."[5]

As civilian nuclear power progressed to the stage of application, and as the defense community came to demand new and improved nuclear weapons, the GAC was pulled away from the basic science issues with which it had been originally preoccupied. Civilian and defense science were identified with new technical priorities, resulting in a breakdown of the boundary between the basic sciences and engineering.[6] In the next era of GAC history the engineers became dominant.

The problem of official secrecy always confronted the GAC. The Atomic Energy Act of 1946, which "represented a novel attempt to define one entire area of information that was to be subject to stringent government control," placed under restriction "all data concerning the manufacture or utilization of atomic weapons, the production of fissionable materials, or the use of fissionable material in the production of power."[7] The Committee constantly had to consider whether secrecy in all respects was contributing to administrative efficiency. Since World War II the scientific community has criticized executive secrecy. The growing involvement of government in the sponsorship of scientific research meant that scientists in and out of public service grew to have a vested interest in governmental procedures and policies governing the release of information in their own professional fields.[8] Members were painfully aware that the progress of scientific discovery was often impeded by overzealous security restrictions.

GAC members were familiar with both sides of the problem. They not only knew how frustrating official security restrictions were when those restrictions applied to them, but they also knew what the government was keeping secret from the rest of the scientific community. Because so much of the work of the early GAC was conducted under conditions closed to the public, members were free to express their views away from public scrutiny. When they felt compelled to bring a crucial matter to the public, however, they sometimes discovered that security restrictions left them "shouting in a cave" occupied only by other equally restricted inhabitants. While no one would deny that the Committee was obligated to protect vital state secrets, it may be fair to inquire why this highly influential group did not insist on declassification of nontechnical matters of social and political importance.

The mature GAC, 1964–1974: Technocrats, engineers, and applications

In the decade of the 1960s nuclear power technology was no longer simply a theoretical exercise but a problem of hard engineering that was being shaped into a reality. Untested theories proposed years earlier now had to prove operative in actual chemical and mechanical application. A proliferation of civilian and defense reactors meant the AEC no longer confronted the severe shortages of fission materials it had grappled with years earlier. The decision to proceed with light-water reactor technology had closed down numerous lines of alternative research and experimentation pursued under AEC sponsorship in the 1950s.[9]

The application stage of nuclear power carried with it risks and dangers. Incidents at the Rocky Flats Arsenal near Denver and at Windscale Pile No. 1 in Britain in the late 1950s were harbingers of nuclear energy's problems in the 1960s. The death of three workers at the army test reactor in Idaho Falls in 1961, as well as other accidents, caused public alarm. In 1966 the Fermi reactor, located near Detroit, suffered a near-disastrous core meltdown that resulted in the reactor's complete abandonment. Many believed that the Fermi accident came close to causing widespread exposure of the surrounding population to potentially lethal amounts of radioactive substances.

Nuclear power technology embodied the new challenge of spent-fuel reprocessing and the new responsibility of storing burgeoning quantities of high-level nuclear waste. In 1963 work began on a West Valley, New York, reprocessing facility, which was supposed to recover and store spent reactor fuel, thereby adding economies in fuel costs for reactor operators and reducing to a degree the volume of nuclear waste requiring long-term storage. The facility began operation in 1966 but operated ineffectively, intermittently, and with unacceptably high levels of contamination and was eventually abandoned by its corporate owner. The problem of storage of high-level nuclear waste also became increasingly controversial; methods of long-term storage have been researched, but in areas where repositories are to be constructed, their safety is still highly disputed.

The GAC followed the progress and problems of nuclear power in the 1960s. With the possible exception of Walter H. Zinn, a retiree of

Combustion Engineering, there were never representatives of nuclear reactor vendor firms on the Committee, but executives of nuclear electric utilities served through the 1960s and early 1970s. Promoting and perfecting commercial nuclear power became a central obligation of the Committee.

In this period the AEC and the GAC had to confront an increasing number of scientific and medical reports that contested the adequacy of the government's radioactivity exposure standards. In 1959 Ernest J. Sternglass, a scientist who had specialized in the effects of radiation on humans, published a study that contradicted the official view that fallout was harmless. Relatively high levels of Sr-90 were discovered in milk and in the bone tissue of children in the United States.[10] Two years later fifty thousand people marched in Trafalgar Square in London to protest atomic bomb testing. In 1966, a study of the effects of low-level radiation exposure concluded that there was no "safe" threshold for human exposure yet identified.[11]

These matters thrust the GAC into unfamiliar social, economic, and political realms. The appointment of physician John C. Bugher to the Committee in 1964 added a new advisory dimension to its work. He was followed in 1970 by another physician, James H. Sterner. These appointments helped to reduce the disciplinary narrowness characteristic of previous GACs and sensitized the Committee to the health and environmental risks accompanying some of its recommendations. Nevertheless, because in this period the Committee had to address an array of controversial problems not resolvable through use of the scientific method alone, the GAC lost much of its prestige in the scientific establishment.

There is perhaps no better example of the Committee's problems and frustrations than its role in Project Plowshare. For almost twenty years the GAC held high expectations that thermonuclear explosives could be put to peaceful civilian use in major construction projects or in mining or storage ventures. The thermonuclear bomb was never sufficiently reconfigured, however, to satisfactorily control radiation emission and ground shock. The Partial Test Ban Treaty of 1963 seriously impeded Plowshare civil construction projects, but it was the U.S. environmental movement that ultimately forced an end to the use of thermonuclear explosives in underground mining and gas stimulation ventures.

The GAC of the 1960s and early 1970s was a body that heavily and directly represented various government, or government contract, laboratories. Many of those who served on the Committee in this period should be considered high-science managers, or technocrats, rather than academically inclined theorists, experimentalists, or bench-science technicians. Many were both technological specialists and bureaucratic officials. Typical of the mature GAC was Herbert Friedman, a space scientist who directed the Naval Research Laboratory's E. O. Hulbert Space Center. Friedman helped the GAC review and assess a wide assortment of rocket and satellite nuclear propulsion projects from 1968 to 1974.

By the early 1970s the world in which both the AEC and the GAC operated underwent a transformation. The JCAE became subject to challenge when Congress created the Office of Technology Assessment in 1972 to help critique science and technology policy proposed by the executive branch.[12] JCAE members were no longer the only congressmen to assess atomic energy.

The JCAE gradually lost jurisdiction over nuclear power and was abolished in 1976. The final group of members conceded that they did not really understand the technology and that they were too close to the nuclear industry itself.[13] The JCAE was replaced by a competing group of two dozen separate committees and subcommittees, each with a fraction of atomic energy jurisdiction.[14] In the mid-1970s atomic energy had little formal institutional identity within the Congress, and few legislative allies.

The AEC itself was buffeted by a variety of forces in its final years. After ten years of steady leadership under Seaborg, James Schlesinger was appointed chairman. His two-year term was characterized by aloof leadership and an unwillingness to rely on the GAC for advice. Matters were not significantly changed during the short chairmanship of Dixie Lee Ray.

The energy crisis of 1973, the environmental movement before that, and the antinuclear movement to follow raised important obstacles in the work of both the AEC and the GAC. The dissolution of the Commission in 1974 did not mark the end of the Committee, but it did force a complete overhaul of the membership. A new era of energy advice was about to begin.

The ERDA GAC, 1975–1977: Interest diversification, temperance, and dissipation

A number of forces dramatically affected the GAC in the mid-1970s. When the AEC was disbanded in 1974, much of its research staff was transferred to the new ERDA and much of its regulatory staff was transferred to the new Nuclear Regulatory Commission. The GAC, with all its statutory authority, was moved to the ERDA where it was to advise the new ERDA administrator just as it had advised the Commission in the past.

By this time, however, there was a new law regulating federal advisory committees, the Federal Advisory Committee Act (FACA) of 1972, which took effect in January 1973. Its chief architect and proponent was Senator Lee Metcalf. The FACA, while acknowledging that advisory committees were a major source of information for federal departments and agencies, sought to correct the abuses and deficiencies that Senator Metcalf and others had identified. For example, some committees were woefully unrepresentative of the interests at issue; many were unbalanced in the number of representatives each interest was accorded; many deliberated in secret and kept few written records of proceedings; a number were found to be composed of an oligarchic, self-perpetuating membership; some met infrequently or spent lavish sums of money for marginal purposes; and most alarming, many operated under conditions of conflicts of interest.

The FACA required that the identities of those giving advice to the government be disclosed, which meant that the employers or institutional affiliations of advisory committee members had to be publicly reported. It attempted to broaden the representation of interests that served on advisory committees. Host agencies were required to publish advance notice and location of forthcoming advisory committee meetings, and these meetings were to be open to the public unless prevented by legitimate official restrictions. Advisory bodies had to report their functions and annual costs. There were to be biennial terminations of federal advisory committees, which meant that the perpetuation of most advisory bodies was subject to official congressional reauthorization. Most important, the FACA compelled advisory committees to render advice, not to assume responsibility in policy formulation or program implementation for the host agency.

The AEC GAC operated with some of the deficiencies Metcalf's committee detected. Under President John F. Kennedy's Executive Order 11007 of 1962, the Justice Department assumed responsibility for the coordination of federal advisory committees. The reforms carried out under this order mandated that advisory committees could only meet with host-agency approval, that committees keep better transcripts of meetings, and that annual reports furnishing names and affiliations of advisory committee members be prepared.[15] In conforming with these regulations the AEC ruled that "scientists on its General Advisory Committee cannot act as private consultants to any private concern doing work sponsored by the Commission."[16] The Kennedy order, however, contained large escape clauses that permitted numerous deviations.[17]

The FACA was more stringent than the Kennedy executive order, but it too was vague on many points. The "balanced" representation called for in the FACA in most cases was interpreted to mean that people representing the public interest — environmental or consumer groups, for example — should be recruited to serve on advisory committees as counterweights to people representing specific business clientele interests.[18] Scientific, as well as industrial, advisory committees were criticized as being out of balance with regard to interest group representation. However, the FACA was not explicit in defining what constituted balance or imbalance in interest group representation.

President Gerald R. Ford's appointment of Charles J. Hitch, Ruth Patrick, and Martin Ward to the ERDA GAC could be considered an effort to add more balance to the interests represented on the Committee. Hitch, an economist and president of Resources for the Future, might be classified as a social scientist and environmentalist. However, he had also been president of the University of California, a major government lab contractor, and in the early 1960s had served under McNamara at the Pentagon. Patrick, a career employee of the Academy of Natural Science in Philadelphia and a botanist, could articulate environmental concerns on the GAC. At the same time, she also served on the boards of the Du Pont Company and the Pennsylvania Power and Light Company, a nuclear electric utility. Ward spoke for labor union interests; at the time of his appointment he was president of the union representing plumbers and pipefitters in the United States and Canada.

Despite Ford's attempt to achieve more balance in interest representation on the ERDA GAC, there was still dissatisfaction with the elite nature of atomic energy advisory groups in general. One long underrepresented interest has been antinuclear power, whose members were frustrated because their arguments were seldom articulated by the scientific establishment consulted so regularly by the AEC: "On one side stands an array of governmental, commercial, and academic proponents committed to the rapid construction of nuclear generating plants and the industries and services they require for support. The scientists, engineers, government and business leaders who have for 30 years shared this objective constitute an impressive concentration of public and private interests."[19] No opponent of nuclear power and no representative of an antinuclear citizen interest group was ever appointed to the AEC or ERDA GAC. Whether this meant that the Committee was unrepresentative of the interests at issue is difficult to judge, given the lack of precision in the FACA standards.

The criteria used by the AEC, and later ERDA, in deciding who would be appointed to the GAC concerned maintenance of disciplinary balance and balance in the representation of the private corporate sector, the university research community, and the government contract laboratories. Given a conflict between disciplinary balance and interest group balance, the effort to sustain disciplinary balance almost always took precedence. A comprehensive analysis of interest representation on the GAC from 1947 to 1977 revealed that the university and corporate research communities were heavily represented. Private corporate executives, however, never held more than three of the Committee's nine seats. The heavy representation of university-affiliated members began a decline in 1963 when President Lyndon B. Johnson appointed a succession of government laboratory science managers to fill vacancies created by departing university professors. According to those who worked with the GAC, the AEC and ERDA went to great lengths to ensure that the Committee did not have too many members from the same contract laboratory or from the same university.[20]

An additional interest representation problem was posed by the diversity of new energy interests that the ERDA had to take up. When the AEC was still in operation in the early 1970s, a variety of interest groups questioned the wisdom of "perpetuating an agency responsible for developing a specific technology," and many argued that "energy producing technologies should be developed and evaluated competitively according to their efficiencies and environmental effects."[21] Added to this was the claim that atomic energy had been overfunded by the government relative to other forms of energy production: "At the outset of the 1970s, 86 percent of all federal energy R&D funds that had been spent since World War II had gone to AEC. It was no wonder that advocates of development in solar, geothermal, and even coal energy felt that they were at a tremendous disadvantage vis-a-vis proponents of nuclear energy. AEC was buttressed by a network of laboratories, contractors, and university centers."[22]

The AEC was not originally conceived to address problems unrelated to nuclear energy and therefore ill prepared to diversify. As a result of the Arab-Israeli War of 1973 and the ensuing Arab oil embargo, the U.S. government was compelled to consider developing a national energy policy that was not simply a mosaic of separate fuel (nuclear power, coal, oil, natural gas, and solar/energy) policies. For this and other reasons, the AEC underwent dissolution.

When the GAC was transferred to ERDA jurisdiction, new sets of energy interests, as well as nuclear energy, had to be represented on the Committee. Coal, natural gas, and solar energy interests, among others, had long been envious of atomic energy's high level of government subsidization and support. Various ERDA offices created to accommodate these energy clientele groups sometimes came into conflict with one another. Often offices that had been transferred out of other departments or agencies and melded into the ERDA continued to operate as if they were independent or never reorganized.

The agenda of one of the early ERDA GAC meetings demonstrates both the new energy interest diversity and the potential for competition and confusion. In November 1975 the ERDA GAC was furnished briefings by ERDA conservation program officials about synthetic fuels, automotive fuels, and waste treatment. This was followed by testimony from the ERDA fossil fuel staff, who spoke about problems in cost sharing, patent policy, pilot plants, demonstration plants, and compilation of a resource inventory. Squeezed into all of this was a briefing by an ERDA nuclear official, who talked about uranium enrichment, standardization in the design of light-water reactor pressure vessels, and the French Phenix breeder reactor.[23]

As atomic energy was subdivided and subsumed within a broad array of energy interests, the Committee became a platform for brokering interests represented by the members. Science advice was no longer confined to the basic or applied sciences; instead, life scientists, social scientists, former political officials, businessmen, and labor people, as well as physicists and engineers, occupied GAC seats. The Committee contained few practicing scientists or engineers and many science administrators. There were few veterans of the Manhattan Project and no world-renowned scientists capable of bridging multiple disciplines, but there were respected public figures dedicated more to sincere public service than to creation of new scientific knowledge. The ERDA GAC was better able to judge the political, economic, and social implications of its recommendations than was its AEC counterpart. But at the same time, the ERDA GAC could not furnish the host agency with the authoritative scientific and technical advice the AEC GAC had long provided.

The movement to give energy a more comprehensive organizational identity with Cabinet-level rank, put the ERDA GAC in jeopardy. Organizers of the Department of Energy (DOE) did not want the new agency to be saddled with a thirty-year-old statutory advisory committee that could independently act as a watchdog over all department programs. Any new general advisory body at DOE was to be an instrument of the department. The Energy Research and Advisory Board (ERAB) assumed many of the duties shouldered by the GAC, among them recommending nominees for the Fermi and Lawrence awards. ERAB's functions are more circumscribed than those of the GAC; it cannot independently fashion its own agenda or launch investigations without DOE permission.

The termination of the ERDA GAC came in September 1977 as the DOE went into operation. The Committee that began with the postwar responsibilities for developing atomic weapons, researching reactors, and stimulating production of fission materials ended with an assignment to file a subcontracted report on the prospects of solar energy.

The GAC elite

The members of the GAC were extraordinary individuals in many respects. Nearly all who served on the Committee were people who had dedicated their careers and intellectual lives to the study and use of atomic energy. The following anecdote demonstrates how exclusive and elite the Committee membership was and how central was their role in the history of atomic energy in the twentieth century.

Committee member Norman F. Ramsey, Jr., was an acclaimed physicist who had directed the "Delivery Group" at the Los Alamos Scientific Laboratory in 1945. It was Ramsey's job to prepare air crews for dropping the atomic bomb. In July 1945, under the direction of William S. Parsons, Ramsey traveled to the small Pacific Island of Tinian where he helped B-29 flight crews test drop dummy versions of the atomic bomb in order to test fusing devices. By July 31 Ramsey, Parsons, and other scientific and military personnel had reassembled the Los Alamos prefabricated weapon, code-named Little Boy. On the morning of August 4 Ramsey and his co-workers watched the bomb-ladened plane take off on its mission to bomb Hiroshima and immediately afterward went to work assembling components of the plutonium-triggered bomb that three days later was detonated over Nagasaki.[24]

Within days of the atomic destruction of Nagasaki, the Imperial Japanese government formally surrendered. When American military occupation forces began to stream into the devastated country, U.S. medical teams were dispatched to Hiroshima and Nagasaki. One of the first American physicians to survey the human and physical damage wrought by the atomic blasts was Dr. Shields Warren, of the navy technical mission of the Joint Commission for the Investigation of the Effects of the Atomic Bomb on Japan. Warren, who observed firsthand the physical and psychological suffering experienced by victims of the atomic explosions, went on to chair the Atomic Casualties Committee of the National Research Council. His friend and colleague, Dr. John C.

Bugher, as a member of Warren's committee traveled to Japan in the years after the war to study the health of Hiroshima and Nagasaki survivors.

Warren frequently testified before the GAC both as an AEC division director and an AEC consultant. Bugher served under Warren in the AEC, succeeding him as director of biology and medicine. Bugher was later appointed to the GAC, serving six years alongside Ramsey. One can only wonder whether these men discussed the fact that one had been in the last group of scientists to dispatch the atomic bombs to Japan and the other among the first American physicians to treat and study the survivors of the bombs' devastation.

Few federal advisory committees have a history as long and distinctive as the GAC. But many other government advisory committees, particularly science advisory committees, have helped to shape public policy and program administration, and their operation should not be assumed to have been trivial, symbolic, or inconsequential. If an advisory committee is composed of people who possess special abilities, or who occupy key extragovernmental positions of critical importance to the host agency, and if the committee addresses a meaningful set of agenda items under a regular meeting schedule, the body will no doubt have a measurable impact on the work of the agency it advises. Federal scientific advisory committees served as an alliance of university, corporate, and governmental research interests and for this reason should be studied in order to better understand the formulation of U.S. science and technology policy.

Formal meetings of the GAC

Year	Meeting	Dates	Location
1947	1	Jan. 3–4	Washington, D.C.
	2	Feb. 2–3	Washington, D.C.
	3	Mar. 28–30	Washington, D.C.
	4	May 30–31, June 1	Washington, D.C.
	5	July 28–29	Washington, D.C.
	6	Oct. 3–5	Washington, D.C.
	7	Nov. 21–23	Washington, D.C.
	Special	Dec. 29–30	Chicago, Ill.
1948	8	Feb. 6–8	Washington, D.C.
	9	Apr. 23–25	Washington, D.C.
	10	June 4–6	Washington, D.C.
	11	Oct. 21–23	Washington, D.C.
1949	12	Feb. 3–5	Washington, D.C.
	13	Apr. 5–6	Washington, D.C.
	14	June 2–4	Washington, D.C.
	15	July 14–15	Berkeley, Calif.
	16	Sept. 22–23	Washington, D.C.
	17	Oct. 28–30	Washington, D.C.
	18	Dec. 2–3	Washington, D.C.
1950	19	Jan. 31, Feb. 1	Washington, D.C.
	20	Mar. 31, Apr. 1	Washington, D.C.
	21	June 1–3	Washington, D.C.
	22	Sept. 10–13	Washington, D.C.
	23	Oct. 30–31, Nov. 1	Los Alamos, N. Mex.
1951	24	Jan. 4–6	Washington, D.C.
	25	Mar. 15–17	Argonne, Ill.
	26	May 8–10	Washington, D.C.
	27	Oct. 11–13	Washington, D.C.
	28	Dec. 12–14	Washington, D.C.
1952	29	Feb. 15–17	Washington, D.C.
	30	Apr. 27–29	Washington, D.C.
	31	June 13–14	Washington, D.C.
	32	Oct. 9–10	Washington, D.C.
1953	33	Feb. 5–7	Washington, D.C.
	34	Mar. 23–24	Washington, D.C.
	35	May 14–16	Washington, D.C.
	36	Aug. 17–19	Washington, D.C.
	37	Nov. 4–6	Washington, D.C.
1954	38	Jan. 6–8	Washington, D.C.
	39	Mar. 31, Apr. 1–2	Washington, D.C.
	40	May 27–29	Washington, D.C.
	41	July 12–15	Sandia and Los Alamos, N.Mex.
	42	Nov. 3–4	Washington, D.C.
	43	Dec. 20–22	Washington, D.C.

Source: AEC GAC meeting information supplied by Anthony A. Tomei (AEC/ERDA, retired). ERDA GAC and Solar Working Group information supplied by William Woodard (DOE, Office of Energy Research).

Year	Meeting	Dates	Location
1955	44	Mar. 2–4	Washington, D.C.
	45	May 2–4	Washington, D.C.
	46	Sept. 21–23	Washington, D.C.
	47	Dec. 13–15	Washington, D.C.
1956	48	Jan. 12–13	Argonne, Ill.
	49	Mar. 28–30	Washington, D.C.
	50	July 16–18	Washington, D.C.
	51	Oct. 29–31	Washington, D.C.
1957	52	Jan. 17–19	Oak Ridge, Tenn.
	53	Apr. 29–30, May 1	Washington, D.C.
	54	July 9–11	Washington, D.C.
	55	Sept. 30, Oct. 1–2	Washington, D.C.
	56	Nov. 21–23	Los Alamos, N.Mex.
1958	57	Feb. 27–28, Mar. 1	Germantown, Md., and Washington, D.C.
	58	May 5–7	Germantown, Md., and Washington, D.C.
	59	July 21–23	Berkeley, Calif.
	60	Oct. 30–31, Nov. 1	Washington, D.C.
1959	61	Jan. 5–7	Germantown, Md., and Washington, D.C.
	62	Mar. 9–11	Savannah River, S.C.
	63	Apr. 9–11	Washington, D.C.
	64	May 4–6	Washington, D.C.
	65	July 20–22	Richland, Wash.
	66	Oct. 28–30	Washington, D.C.
1960	67	Feb. 1–3	Washington, D.C.
	68	Mar. 17–19	Oak Ridge, Tenn.
	69	May 16–18	Germantown, Md., and Washington, D.C.
	70	July 26–28	Germantown, Md., and Washington, D.C.
	71	Oct. 24–26	Argonne, Ill.
1961	72	Jan. 30–31, Feb. 1	Washington, D.C.
	73	Mar. 22–24	Washington, D.C.
	74	Apr. 27–29	Washington, D.C.
	75	July 13–15	Los Alamos, N.Mex.
	76	Oct. 19–21	Washington, D.C.
	77	Nov. 30, Dec. 1	Washington, D.C.
1962	78	Jan. 29–31	Washington, D.C.
	79	Mar. 29–31	Brookhaven, N.Y.
	80	July 9–11	Livermore and Berkeley, Calif.
	81	Oct. 4–6	Washington, D.C.
1963	82	Jan. 7–9	Washington, D.C.
	83	Mar. 18–20	Sandia and Los Alamos, N.Mex.
	84	Apr. 25–27	Washington, D.C.
	85	July 18–20	Argonne, Ill.
	86	Oct. 20–22	Washington, D.C.
1964	87	Jan. 13–15	Washington, D.C.
	88	Apr. 2–4	Sandia, N.Mex.
	89	July 6–8	Washington, D.C.
	90	Oct. 12–14	Cleveland, Ohio, and Washington, D.C.
1965	91	Jan. 11–13	Oak Ridge, Tenn.
	92	Mar. 29–31	Washington, D.C.
	93	July 12–14	Livermore, Calif.
	94	Nov. 1–3	Washington, D.C.

Year	Meeting	Dates	Location
1966	95	Feb. 2–4	Mayaguez, P.R.
	96	Apr. 28–30	Washington, D.C.
	97	July 12–14	Brookhaven, N.Y.
	98	Nov. 2–4	Washington, D.C.
1967	99	Feb. 1–3	Richland, Wash.
	100	May 1–3	Washington, D.C.
	101	Aug. 2–4	Los Alamos, N.Mex.
	102	Nov. 13–15	Washington, D.C.
1968	103	Jan. 24–26	Berkeley, Calif.
	104	May 6–8	Washington, D.C.
	105	July 8–11	Argonne, Ill.
	106	Oct. 14–16	Washington, D.C.
1969	107	Feb. 10–12	Oak Ridge, Tenn.
	108	Apr. 23–25	Washington, D.C.
	109	July 29–31	Idaho Falls, Idaho
	110	Nov. 10–12	Washington, D.C.
1970	111	Feb. 25–27	Savannah River, S.C.
	112	May 4–6	Germantown, Md., and Washington, D.C.
	113	July 20–22	Livermore, Calif.
	114	Nov. 9–11	Washington, D.C.
1971	115	Feb. 23–25	Los Alamos, N.Mex.
	116	May 17–19	Washington, D.C.
	117	Aug. 17–19	Batavia and Argonne, Ill.
	118	Nov. 8–10	Germantown, Md., and Washington, D.C.
1972	119	Feb. 24–26	Scottsdale, Ariz.
	120	May 22–24	Washington, D.C.
	121	Aug. 22–24	Brookhaven, N.Y.
	122	Oct. 31, Nov. 1–2	Washington, D.C.
1973	123	Feb. 13–15	Richland, Wash.
	124	May 9–11	Washington, D.C.
	125	July 9–11	San Francisco (Palo Alto and Berkeley), Calif.
	126	Oct. 16–18	Washington, D.C.
1974	127	Feb. 28, Mar. 1	Oak Ridge, Tenn.
	128	May 1–3	Washington, D.C.
	129	July 29–31	Los Alamos, N.Mex.
	130	Nov. 6–8	Washington, D.C.
1975	1[a]	Oct. 30–31	Washington, D.C.
	2[a]	Nov. 13–14	Washington, D.C.
1976	3[a]	Feb. 4–5	Washington, D.C.
	4[a]	Apr. 7–9	Oak Ridge, Tenn.
	5[a]	June 1–3	Livermore and Oakland, Calif.
	6[a]	Oct. 6–7	Washington, D.C.
	7[a]	Nov. 30, Dec. 1	Argonne, Ill.
1977	8[a]	Mar. 1–2	Washington, D.C.
	9[a]	Apr. 27–29	Los Alamos, N.Mex.
	10[a]	June 7–8	Washington, D.C.
	11[a]	Aug. 23	Washington, D.C.
	12[a]	Sept. 21–22	Golden, Colo.
	1[b]	Nov. 11–12	Washington, D.C.
	2	Dec. 9–10	Washington, D.C.
1978	3	Jan. 11–12	Washington, D.C.

[a]ERDA GAC meetings

[b]The ERDA GAC was terminated on September 30, 1977. The final cohort of ERDA GAC members was invited to join the new ad hoc Solar Working Group of the DOE. The Solar Working Group was officially terminated April 1, 1977.

The major atomic energy laboratories

FROM THE OUTSET of AEC formal operations, there was a high concentration of industrial and academic contractors in AEC's laboratory empire. In the 1963 budget year, for example, almost three-quarters of all AEC contractor operating cost payments were paid to only seven contractors. Two of these seven were universities: the University of California and the University of Chicago. The remaining five major contractors were huge industrial or commercial firms: Union Carbide Corporation, General Electric Company, Bendix Corporation, Du Pont Company, and Sandia Corporation, which operated as a subsidiary of American Telephone and Telegraph Company–Western Electric Company–Bell Telephone Laboratories.[1] By June 1974, the cumulative federal appropriation for AEC's programs totaled nearly $60 billion, with the vast majority of this funding devoted to contract laboratory research.

According to a 1982 Department of Energy (DOE) report, there have been twelve long-standing multiprogram laboratories (the term *multiprogram* denoted a laboratory that derived its activities and support from an AEC/ERDA program office). This was a matrix form of organization; each laboratory budget was not a separate line item in the AEC or ERDA budgets, but a "composite of several allocations determined by negotiations between the program offices and the laboratory." The laboratories reported to the program offices for which they worked.[2] Because the Hanford Engineering Development Laboratory, the Idaho Nuclear Engineering Laboratory, and the Savannah River National Laboratory have long concentrated almost exclusively in a single program area, DOE considers them multiprogram laboratories in name only.[3] If these three facilities are omitted from the group, there are nine formal multiprogram laboratories, and six of these have emerged as national laboratories.

The designation *national laboratory* came from the official proclamation that these laboratories were guardians of "national trust" missions owing to their work in high-energy or nuclear physics, in the radiobiological sciences, and in nuclear medicine research.[4] The Argonne, Brookhaven, Lawrence Berkeley, Lawrence Livermore, Los Alamos, and Oak Ridge labs are genuine multiprogram national laboratories, although Lawrence Berkeley has not always been designated as such. The Pacific Northwest and Ames labs function as multiprogram facilities but are not classified as national laboratories in a formal sense. Sandia is a national laboratory, but only in recent history has it come to fit the multiprogram classification.

Whether a facility is a national laboratory or not, and whether a lab operates in a multiprogram or single program mode is not critical in this analysis. In a general sense, however, labs with national laboratory status have grown to be huge and expensive complexes. In competition for funding, multiprogram labs usually fare better than do single-program dependent ones. Among multiprogram labs, national laboratories usually secure more financial support than do those that do not enjoy this status.

The following overview represents a summary of the work and accomplishments of the ten major AEC laboratories that were frequently the objects of GAC discussions. University contract labs are discussed first, then industrial contract labs.

Los Alamos Scientific Laboratory

The Los Alamos Scientific Laboratory has long been a premier national research facility. Located thirty-six miles northwest of Santa Fe, New Mexico, the institution has been, and at this writing remains, under the management of the University of California at Berkeley. The UC-Berkeley contract was signed in January 1943.[5] Los Alamos was created as a supersecret laboratory of the Manhattan Project in World War II, and J. Robert Oppenheimer was the first director. Under army supervision and administration, Los Alamos scientists successfully exploded the first atomic bomb at Alamogordo, New Mexico, on July 16, 1945. These scientists also produced the atomic bombs dropped on Hiroshima and Nagasaki in August 1945.

From the beginning, the Los Alamos lab has been directed toward designing, building, and testing nuclear devices. Along with the Sandia and Lawrence Livermore laboratories, Los Alamos increases and maintains the nation's stockpile of atomic weapons. In the postwar era, Los

Alamos became the prime contractor for work on AEC's Rover Project, which was intended to explore the scientific and technical feasibility of nuclear rocket propulsion.[6] This project failed to produce an earth-launched reactor-propelled rocket, but technical work and reactor miniaturization advanced by Rover contributed to development of nuclear propulsion plants for unmanned satellites and exploratory spacecraft.

Los Alamos scientists performed much of the research and testing of Project Plowshare (involving peaceful uses of nuclear explosives). For example, nuclear explosives were detonated underground in the Gnome experiment and in subsequent tests to ascertain whether they could be used for mineral resource extraction.[7]

In the 1950s, Los Alamos underwent some diversification as it assumed new scientific and technical duties in nonweapons fields. The lab has conducted extensive research of nuclear fission, including isotope separation by laser induction and testing of advanced reactor fuel elements. Los Alamos researchers modeled nuclear reactor accidents for the Nuclear Regulatory Commission in the 1970s. Los Alamos scientists have evaluated the biomedical consequences of nuclear energy production and have investigated various methods of high-level nuclear waste storage and disposal. The lab continues to pursue fusion energy research as well as a wide variety of nonnuclear experimental programs.[8]

Many of the GAC's early members had worked at Los Alamos during and after World War II, foremost among them Oppenheimer, Enrico Fermi, and Edward Teller. Los Alamos had no full-time career employee on the GAC until 1964, when physicist Darol K. Froman was appointed to the GAC by President Lyndon B. Johnson. Two years later, Jane H. Hall, also a physicist of the lab, was appointed by President Johnson to replace Froman. Hall served on the committee until late 1972, so Los Alamos had eight continuous years of direct representation on the GAC. The lab enjoyed years of support from GAC members, who periodically visited the institution to conduct research and experimentation and who exhibited a fondness and protective attitude toward the Los Alamos facility and its researchers.

Ernest O. Lawrence Berkeley Radiation Laboratory

The University of California's Berkeley Radiation Laboratory was established in 1936 by Ernest O. Lawrence, who won a 1939 Nobel Prize in physics for his invention of the cyclotron and for his achievements in particle accelerator research. After his death in 1958, the facility was renamed in his honor. Although the real property and physical plant of the Berkeley lab is small compared with other major AEC labs, Berkeley has occupied a central role in atomic energy research. The lab, in conjunction with the university, has trained hundreds of graduate students, many of whom have gone on to scientific and engineering careers with universities, industry, or government research laboratories.

The Berkeley Radiation Laboratory played a key role in the wartime Manhattan Project. Glenn T. Seaborg and Edwin M. McMillan discovered the element plutonium in experiments conducted at the facility. Moreover, the electromagnetic separation process for uranium isotope separation was developed at this research center. These and other accomplishments realized in Berkeley laboratory work helped to make the atomic bomb a reality.

Besides defense-related work, the Berkeley laboratory has long pursued experimentation in high-energy physics, nuclear physics, and other basic energy sciences. The lab is part of the UC-Berkeley campus and draws scientific and engineering talent from the faculty and graduate student body of the university. The Berkeley lab has been highly innovative in the construction and operation of various types of particle accelerators, such as the HILAC linear accelerator, the Bevatron (a proton synchrotron), and an eighty-eight-inch cyclotron.[9] Later, by linking together accelerators, the lab produced the Super-HILAC accelerator system.

Atomic energy officials have long considered Berkeley a national laboratory in all but name. The Berkeley lab today holds the formal national laboratory title. However, at various times Berkeley lab officials had found it advantageous to avoid formal national laboratory designation identifying it as an AEC research center.[10]

UC-Berkeley and its campus laboratory have long enjoyed strong GAC representation. Members McMillan, Teller, and Kenneth S. Pitzer each had a long association with the university and the lab. Seaborg at one time was chancellor at UC-Berkeley, and he pursued much of his scientific career at the Berkeley lab. Seaborg was not only an initial GAC member but went on to become AEC chairman from 1961 to 1971. Charles J. Hitch, an economist by training, had been president of UC-Berkeley shortly before he was appointed to the GAC in 1975.

Ernest O. Lawrence Livermore National Laboratory

In 1950 a branch of the Berkeley Radiation Laboratory was established at the site of a planned University of California accelerator facility in the Livermore Valley about fifty miles due east of San Francisco. In July 1952 the AEC opened the facility as a national laboratory. The facility was initially led by Teller, Lawrence, and Herbert F. York.[11] In the fall of 1951 and winter of 1952, Teller had become highly dissatisfied with the work environment of the Los Alamos lab and pressed for establishment of a second major weapons laboratory to concentrate on thermonuclear weapons. When the AEC and GAC did not readily agree to Teller's demand for a new lab, he took his case to General James A. Doolittle and Secretary of the Air Force Thomas K. Finletter. Doolittle, Finletter, and other major air force officials were receptive to Teller's requests and they convinced Secretary of Defense Robert A. Lovett to urge the administration to create the facility. According to Teller, once the air force began its efforts, AEC and GAC opposition to the Teller proposal melted away. At the behest of Teller, Lawrence, and York, the AEC approved UC-Berkeley's proposal and construction began at the Livermore location.[12] It was renamed in honor of Lawrence, as was the Berkeley Radiation Laboratory, in 1958. For many years Livermore and Berkeley "were considered two branches of the same institution, but eventually the vast differences in their missions and characters led to disassociation."[13]

From the very beginning, Livermore has been in continuous competition with Los Alamos in weapons research work. Originally organized as a weapons laboratory dedicated to pursuit of thermonuclear weapon research and development, Livermore continued to serve this mission but absorbed other responsibilities as well. The Livermore lab initiated and sustained Project Plowshare, established with the help of the Joint Committee on Atomic Energy (JCAE) and led by Teller. "Plowshare developed according to Livermore's interests and served those interests. It applied a technology with which Livermore was familiar in a manner amenable to study by Livermore's staff."[14]

The Livermore lab has also been the site of extensive applied research work in ramjet and rocket propulsion, as well as in nuclear weaponry. Scientists there made significant contributions to the development of nuclear warheads for air force Minuteman and navy Polaris missiles.[15]

Livermore has invested sizable resources and scientific talent in work on magnetic fusion, laser fusion energy, and isotope separation. The lab has several large laser fusion facilities, an extremely powerful particle accelerator, a magnetic fusion instrument complex, and a wide array of other research facilities.[16] In the late 1970s and into the 1980s, Livermore assumed a major role in the development of particle beam technology. The lab is expected to perfect a new generation of space-based weapons and antimissile systems under President Ronald W. Reagan's Strategic Defense Initiative.

In the realm of nondefense research, Livermore lab has conducted experimental work in coal gasification. In medical research, the lab has helped establish the new field of flow cytogenetics to analyze chromosomes. Livermore-created technologies in the field of toxicology have helped facilitate research in human somatic mutation and may lead to advances in preventive medicine against cancer and other diseases.

A number of GAC members from UC-Berkeley worked at various times at Livermore. Teller pursued research at this lab while he served as a member of the GAC from 1956 to 1958. He resigned from the GAC stating that since he was being appointed director of Livermore, GAC membership might pose a conflict of interest. Michael M. May acted as an at-large executive of Livermore during his term of GAC service from 1972 to 1977. Although Livermore never enjoyed the degree of GAC representation Los Alamos did, the research complex had many spokesmen and patrons on the Committee.

Argonne National Laboratory

The Argonne National Laboratory, located about twenty miles west of Chicago, evolved from the wartime Metallurgical Laboratory of the University of Chicago. The Metallurgical lab had been another center of Manhattan Project research. The Manhattan District's postwar Advisory Committee on Research and Development recommended that the Metallurgical Laboratory be transformed into Argonne, a "permanent national laboratory for nuclear research."[17]

Among the major achievements of scientists working at this lab were the demonstration of the first controlled nuclear chain reaction and the design and construction supervision of the Hanford plutonium production reactors with Du Pont. After its formal christening as a national laboratory in 1946, scientists and engineers at Argonne, working with Bettis Laboratory (a Westinghouse Electric Corporation Pittsburgh research facility), did some of the initial design work on the naval nuclear reactor for the Nautilus atomic submarine.[18] On January 1, 1948, Argonne was named AEC's central reactor laboratory.[19]

Argonne is most noted for its valuable contributions to the research, design, and development of the boiling-water nuclear reactor. Its prototype, the experimental boiling-water reactor, was put in operation at Argonne and became the model for a generation of nuclear reactors built by the General Electric Company. Argonne engineers also designed the AEC's Savannah River plutonium production reactors, which yield the fissionable materials needed by the AEC weapons laboratories and ultimately by the armed services. Furthermore, Argonne scientists have been at the forefront of research and development of the liquid-metal-cooled fast breeder reactor. Allied with researchers of the Oak Ridge National Laboratory, Argonne investigators addressed the problem of reprocessing spent reactor fuel through work on the Redox process of radioactive decontamination.

Argonne has also advanced the study of high-energy physics. Equipped with a zero-gradient synchrotron, the Intense Pulsed Neutron Source-1, and other elaborate research facilities, Argonne has been a leader in nuclear physics experimentation. Argonne scientists have explored magnetohydrodynamic generators of electricity and have conducted high-energy physics bubble chamber experiments through the lab's huge high-field superconducting magnets.[20]

In the decade of the 1970s, Argonne has been the scene of biological research directed to development of new diagnostic tools to aid, by separating and mapping human serum proteins, in the detection of human diseases. Lab researchers at Argonne developed liposome encapsulation, which has been used in cancer chemotherapy and has helped pharmaceutical companies test their anticancer agents.[21]

Many of those who served on the GAC worked at Argonne while holding academic appointments at the University of Chicago, among them Fermi, Willard F. Libby, and Warren C. Johnson. Cyril S. Smith had been a leader of the original metallurgical lab, which later formed the foundation of the Argonne lab. Walter H. Zinn, a later GAC appointee, served as director of Argonne for most of the 1950s. Stephen Lawroski, who served on the GAC from 1964 through 1970, was the only GAC member to be in the active employ of Argonne while serving on the Committee.

Enrico Fermi National Accelerator Laboratory

A short distance from the Argonne lab is the Enrico Fermi National Accelerator Laboratory at Batavia, Illinois. In 1962, the Lawrence Berkeley Radiation Laboratory proposed a design study for a new proton synchrotron that would be at least one hundred times more powerful than the conventional Bevatron accelerator of that time. Because of the immense size and high cost of such a facility and the implications it would have for the future of high-energy physics, a scientific committee (the Ramsey panel) was impaneled by the AEC and the President's Science Advisory Committee to advise on the project. The Berkeley design that had sparked original interest in the endeavor was not the only design the panel reviewed, but in 1963 the panel selected the Berkeley 200-Bev proton accelerator design for the new machine.

With the permission of the JCAE in 1965, the AEC asked the National Academy of Sciences to appoint a site evaluation committee for the envisioned national accelerator laboratory.[22] By December 1966, the AEC announced the site selection committee's choice; the new facility would be built at Batavia, Illinois. The facility was named in honor of preeminent physicist and early GAC member Fermi who had passed away a decade earlier. Construction of the Fermi lab began in 1969 and the accelerator began operation in 1972, operated under contract by a consortium of universities incorporated as the Universities Research Association. The leading U.S. center for research experimentation in high-energy physics, the National Accelerator Laboratory commands more scientific attention and government funding than other U.S. laboratories operating accelerators.

Edwin L. Goldwasser of the University of Illinois at Urbana was appointed to the GAC by President Johnson in 1966. Several months after his appointment, Goldwasser assumed the post of associate director of the National Accelerator Laboratory. During his six-year GAC term, Goldwasser was able to share his laboratory's interests and concerns with other Committee members.

Brookhaven National Laboratory

Another major AEC contract laboratory managed by a university consortium is the Brookhaven National Laboratory. It began operation in January 1947 on the grounds of a defunct military troop-staging area. Located about seventy miles to the east of New York City near Upton, Long Island, Brookhaven has been operated under contract by Associated Universities, Inc. (AUI), a nonprofit educational corporation. AUI is run by an eighteen-member board of directors, with two representatives on the board from each of AUI's nine sponsoring universities: Columbia, Cornell, Harvard, Johns Hopkins, Princeton, and Yale universities, the Massachusetts Institute of Technology, and the universities of Pennsylvania and Rochester.

Brookhaven conceives, develops, constructs, and operates large and complex research facilities devoted to studying the fundamental properties of matter.[23] Scientific disciplines that have been heavily represented at Brookhaven include high-energy, nuclear, and solid state physics, chemistry, and biology. Brookhaven operates the National Synchrotron Light Source, the alternating-gradient synchrotron, a high-flux beam reactor, and a medical research reactor. Over 1000 faculty guest appointments to Brookhaven are made each year, and the facilities have been heavily utilized by laboratory staff and research visitors. Nobel prizes for physics in 1976 and in 1980 were awarded to scientists who as Brookhaven visitors made discoveries that later earned them the award.[24]

In addition, Brookhaven researchers have advanced the studies of liquid-metal fast breeder reactor technology, high-level radioactive waste disposal technology, the industrial application of high-intensity ionizing radiation, and general reactor physics.[25] Brookhaven people have been highly successful in biological and medical studies of the effects of radiation in the production and use of chemical substances with energy potential.

The Brookhaven lab has made possible great strides in the study of genetics. Brookhaven inventions have facilitated testing and manufacture of radiopharmaceuticals. In the 1970s, Brookhaven life scientists perfected the therapeutic use of L-dopa for treatment of Parkinson's disease. Other Brookhaven biomedical research has helped doctors and medical researchers to understand regional metabolic activity in the brain.

It has been long-standing Brookhaven lab policy to pursue unclassified lines of research exclusively. Brookhaven once operated one of the first air-cooled graphite test reactors, but that reactor has been decommissioned for many years and is exhibited in public tours.

A great many GAC members have been affiliated with one or more of the nine northeastern Ivy League universities that direct Brookhaven's contractor operator, AUI. However, only two GAC members have had close ties to AUI; after departing the Columbia University faculty and GAC membership, Isidor I. Rabi became president of AUI in 1960, and Gerald F. Tape, an executive of AUI, served on the GAC during its final two years of operation (1975–1977).

Oak Ridge National Laboratory

Oak Ridge National Laboratory has been a key government laboratory with a long and distinguished history. Located near its namesake city in eastern Tennessee, this lab has been managed for many years by

Union Carbide Nuclear Company, a subsidiary of Union Carbide Corporation. While the lab has a contractual association with Union Carbide's subsidiary, "an exceptional amount of decentralized authority [is] vested in it by Union Carbide."[26]

Originally called the Clinton Laboratories, or Clinton Engineer Works, the Oak Ridge facilities were chartered simultaneously with the Los Alamos laboratory in January 1943. The lab began as an expansive industrial facility containing a gaseous-diffusion plant and an electromagnetic isotope separation plant, both used in the enrichment of uranium.[27] One of the lab's first experimental structures was a plutonium production pilot plant built by Du Pont under subcontract to the University of Chicago. The plutonium generated by this plant went to Manhattan Project bomb fabrication work. A small amount of this plutonium was used for the bomb detonated over Nagasaki on August 9, 1945. For one year after the war, the Monsanto Company operated the Clinton labs. When Monsanto disengaged from its contract, Union Carbide created a subsidiary firm that assumed control of the lab, which was renamed the Oak Ridge National Laboratory.

From a managerial vantage point, Oak Ridge may be the government's most sophisticated research laboratory. Through the office of the independent Oak Ridge Institute of Nuclear Studies (ORINS), university faculty and student scientists have arranged visitations to the Oak Ridge laboratory. In 1965, ORINS was brought into Oak Ridge Associated Universities (ORAU). In formal terms, the organization is an incorporation of universities in the South. It manages "the terms under which faculty and graduate students are selected and given leave and funds to undertake research at a government installation."[28] ORINS/ORAU has served as an educational intermediary between the Oak Ridge laboratory and southern universities.

Besides furnishing access to university researchers, Oak Ridge has involved researchers from private industry.[29] The lab has assumed a major educational and training function geared to serve both the business and academic communities. Moreover, Oak Ridge has had a long-standing policy of pursuing non-AEC work in order to diversify its program. For example, the lab has launched efforts in the desalination of seawater with Department of Interior sponsorship; basic research in molecular biology supported by the National Institutes of Health; civil defense work for the Office of Civil Defense; and environmental studies underwritten by the National Science Foundation.[30]

Oak Ridge is credited with advancing the development of nuclear reactor technology, chemical technology, and fusion energy research.

The lab has made possible dramatic increases in radioisotope production and has made discoveries in basic research of chemistry, physics, metallurgy, and biology.[31]

In the field of nuclear medicine, Oak Ridge has long been a principal developer for models and techniques to estimate radiation doses received by humans. Since 1945, the laboratory has achieved numerous breakthroughs in the production of radionuclides for medical use. Some of the radiopharmaceuticals made at the lab have been used in the study of heart disease and brain tumors.[32]

In reactor development, Oak Ridge technicians and scientists conducted extensive studies on thermal breeder reactor systems and on high-temperature gas-cooled reactors, both for possible civilian power application. Oak Ridge defense projects served the army's Nuclear Power Program and the air force's Aircraft Nuclear Propulsion Program. The first high-flux test reactor and materials testing reactor were Oak Ridge achievements as well.[33]

The Oak Ridge lab has been one of the nation's chief suppliers of stable radioisotopes. It is a major center of research on thermonuclear power and neutron radiation damage to metals. It has led exploration of nuclear fuel reprocessing, having hosted research programs that created the fuels Purex (1953), Thorex (1958), and Remotex (1980). The first two processes are used at fuel reprocessing plants throughout the world.[34] Oak Ridge manages and maintains operation of an isotope separation facility and high-flux isotope reactor, an electron linear accelerator and isochronous cyclotron, and a transuranium processing plant. Among the eight major user facilities at the lab are two accelerators and a neutron scattering facility.[35]

Oak Ridge has hosted research visits by many scientists and engineers who served on the GAC but never had an employee appointed to the Committee. Oak Ridge officials were, however, frequently invited to attend and participate in GAC meetings.

Hanford Works and Pacific Northwest Laboratory

The Hanford atomic energy facilities in Washington State evolved conjointly with the Clinton (later Oak Ridge) and Los Alamos labs under the Manhattan Project. Du Pont built the huge reactors that produced plutonium for the atomic bomb. In May 1946, General Electric became Hanford's new industrial contract manager. While the facility began operation as a production plant, research lab operations emerged at the site in 1956. In January 1964, the General Electric Hanford contract was segmented and transferred to a number of other contractors "in an effort to widen industrial participation and stimulate economic diversification."[36] About that time, Battelle Memorial Institute assumed management of the Hanford laboratory. Battelle, which promoted private as well as AEC contract work at Hanford, took over the laboratory portion of the Hanford complex named the Pacific Northwest Laboratory (PNL).[37]

Originally, Hanford, Oak Ridge, and Los Alamos began as company towns in which the U.S. government owned all the land and buildings. The three laboratories spawned by the Manhattan Project became so large they were referred to as "atomic cities." "No one could even visit Oak Ridge or Los Alamos without a Commission pass, much less live there without permission."[38] In this regard Richland, Washington, was also an "atomic city," created largely by the mammoth Hanford production plant. In the case of both Hanford and Oak Ridge, the research laboratories were only a fraction of the total physical plant. The production plants on these government reservations employed several thousand workers.

For three decades Hanford scientists and engineers have investigated nuclear power with a special preoccupation with matters pertaining to reactor core fuel performance, reactor core life, nuclear plant safety, and nuclear plant factor analysis of instrumentation and human control. The laboratory set forth the technical, health, and environmental basis for private sector use of plutonium and uranium mixed-oxide fuels in light-water nuclear reactors (1960–1970). PNL has identified effective decontamination techniques for metal surfaces and has engineered a more economical dry-cooling-tower technology for nuclear power plants.[39]

Throughout its history of operation the Hanford lab has studied the health and environmental effects of radionuclides. Instruments and procedures developed at the lab have been applied in studies of the human health effects of radioactive elements, and these studies have been the basis for issuance of official radiation exposure standards.

Many of the original Hanford Works buildings have been closed; many of the remaining ones are operated by industrial contractors for the government. PNL continues management of several life science labs, a marine research lab, a critical mass lab, a nuclear waste vitrification lab, and a steam generator examination facility.[40] Battelle pursues contract research for numerous private corporate clients at PNL; this diversification has helped "offset the (local area economic) hardships caused by the cutbacks in plutonium production" at the old Hanford Works.[41]

Hanford and PNL never had a direct employee representative on the GAC. One GAC member, Hartley Rowe, had worked as a top engineer in the construction of the original Hanford plant. Another member, Eugene P. Wigner, had performed invaluable design calculations for the plutonium-producing piles at Hanford. Du Pont's Hood Worthington, a GAC colleague of Rowe's in 1947 and 1948, also had made major contributions to the original construction of the Hanford Works.

Sandia National Laboratory

Sandia National Laboratory, originally an extension of the Los Alamos lab, was formally detached and established as a major AEC laboratory in 1949. With the bulk of its facilities located outside of Albuquerque, New Mexico, the Sandia lab is operated under contract by Sandia Corporation, a nonprofit subsidiary of Western Electric. Sandia is responsible for helping to develop "safe, reliable, deliverable, field-ready weapons using the nuclear devices" fabricated and tested by Los Alamos and other major laboratories. In precise terms, Sandia performs the research and development required to incorporate nuclear devices into operational weapons.[42]

Among Sandia's accomplishments have been advances in guided missile technology and the production and testing of missiles capable of conveying nuclear warheads. Sandia work helped to bring about intermediate and intercontinental range ballistic missiles.[43] The lab has been for many years responsible, along with private industry, for improving the technology needed for radiation-tolerant, large-scale integrated circuits, especially radiation hardening of microelectronics equipment. This work is intended to help military technologies function through circumstances that might be encountered in a nuclear war. Besides serving a national security purpose, this work also benefits commercial nuclear reactor instrumentation, satellite-based equipment users, and the U.S. space program.[44]

Sandia has also worked on peaceful applications of nuclear explosives under Project Plowshare. In 1970, the lab branched into research on laser fusion, geothermal energy, and solar energy.[45] However, the lab's cardinal responsibility is to continue to build and safely maintain the stockpile of atomic bombs and warheads the government requires.

The GAC played a part in the establishment of the Sandia laboratory. In June 1947, the Committee helped to decide on the location of this new laboratory. The site selection group ultimately recommended that it be constructed near Albuquerque, New Mexico. UC-Berkeley, the lab's original operator, asked permission to disengage from its contract in December 1948, explaining that the industrial orientation of Sandia was not amenable to the university's research orientation.[46] It may have been, however, that the university had no desire then to direct a weapons experimentation and warehouse facility so completely identified with the military.

In the effort to find another operator for the lab, AEC General Manager Carroll L. Wilson and AEC Engineering Division Director Roger S. Warner approached James B. Fisk of Bell Laboratories only a few months after Fisk had resigned from the post of AEC Research Division director.[47] Wilson and Warner suggested to Fisk that Bell Laboratories should become the new industrial contractor for Sandia. Wilson and Warner also asked Oliver E. Buckley, a GAC member and then president of Bell labs, if his firm would take charge of Sandia.[48]

After a period of assessment, and at the personal invitation of President Harry S. Truman, Bell executives agreed to direct Sandia. Western Electric, a major American Telephone and Telegraph Company subsidiary, became the industrial contractor of Sandia through formation of its own subsidiary, the Sandia Corporation. At Meeting 14 in June 1949, Oppenheimer voiced satisfaction on learning that Sandia was to gain a new contractor. Buckley, whose company was to indirectly manage the lab, abstained from this and other GAC deliberations that involved Sandia.[49]

Sandia's activities were totally defense-related until 1973. After that time, approximately one-quarter of Sandia's staff performed work in nondefense research areas.[50] No Sandia employee ever served on the GAC, and the lab was perceived by the scientific community as a hardware-oriented engineering laboratory.

Ames Laboratory

The smallest of the nine multipurpose laboratories is located in Ames, Iowa. Operated under contract by Iowa State University (ISU), the facility conducts basic research in materials and chemical sciences. The lab prepares high-purity metals, alloys, compounds, and single crystals. Ames researchers pursue projects in high-energy physics, nuclear physics, and solar energy technology. The lab offers year-round appointments to ISU faculty and provides graduate student training, not unlike the Lawrence Berkeley lab.

Ames scientists have made contributions in the efficient reduction

and purification of uranium, thorium, the rare earths, zirconium, haf-
nium, yttrium, and vanadium. Essentially all uranium used in the western world has been prepared through processes developed by Ames.
Moreover, the rare earth industry continues to be heavily dependent on
the basic separations and chemical, metallurgical, and materials characterization achievements of this laboratory, which has pursued this kind
of work since 1940.[51] The lab never had a direct representative on the
GAC.

Biography of Anthony A. Tomei

ANTHONY A. TOMEI was born in Williamsport, Pennsylvania, attended business school in Philadelphia, and in 1940 commenced federal service with the War Department in Washington, D.C. On entry into the military service in the spring of 1942, he was assigned to the Office of the Combined Chiefs of Staff in Washington. He was transferred to the Operational Research Section of Headquarters, VIII Fighter Command, near Watford, England, in the summer of 1943. It was there that he began working with scientists. In the summer of 1944 he was transferred to Headquarters, U.S. Strategic Bombing Survey, in London, from which he performed field trips to France, Italy, and Germany to gather early data about the accuracy and effectiveness of U.S. bombing missions. In fall 1945 he was honorably discharged and soon after reentered federal service. During this period he attended George Washington University and the University of Maryland at College Park.

The Atomic Energy Commission began operation on January 1, 1947, and Tomei joined the AEC headquarters staff in the spring of that year. Recruited by John H. Manley, the secretary to the AEC GAC, Tomei advanced through the ranks until he became the GAC secretary in the early 1960s. He was in attendance at all but 4 of the 130 AEC GAC meetings and was also present for the first two ERDA GAC meetings.

Initially, Tomei worked closely with the GAC secretary and when appointed secretary he performed his duties in close collaboration with the chairman. Among these duties were the following:

1. Planning, coordinating, and making all arrangements for the meetings of the Committee and its subcommittees and ad hoc committees, both in Washington and away at field offices, laboratories, and elsewhere.

2. Finalizing the meeting agenda; writing the detailed minutes for GAC approval and transmittal to the AEC; and receiving the chairman's summary reports for incorporation into final form and transmittal to the AEC chairman.

3. Scheduling the GAC role in the two annual AEC awards, one national (Lawrence) and presented by the AEC chairman and the other, international (Fermi) and presented by the president; with GAC advice, recruiting experts from the pertinent energy disciplines to screen initially the nominations for the Lawrence Award; presenting the findings and the nominations for the international award to be presented to the GAC in comprehensive form for final selections and transmittal to the AEC and the president for approval.

4. Effecting liaison among the Committee members at their home offices with government officials and executives in private industry who operated AEC laboratories.

Tomei retired from the GAC office, and from federal service, in mid-1975.

NOTES

Chapter 1. Government science advice and the GAC

1. Richard S. Westfall, *A Biography of Isaac Newton* (Cambridge, Engl.: Cambridge University Press, 1980), pp. 551–54, 623.

2. Martin L. Perl, "The Scientific Advisory System: Some Observations," in *Knowledge, Politics, and Public Policy,* ed. Philip H. Melanson (Cambridge, Mass.: Winthrop Publishers, 1973), p. 167.

3. Don K. Price, *The Scientific Estate* (Cambridge, Mass.: The Belknap Press of Harvard University Press, 1965), p. 138.

4. Perl, 1973, p. 160.

5. Ibid., p. 165.

6. Daniel S. Greenberg, *The Politics of Pure Science* (New York: The New American Library, 1967), p. 8.

7. Daniel Ford, *The Cult of the Atom* (New York: Simon and Schuster, 1982), p. 24.

8. David E. Lilienthal, *Atomic Energy: A New Start* (New York: Harper and Row, 1980), p. 30.

9. Price, 1965, p. 55.

10. Ibid., p. 15; see also David Dickson, *The New Politics of Science* (New York: Pantheon Books, 1984).

11. See Richard Hirsch and Joseph J. Trento, *The National Aeronautics and Space Administration* (New York: Praeger Publishers, 1973).

12. Price, 1965, p. 80.

13. Ibid., p. 46.

14. Grant McConnell, *Private Power and American Democracy* (New York: Vintage Books, 1970), p. 275.

15. Price, 1965, p. 12.

16. David Truman, *The Governmental Process: Political Interests and Public Opinion* (New York: Alfred A. Knopf, 1951), pp. 458–59.

17. Joseph A. Pika, "Federal Advisory Committees: Links between Agencies and Their Publics" (Paper delivered at the Northeastern Political Science Association, Newark, N.J., 12–14 November 1981), p. 19.

18. U.S. AEC General Advisory Committee, "Problems Presented by Radioactive Fallout: Statement by the General Advisory Committee of the U.S. Atomic Energy Commission," *Bulletin of the Atomic Scientists* 15(June 1959):258–59.

19. David S. Brown, "The Management of Advisory Committees: An Assignment for the '70's," *Public Administration Review* 32(July/August 1972):334–42. See also Truman, 1951, pp. 458–59.

20. See Thomas R. Wolanin, *Presidential Advisory Commissions* (Madison: University of Wisconsin Press, 1975); Frank Popper, *The President's Commissions* (New York: Twentieth Century Fund, 1970); Thomas E. Cronin and Sanford D. Greenberg, eds., *The*

Presidential Advisory System (New York: Harper and Row, 1969); William T. Golden, ed., *Science Advice to the President* (New York: Pergamon Press, 1980); Perl, 1973; and Thaddeus J. Trenn, *America's Golden Bough: The Science Advisory Intertwist* (Cambridge, Mass.: Oelgeschlager, Gunn and Hain, Publishers, 1983). Wolanin, Popper, and Cronin and Sanford examine the operation and function of presidential science advisory committees. Golden and Perl investigate the president's science advisory network. Trenn's book is a comparative analysis of federal science advisory committees that gives especial attention to the President's Science Advisory Committee but has only a short reference to the AEC GAC.

21. Thomas E. Cronin and Norman C. Thomas, "Federal Advisory Processes: Advice and Discontent," *Science* 26(February 1971):771–79).

22. Brown, 1972, p. 335.

23. Ibid.

24. Ibid.

25. McConnell, 1970, p. 258.

26. Leslie Gordon, "Government Controls in Peace and War," *Bulletin of the Business Historical Society,* vol. 20 (April 1946). See also A. Lee Fritschler and Bernard H. Ross, *Business Regulation and Government Decision-Making* (Boston: Little, Brown and Co., 1980).

27. Brown, 1972, p. 338.

28. Henry Fairlie, "Help from Outside," in Cronin and Greenberg, 1969, pp. 144–45.

29. For a study of the ACRS, see David Okrent, *Nuclear Reactor Safety: On the History of the Regulatory Process* (Madison: University of Wisconsin Press, 1981).

30. The term "national laboratory" is used in this study for the following laboratories: Lawrence Berkeley Radiation Laboratory, Lawrence Livermore National Laboratory, Los Alamos Scientific Laboratory, Oak Ridge National Laboratory, Argonne National Laboratory, Sandia National Laboratory, Brookhaven National Laboratory, Fermi National Accelerator Laboratory, and the Hanford Works and Pacific Northwest Laboratory. The Los Alamos Scientific Laboratory was renamed the Los Alamos National Laboratory in 1979. The former name is used here because it was the designation used in the time of the GAC.

Chapter 2.   GAC origin, purpose, members, and procedures

1. Atomic Energy Act of 1954, Sec. 157b(3). This appears in U.S. Congress, Joint Committee on Atomic Energy, *Atomic Energy Legislation through the 94th Congress, 2d Session* (Washington, D.C.: U.S. Government Printing Office, March, 1977). See also Richard G. Hewlett and Oscar E. Anderson, Jr., *The New World: An Official History of the U.S. Atomic Energy Commission 1939–1946,* vol. 1 (University Park: Pennsylvania State University Press, 1962), p. 648.

2. Richard G. Hewlett and Francis Duncan, *Atomic Shield: An Official History of the U.S. Atomic Energy Commission 1947–1952,* vol. 2 (University Park: Pennsylvania State University Press, 1969), p. 16.

3. Atomic Energy Act of 1954, Sec. 157b(3).

4. Adrian Kuyper, "A Look at the New Atomic Energy Law," *Bulletin of the Atomic Scientists* 10(December 1954):389–92.

5. Hewlett and Duncan, 1969, p. 486.

6. Hewlett and Anderson, 1962, p. 648.

7. Steven L. Del Sesto, *Science, Politics, and Controversy: Civilian Nuclear Power in the United States, 1946–1974* (Boulder, Colo.: Westview Press, 1979), p. 21.

8. Daniel Ford, *The Cult of the Atom* (New York: Simon and Schuster, 1982), p. 33.

9. Hewlett and Duncan, 1969, p. 16.

10. Corbin Allardice and Edward R. Trapnell, *The Atomic Energy Commission* (New York: Praeger Publishers, 1974), p. 63.

11. Ibid.,

12. Draft Minutes of GAC Meeting 17, 28–30 October 1949, U.S. Department of Energy Archives, Germantown, Md. Although labeled "Draft Minutes," these are the official minutes of the GAC and so the word "draft" has been dropped in subsequent citations.

13. Anthony A. Tomei, "An Account of the Administrative and Organizational Practices and Procedures of the General Advisory Committee," unpublished document, 8 June 1956, U.S. Department of Energy Archives, Germantown, Md., p. 27.

14. For a thorough study of the operation and history of the JCAE, see Harold P. Green and Alan Rosenthal, *Government of the Atom* (New York: Atherton Press, 1963).

15. David E. Lilienthal, *Atomic Energy: A New Start* (New York: Harper and Row, 1980), p. 92.

16. Ford, 1982, p. 43.

17. Minutes of GAC Meeting 2, 2 February 1947, p. 2.

18. Tomei, 1956, p. 4.

19. Del Sesto, 1979, p. 21.

20. Don K. Price, *The Scientific Estate* (Cambridge, Mass.: The Belknap Press of Harvard University Press, 1965), p. 155.

21. Tomei, 1956, p. 4, and Hewlett and Duncan, 1969, p. 16.

22. Ford, 1982, p. 32.

23. Allardice and Trapnell, 1974, p. 62.

24. Harold Orlans, *Contracting for Atoms* (Washington, D.C.: The Brookings Institution, 1967), pp. 183–85.

25. Minutes of GAC Meeting 5, 28–29 July 1947.

26. Hewlett and Anderson, 1962, p. 648.

27. U.S. Congress, Senate Committee on Governmental Affairs, Subcommittee on Reports, Accounting, and Management, *Energy Advisers: An Analysis of Federal Advisory Committees Dealing with Energy,* a report prepared by Susan R. Abbasi and Alfred R. Greenwood (Washington, D.C.: U.S. Government Printing Office, March 1977), p. 176 (hereafter called Abbasi and Greenwood, 1977).

28. Anthony A. Tomei, telephone interview with author, 4 June 1984.

29. Orlans, 1967, p. 188.

30. Abbasi and Greenwood, 1977, p. 175.

31. Martin L. Perl, "The Scientific Advisory System: Some Observations," in *Knowledge, Politics, and Public Policy,* ed. Philip H. Melanson (Cambridge, Mass.: Winthrop Publishers, 1973), p. 162.

32. GAC Secretary Fisher Howe to Robert J. Hart, manager, Oak Ridge Operations Office, letter, 23 February 1976, U.S. Department of Energy Archives, Germantown, Md. (Howe's boldface).

33. Minutes of GAC Meeting 2, 2–3 February 1947, p. 2.

34. Minutes of GAC Meeting 4, 30–31 May and 1 June 1947, p. 5.

35. See Robert C. Williams and Philip L. Cantelon, eds., *The American Atom* (Philadelphia: University of Pennsylvania Press, 1984), pp. 141–75.

36. Minutes of Meeting 2, 2–3 February 1947, p. 7.

37. Ibid., pp. 1, 9, 10.

38. Tomei, 1956, p. 4.

39. Jaques Cattell, ed., *American Men and Women of Science,* 14th ed. (New York: R. R. Bowker Co., 1979), p. 330.

40. Jaques Cattell, ed., *American Men and Women of Science,* 12th ed. (New York: R. R. Bowker Co., 1972), p. 1031.

41. U.S. Congress, Joint Committee on Atomic Energy, *Atomic Energy Legislation through the 94th Congress, 2d Session* (Washington, D.C.: U.S. Government Printing Office, March 1977), p. 59.

42. In 1974, Congress substituted the words "after consultation with" for the words "upon recommendation of [the GAC]." See P.L. 93-276 (88 Stat. 115), sec. 201. This change reflected some congressional disapproval of the GAC on the grounds that the

Committee retained too much power in the assignment of these awards. A source who prefers to remain anonymous says dissension within the JCAE resulted from the GAC's unwillingness to grant Lewis L. Strauss a Fermi Award in the early 1970s because the GAC members of the period still harbored animosity toward Strauss for his role in the Oppenheimer affair of the mid-1950s. Apparently AEC Chairman James Schlesinger and Representative Craig Hosmer had pressed the Committee to grant Strauss the award, and they tried to bypass the GAC by amending the Atomic Energy Act of 1946 to relegate the GAC to a mere consulting role in conferral of scientific awards. As it turned out, by the time the amendment was approved, Strauss had died (the Fermi cannot be awarded posthumously).

43. Amitai Etzioni, *Modern Organizations* (Englewood Cliffs, N.J.: Prentice-Hall, 1964), p. 59.

44. Ibid., p. 62.

45. Minutes of GAC Meeting 42, 3–4 November 1954, p. 33.

46. AEC Chairman Lewis L. Strauss to President Dwight D. Eisenhower, letter of 15 November 1954, U.S. Department of Energy Archives, Germantown, Md. The GAC had advocated that the Fermi Award be nontaxable, and this was mentioned in the Strauss letter.

47. The years in which no one was nominated and no award conferred were (at this writing) 1960, 1965, 1967, 1973, 1974, 1975, 1977, and 1979.

48. Alvin W. Trivelpiece, Director, U.S. Department of Energy, Office of Energy Research, "Enrico Fermi Award," letter announcement of 15 April 1983 (hereafter cited as Trivelpiece, 1983).

49. Alvin W. Trivelpiece, Director, U.S. Department of Energy, Office of Energy Research, "Enrico Fermi Award," letter announcement of 1 March 1984.

50. Memorandum of Gerald F. Tape to AEC Chairman Glenn T. Seaborg et al., 18 May 1964, U.S. Department of Energy Archives, Germantown, Md.

51. Memorandum of Joseph F. Hennessey to AEC Chairman Glenn T. Seaborg et al., "Background Information on Fermi and Lawrence Awards," 31 January 1966 (hereafter referred to as Hennessey memo, 1966).

52. Trivelpiece, 1983.

53. William Woodard, Energy Research Advisory Board Office of the Department of Energy, interview with author, 18 April 1983.

54. In the AEC era, the GAC customarily listed the topics of awards for evening sessions, after the regular agenda topics (weapons, reactors, materials research) had been handled. This information was provided by former GAC Secretary Anthony A. Tomei in a letter to the author dated 29 July 1985.

55. While it is true that life scientists are eligible for the Fermi Award and that winners Stafford L. Warren and Shields Warren were life scientists, the Lawrence Award seems to be more explicit in specifying the eligibility of life scientists.

56. Trivelpiece, 1983.

57. Hennessey memo, 1966, p. 3.

58. Ibid., p. 4.

59. Ibid., p. 7.

60. In the AEC era, however, the GAC recruited panels in five disciplines to perform the initial screening of the nominations for the Lawrence Award. This done, the GAC would convene in closed evening session during a regular meeting to review the panels' selections and to discuss nominations before voting its recommendations. This information was provided by Anthony A. Tomei in a letter to the author dated 29 July 1985.

Chapter 3.   Knowledge specializations and career histories of GAC members

1. Don K. Price, *The Scientific Estate* (Cambridge, Mass.: The Belknap Press of Harvard University Press, 1965), p. 138.

2. Harvey Brooks, "The Scientific Adviser," in *Scientists in National Policy-Making,* ed. Robert Gilpin and Christopher Wright (New York: Columbia University Press, 1964), p. 81.

3. Martin L. Perl, "The Scientific Advisory System: Some Observations," in *Knowledge, Politics, and Public Policy,* ed. Philip H. Melanson (Cambridge, Mass.: Winthrop Publishers, 1973), p. 160.

4. W. Henry Lambright, *Governing Science and Technology* (New York: Oxford University Press, 1976), p. 28.

5. Richard G. Hewlett and Oscar E. Anderson, Jr., *The New World: An Official History of the Atomic Energy Commission 1939–1946,* vol. 1 (University Park: Pennsylvania State University Press, 1962), p. 648.

6. Price, 1965, p. 30.

7. Ibid., pp. 55, 23.

8. Ibid., p. 46.

9. Ibid., p. 149.

10. Irvin C. Bupp and Jean-Claude Derian, *The Failed Promise of Nuclear Power: The Story of Light Water* (New York: Basic Books, 1978), pp. 181, 183, 189.

11. Ibid., p. 183.

12. Daniel Ford, *The Cult of the Atom* (New York: Simon and Schuster, 1982), p. 34.

13. Minutes of Meeting 22, 10–13 September 1950, U.S. Department of Energy Archives, Germantown, Md., p. 17.

14. Hewlett and Anderson, 1962, pp. 56, 635.

15. Lambright, 1976, p. 9.

16. Price, 1965, p. 148.

17. Ibid., pp. 124, 133, 151, quote from p. 133.

18. Ibid., p. 123.

19. Ibid., p. 107.

20. Richard G. Hewlett and Francis Duncan, *Atomic Shield: An Official History of the U.S. Atomic Energy Commission 1947–1952,* vol. 2 (University Park: Pennsylvania State University Press, 1969), pp. 16, 188.

21. Ibid., p. 666.

22. *Energy Policy,* 2d ed. (Washington, D.C.: Congressional Quarterly, March 1981), p. 141.

23. *National Journal,* 21 August 1976, pp. 1183–85; 15 January 1977, p. 117.

24. First Boston underwrites and distributes loans and capital issues and is a dealer in securities for government, municipal, and corporate bond issues. It also sells investors short-term unsecured promissory notes purchased from industrial concerns. See *Moody's Bank and Finance Manual,* vol. 2, 1976, p. 1456, and vol. 2, 1977, p. 1475.

25. Shearson is an investment brokerage firm that deals in securities, brokers commodity transactions, engages in investment banking and investment management, and sponsors or participates in the underwriting and distribution of securities for corporate and municipal bond issues. See *Moody's Bank and Finance Manual,* vol. 2, 1976, p. 1417, and vol. 2, 1977, p. 1401.

Chapter 4.   Career path associations of GAC members

1. Thaddeus J. Trenn, *America's Golden Bough: The Science Advisory Intertwist* (Cambridge, Mass.: Oelgeschlager, Gunn, and Hain Publishers, 1983), p. 35.

2. Richard G. Hewlett and Francis Duncan, *Atomic Shield: An Official History of the U.S. Atomic Energy Commission 1947–1952,* vol. 2 (University Park: Pennsylvania State University Press, 1969), p. 16.

3. Richard G. Hewlett and Oscar E. Anderson, Jr., *The New World: An Official History of the U.S. Atomic Energy Commission 1939–1946,* vol. 1 (University Park: Pennsylvania State University Press, 1962), p. 2.

4. Froman continued working at the Los Alamos Scientific Laboratory until 1962. From 1949 to 1951 he served as assistant director of weapons development and then worked eleven years as technical associate director. He was scientific director for the Douglas Aircraft Company from 1963 to 1969.

5. Like Froman, Hall dedicated her postwar career to work at the Los Alamos Scientific Laboratory.

6. Peter Goodchild, *J. Robert Oppenheimer: Shatterer of Worlds* (Boston: Houghton Mifflin, 1981), p. 71. According to Sam Allison, as quoted by Goodchild, when Oppenheimer began to draw up plans for the Los Alamos lab he had little appreciation of how big it would grow to be and how complicated its administration would become.

7. Hewlett and Anderson, 1962, p. 54.

8. Goodchild, 1981, p. 59.

9. Hewlett and Anderson, 1962, p. 25.

10. Trenn, 1983, p. 16.

11. Hewlett and Anderson, 1962, p. 41.

12. Trenn, 1983, p. 18.

13. Hewlett and Anderson, 1962, p. 41.

14. Trenn, 1983, pp. 18–19.

15. Ibid., p. 19.

16. Hewlett and Anderson, 1962, pp. 62, 63, 203.

17. Ibid., pp. 246, 313.

18. Ibid., pp. 55, 56, 179, 180, 195.

19. Ibid., p. 297.

20. Trenn, 1983, p. 19.

21. Hewlett and Duncan, 1969, p. 667.

22. Ibid.

23. Trenn, 1983, p. 38.

24. Ibid., p. 35.

25. Trenn, 1983, p. 48.

26. Ibid., p. 53.

27. Ibid.

28. Ibid., p. 62.

29. William Wells, "Science Advice and the Presidency: An Overview from Roosevelt to Ford," in *Science Advice to the President,* ed. William T. Golden (New York: Pergamon Press, 1980), p. 225.

30. Trenn, 1983, p. 68.

31. Ibid., p. 69.

32. Ibid., p. 82.

33. Ibid., p. 75.

34. Ibid., p. 87.

Chapter 5.   The GAC and the great atomic energy laboratories

1. Glenn T. Seaborg and Daniel M. Wilkes, *Education and the Atom* (New York: McGraw-Hill Book Company, 1964), p. 4.

2. Between 1939 and 1945, the vast majority of federal research and development was performed by the government's own labs. By 1945, the U.S. government had spent in excess of $1.5 billion on Manhattan Project laboratory work. See W. Henry Lambright, *Governing Science and Technology* (New York: Oxford University Press, 1976), p. 17. According to a table of monthly statements for the Manhattan Engineer District, for the period August 1942 through December 1946, the federal government spent $2,191,458,000 (or $2.2 billion). See Richard G. Hewlett and Oscar E. Anderson, Jr., *The New World: An*

Official History of the United States Atomic Energy Commission 1939–1946, vol. 1 (University Park: Pennsylvania State University Press, 1962), p. 724.

3. Harold Orlans, *Contracting for Atoms* (Washington, D.C.: The Brookings Institution, 1967), p. 5.

4. Albert H. Teich, "Bureaucracy and Politics in Big Science: Relations between Headquarters and the National Laboratories in AEC and ERDA," reprinted in *The Role of the National Energy Laboratories in ERDA and Department of Energy Operations: Retrospect and Prospect,* Appendix V, a report prepared for the U.S. House of Representatives, Committee on Science and Technology, Subcommittee on Advanced Energy Technologies and Energy Conservation Research, Development, and Demonstration (Washington, D.C.: U.S. Government Printing Office, 1978), pp. 352–53 (hereafter cited as Teich, 1978).

5. Harold Orlans, 1967, p. 5.

6. Richard G. Hewlett and B. J. Dierenfield, *The Federal Role and Activities in Energy Research and Development 1946–1980: An Historical Summary* (Gaithersburg, Md.: History Associates, 1983), pp. 21–22.

7. Ibid., pp. 21–22.

8. Joseph Boskin and Fred Kinsky, *The Oppenheimer Affair* (Beverly Hills, Calif.: Glencoe Press, 1968), p. 28.

9. Ibid., pp. 29–30.

10. For a fascinating and detailed history of the early Los Alamos Scientific Laboratory, see James W. Kunetka, *City of Fire: Los Alamos and the Atomic Age, 1943–1945,* rev. ed. (Albuquerque: University of New Mexico Press, 1979).

11. Hans A. Bethe, "Comments on the History of the H-Bomb," *Los Alamos Science* (Fall 1982):43–53, quote from p. 45.

12. Boskin and Kinsky, 1968, pp. 38–39.

13. Ibid., p. 39.

14. Teich, 1978, p. 359.

15. Minutes of GAC Meeting 38, 8 January 1954, U.S. Department of Energy Archives, Germantown, Md., p. 1.

16. Daniel Ford, *The Cult of the Atom* (New York: Simon and Schuster, 1982), p. 32.

17. Minutes of GAC Meeting 2, 2–3 February 1947, p. 3.

18. Ibid., p. 6.

19. Ibid., p. 4.

20. Ibid., p. 4.

21. Ibid., p. 5.

22. Sam Cohen, *The Truth about the Neutron Bomb* (New York: William Morrow and Co., 1983).

23. Minutes of GAC Meeting 2, 2 February 1947, p. 3.

24. Minutes of GAC Meeting 28, 12–14 December 1951, p. 8.

25. Don K. Price, *The Scientific Estate* (Cambridge, Mass.: The Belknap Press of Harvard University Press, 1965), p. 75.

26. Teich, 1978, p. 359.

27. Orlans, 1967, p. 77.

28. GAC Chairman Isidor I. Rabi to AEC Chairman Lewis L. Strauss, letter, 8 January 1954, p. 1, U.S. Department of Energy Archives, Germantown, Md.

29. Minutes of GAC Meeting 38, 8 January 1954, pp. 1–2.

30. Minutes of GAC Meeting 36, 17–19 August 1953, p. 44.

31. Minutes of GAC Meeting 15, 15 July 1949, p. 12.

32. Minutes of GAC Meeting 22, 10–13 September 1950, p. 16.

33. Ibid.

34. Minutes of GAC Meeting 35, 14–16 May 1953, p. 33.

35. Minutes of GAC Meeting 43, 20–22 December 1954, p. 26.

36. GAC Chairman Isidor Rabi to AEC Chairman Lewis L. Strauss, letter of 30 July 1956, p. 1, U.S. Department of Energy Archives, Germantown, Md. For a thorough, scholarly history of Project Sherwood and fusion energy research, see Joan Lisa Brom-

berg, *Fusion: Science, Politics, and the Invention of a New Energy Source* (Cambridge, Mass.: MIT Press, 1982).

37. Teich, 1978, p. 351.

38. Minutes of GAC Meeting 15, 15 July 1949, p. 9.

39. Minutes of GAC Meeting 22, 4th Session, 10-13 September 1950, p. 17.

40. Minutes of GAC Meeting 26, 8-10 May 1951, p. 22.

41. Teich, 1978, pp. 355-56.

42. Peter B. Natchez and Irvin C. Bupp, "Policy and Priority in the Budgetary Process," *American Political Science Review* 67(September 1973):951-63, quote from p. 963.

43. Ibid., p. 960.

44. Bromberg, 1982, p. 114. "Toy Top," built under the direction of Livermore's Frederic H. Coensgen in 1954, was designed to test a new method for the construction of high-field, fast-pulsed magnets.

45. Ibid., p. 115.

46. Minutes of GAC Meeting 35, 14-16 May 1953, p. 33.

47. Ibid.

48. Ibid., p. 37.

49. Ibid.

50. Ibid.

51. Teich, 1978, p. 382.

52. Anthony A. Tomei, "An Account of the Administrative and Organizational Practices and Procedures of the General Advisory Committee," unpublished document, 8 June 1956, U.S. Department of Energy Archives, Germantown, Md., p. 77.

53. Minutes of GAC Meeting 47, 13-15 December 1955, pp. 16-17.

54. Minutes of GAC Meeting 2, 2 February 1947, p. 6.

55. Minutes of GAC Meeting 35, 14-16 May 1953.

56. Minutes of GAC Meeting 47, 13-15 December 1955, p. 17.

57. Minutes of ERDA GAC Meeting 1, 30-31 October 1975, U.S. Department of Energy, Energy Research Advisory Board Office.

58. Minutes of ERDA GAC Meeting 8, 1-2 March 1977.

59. Allen C. Allison, "News Roundup," *Bulletin of the Atomic Scientists* 16(January 1960), p. 31.

60. Price, 1965, p. 81.

61. Minutes of GAC Meeting 47, 13-15 December 1955, pp. 17-18.

62. Ibid.

63. Ibid., p. 20.

64. Teich, 1978, p. 378.

65. Robert C. Williams and Philip L. Cantelon, eds., *The American Atom* (Philadelphia: University of Pennsylvania Press, 1984), p. 79.

66. The best history of the atomic airplane is W. Henry Lambright, *Shooting Down the Nuclear Plane,* vol. 104 (Syracuse, N.Y.: Inter-University Case Program, 1967), pp. 1-33.

67. Richard G. Hewlett and Francis Duncan, *Atomic Shield: An Official History of the U.S. Atomic Energy Commission 1947-1952,* vol. 2 (University Park: Pennsylvania State University Press, 1969), p. 72.

68. Ibid., p. 208; see also Lambright, 1967, p. 5.

69. Minutes of GAC Meeting 7, 21-23 November 1947.

70. Hewlett and Duncan, 1969, pp. 73, 190.

71. Lambright, 1967, p. 5.

72. Hewlett and Duncan, 1969, p. 212.

73. Harry S. Baer, Jr., "Nuclear Power for Aircraft," *Flying,* June 1957, p. 25 (cited in Lambright, 1967, p. 1).

74. Hewlett and Duncan, 1969, p. 490.

75. Lambright, 1967, p. 7.

76. Ibid., p. 8.

77. Eugene P. Wigner to Isidor I. Rabi, letter of 22 September 1955, U.S. Department of Energy Archives, Germantown, Md.

78. In Lambright 1967, p. 6, the direct and indirect cycles were described:

> [In the direct cycle], air entered through a compressor, was forced into the reactor, and was heated by the fuel elements. After passing through the turbine, where energy was extracted to drive the compressor, the heat was expelled at high velocity through the exhaust nozzle. In the indirect cycle, the heat generated in the reactor was absorbed by a liquid metal coolant that flowed through the reactor core. The coolant then flowed through an intermediate heat exchanger where the heat was transferred to a secondary loop. The hot liquid metal was then pumped to the jet engine, which contained radiators where the heat was given up by the liquid metal and imparted to the air system flowing through the engine. Thus, the air was heated directly by the reactor in the direct cycle and indirectly by the reactor in the indirect cycle.

79. Minutes of GAC Meeting 46, 21–23 September 1955, p. 28.

80. Lambright, 1967, p. 13.

81. Ibid., p. 15. Lambright indicates the navy had argued that a major advantage of the atomic seaplane was the lessened risk of human radiation exposure compared with a land-based nuclear plane.

82. Minutes of GAC Meeting 52, 17–19 January 1957, p. 21.

83. Lambright, 1967, p. 3. According to Lambright, "Anyone standing unprotected within 100 feet of the bare core of a nuclear reactor would receive a lethal dose of radiation in a few minutes." Most land-based reactors of the period were shielded by six feet of concrete. To reduce shield weight, the plane would have to be propelled by "a very small reactor capable of releasing a great deal of energy." This required a reactor that would have to operate at temperatures about 500 percent higher than those in the first atomic submarine.

84. Ibid., p. 4.

85. Warren C. Johnson to Lewis L. Strauss, letter, 10 December 1957, U.S. Department of Energy Archives, Germantown, Md.

86. Lambright, 1967, p. 13.

87. Richard G. Hewlett and Jack M. Holl, *Atoms for Peace and War: A History of the United States Atomic Energy Commission,* vol. 3 (unpublished manuscript, 1986), chap. XIX, p. 2.

88. Lambright, 1967, p. 21.

89. Stephen Hilgartner, Richard C. Bell, and Rory O'Connor, *Nukespeak: The Selling of Nuclear Technology in America* (New York: Penguin Books, 1982), p. 47.

90. Lambright, 1967, p. 32.

91. Hewlett and Holl, 1986, chap. XIX, p. 2.

92. Teich, 1978, p. 345.

Chapter 6. The GAC and the Project Super controversy

1. John H. Manley, telephone conversation with author, 7 September 1986.

Many scholarly studies have pieced together information about the Committee's meetings on this subject. One of the most illuminating is Herbert York, *The Advisers: Oppenheimer, Teller, and the Superbomb* (San Francisco: W. H. Freeman, 1976). Manley, the first GAC secretary, petitioned the AEC in 1973 to declassify some GAC documents regarding the Committee's October 1949 meeting regarding Project Super. These records were declassified on 24 March 1973.

The overview in this chapter of what happened at the time of these GAC meetings blends GAC archival records with secondary source accounts. Richard G. Hewlett and

Francis Duncan, *Atomic Shield: An Official History of the Atomic Energy Commission 1947–1952,* vol. 2 (University Park: Pennsylvania State University Press, 1969), offers a detailed account of events in this period, but the work does not present the actual meeting records of these sessions because the book was researched and written before 1969, and these records were still classified. Most of the documents referred to were researched at the U.S. Department of Energy Archives. Many of these materials appear in York's book as well as in a documentary collection, Robert C. Williams and Philip L. Cantelon, eds., *The American Atom* (Philadelphia: University of Pennsylvania Press, 1984).

2. Peter Goodchild, *J. Robert Oppenheimer: Shatterer of Worlds* (Boston: Houghton Mifflin Company, 1981), p. 53.

3. See Hans A. Bethe, "Comments on the History of the H-Bomb," in *Los Alamos Science* (Fall 1982):43–53. According to Bethe, the so-called "classical super" became technically feasible only after years of concerted theoretical research that in the later years received a major boost from new, high-speed computing machines capable of complex mathematical calculation and information storage.

4. Anthony A. Tomei, "An Account of the Administrative and Organizational Practices and Procedures of the General Advisory Committee," unpublished document, 8 June 1956, U.S. Department of Energy Archives, Germantown, Md., p. 30.

5. Hewlett and Duncan, 1969, pp. 363–66. Oppenheimer had actually written the draft of the panel's conclusion that the observed phenomena were "consistent with the view that the origin of the fission products was the explosion of an atomic bomb" on 29 August 1949.

6. Ibid.

7. York, 1976, pp. 33–34.

8. Tomei, 1956, p. 31.

9. Hewlett and Duncan, 1969, p. 379.

10. Goodchild, 1981, p. 202. It is noteworthy that Oppenheimer could not recall reading Seaborg's pro-Super letter to the GAC at its October 1949 meeting. In 1954, security officials used against him his failure to recall reading the letter to the Committee. Goodchild indicates that Cyril S. Smith remembered that Oppenheimer had read Seaborg's letter to the GAC at the October 29, 1949 meeting. This is further confirmed by Anthony Tomei, administrative assistant to the GAC at the time, who was present at the session when the letter was read.

11. Williams and Cantelon, 1984, p. 118.

12. George F. Kennan, *The Nuclear Delusion: Soviet-American Relations in the Atomic Age* (New York: Pantheon Books, 1983), p. xv.

13. Ibid., p. xvi.

14. Ibid. Kennan reproduced this quote from his original January 1950 paper to Secretary of State Acheson.

15. Ibid., p. xvii.

16. Hewlett and Duncan, 1969, pp. 381–82.

17. Williams and Cantelon, 1984, p. 118.

18. Hewlett and Duncan, 1969, p. 382.

19. Warner R. Schilling, "The H-Bomb Decision: How to Decide without Actually Choosing," *Political Science Quarterly* 77(March 1961):24–46, quotes from pp. 25 and 27.

20. Williams and Cantelon, 1984, p. 119.

21. Goodchild, 1981, p. 200.

22. Ibid. When Oppenheimer stated his views, following the comments of Committee members, he indicated that he was surprised by the support government officials seemed to be giving to an all-out program for development of the superbomb. In expressing his gratification with the GAC recommendation against accelerated thermonuclear weapon development, he remarked, "I am glad you feel this way, for if it had not come out this way, I would have had to resign as Chairman." John H. Manley, in a telephone call to the author 7 September 1986, said he does not believe this quotation is accurate. Manley contends that at this point there was a paucity of informed officials advocating an accelerated superbomb program.

23. Williams and Cantelon, 1984, pp. 119–20.

24. Minutes of GAC Meeting 17, 28–30 October 1949, U.S. Department of Energy Archives, Germantown, Md.; see also Williams and Cantelon, 1984, pp. 125–26.

25. Minutes of GAC Meeting 2, 2–3 February 1947, p. 3.

26. Manley, 1986.

27. Hewlett and Duncan, 1969, p. 384.

28. Jonathan Schell, *The Fate of the Earth* (New York: Alfred A. Knopf, 1982), p. 146.

29. Hewlett and Duncan, 1969, p. 384.

30. Minutes of GAC Meeting 17, 28–30 October 1947; see also Williams and Cantelon, 1984, pp. 126–27.

31. York, 1976, p. 54.

32. Ibid., p. 47.

33. Williams and Cantelon, 1984, p. 123.

34. "U.S. AEC General Advisory Committee Report on the 'Super,' " 30 October 1949, Historical Document Number 349, U.S. Department of Energy Archives, Germantown, Md., p. 7; see also Williams and Cantelon, 1984, pp. 123–24.

35. Williams and Cantelon, 1984, p. 124; see also Schilling, 1961, p. 33. According to Schilling, this led most Committee members to conclude that "the military purposes of the United States would be much better served by the A-bombs and the A-bomb developments which would otherwise have to be foregone or postponed."

36. Williams and Cantelon, 1984, p. 124.

37. Hewlett and Duncan, 1969, p. 379.

38. Schilling, 1961, p. 32.

39. Williams and Cantelon, 1984, p. 125.

40. York, 1976, p. 60.

41. Ibid., p. 71.

42. Ibid., pp. 66–67.

43. Ibid., p. 62.

44. Ibid., p. 55.

45. Ibid., p. 12.

46. Hewlett and Duncan, 1969, p. 385.

47. York, 1976, p. 57.

48. Schilling, 1961, p. 35.

49. Williams and Cantelon, 1984, p. 128.

50. Ibid., p. 129.

51. Ibid., p. 130.

52. Ibid., pp. 130–31; see also York, 1976, p. 59.

53. Williams and Cantelon, 1984, p. 130.

54. York, 1976, p. 9.

55. Schilling, 1961, p. 34.

56. Hewlett and Duncan, 1969, p. 393.

57. Schilling, 1961, p. 30. Study groups were formed in each of the three representatives' departments, and their research findings and advice were forwarded to President Truman in the weeks before he finally decided to officially approve an accelerated U.S. superbomb program. When the special working group of the NSC finally met to advise on Project Super, Acheson, backed by Johnson, set out recommendations supporting increased thermonuclear weapon research. Lilienthal was outvoted, but did succeed in expressing his reservations about the weapon directly to the president.

58. York, 1976, p. 69.

59. Ibid.

60. Goodchild, 1981, pp. 203–4.

61. Hewlett and Duncan, 1969, p. 400.

62. York, 1976, p. 62.

63. Hewlett and Duncan, 1969, p. 402.

64. Schilling, 1961, p. 43.

65. Ibid., p. 35.

66. Williams and Cantelon, 1984, p. 131; see also Tomei, 1956, p. 33.

67. Schilling, 1961, p. 38.

68. Richard Pfau, *No Sacrifice Too Great: The Life of Lewis L. Strauss* (Charlottesville: University Press of Virginia, 1984), p. 122.

69. Schilling, 1961, p. 44.

70. York, 1976, p. 5.

71. GAC administrative assistant Tomei points out that the official reason Oppenheimer lost his AEC security clearance in 1954 stemmed from his failure to divulge completely his political associations before and during World War II. Nevertheless, the matter of Oppenheimer's stand on the H-bomb was extensively explored in the AEC hearings, which resulted in the cancellation of his clearance.

72. Williams and Cantelon, 1984, p. 146.

73. Philip M. Stern with Harold P. Green, *The Oppenheimer Case: Security on Trial* (New York: Harper and Row, 1969), pp. 148–49.

74. Minutes of GAC Meeting 28, 12–14 December 1951, p. 29.

75. Martin L. Perl, "The Science Advisory System," in *Knowledge, Politics, and Public Policy,* ed. Philip H. Melanson (Cambridge, Mass.: Winthrop Publishers, 1973), p. 167.

76. Edward Teller, *Energy from Heaven and Earth* (San Francisco: W. H. Freeman and Co., 1979), p. 154.

77. Ibid., p. 155.

78. York, 1976, p. 71, excerpted from an article by Teller entitled "Back to the Laboratories."

79. Ibid., p. 65.

80. Bethe, 1982, p. 49.

81. Ibid., p. 45.

82. Ibid., p. 48. According to Bethe, Project Super research at Los Alamos was foundering in January 1951. The entire research project could not advance until major theoretical impediments were overcome. By March 1951 Teller and Ulam published a paper that contained half of the new concept needed to make the classic superbomb technically realizable. A month later Teller calculated the very important second half of the new concept. Bethe claims that the twin theoretical breakthroughs were about as surprising to him as the discovery of fission had been to physicists in 1939.

83. Pfau, 1984, p. 133.

84. Hewlett and Duncan, 1969, p. 569.

85. Minutes of GAC Meeting 28, 12–14 December 1951, p. 10.

86. Ibid., p. 11.

87. Ibid.

88. Ibid., p. 12.

89. Ibid., p. 13.

90. Ibid., p. 14.

91. Ibid., p. 27.

92. Hewlett and Duncan, 1969, p. 570.

93. Minutes of GAC Meeting 28, 12–14 December 1951, p. 28.

94. Ibid.

95. Hewlett and Duncan, 1969, p. 571. The work delegated to the new facilities basically involved production concerns, not field testing. Los Alamos retained exclusive responsibility for testing weapons through detonation.

96. Minutes of GAC Meeting 28, 12–14 December 1951, p. 30.

97. Hewlett and Duncan, 1969, pp. 581–84.

98. The Franck Report raised moral and ethical objections to use of the atomic bomb. Conant and Oppenheimer had been central figures in the debate about use of the atomic bomb. They had read the Franck Report as members of the Interim Committee that was to consider the future of U.S. weapons development, and they approved use of the atomic bomb.

99. Schilling, 1961, p. 36.

100. Bethe, 1982, p. 47.

101. Ibid., p. 48.

102. Goodchild, 1981, p. 210.

Chapter 7.   The GAC and Project Gabriel

1. Minutes of GAC Meeting 2, 2 February 1947, U.S. Department of Energy Archives, Germantown, Md., p. 3.

2. Jonathan Schell, *The Fate of the Earth* (New York: Alfred A. Knopf, 1982), pp. 12–13, 19.

3. Richard G. Hewlett and Jack M. Holl, *Atoms for Peace and War: A History of the United States Atomic Energy Commission 1952–1960*, vol. 3 (unpublished manuscript, 1986), chap. IX, p. 21. The AEC division of biology and medicine first sponsored research on the radiological hazards of nuclear explosions in 1949. Early conclusions were that it would require the detonation of one hundred thousand weapons of the Nagasaki type to reach the doomsday level. Given the remoteness of this actually occurring, the division staff lightly gave fallout study the code name Project Gabriel.

4. Ibid., p. 22. Possibly to suggest that strontium-90 could be as widely distributed over the earth's surface as solar energy, Libby and his colleagues began referring to their work as Project Sunshine. By the end of 1953 the AEC division of biology and medicine furnished $3.3 million to fund seventy basic research projects related to Gabriel.

5. Minutes of GAC Meeting 36, 17–19 August 1953.

6. Schell, 1982, p. 62.

7. Minutes of GAC Meeting 36, 17–19 August 1953.

8. Ibid., p. 13.

9. Ibid., p. 14.

10. Robert C. Williams and Philip L. Cantelon, eds., *The American Atom* (Philadelphia: University of Pennsylvania Press, 1984), pp. 181–83. The table cited and reproduced in this book appeared originally in *Stockholm Peace Research Institute Yearbook of World Armaments and Disarmament, 1968/69* (New York: Humanities Press, 1969), p. 242.

11. Schell, 1982, p. 46; see also Robert A. Divine, *Blowing on the Wind: The Nuclear Test Ban Debate 1954–1960* (New York: Oxford University Press, 1978), p. 316. Divine said the AEC estimated the biggest Soviet explosion to be 58 megatons.

12. Minutes of GAC Meeting 36, 17–19 August 1953, p. 14.

13. George B. Kistiakowsky, *A Scientist at the White House* (Cambridge, Mass.: Harvard University Press, 1976), p. 302; see also Divine, 1978, p. 319.

14. Richard G. Hewlett and Francis Duncan, *Atomic Shield: An Official History of the U.S. Atomic Energy Commission 1947–1952*, vol. 2 (University Park: Pennsylvania State University Press, 1969), p. 114.

15. Minutes of GAC Meeting 28, 12–14 December 1951, p. 8.

16. Ibid.

17. Kosta Telegadas, "Announced Nuclear Detonations, United States, United Kingdom, Union of Soviet Socialist Republics," Office of Meteorological Research, U.S. Weather Bureau, November 1959, *Hearings on Fallout from Nuclear Weapons Tests,* vol. 3, app. I, a report prepared for the U.S. Congress, Joint Committee on Atomic Energy, Special Subcommittee on Radiation, 86th Cong., 1st sess. (Washington, D.C.: U.S. Government Printing Office, 1959), p. 4. The original document lists an incorrect year; it should be 1958. The hearing record in which it appeared came out in May 1959, and the hearing days were May 5–8.

18. Minutes of GAC Meeting 36, 17–19 August 1953, p. 15.

19. Kistiakowsky, 1976, p. 326.

20. Minutes of GAC Meeting 36, 17–19 August 1953, p. 15.

21. Ibid.

22. Ibid.

23. Ibid., p. 16.

24. Kistiakowsky, 1976, p. 284. As late as March 27, 1960, the issue of the Sr-90 in American wheat introduced by nuclear weapons testing in 1958 was still a controversial and heated public problem. According to Kistiakowsky, the Federal Radiation Council helped advise the Eisenhower administration how to explain the risk and probability of health danger posed by traces of Sr-90 in the typical American diet.

25. Minutes of GAC Meeting 36, 17–19 August 1953, p. 16.

26. Ibid.

27. Ibid., p. 17.

28. Divine, 1978, p. 42.

29. Minutes of GAC Meeting 39, 31 March and 1–2 April 1954.

30. Minutes of GAC Meeting 36, 17–19 August 1953, p. 17.

31. Telegadas, 1959, p. 4; see also Divine, 1978, p. 17.

32. Schell, 1982, pp. 53, 74.

33. "Hydrogen Blast Astonished Scientists, Eisenhower Says," *New York Times* (25 March 1954), p. 1:2.

34. "Inquiry Is Begun in Hydrogen Test," *New York Times* (20 March 1954), p. 3:8. For a more complete account of what happened to the twenty-three Japanese fishermen contaminated by the blast, see Ralph E. Lapp, *The Voyage of the Lucky Dragon* (New York: Harper Brothers Publishers, 1957).

35. See Jaques Cattell, ed., *American Men and Women of Science,* 12th ed. (New York: Jaques Cattell Press/R. R. Bowker, Co., 1971), p. 5658. In later years Scoville held senior positions at the Central Intelligence Agency (1955–1963) and in the Arms Control and Disarmament Agency (1963–1969).

36. Minutes of GAC Meeting 40, 27–29 May 1954, p. 21.

37. Divine, 1978, p. 4.

38. Distances are map approximations.

39. "U.S. Will Pay Marshall Islanders," *New York Times* (28 June 1983), sec. 1, p. 6. The article reported that the United States planned to pay the government of the Marshall Islands $183.7 million over the following fifteen years for injuries and damages resulting from nuclear testing in the islands thirty years ago.

40. Divine, 1978, pp. 30–31.

41. Minutes of GAC Meeting 40, 27–29 May 1954, p. 27.

42. Ibid.

43. Ibid.

44. Minutes of GAC Meeting 51, 29–31 October 1956.

45. Divine, 1978, p. 34.

46. GAC Prepared Statement to the AEC, May 7, 1958. GAC Chairman Warren C. Johnson to AEC Chairman Lewis L. Strauss, letter report on Meeting 58, 7 May 1958, U.S. Department of Energy Archives, Germantown, Md., p. 3.

47. Ibid., pp. 3–4 (Johnson's italics).

48. General Advisory Committee of the U.S. Atomic Energy Commission, "Problems Presented by Radioactive Fallout," *Bulletin of the Atomic Scientists* 15(June 1959):258–59.

49. "Editorial Comment by E. R.," *Bulletin of the Atomic Scientists* 15(June 1959):259. The initials probably stand for those of the editor, Eugene Rabinowich.

50. Ralph E. Lapp, "A Criticism of the GAC Report," *Bulletin of the Atomic Scientists* 15(September 1959), pp. 311–12, 320.

51. Kistiakowsky, 1976, p. 424. For an excellent insider's account of the history of the Test Ban negotiation period, see Glenn T. Seaborg with Benjamin S. Loeb, *Kennedy, Khrushchev, and the Test Ban* (Berkeley: University of California Press, 1981).

52. In a letter sent to the author June 17, 1985, Anthony A. Tomei contends that the GAC was merely following its statutory charter by offering advice on scientific and technical matters of a general nature "unconstrained by any lack of disciplinary representation

apparent in the composition of the committee." This may be a valid claim, but the great scientific stature of the GAC gave its advice more influence inside the AEC than did advisories of departmentally impaneled medical advisory committees. A general advisory committee, of course, does have license to move beyond its charge in scientific and technical matters and offer speculations on matters far beyond its area of expertise.

53. Hewlett and Holl, 1986, chap. IX, p. 21. Later Gabriel studies had used Sr-90 as the critical factor in determining the number of weapon detonations that constituted a radiological hazard. Not until the Upshot-Knothole tests in 1953, however, was it evident that Sr-90 could be widely distributed over the northern hemisphere, not only by nuclear war but also as fallout from testing.

54. Divine, 1978, p. 34.

55. Hewlett and Holl, 1986, chap. IX, p. 22.

Chapter 8.   The GAC and Project Plowshare

1. Stephen Hilgartner, Richard C. Bell, and Rory O'Connor, *Nukespeak: The Selling of Nuclear Technology in America* (New York: Penguin Books, 1983), p. 41.

2. See Richard G. Hewlett and Francis Duncan, *Atomic Shield: An Official History of the U.S. Atomic Energy Commission 1947–1952,* vol. 2 (University Park: Pennsylvania State University Press, 1969); Hilgartner et al., 1983; and U.S. Atomic Energy Commission, *Major Activities in the Atomic Energy Programs* (Washington, D.C.: U.S. Government Printing Office, 1963), p. 10 (hereafter cited as U.S. AEC, *Major Activities*).

3. Hilgartner et al., 1983, p. 43.

4. Ibid.

5. Irvin C. Bupp, "Priorities in Nuclear Technology: Program Prosperity and Decay in the United States Atomic Energy Commission, 1956–1971" (Ph.D. diss., Department of Government, Harvard University, 1971), p. 180 (cited in Albert H. Teich, "Bureaucracy and Politics in Big Science: Relations between Headquarters and the National Laboratories in AEC and ERDA," in *The Role of the National Energy Laboratories in ERDA and Department of Energy Operations: Retrospect and Prospect,* app. V, a report to the U.S. House, Committee on Science and Technology, Subcommittee on Advanced Energy Technologies and Energy Conservation Research, Development, and Demonstration, 95th Cong., 2d sess., 1978, p. 373).

6. David B. Brooks and John V. Krutilla, *Peaceful Use of Nuclear Explosives: Some Economic Aspects* (Baltimore: The Johns Hopkins University Press for Resources for the Future, 1969), p. 1.

7. Ibid., p. 5.

8. Glenn T. Seaborg with Benjamin S. Loeb, *Kennedy, Khrushchev, and the Test Ban* (Berkeley: University of California Press, 1981), p. 248.

9. Peter deLeon, "A Theory of Policy Termination," in *The Policy Cycle,* Judith V. May and Aaron Wildavsky, eds. (Beverly Hills, Calif.: Sage Publications, 1978), pp. 280–99.

10. Robert A. Divine, *Blowing on the Wind: The Nuclear Test Ban Debate 1954–1960* (New York: Oxford University Press, 1978), pp. 157–58.

11. U.S. Atomic Energy Commission, *Progress in Peaceful Uses of Atomic Energy,* vol. 23 (Washington, D.C.: U.S. Government Printing Office, July-December, 1957), p. 276.

12. Seaborg, 1981, pp. 247–48.

13. Ibid., p. 244.

14. U.S. AEC, *Major Activities,* 1963, p. 222.

15. Ibid., 1964, p. 171.

16. U.S. AEC, *Research on Power from Fusion,* vol. 24 (Washington, D.C.: U.S. Government Printing Office, January-June, 1958), p. 15 (hereafter cited as U.S. AEC, *Research,* 1958).

17. Seaborg, 1981, p. 196.
18. Hilgartner et al., 1983, p. 50.
19. U.S. AEC, *Major Activities,* 1963, p. 228.
20. Seaborg, 1981, p. 197.
21. Hilgartner et al., 1983, pp. 50-51.
22. U.S. AEC, *Major Activities,* 1964, p. 176.
23. U.S. AEC Memorandum for the Record of July 6, 1972, Checklist of Commission Meeting with the General Advisory Committee, May 24, 1972, U.S. Department of Energy Archives, Germantown, Md. (hereafter cited as U.S. AEC Memorandum, 1972).
24. U.S. AEC, *Major Activities,* 1967, p. 204.
25. Ibid., 1966, p. 246.
26. Willard F. Libby, "Nuclear Energy: Some New Aspects," in *Bulletin of the Atomic Scientists* 15(June 1959):240-44, quote from p. 242.
27. Seaborg, 1981, pp. 196-98.
28. Minutes of GAC Meeting 95, 2-4 February 1966, U.S. Department of Energy Archives, Germantown, Md., p. 26. The official quoted is John S. Kelly, then director of the AEC Office of Peaceful Nuclear Explosives.
29. U.S. AEC, *Major Activities,* 1967, p. 205.
30. Minutes of GAC Meeting 123, 15 February 1973, p. 18.
31. Ibid., p. 19.
32. Ibid.
33. U.S. AEC, *Major Activities,* 1968, p. 202.
34. Ibid.
35. U.S. AEC Memorandum, 1972.
36. U.S. AEC, *Major Activities,* 1958, p. 51.
37. Ibid., 1964, p. 165.
38. U.S. AEC, *Major Activities,* 1969, p. 202.
39. Brooks and Krutilla, 1969, p. 12.
40. U.S. AEC, *Major Activities,* 1965, p. 203.
41. See "Reported Nuclear Test Explosions, 1945-68" in *Stockholm Peace Research Institute Yearbook of World Armaments and Disarmament, 1968/1969* (New York: Humanities Press, 1969), p. 242, cited in Robert C. Williams and Philip L. Cantelon, eds., *The American Atom* (Philadelphia: University of Pennsylvania Press, 1984), pp. 181-83.
42. U.S. AEC, *Major Activities,* 1960, p. 153.
43. Ibid., 1961, p. 210.
44. U.S. AEC, *Research,* 1958, p. 52.
45. U.S. AEC, *Major Activities,* 1960, p. 153.
46. Ibid., 1961, pp. 212-13.
47. Ibid., pp. 210-11.
48. Ibid., 1962, p. 254.
49. Anthony A. Tomei for Robert A. Charpie to AEC Commissioners, letter report of planned agenda for GAC Meeting 78, 29-31 January 1962, 16 January 1962, U.S. Department of Energy Archives, Germantown, Md.
50. U.S. AEC, *Research,* 1958, p. 15.
51. U.S. AEC, *Major Activities,* 1959, p. 93.
52. Ibid., 1961, pp. 215-16.
53. Ibid., 1962, p. 253.
54. Ibid., pp. 250-51.
55. Ibid., 1963, p. 217.
56. Brooks and Krutilla, 1969, p. 36.
57. U.S. AEC, *Major Activities,* 1963, p. 227.
58. Ibid.
59. Brooks and Krutilla, 1969, p. 36.
60. U.S. AEC, *Major Activities,* 1965, p. 196.
61. Brooks and Krutilla, 1969, p. 37.
62. Ibid., p. 39.

63. Hilgartner, 1983, p. 50.

64. George B. Kistiakowsky, *A Scientist at the White House* (Cambridge, Mass.: Harvard University Press, 1976), p. 365.

65. U.S. AEC, *Major Activities,* 1962, p. 263.

66. Ibid., 1964, pp. 164–65.

67. Ibid., 1966, p. 252.

68. Ibid., 1963, pp. 210–13.

69. Ibid., p. 210.

70. Ibid., 1964, p. 159.

71. This point was expressed by Gerald F. Tape before the GAC. See Minutes of GAC Meeting 95, 2–4 February 1966, p. 25.

72. Anthony A. Tomei to AEC Commissioners, letter report of planned agenda for GAC Meeting 95, 2–4 February 1966, 4 January 1966, U.S. Department of Energy Archives, Germantown, Md.

73. U.S. AEC, *Major Activities,* 1968, pp. 196–97.

74. Ibid.

75. Ibid., p. 198.

76. Brooks and Krutilla, 1969, p. 39.

77. Atlantic-Pacific Interocean Canal Study Commission, *Interocean Canal Studies* (Washington, D.C.: U.S. Government Printing Office, 1970), p. 37 (hereafter cited as Canal Study Commission, 1970).

78. Ibid., p. 40.

79. Jerome Weisner and Herbert York, "National Security and the Nuclear Test Ban," *Scientific American* 211(October 1964):27–35, quote from p. 28. This was a pre–Vietnam War estimation.

80. Canal Study Commission, 1970, pp. 43–44.

81. U.S. AEC, *Major Activities,* 1970, pp. 201–2.

82. Canal Study Commission, 1970, p. 40.

83. U.S. AEC, *Major Activities,* 1970, p. 42.

84. Ibid.

85. Ibid., 1971, p. 139.

86. U.S. AEC, *Annual Report to Congress: Operating and Developmental Functions,* vol. 1 (Washington, D.C.: U.S. Government Printing Office, 1974), p. 26.

87. U.S. AEC, *Major Activities,* 1971, pp. 142–43.

88. deLeon, 1978, p. 280.

Chapter 9.   The GAC and the great accelerator debates

1. Martin L. Perl, "The Scientific Advisory System: Some Observations," in *Knowledge, Politics, and Public Policy,* ed. Philip H. Melanson (Cambridge, Mass.: Winthrop Publishers, 1973), p. 168.

2. Don K. Price, *The Scientific Estate* (Cambridge, Mass.: The Belknap Press of Harvard University Press, 1965), pp. 66–67.

3. Ibid., p. 2.

4. Ibid., p. 16.

5. Donald A. Strickland, *Scientists in Politics: The Atomic Scientists Movement, 1945–46* (West Lafayette, Ind.: Purdue University Studies, 1968), pp. 3, 72. Strickland's study is an excellent account of the role played by physical scientists in lobbying on the May-Johnson Bill and on the McMahon Bill; the latter would eventually be enacted into law as the Atomic Energy Act of 1946.

6. Price, 1965, p. 81.

7. Grant McConnell, *Private Power and American Democracy* (New York: Vintage Books, 1970), p. 164.

8. Glenn T. Seaborg and Daniel M. Wilkes, *Education and the Atom* (New York: McGraw-Hill Book Company, 1964), p. 8.

9. Ibid., p. 27.

10. Ibid., p. 40.

11. Richard S. Morse worked for MIT's Development Foundation, Inc., while on the GAC.

12. Helen C. Allison, "News Roundup," *Bulletin of the Atomic Scientists* 15(June 1959):269.

13. Minutes of GAC Meeting 29, 15–17 February 1952, U.S. Department of Energy Archives, Germantown, Md., p. 16.

14. David Z. Robinson, "Resource Allocation in High Energy Physics," in *Science Policy and the University,* ed. Harold Orlans (Washington, D.C.: The Brookings Institution, 1968), p. 165.

15. U.S. Congress, Joint Committee on Atomic Energy, "High Energy Physics Program: Report on National Policy and Background Information," 89th Cong., 1st sess. (Washington, D.C.: U.S. Government Printing Office, February 1965), p. 9 (hereafter cited as High Energy Physics Program, 1965).

16. Ibid., p. 10.

17. Robinson, 1968, p. 166 fn.

18. High Energy Physics Program, 1965, p. 173. A linear accelerator is a long straight tube in which charged particles are accelerated by high-frequency electric fields. A synchrotron accelerator is one in which charged particles are accelerated around a circular path of essentially constant radius by a radio-frequency electric field. The magnetic guiding and focusing fields of the magnet are increased to match the energy gained by the particles, thereby maintaining them at a constant radius.

19. Robinson, 1968, p. 166 fn.

20. Ibid., p. 170.

21. Minutes of GAC Meeting 33, 5–7 February 1953, p. 2. The Committee referred to the item as "Dr. Platt's letter."

22. High Energy Physics Program, 1965, p. 19.

23. W. Henry Lambright, *Governing Science and Technology* (New York: Oxford University Press, 1976), p. 31.

24. Minutes of GAC Meeting 36, 17–19 August 1953, p. 45.

25. Ibid., p. 46.

26. Ibid.

27. Ibid., p. 45.

28. Robinson, 1968, p. 166.

29. Minutes of GAC Meeting 43, 20–22 December 1954, p. 23.

30. By the mid-1950s the MURA grew to include fifteen major midwest universities that had a special center for the design and construction of an accelerator. See Robinson, 1968, p. 171.

31. See Donald R. Fleming, "The Big Money and the High Politics of Science," *Atlantic,* August 1965, pp. 41–45.

32. Minutes of GAC Meeting 42, 3–4 November 1954, p. 31.

33. According to Anthony A. Tomei, former GAC secretary, in a letter to the author of 29 July 1985, "The GAC never really believed it could enter into a 'conflict-of-interest' situation. It had said in meetings that it *advised,* not *decided,* on issues. But, it is true that a few GAC members were quite sensitive to the possibility that there would be any *appearance* of a conflict of interest" (Tomei's italics).

34. Minutes of GAC Meeting 42, 3–4 November 1954, p. 31.

35. Ibid., p. 32.

36. Ibid., p. 33.

37. Robinson, 1968, p. 171.

38. Ibid., p. 173.

39. Fleming, 1965, p. 43; Harold Orlans, *Contracting for Atoms* (Washington, D.C.: The Brookings Institution, 1967), pp. 51–52.

40. Robinson, 1968, p. 173.

41. For an excellent study of President Johnson's role in the space program see John M. Logsdon, *The Decision to Go to the Moon* (Cambridge, Mass.: MIT Press, 1970), especially pp. 22, 67–71, 82, and 112.

42. Minutes of GAC Meeting 42, 3–4 November 1954, p. 30.

43. Ibid., p. 31.

44. Minutes of GAC Meeting 43, 20–22 December 1954, p. 23.

45. Ibid.

46. Ibid.

47. Minutes of GAC Meeting 47, 13–15 December 1955, p. 19.

48. Ibid., p. 28.

49. High Energy Physics Program, 1965, p. 166.

50. Robinson, 1968, p. 167.

51. Ibid.

52. Ibid., pp. 167–68.

53. High Energy Physics Program, 1965, p. 92.

54. Charles O. Jones, *An Introduction to the Study of Public Policy*, 3d ed. (Monterey, Calif.: Brooks/Cole Publishing Company, 1984), p. 247.

55. Verbatim Minutes of GAC Meeting 4, 31 May 1947, p. 11.

Chapter 10.   The life cycle of an elite scientific advisory committee

1. Don K. Price, *The Scientific Estate* (Cambridge, Mass.: The Belknap Press of Harvard University Press, 1965), p. 105.

2. Richard G. Hewlett and Francis Duncan, *Atomic Shield: An Official History of the U.S. Atomic Energy Commission 1947–1952*, vol. 2 (University Park: Pennsylvania State University Press, 1969), p. 16.

3. Steven L. Del Sesto, *Science, Politics, and Controversy: Civilian Nuclear Power in the United States, 1946–1974* (Boulder, Colo.: Westview Press, 1979), p. 21.

4. Irvin C. Bupp and Jean-Claude Derian, *The Failed Promise of Nuclear Power: The Story of Light Water* (New York: Basic Books, 1978), p. 6.

5. Daniel Ford, *The Cult of the Atom* (New York: Simon and Schuster, 1982), p. 60.

6. Price, 1965, p. 55.

7. Francis E. Rourke, *Secrecy and Publicity: Dilemmas of Democracy* (Baltimore: The Johns Hopkins University Press, 1966), pp. 50–51.

8. Rourke, 1966, p. 28.

9. For a thorough historical analysis of atomic reactor research that explains why the United States chose to pursue the light-water-cooled reactor technology, see George T. Mazuzan and J. Samuel Walker, *Controlling the Atom: The Beginnings of Nuclear Regulation 1946–1962* (Berkeley: University of California Press, 1984).

10. Leslie J. Freeman, *Nuclear Witnesses: Insiders Speak Out* (New York: W. W. Norton and Co., 1981), p. xxi.

11. John W. Gofman and Arthur R. Tamplin, *Poisoned Power: The Case against Nuclear Power Plants* (Emmaus, Pa.: Rodale Press, 1971), pp. 63–89.

12. W. Henry Lambright, *Governing Science and Technology* (New York: Oxford University Press, 1976), p. 24.

13. Ford, 1982, p. 226.

14. Bupp and Derian, 1978, p. xxii.

15. Joseph A. Pika, "Federal Advisory Committees: Links between Agencies and Their Publics" (Paper delivered at the Northeastern Political Science Association, Newark, N.J., 12–14 November 1981), p. 7.

16. "New Scientific Consultant Policy," *Bulletin of the Atomic Scientists* 18(May 1962):43–44.

17. Grant McConnell, *Private Power and American Democracy* (New York: Vintage Books, 1970), p. 280.

18. U.S. Congress, Senate Committee on Governmental Affairs, Subcommittee on Reports, Accounting, and Management, *Energy Advisers: An Analysis of Federal Advisory Committees Dealing with Energy,* a report prepared by Susan R. Abbasi and Alfred R. Greenwood (Washington, D.C.: U.S. Government Printing Office, March 1977), p. 20.

19. Bupp and Derian, 1978, p. 10.

20. This point was confirmed by Anthony A. Tomei, former GAC secretary, in the case of the AEC GAC.

21. Elizabeth S. Rolph, *Nuclear Power and Public Safety: A Study in Regulation* (Lexington, Mass.: Lexington Books, 1979), p. 155.

22. Lambright, 1976, p. 33.

23. Minutes of ERDA GAC Meeting 2, 13–14 November 1975, U.S. Department of Energy, Energy Research Advisory Board.

24. Richard G. Hewlett and Oscar E. Anderson, Jr., *The New World: An Official History of the U.S. Atomic Energy Commission 1939–1946,* vol. 1 (University Park: Pennsylvania State University Press, 1962), pp. 399–401.

Appendix B.   The major atomic energy laboratories

1. Harold Orlans, *Contracting for Atoms* (Washington, D.C.: The Brookings Institution, 1967), p. 14.

2. Albert H. Teich, "Bureaucracy and Politics in Big Science: Relations between Headquarters and the National Laboratories in AEC and ERDA," in *The Role of the National Energy Laboratories in ERDA and Department of Energy Operations: Retrospect and Prospect,* a report prepared for the U.S. House, Committee on Science and Technology, Subcommittee on Advanced Energy Technologies and Energy Conservation Research, Development and Demonstration, 95th Cong., 2d sess. (Washington, D.C.: U.S. Government Printing Office, January 1978), p. 355.

3. U.S. Department of Energy, Energy Research Advisory Board, Multiprogram Laboratory Panel, "Preliminary Report on the Multiprogram National Laboratories," unpublished document, March 1982 (hereafter cited as ERAB Panel, 1982), pp. 10–11.

4. Ibid., p. 7.

5. Orlans, 1967, p. 18.

6. John F. Hogerton, *The Atomic Energy Deskbook* (New York: Reinhold Publishing Corp., 1963), p. 284.

7. Ibid.

8. ERAB Panel, 1982, app. D, p. 6.

9. Hogerton, 1963, p. 133; ERAB Panel, 1982, app. D, p. 4.

10. Minutes of GAC Meeting 15, 15 July 1949, U.S. Department of Energy Archives, Germantown, Md., p. 11. At this meeting Seaborg was quoted as saying, "Berkeley is not really a national laboratory in matters of policy or in the minds of American scientists."

11. Orlans, 1967, p. 82.

12. Edward Teller with Allen Brown, *The Legacy of Hiroshima* (Garden City, N.Y.: Doubleday and Co., 1962), pp. 59–61.

13. Teich, 1978, p. 354.

14. Ibid., p. 374.

15. Orlans, 1967, p. 83.

16. ERAB Panel, 1982, app. D, p. 5.

17. Teich, 1978, p. 353.

18. Hogerton, 1963, p. 30.

19. Teich, 1978, p. 371.

20. ERAB Panel, 1982, app. E, p. 3.

21. Ibid., p. 4.

22. Richard G. Hewlett and B. J. Dierenfield, *The Federal Role and Activities in Energy Research and Development 1946–1980: A Historical Summary* (Gaithersburg, Md.: History Associates, Inc., 1983), p. 51.

23. ERAB Panel, 1982, app. D, p. 3.

24. Ibid., app. E, p. 5.

25. Hogerton, 1963, p. 83.

26. Orlans, 1967, p. 73.

27. Teich, 1978, p. 352.

28. Orlans, 1967, p. 61.

29. ERAB Panel, 1982, app. D, p. 7.

30. Teich, 1978, p. 369.

31. Hogerton, 1963, p. 372.

32. ERAB Panel, 1982, app. E, p. 15.

33. Hogerton, 1963, p. 372.

34. ERAB Panel, 1982, app. E, p. 15.

35. Ibid., app. D, p. 17.

36. Orlans, 1967, pp. 18, 23.

37. Ibid., p. 25.

38. Richard G. Hewlett and Francis Duncan, *Atomic Shield: An Official History of the U.S. Atomic Energy Commission 1947–1952,* vol. 2 (University Park: Pennsylvania State University Press, 1969), p. 36.

39. ERAB Panel, 1982, app. E, p. 17.

40. Ibid., app. D, p. 8.

41. Teich, 1978, pp. 354–55.

42. Hogerton, 1963, p. 490.

43. A very early reference to this work can be found in Minutes of GAC Meeting 23, 30–31 October and 1 November 1950.

44. ERAB Panel, 1982, app. D, p. 22.

45. Teich, 1978, p. 354.

46. Minutes of GAC Meeting 4, 30–31 May and 1 June 1947, p. 3.

47. Hewlett and Duncan, 1969, p. 177.

48. Orlans, 1967, p. 177.

49. Minutes of GAC Meeting 14, 2–4 June 1949, p. 18.

50. ERAB Panel, 1982, app. E, p. 20.

51. Ibid., p. 1.

BIBLIOGRAPHY

Books, articles, and reports

Allardice, Corbin, and Edward R. Trapnell. *The Atomic Energy Commission.* New York: Praeger Publishers, 1974.

Allison, Allen C. "News Roundup." *Bulletin of the Atomic Scientists* 16(January 1960):31.

Allison, Helen C. "News Roundup." *Bulletin of the Atomic Scientists* 15(June 1959):269.

Atlantic-Pacific Interocean Canal Study Commission. *Interocean Canal Studies.* Washington, D.C.: U.S. Government Printing Office, 1970.

Baer, Harry S., Jr. "Nuclear Power for Aircraft." *Flying,* June 1957, p. 25.

Bethe, Hans A. "Comments on the History of the H-Bomb." *Los Alamos Science* (Fall 1982):43–53.

Boskin, Joseph, and Fred Kinsky. *The Oppenheimer Affair.* Beverly Hills, Calif.: Glencoe Press, 1968.

Bromberg, Joan Lisa. *Fusion: Science, Politics, and the Invention of a New Energy Source.* Cambridge, Mass.: MIT Press, 1982.

Brooks, David B., and John V. Krutilla. *Peaceful Use of Nuclear Explosives: Some Economic Aspects.* Baltimore: The Johns Hopkins University Press for Resources for the Future, 1969.

Brooks, Harvey. "The Scientific Adviser." In *Scientists in National Policy-Making,* edited by Robert Gilpin and Christopher Wright. New York: Columbia University Press, 1964.

Brown, David S. "The Management of Advisory Committees: An Assignment for the '70's." *Public Administration Review* 32(July/August 1972):334–42.

Bupp, Irvin C. "Priorities in Nuclear Technology: Program Prosperity and Decay in the United States Atomic Energy Commission, 1956–1971." Ph.D. diss., Harvard University, 1971.

Bupp, Irvin C., and Jean-Claude Derian. *The Failed Promise of Nuclear Power: The Story of Light Water.* New York: Basic Books, 1978.

Cardozo, Michael H. "The Federal Advisory Committee Act in Operation." *Administrative Law Review* 33(Winter 1981):1–62.

Cattell, Jaques, ed. *American Men of Science.* 9th ed. New York: R. R. Bowker, 1955.

———. *American Men of Science.* 10th ed. New York: R. R. Bowker, 1960.

———. *American Men of Science.* 11th ed. New York: R. R. Bowker, 1969.

———. *American Men and Women of Science.* 12th ed. New York: R. R. Bowker, 1971.

_____. *American Men and Women of Science.* 13th ed. New York: R. R. Bowker, 1976.

_____. *American Men and Women of Science.* 14th ed. New York: R. R. Bowker, 1979.

Cohen, Sam. *The Truth about the Neutron Bomb.* New York: William Morrow and Co., 1983.

Cronin, Thomas E., and Sanford D. Greenberg, eds. *The Presidential Advisory System.* New York: Harper and Row, 1969.

Cronin, Thomas E., and Norman C. Thomas. "Federal Advisory Processes: Advice and Discontent." *Science* 26(February 1971):771–79.

Davis, David Howard. *Energy Politics.* 2d ed. New York: St. Martin's Press, 1978.

deLeon, Peter. "A Theory of Policy Termination." In *The Policy Cycle,* edited by Judith V. May and Aaron Wildavsky. Beverly Hills, Calif.: Sage Publications, 1978.

Del Sesto, Steven L. *Science, Politics, and Controversy: Civilian Nuclear Power in the United States, 1946–1974.* Boulder, Colo.: Westview Press, 1979.

Dickson, David. *The New Politics of Science.* New York: Pantheon Books, 1984.

Divine, Robert A. *Blowing on the Wind: The Nuclear Test Ban Debate, 1954–1960.* New York: Oxford University Press, 1978.

"Editorial Comment by E. R." *Bulletin of the Atomic Scientists* 15(June 1959):259.

Energy Policy, 2d ed. Washington, D.C.: Congressional Quarterly, March 1981.

Etzioni, Amitai. *Modern Organizations.* Englewood Cliffs, N.J.: Prentice-Hall, 1964.

Fairlie, Henry. "Help from Outside." In *The Presidential Advisory System,* edited by Thomas E. Cronin and Sanford D. Greenberg. New York: Harper and Row, 1969.

Fleming, Donald R. "The Big Money and the High Politics of Science." *Atlantic,* August 1965, pp. 41–45.

Ford, Daniel. *The Cult of the Atom.* New York: Simon and Schuster, 1982.

Freeman, Leslie J. *Nuclear Witnesses: Insiders Speak Out.* New York: W. W. Norton and Co., 1981.

Fritschler, A. Lee, and Bernard H. Ross. *Business Regulation and Government Decision-Making.* Boston: Little, Brown and Company, 1980.

Garrison, Lloyd K. "Oppenheimer Requests Review." *Bulletin of the Atomic Scientists* 10(June 1954):251–54.

General Advisory Committee of the U.S. Atomic Energy Commission. "Problems Presented by Radioactive Fallout." *Bulletin of the Atomic Scientists* 15(June 1959):258–59.

Gilpin, Robert, and Christopher Wright, eds. *Scientists and National Policy Making.* New York: Columbia University Press, 1964.

Gofman, John W., and Arthur R. Tamplin. *Poisoned Power: The Case against Nuclear Power Plants.* Emmaus, Pa.: Rodale Press, 1971.

Golden, William T., ed. *Science Advice to the President.* New York: Pergamon Press, 1980.

Goodchild, Peter. *J. Robert Oppenheimer: Shatterer of Worlds.* Boston: Houghton Mifflin Co., 1981.

Goodwin, Craufurd D., ed. *Energy Policy in Perspective.* Washington, D.C.: The Brookings Institution, 1981.

Gordon, Leslie. "Government Controls in Peace and War." *Bulletin of the Business Historical Society* 20(April 1946):1–5.

Green, Harold P., and Alan Rosenthal. *Government of the Atom.* New York: Atherton Press, 1963.

Greenberg, Daniel S. *The Politics of Pure Science.* New York: The New American Library, 1967.

Hewlett, Richard G., and Oscar E. Anderson, Jr. *The New World: An Official History of the U.S. Atomic Energy Commission 1939–1946.* Vol. 1. University Park: Pennsylvania State University Press, 1962.

Hewlett, Richard G., and B. J. Dierenfield. *The Federal Role and Activities in Energy Research and Development 1946–1980: A Historical Summary.* Gaithersburg, Md.: History Associates, 1983.

Hewlett, Richard G., and Francis Duncan. *Atomic Shield: An Official History of the U.S. Atomic Energy Commission 1947–1952.* Vol. 2. University Park: Pennsylvania State University Press, 1969.

_____. *Nuclear Navy, 1946–1962.* Chicago: The University of Chicago Press, 1974.

Hewlett, Richard G., and Jack M. Holl. *Atoms for Peace and War: A History of the United States Atomic Energy Commission, 1952–1960.* Vol. 3. Unpublished manuscript.

Hilgartner, Stephen, Richard C. Bell, and Rory O'Connor. *Nukespeak: The Selling of Nuclear Technology in America.* New York: Penguin Books, 1983.

Hirsch, Richard, and Joseph J. Trento. *The National Aeronautics and Space Administration.* New York: Praeger Publishers, 1973.

Hitch, Charles. *Decision Making for Defense.* Berkeley: University of California Press, 1965.

_____. *Resources for an Uncertain Future.* Baltimore: The Johns Hopkins University Press for Resources for the Future, 1978.

Hodgetts, J. E. *Administering the Atom for Peace.* New York: Atherton Press, 1964.

Hogerton, John F. *The Atomic Energy Deskbook.* New York: Reinhold Publishing, 1963.

"Hydrogen Blast Astonished Scientists, Eisenhower Says." *New York Times,* 20 March 1954, p. 3.

"Inquiry Is Begun in Hydrogen Test." *New York Times,* 20 March 1954, p. 3.

Jones, Charles O. *An Introduction to the Study of Public Policy.* Monterey, Calif.: Brooks/Cole Publishing Co., 1984.

Kennan, George F. *The Nuclear Delusion: Soviet-American Relations in the Atomic Age.* New York: Pantheon Books, 1983.

Kistiakowsky, George B. *A Scientist at the White House.* Cambridge, Mass.: Harvard University Press, 1976.

Kuhn, James W. *Scientific and Managerial Manpower in Nuclear Industry.* New York: Columbia University Press, 1966.

Kunetka, James W. *City of Fire: Los Alamos and the Atomic Age, 1943–1945.* Rev. ed. Albuquerque: University of New Mexico Press, 1979.

Kuyper, Adrian. "A Look at the New Atomic Energy Law." *Bulletin of the Atomic Scientists* 10(December 1954):389–92.

Lambright, W. Henry. *Governing Science and Technology.* New York: Oxford University Press, 1976.

————. *Shooting Down the Nuclear Plane*. Vol. 104. Syracuse, N.Y.: Inter-University Case Program, 1967.

Lapp, Ralph E. "A Criticism of the GAC Report." *Bulletin of the Atomic Scientists* 15(September 1959):311–12, 320.

————. *The Voyage of the Lucky Dragon*. New York: Harper Brothers Publishers, 1957.

Libby, Leona Marshall. *The Uranium People*. New York: Crane Russak and Charles Scribner's Sons, 1979.

Libby, Willard F. "Nuclear Energy: Some New Aspects." *Bulletin of the Atomic Scientists* 15(June 1959):240–44.

Lilienthal, David E. *Atomic Energy: A New Start*. New York: Harper and Row Publishers, 1980.

Logsdon, John M. *The Decision to Go to the Moon*. Cambridge, Mass.: MIT Press, 1970.

Lovins, Amory B., and L. Hunter Lovins. *Brittle Power: Energy Strategy for National Security*. Andover, Mass.: Brickhouse Publishing, 1982.

Lowi, Theodore J. *The End of Liberalism: Ideology, Policy and the Crisis of Public Authority*. New York: W. W. Norton and Co., 1969.

McConnell, Grant. *Private Power and American Democracy*. New York: Vintage Books, 1970.

Mazuzan, George T., and J. Samuel Walker. *Controlling the Atom: The Beginnings of Nuclear Regulation 1946–1962*. Berkeley: University of California Press, 1984.

Metzger, H. Peter. *The Atomic Establishment*. New York: Simon and Schuster, 1972.

Moody's Bank and Finance Manual. Vol. 2, 1976, and vol. 2, 1977. New York: Investor's Services, 1976 and 1977.

Natchez, Peter B., and Irvin C. Bupp. "Policy and Priority in the Budgetary Process." *American Political Science Review* 67(September 1973):951–63.

National Archives and Records Service. *Weekly Compilation of Presidential Documents*. Vols. 1–53 (selective) for GAC appointment announcements. Washington, D.C.: General Services Administration, 1965 to 1977.

National Journal 34(21 August 1976):1183–85.

National Journal 3(15 January 1977):117.

Nelkin, Dorothy, ed. *Controversy: The Politics of Technical Decisions*. Beverly Hills, Calif.: Sage Publications, 1979.

Nelson, William R., ed. *The Politics of Science*. New York: Oxford University Press, 1968.

"New Scientific Consultant Policy." *Bulletin of the Atomic Scientists* 18(May 1962):43–44.

Okrent, David. *Nuclear Reactor Safety: On the History of the Regulatory Process*. Madison: University of Wisconsin Press, 1981.

Orlans, Harold. *Contracting for Atoms*. Washington, D.C.: The Brookings Institution, 1967.

————. "Developments in Government Policies toward Science and Technology." In *Public Science Policy and Administration,* edited by Albert H. Rosenthal. Albuquerque: University of New Mexico Press, 1973.

————, ed. *Science Policy and the University*. Washington, D.C.: The Brookings Institution, 1968.

Pelham, Ann. *Energy Policy.* 2d ed. Washington, D.C.: Congressional Quarterly, 1981.

Perl, Martin L. "The Scientific Advisory System: Some Observations." In *Knowledge, Politics, and Public Policy,* edited by Philip H. Melanson. Cambridge, Mass.: Winthrop Publishers, 1973.

Pfau, Richard. *No Sacrifice Too Great: The Life of Lewis L. Strauss.* Charlottesville: University Press of Virginia, 1984.

Pika, Joseph A. "Federal Advisory Committees: Links between Agencies and Their Publics." Paper presented at the Northeastern Political Science Association, Newark, N.J., 12–14 November 1981.

Popper, Frank. *The President's Commissions.* New York: Twentieth Century Fund, 1970.

Price, Don K. *The Scientific Estate.* Cambridge, Mass.: The Belknap Press of Harvard University Press, 1965.

Primack, Joel, and Frank von Hippel. *Advice and Dissent: Scientists in the Political Arena.* New York: Basic Books, 1974.

Reagan, Michael D. *Science and the Federal Patron.* New York: Oxford University Press, 1969.

"Reported Nuclear Test Explosions." In *Stockholm Peace Research Institute Yearbook of Armaments and Disarmament, 1968/1969.* New York: Humanities Press, 1969.

Ripley, Randall B., and Grace A. Franklin. *Congress, the Bureaucracy and Public Policy.* Rev. ed. Homewood, Ill.: Dorsey Press, 1980.

Robinson, David Z. "Resource Allocation in High Energy Physics." In *Science Policy and the University,* edited by Harold Orlans. Washington, D.C.: The Brookings Institution, 1968.

Rolph, Elizabeth S. *Nuclear Power and Public Safety: A Study in Regulation.* Lexington, Mass.: Lexington Books, 1979.

Rosenbaum, Walter A. *Energy, Politics, and Public Policy.* Washington, D.C.: Congressional Quarterly Press, 1981.

Rourke, Francis E. *Secrecy and Publicity: Dilemmas of Democracy.* Baltimore: The Johns Hopkins University Press, 1966.

Rouze, Michel. *Oppenheimer: The Man and His Theories.* Translated by Patrick Evans. New York: Paul S. Erikkson, 1965.

Schell, Jonathan. *The Fate of the Earth.* New York: Alfred A. Knopf, 1982.

Schilling, Charles W., ed. *Atomic Energy Encyclopedia in the Life Sciences.* Philadelphia: W. B. Saunders Co., 1964.

Schilling, Warner R. "The H-Bomb Decision: How to Decide without Actually Choosing." *Political Science Quarterly* 76(March 1961):24–46.

Schooler, Dean, Jr. *Science, Scientists, and Public Policy.* New York: Free Press, 1971.

Seaborg, Glenn T., with Benjamin S. Loeb. *Kennedy, Khrushchev, and the Test Ban.* Berkeley: University of California Press, 1981.

Seaborg, Glenn T., and Daniel M. Wilkes. *Education and the Atom.* New York: McGraw-Hill Book Company, 1964.

Seidman, Harold. *Politics, Position, and Power.* 2d ed. New York: Oxford University Press, 1975.

Shrader-Frechette, K. S. *Nuclear Power and Public Policy.* Boston: Reidel Publishing Co., 1980.

Stern, Philip M., with Harold P. Green. *The Oppenheimer Case: Security on Trial.* New York: Harper and Row, 1969.

Strickland, Donald A. *Scientists in Politics: The Atomic Scientists Movement 1945–1946.* West Lafayette, Ind.: Purdue University Studies, 1968.

Sullivan, Linda E., and Anthony T. Kruzas, eds. *Encyclopedia of Government Advisory Organizations.* Detroit: Gale Research, 1975.

Teich, Albert H. "Bureaucracy and Politics in Big Science: Relations between Headquarters and the National Laboratories in AEC and ERDA." In *The Role of the National Energy Laboratories in ERDA and Department of Energy Operations: Retrospect and Prospect,* report prepared for the U.S. House of Representatives Committee on Science and Technology, Subcommittee on Advanced Energy Technologies and Energy Conservation Research, Development, and Demonstration, 95th Cong., 2d sess. Washington, D.C.: U.S. Government Printing Office, 1978.

Telegadas, Kosta. "Announced Nuclear Detonations, United States, United Kingdom, Union of Soviet Socialist Republics." In *Hearings on Fallout from Nuclear Weapons Tests,* vol. 3, app. I. Report prepared for U.S. Congress, Joint Committee on Atomic Energy, Special Subcommittee on Radiation, 86th Cong., 1st sess. Washington, D.C.: U.S. Government Printing Office, 1959.

Teller, Edward. *Energy from Heaven to Earth.* San Francisco: W. H. Freeman and Co., 1979.

Teller, Edward, with Allen Brown. *The Legacy of Hiroshima.* Garden City, N.Y.: Doubleday, 1962.

Trenn, Thaddeus J. *America's Golden Bough: The Science Advisory Intertwist.* Cambridge, Mass.: Oelgeschlager, Gunn and Hain, Publishers, 1983.

Truman, David B. *The Governmental Process: Political Interests and Public Opinion.* New York: Alfred A. Knopf, 1951.

U.S. AEC General Advisory Committee. "Problems Presented by Radioactive Fallout: Statement by the General Advisory Committee of the U.S. Atomic Energy Commission." *Bulletin of the Atomic Scientists* 15(June 1959):258–59.

U.S. Congress, Joint Committee on Atomic Energy. *Atomic Energy Legislation through the 94th Congress, 2d Session.* Washington, D.C.: U.S. Government Printing Office, March 1977.

U.S. Congress, Joint Committee on Atomic Energy. *High Energy Physics Program: Report on National Policy and Background Information.* 89th Cong., 1st sess. Washington, D.C.: U.S. Government Printing Office, February 1965.

U.S. Congress. Senate. Committee on Governmental Affairs, Subcommittee on Reports, Accounting, and Management. *Energy Advisers: An Analysis of Federal Advisory Committees Dealing with Energy.* Report prepared by Susan R. Abbasi and Alfred R. Greenwood. 94th Cong., 2d sess. Washington, D.C.: U.S. Government Printing Office, 1977.

U.S. Nuclear Regulatory Commission, Office of Nuclear Reactor Regulation. *Owners of Nuclear Power Plants.* NUREG-0327, rev. 2. Washington, D.C.: U.S. Government Printing Office, 1979.

"U.S. Will Pay Marshall Islanders." *New York Times,* 28 June 1983, sec. 1, p. 6.

Weisner, Jerome, and Herbert York. "National Security and the Nuclear Test Ban." *Scientific American,* October 1964, pp. 27–35.

Wells, William. "Science Advice and the Presidency: An Overview from Roosevelt to Ford." In *Science Advice to the President,* edited by William T. Golden. New York: Pergamon Press, 1980.

Westfall, Robert S. *A Biography of Isaac Newton.* Cambridge, Engl.: Cambridge University Press, 1980.

Who's Who in Atoms. Vol. 1. London: Vallancey Press, 1960.

Who's Who in Atoms. Vol. 2. 5th ed. London: Harrap Research Publications, 1969.

Widditsch, Ann. "News Roundup." *Bulletin of the Atomic Scientists* 17(April 1961):163.

Williams, Robert C., and Philip L. Cantelon, eds. *The American Atom.* Philadelphia: University of Pennsylvania Press, 1984.

Wolanin, Thomas R. *Presidential Advisory Commissions.* Madison: University of Wisconsin Press, 1975.

York, Herbert. *The Advisers: Oppenheimer, Teller, and the Superbomb.* San Francisco: W. H. Freeman and Co., 1976.

Zuckerman, (Lord) Solly. "The Function of Scientific Advisers." *Minerva: A Review of Science Learning and Policy* 19(Spring 1981):186–95.

Atomic Energy Commission, ERDA, and Department of Energy publications and documents

U.S. Atomic Energy Commission. *Annual Report to Congress: Operating and Developmental Functions.* Washington, D.C.: U.S. Government Printing Office, 1974.

_____. *Major Activities in the Atomic Energy Programs.* Washington, D.C.: U.S. Government Printing Office, 1958–1971, inclusive.

_____. *Progress in Peaceful Uses of Atomic Energy.* Vol. 23. Washington, D.C.: U.S. Government Printing Office, July–December 1957.

_____. *Research on Power from Fusion.* Vol. 24. Washington, D.C.: U.S. Government Printing Office, 1958.

U.S. Department of Energy. Assistant Secretary, Management and Administration, Office of the Executive Secretary, History Division. *Energy History Chronology from World War II to the Present.* Report prepared by Prentice C. Dean. 1982.

_____. Energy Research Advisory Board, Multiprogram Laboratory Panel. "Preliminary Report on the Multiprogram National Laboratories." March 1982.

_____. Energy Research Advisory Board Office. Hennessey, Joseph F., "Background Information on Fermi and Lawrence Awards." Memorandum to AEC Chairman Glenn T. Seaborg, et al. 31 January 1966.

_____. Energy Research Advisory Board Office. Minutes of ERDA General Advisory Committee Meetings, 1975–1977 inclusive. Unclassified records only.

_____. Office of Energy Research. "Enrico Fermi Award." Letter announcement by Alvin W. Trivelpiece. 15 April 1983.

_____. Office of Energy Research. "Enrico Fermi Award." Letter announcement by Alvin W. Trivelpiece. 1 March 1984.

U.S. Department of Energy Archives, Germantown, Md. Draft Minutes and verbatim transcriptions of AEC General Advisory Committee Meetings, 1947–1975 inclusive. Unclassified or declassified records only.

_____. Howe, Fisher, to Robert J. Hart. 23 February 1976.

_____. Johnson, Warren C., to Lewis L. Strauss. 9 November 1956.

_____. Johnson, Warren C., to Lewis L. Strauss. 10 December 1957.

_____. Johnson, Warren C., to Lewis L. Strauss. 7 May 1958.

_____. Rabi, Isidor I., to Lewis L. Strauss. 8 January 1954.

_____. Rabi, Isidor I., to Lewis L. Strauss. 30 July 1956.

_____. Strauss, Lewis L., to Dwight D. Eisenhower. 15 November 1954.

_____. Tape, Gerald F., to Glenn T. Seaborg, et al. Memorandum. 18 May 1964.

_____. Tomei, Anthony A. "An Account of the Administrative and Organizational Practices and Procedures of the General Advisory Committee." 8 June 1956.

_____. Tomei, Anthony A., for Robert A. Charpie to the AEC Commissioners. 16 January 1962.

_____. Tomei, Anthony A., to AEC Commissioners. 4 January 1966.

_____. Tomei, Anthony A., to General Advisory Committee. U.S. ERDA Memorandum. 18 February 1975.

_____. "U.S. AEC General Advisory Committee Report on the 'Super.' " Historical Document Number 349. 30 October 1949.

_____. "U.S. AEC Memorandum for the Record of July 6, 1972. Checklist of Commission Meeting with the General Advisory Committee, May 24, 1972." 6 July 1972.

_____. Wigner, Eugene P., to Isidor I. Rabi. 22 September 1955.

U.S. Energy Research and Development Administration. "Annual Report on Federal Advisory Committee." Interagency Report Control No. 1121-GSA-AN, Standard Form 248 (Rev. 5-76). Prepared by Fisher Howe, Secretary, General Advisory Committee. 1977.

_____. "Memorandum: G.A.C. Members, Chairmen, and Technical Assistants," supplied by Anthony A. Tomei to General Advisory Committee files. 18 February 1975.

Personal communications

Manley, John H. Interview with author, by telephone. 7 September 1986.

Tomei, Anthony A. Interview with author. Williamsport, Pennsylvania, 4 June 1984.

_____. Letter to author. 29 July 1985.

Woodard, William. Interview with author. 18 April 1983.

INDEX

Abelson, Philip H.: and atomic sub feasibility report, 75; and Carnegie Institution posts, 74–75, 218; as codiscoverer of neptunium, 74; education of, 95; multidisciplinary talent of, 47; at Naval Research lab, 74, 101; as NDRC member, 103–4; and Oak Ridge, 74–75, 103–4; and OSRD interaction, 101; as Project Plowshare adviser, 75; as Ramsey panel member, 234; as *Science* edior, 75; scientific contributions of, 127; and tracers and organic geochemistry, 75
ABM. *See* Antiballistic missile system
Accelerators. *See* Particle accelerators
Acheson, Dean G.: criticizes GAC, 241; endorses second lab proposal, 168; and Kennan advises, 144–45; and Project Super, 154; and Truman's H-bomb decision, 160
Administrative estate, 51
Advanced Research Projects Agency, 191
Advisory Committee on Reactor Safeguards, 18, 80
AEC. *See* Atomic Energy Commission
Aircraft Nuclear Propulsion: builds American scientific prestige, 139; cost estimates for, 136, 140; and direct and indirect cycles, 281n.78; and GAC Reactors Subcommittee, 139; GAC rejection of, 138–39, 241; GAC supervises program of, 241; history of, 135–40; McNamara cancels, 139; and Nuclear Energy for Propulsion of Aircraft, 135–36; and nuclear seaplane, 138; Oak Ridge budgetary interest in, 126; Price supports, 139
Air Force, U.S.: and Livermore creation, 168; and Long Range Detection System, 143; and nuclear airplane, 135–40
Alamogordo, N.M., 257
American Association for the Advancement of Science, 215

American Telephone and Telegraph Co., 80
Ames Laboratory, 116, 269–70
Anamosa, Harold S., 40–41
ANL. *See* Organic National Laboratory
ANP. *See* Aircraft Nuclear Propulsion
Antiballistic missile system: and light sentinel dispute, 109; and proposed test ban treaty effects, 183–84
Antinuclear movement, 244–45, 247
Arab-Israeli War of 1973, 248
Arab oil embargo, 248
Argonne National laboratory, 261–62: in accelerator competition, 224, 228–30; as AEC contract lab, 13; funding of in 1947, 115; as GAC meeting site, 28; and W. Johnson, 228–29; and Lawroski, 79, 262; as multiprogram national lab, 257; as University of Chicago contract operator, 115; and Zinn, 66, 110, 133, 262
Argonne Universities Association, 217
Army Corps of Engineers: and Project Plowshare, 193, 199; studies Project Gnome site, 202; transfers Manhattan Project to AEC, 114
Associated Midwest Universities, 217
Associated Universities, Inc.: Composition of board, 225, 263; as contract operator of Brookhaven, 115, 225, 263; and Glennan, 82; and Rabi, 57, 225, 264; and Tape, 67
Atlantic-Pacific Interocean Canal Project: history of, 204–8; Project Plowshare investigates for, 190, 194; nuclear explosives application for, 200–201; Teller supports, 193, 204
Atomic Casualties, Committee on, 86, 250–51
Atomic Energy Act of 1946: creates AEC, 16; creates GAC, 10–11, 16; GAC interprets research intent of, 223; and Joint Committee on Atomic Energy, 10, 16;